$\frac{dy}{t}$

THE PLEASURE HAUNTS OF LONDON

BAGNIGGE WELLS
The Long Room

THE
PLEASURE HAUNTS
OF LONDON

*during four
centuries*

by

E. Beresford Chancellor

*London
Constable & Company Ltd
Houghton Mifflin Company
Boston & New York
1925*

PRINTED IN GREAT BRITAIN BY RICHARD CLAY & SONS, LIMITED,
BUNGAY, SUFFOLK.

FOREWORD

In the following pages I have attempted to give some account of the Pleasure Haunts of London from the days of the Tudors to our own time. The subject is a large one, and I have, therefore, been obliged to keep what I had to say within drastic limits. I have, however, endeavoured to include all the essential information possible, and by references to works which are specifically allocated to the various subjects dealt with, have indicated to those anxious for further information the sources whence it may be gained.

Certain books, mostly scarce ones now, have been written on special phases of my subject, but there is none which, so far as I know, combines information on it as a whole; and I am, therefore, emboldened to hope that this volume may be considered as filling a gap, if a gap can possibly be found, in the vast library concerned with London and its variegated life.

E. B. C.

I have to thank Mr. Oliver Bernard for the loan of the rare work by Brayley on the Theatres, from which some of the illustrations have been copied; and also Messrs. Tregaskis & Co. of Museum Street for the loan of a very scarce book from which certain details have been extracted for incorporation in this volume.

CONTENTS

LIST OF ILLUSTRATIONS

THE PLEASURE HAUNTS OF LONDON DURING FOUR CENTURIES

INTRODUCTION

THE English have, on the showing of other more temperamental peoples, been accustomed to take their pleasures sadly. Like all generalizations, especially those due to inadequate knowledge or determined perversity, the charge is wholly absurd and unfounded.

The truth is that from earliest times, when the old chronicler, FitzStephen, records the sports and pastimes and amusements of his twelfth-century day, down to our own period, we have been a people devoted to pleasure in all its forms; and one has only to glance through the annals of social life from the sixteenth century downwards to realise that the English have been, and are, as essentially pleasure-loving as other nations, and quite as joyous in its pursuit.

In the days of the Tudors bull- and bear-baiting, with a gradually awakened attraction towards the theatre, were the staple amusements of the people—amusements that survived, and in the case of the theatre with ever-increasing zest, into the succeeding centuries. In the time of the Georges cock-fighting, and gambling (for lotteries attracted the class that had not opportunities of playing in other ways), and a growing delight in public amusements of the Ranelagh and Vauxhall type became chiefly popular; while the extraordinary development of the theatre,

B

at a later time, and the extension of popular amusements in the form of pugilistic encounters in one
direction, and the more simple delights of tea-gardens
and "shows" in another, have proved, what is so
markedly patent to-day, that it is through the eye
that the people prefers chiefly to recreate itself.

I shall endeavour to describe those haunts in which,
in successive ages, pleasure has been provided and
sought in London. We shall see that under the Tudors
such centres were to be found in the bear- and bull-
baiting rings at Hockley in the Hole, in Clerkenwell,
on Bankside, on the Surrey shore of the river, and
elsewhere; that, later, the rise of the theatres alternated
with, and almost superseded, these more savage
delights; we shall see that, in the time of the Stuarts,
pleasure gardens came into existence and enjoyed
much popularity, and the Mulberry Garden and the
Spring Gardens, and Foxhall (a precursor of the
better-known Vauxhall of a later day) were largely
patronized, and appealed to all classes. When we
reach the eighteenth century, we are confronted with
an extension of such resorts which, before the period
had closed, were innumerable; Ranelagh and Vauxhall
and Marylebone Gardens contending in popularity
with the gatherings at Mrs. Cornelys's rooms in Soho
and with the Pantheon, which proved her most
formidable rival. During this time, too, the annual
Fairs drew vast crowds whose boisterous and noisy
demeanour resulted, in course of time, in their
suppression.

With the Regency the full-blooded eighteenth
century may be said to have reached a climax, and
gradually to have shed that decorative character, both
in manners and dress, which makes us so lenient to
the vagaries of the earlier portion of it. For it was
during the early years of the nineteenth century that
a rather vulgar form of life began, and, owing to
the example set by various members of the "ton,"

as it was called, with a compliant head-piece in the
Regent himself, the development occurred of that
faſt life of which the popular exemplification is to be
found in the books of Pierce Egan, and the more
lurid character judged by the number of those houses
of ill-fame of which the notorious White House
in Soho and the eſtablishments of Mrs. Berkeley
and others, are outſtanding examples; while such
places as the Cider Cellars in Maiden Lane, and the
Cole Hole in the Strand, the Oyſter Saloon in Bridges
Street, and "The Holy Land" further eaſt, were well-
known resorts of those who were ultra-bohemian in
their taſtes or were amused to find themselves in a
queſtionable environment.

At this period, too, gambling hells ſtarted up and
multiplied exceedingly in all quarters, with Crockfords
as a sort of chief Temple of Chance, flanked by many
less obtrusive centres in the immediate neighbourhood.
Vauxhall took on a new lease of life, and made a hiſtory
for itself under the famous Simpson, almoſt, if not
quite, equalling its fame in the days when Cheſterfield
was to be seen there and Horace Walpole recorded
its doings.

Fresh developments of the same idea sprang up
in those days in the form of Rosherville Gardens and
Cremorne, both deſtined to survive till a period
within living memory. Greenwich, too, became famous
not only for its whitebait, but for that political *aura*
which spread itself from the ship with its dinner-table
surrounded by illuſtrious ſtatesmen; while the "Maria
Wood" floated peacefully on the Thames, and formed
a sort of later recrudescence of "The Folly" of an
earlier day.

If such things as these may be regarded as the
outſtanding exemplifications of the pleasures of the
nation, there were, of course, innumerable other
resorts which pandered to particular taſtes, and
which formed lesser *foci* of amusement.   Even in the

sixteenth century we find dancing indulged in by all classes, if not in special centres, at least generally on those open spaces which were then within easy distance of inhabited London, where, too, gymnastic games were as popular as football and cricket are to-day. Tennis and bowls were indulged in by the upper classes in spots set aside for the games, and in the winter skating was as popular as it had been when FitzStephen tells us how the citizens in his day enjoyed it on "the Great Fenne or Moore which watereth the wals of the Citie on the north side." Cock-fighting, which in the days of this early chronicler chiefly consisted in the archaic form of schoolboys throwing stones at cocks, first became an organized sport in Henry VIII.'s time, when the earliest known cockpit was formed, and survived well into the nineteenth century.

The Annual Fairs held in London, the chief of which was that of Bartholomew, formed, for a certain period each year, recurring pleasure haunts which drew to their variegated attractions all classes of society; while with the coming of the seventeenth and eighteenth centuries, the river became, not only a recognized means of transit and commerce, but also a pleasure resort which communicated with other pleasure haunts at various spots on its banks. At certain intervals what we know as a good old-fashioned winter, which in the retrospect seems so picturesque but which must actually have been attended by many serious *désagrémens*, resulted in the Thames being frozen over, and those Frost Fairs, concerning which quite a little literature is extant, formed for certain weeks a novel and much-appreciated form of amusement to the Londoner, who experienced an added pleasure in visiting quite usual and accustomed shows because they were exhibited in a strange environment.

As time went on the unsophisticated pleasures of numberless tea-gardens and spas (for wherever a well was to be found, its owner managed somehow to endow it with medicinal properties, and thus added to its attractions among a people notoriously ready to embrace quack medicines) gave place to haunts of less reputable character: night-cellars and gambling hells, and such-like resorts; and the early years of the nineteenth century, the days when the Toms and Jerrys of society were on the prowl and the compliant fair were known as Cyprians, saw a great increase in such places.

Indeed, the word pleasure connotes equally both innocent, and what may be euphemistically termed sophisticated, amusement, and London, in common with every great city, has always possessed its regular resorts for the latter. My account of the pleasure haunts would be incomplete did I not touch on such as these, and I shall, therefore, have something to say (I hope without offence) on a matter which is perennial but will always remain debatable. It was during this time, too, that there arose another form of amusement which developed as the years went on, but which, to-day, has sunk entirely into desuetude. I mean that rage for panoramas, dioramas, and such-like "shows" with which our forbears were accustomed to combine amusement and instruction, which began to take so firm a hold of the nation during the earlier years of the Victorian era. It was a time when people became excited over diving-bells, when the Royal Institution was a power in the land, when history and geography were eagerly absorbed through eyes that ranged round the Panorama in Leicester Square and the Diorama in the Regent's Park. There was a sort of educational *aura* about, and the words of Faraday and Davy had weight. Indeed, England was by now quite prepared to make a success of what was to become for a time one of the greatest pleasure-cum-instruction haunts London has ever known—the Great Exhibition of 1851. The pages of

"The Illustrated London News" revealed the glassy wonders of that amazing conception. Thence one visualized its marvels amid those palm-adorned alleys whose great glass roof alone intervened between the blue sky and the green grass of Hyde Park, with all the world swarming in and out of the human bee-hive, with M. Soyer providing the culinary art of his genius in adjacent Gore House, whence the gorgeous lady and the superb beau had but lately fled, and Prince Albert, as a sort of presiding deity, such a deity as he seems still to be, sitting attentive beneath his gothic multi-coloured canopy with all the ends of the world attendant in marble at his feet, serene, complacent, full of knowledge—a kind of royal schoolmaster abroad.

The undoubted success of that super-show has, I cannot but think, left its influence on our social life; it has been the pioneer not only of the second exhibition of 1862, but also of that series of not dissimilar ones with which we have been familiar in our own times, from the Fisheries, the Healtheries, the Colinderies, and such-like (in whose names the English language was disguised out of all seeming), to the White City of Imré Kiralfy's contriving, and the Wembley of to-day.

Such expositions of national and international activity have obviously been but intermittent, but they have formed, apart from their more serious intention, a means of pleasure and amusement with which not even the recognized vagaries of our climate has been able to interfere.

There is another form of amusement which has been almost as intermittent—I mean roller-skating; in later days alternating with skating on manufactured ice itself. The curious way in which this form of recreation has bobbed up and down, so to phrase it, during the last half-century is very remarkable. A decade or so has usually elapsed between the periods of its resuscitation. It first made its appearance in the 'seventies of the last century, and all the world became bitten with the passion for gyrating on wheels—not unnaturally in a country whence the good old winters (with marked exceptions such as in 1881 and 1891 and so forth) seemed to have departed, and real ice-skating was limited to very short periods and generally to very distant parts of the country. Skating-rinks sprang up everywhere, not only in the metropolis, but in all the chief towns, and in London high society disported itself on that marble floor which Prince's Club (where Cadogan Square is now) added to its other attractions. And then suddenly the craze died; to have a re-incarnation at intervals, until but a few years ago when Holland Park resounded to the whirr of the unaccustomed wheels, and Princes' (a recrudescence in name only of the original club), greatly daring, produced a surface on which ordinary skates were possible.

Half a century and more ago, too, the Music Hall became a pioneer in the land, and the young 'Varsity blade made the Alhambra and the Empire the objective of his nascent manhood. Since those days music-halls have increased and multiplied. They are the same yet not the same, and those familiar with their forerunners will seek in vain for that lounge where the fair ones of the town were wont to fore-gather, and where the performance was one of the least of the attractions to the majority of those who haunted them—with vacuous eye-glass, a cane (for sucking) and a gardenia—the "La-di-da young man" of Gilbert's irony. In those days dancing (except in quite low haunts—although we had no Mabille or Bal Bullier in London) was confined for most people to private houses; to-day Dance Clubs, Night Clubs, cabarets, and their congeners have sprung up on all sides, and private houses are only occasionally disturbed by the tramp of youthful feet. Nor is it, I believe, only from the youth of the period that most of these new haunts are recruited; the middle-aged, even the old, have become the chief protagonists, and the young, ramparted about with cigarette-smoke and many cocktails, watch with unaffected boredom the gyrations of their elders in those solemn measures which are so marked a change from the mazy whirls and the ever-increased speed of the valse, and the determined abandon of the gallop of former years.

Besides such haunts of pleasure as I have adumbrated, there have been others in London of a more unexpected character, and it will be news to many to learn that in a spot to-day covered with houses and forming a quite well-known residential quarter, once existed a race-course whose attractions at least for a time were a marked feature of the Civic pleasure-life. I refer to the race-course that existed on Notting Hill, details of which will be found in the body of this work.

Pugilism, in the eighteenth and especially in the earlier years of the nineteenth century, was popular, and although many of those famous contests with which the well-known names of Ben Sayers, Broughton, and such-like exponents are associated, took place outside the city, there were special centres, as there are to-day, where rings existed and prize-fights occurred.

Nor should the river be forgotten as a medium for the exhibition of a different kind of attraction, when races were held at Fulham and Putney reaches; when the 'Varsity boat-race itself started, as it starts to-day, at a spot which may properly be regarded as part and parcel of London, and where, occasionally, such weird and unexpected sights as that of a clown passing down the stream in a tub drawn by swans (or was it geese?) might have been seen exhibited to the eyes of a wondering crowd.

Indeed any place where the populace congregates for amusement or sight-seeing may be termed a pleasure haunt, and so there must be included in this rapid survey such unexpected *milieux* as Bridewell, where, in the eighteenth century, a certain class of people, chiefly from the higher stratas of society, were accustomed to congregate to see the whippings administered to the prisoners from those mixed motives of cruelty and sensuality which are to be found in some disordered imaginations.

The ravings of madness at Bedlam, too, attracted the curious to visit the unhappy inmates, not with a view to ameliorate their lot, but to watch, as the ladies in one of Hogarth's well-known prints are watching, the indecent actions and irresponsible contortions of lunacy. The author of "The London Spy" has preserved a record of this fashion in a passage in that work, by which the motives of the visitors are but too plainly indicated.

Still other haunts of pleasure (for there is no doubt that the crowds that congregated were actuated by delight in seeing fellow-men and women ill used, and generally took active steps themselves to exacerbate their lot) were the pillories which at one time stood at certain recognized spots in the city, and generally exhibited some malefactor to the organized indignities of the mob. From the days when political writers like Prynne, in the seventeenth century, to Defoe, in the eighteenth, were thus exposed to the hostile attentions of the people, the pillory may be said to have formed one of those free shows which, together with the procession of the Lord Mayor through the city or earlier by river, or the sovereign going in state to the Houses of Parliament, gave an opportunity for the people to enjoy something for which they did not pay, and in the case of the pillory to exhibit that love of exercising their cruelty on something that was powerless to retaliate.

Such forms of pleasure haunts as these are, of course, to be differentiated from those which have

had actual premises of their own, and with which
I deal in the following pages, but at the same time
they should, I think, properly be mentioned, because
they pandered to certain pleasure-loving propensities.

Pleasure is a curious thing to define; and if some
found it in the rural delights of gardens and others
in the hotbeds of iniquity, some in pelting a miserable
head fixed in a hole of the pillory, and others in going
to see men and women hanged at Tyburn and Newgate, there were many whose tastes were so catholic
as to lead them to all these "shows" as they came
along, and to cause them to take an equal interest
in what delighted the eye or excited the imagination.
That this still holds good is proved by the variety
of pleasure haunts that exist to-day, and the hold
all of them appear to have on the popular mind; and
many who form the crowds at football and cricket
matches are those that fill the theatres and the cinemas,
and are later to be found in the night clubs and
cabarets.

What seems to emerge from a study of the pleasure
haunts through the last few centuries is that in this
respect human nature remains much as it ever was:
the man who watches a contest between two prize-
fighters at the National Sporting Club (say) is of
the same fibre as he who grew excited at the ring in
the days of the earlier Georges, and as he who delighted
in what was equally an exhibition of skill between
bears and bulls and dogs in the time of the Tudors.

The love of dramatic performances has been
perennial from the time of Elizabeth; and dancing,
if now and again it has exhibited specially marked
phases of popularity, in one of which we now rather
wonderingly find ourselves, has always been part and
parcel of the lighter side of our civic existence. That
we now no longer delight in such full-blooded forms
of recreation, as did our Tudor and Stuart forbears,
is due to that gradual emollience in manners and

customs which Time generally brings in its train.
At the same time it will be found that, given the
different manners and customs of different periods,
the recreations of the people bear a not undue
similarity throughout the ages, and the haunts where
such were sought, if changed in *venue*, can still boast
a certain resemblance to each other. Thus the early
theatres in Shoreditch and Bankside were precursors
of those in Dorset Gardens, Salisbury Square, and
Lincoln's Inn Fields, which were to be succeeded by
the Covent Garden and Drury Lane of the eighteenth
century and of to-day, and by those smaller houses
in the Strand—the Olympic, the Globe and so forth—
which have now given place to a colony of such
haunts all over London; while the Old Vic preserves
still some of the characteristics of the earlier Surrey
and Coburg Theatres, where the transpontine drama
with all that it connoted held sway during the earlier
half of the last century.

Again, if, as is the case, our music-halls have departed from their old form as well as the form of the
entertainments they provided, they are the legitimate
successors of those earlier ones, some of which living
people remember. If, too, just now such things are
no longer popular, haunts like the Earl's Court
Exhibitions had a certain something in common with
the Vauxhall and Ranelagh of an earlier day, and the
dancing centres and night clubs are but a more
popular form of the entertainments provided by
Mrs. Cornelys and the Pantheon of the eighteenth
century; with links between them formed by such
places as Cremorne and Rosherville.

No longer, indeed, are we excited by balloon
ascents; no longer do we crowd to look at the dioramas
and panoramas of our fathers' days. We are become
far too sophisticated to grow lyric, as our forbears
did, over a diving-bell, or to enjoy the simple pleasures
of a German Reeds' entertainment. But the Hall of

Mystery in Langham Place is still as popular as it was in the Egyptian Hall whose oriental façade Piccadilly has long forgotten; and Lords and the Oval and Lillie Bridge draw vaster crowds than the last century would have dreamed possible. Clubs are more numerous than they ever were, and bridge claims those who at an earlier day regarded whist as the king of card-games. We have to go much further than Notting Hill for our racing; and if we can play tennis and racquets in London, as, indeed, our ancestors could in Charles II.'s time, we can also swim there without having to go, as the seventeenth and eighteenth centuries had to go, to what were then the outskirts of the city.

The Coffee-houses and Chocolate-houses of the past may, too, be said to have a recrudescence in the innumerable facilities offered by well-known firms, and the future topographer will have to be as much concerned with Corner Houses as those of to-day are with Ozinda's and the Grecian. Taverns have given place to what we call (so much less picturesquely) Public Houses; inns, with their galleried yards and their exiguous parlours, have been succeeded by immense caravanserais in which the visitor, if he be known at all, is known (like a convict) by a number, and mine host is represented by a body of gentlemen who meet in a board-room and are harassed by tremendous questions of policy, like Cabinet Ministers.

As will be seen in the following pages, I have endeavoured to trace the evolution of pleasure in London by recording the history of its haunts from the time of the Tudors downwards. In this survey are included the Bear- and Bull-baiting Rings, the Theatres, the Pleasure Gardens, such famous resorts as Ranelagh and Vauxhall, the rooms of Mrs. Cornelys and Mr. Almack; the less reputable haunts associated with the name of the notorious Mrs. Berkeley and others; the Tea-gardens and Wells of a more unsophisticated section of the people; as well as such more widely popular "shows" as exhibitions, both of the 1851 and the Earl's Court description. Many subsidiary places where pleasure has been sought and achieved have also entered into my scheme, and have received a more or less extended notice as their importance or otherwise suggests; in fact, wherever in London "love or gold can . . . buy entertainment," as Shakespeare phrases it, that spot I have endeavoured to describe and illustrate with the hope that what has in the past afforded pleasure in itself may again be the means of giving some to those who read its annals.

CHAPTER I

TUDOR London has almost wholly disappeared. You may roam the city from west to east, and find practically nothing of that architecturally picturesque period remaining. So thoroughly did the Great Fire do its devastating work that, with the exception of the famous block of old houses in Holborn, and such relics of a still earlier day as have survived in St. Bartholomew's, Smithfield and the Tower and a few churches, together with the Abbey, and the gatehouse of St. James's Palace, there is practically nothing to show us what London looked like when Henry ruled and Elizabeth, and Shakespeare headed that amazing constellation which laid the foundation of our dramatic literature.

Shakespeare's London is, indeed, so far as architectural remains show, almost as much obliterated as Chaucer's. And yet, so dominating was that period, so tremendous the influence it exerted, so insistent the mark it left on our national life, that we somehow seem to know it better than later ages whose remains are around us.

You can go from Charing Cross to Liverpool Street without seeing a single building recalling the spacious days of Queen Bess, yet, through the reconstruction of historians and topographers, you can visualize that period at a hundred spots on the route; Bankside is now a miserable congeries of dilapidated wharves and warehouses (where there should be an embankment), or of modern commercial buildings,

14

and ill-inhabited, as the old writers used to put it, houses, with not a trace of those splendid ecclesiastical palaces which once rose there; and yet with the magic name of Shakespeare, the touchstone by which so many writers have been able to revivify the London of his day, you can reconstruct, at least in the mind's eye, those theatres with which he was identified and, indeed, that whole area which his genius has forever illumined.

And it is in the theatre that the amusements of Tudor times found their best and most characteristic expression. The bull- and bear-baiting, with which Bankside is so closely identified, were actually earlier *media* of entertainment, indeed they were in Tudor times but a continuation of such things as had been popular in the twelfth century, and they were destined to survive well into the days of the Stuarts; but, after all, they were a survival of barbarism, whereas the theatre was the beginning of a more intellectual conception of amusement, if not, indeed, of life itself, and as such claims priority.

Humanity has always delighted in shows, and the plays of the sixteenth century were but a development (but what a development!) of those "mysteries" and "mummers" which had been previously the only forms of dramatic performance known to unsophisticated generations.

In such well-known works as Strutt's "Sports and Pastimes of the People of England," and Brand's "Popular Antiquities" will be found, in addition to a vast amount of information on the sports and amusements of the Londoner in pre-Tudor days, much bearing on this and later periods; and just as the horse-races on Notting Hill in the earlier part of the nineteenth century were anticipated by horse-races in the Middle Ages,[1] and the baiting of animals

[1] Fitzstephen (temp. Henry II.) says horses were matched against each other in West Smithfield in his time; but it would seem rather to prove their excellence as saleable objects than for actual sport.

under the Tudors was but a continuation of what had happened under the Normans and the Plantaganets, so the dramatic performances of the period we are considering were but an outcome of those miracle plays and mysteries with which from time immemorial the people of London, and, indeed, of every part of the country, were familiar.

But before Elizabethan days no special buildings had been constructed specially for such exhibitions. A rough-and-ready structure, where one was used at all, was set up wherever convenience dictated, and miracles, so called because they consisted of sacred plays or representations of the miracles said to have been performed by the holy confessors, were exhibited, as were the "Mystery" plays, in all sorts of places: here in the hall of the king's palace; there in some church, although this latter custom was prohibited by Bishop Bonner, in 1542, by proclamation; and one of the few actual sites identified with early performances of such plays was Skinner's Wells, near Smithfield, where, in 1391, the parish clerks of London exhibited a play which lasted for three days, and whose performance was attended by the King, Richard II, and his court. Indeed, Skinner's Wells appears to have been something in the nature of a regular haunt for dramatic performers, for Stow tells us that, in 1409, "a great play" was performed there, lasting eight days, "where were to see the same the most part of the Nobles and Gentles in England." Skinner's Wells is traditionally said to have occupied a site on the west side of the Church of St. James, Clerkenwell,[1] and its proximity to Smithfield, where jousts and tournaments were of frequent occurrence, and the chief market of London existed and Bartholomew Fair, founded by Rahere in the time of Henry I.,

[1] Skinner Street and Market Street preserve its memory. See for account of it Cromwell's " History of Clerkenwell." In Rocque's Map of 1745, the Skin Market is shown on the site.

was held for three feverish days in the year, made this spot a recognized centre for popular amusement as well as of commerce.

But it is with pleasure haunts that we are here concerned, and in the direction of the drama the first theatre, as such,[1] which is known to have existed in London, was that in the precincts of the old Holywell Priory, in Shoreditch, with which the name of James Burbage is associated. After the Dissolution a large portion of the estate on which the Priory stood was purchased by one Henry Webb, in 1544, and half of this property later passed to Giles Allen, from whom James Burbage, a joiner and an important member of the Earl of Leicester's company of players, obtained a twenty-one years' lease, on April 13, 1576, "of houses and land situated between Finsbury Field and the public road from Bishopsgate to Shoreditch Church."[2] The lease, we are told, was obtained with the express object of a playhouse being erected on part of the site.

The late Halliwell-Phillipps gives minute details as to the topography of this area, and in the well-known map of Agas, *circa* 1560–70, and that of Braun and Hogenberg of 1572, the position to be occupied but a few years later by London's first theatre is plainly shown. Stow, in referring to Holywell Priory, mentions the demolition of the church, the building of lodgings

[1] It would appear that hitherto the miracle plays and so forth were exhibited on a sort of movable scaffold on wheels, containing two rooms, the lower one used as a dressing-room and the higher one as the stage, without a covering. These peripatetic "theatres" moved from street to street, in some of which scaffolds and stages were erected for the convenience of witnessing the performance, and were, no doubt, occupied by the quality and were paid for, the populace viewing the show as well as they could from the ground, on which they sat or stood. See the description of one of these left by Archdeacon Rogers (who flourished during the sixteenth century at Chester), and quoted by Thomas Sharp in his "Coventry Pageants," 1825. The name of *stage*-plays may well have arisen from this custom.

[2] "Early London Theatres," by T. Fairman Ordish, 1894.

C

for noblemen and others, "and neare thereunto are builded," he adds, "two publique houses for the acting and shewe of comedies, tragedies, and histories for recreation, whereof the one is called The Curtain and the other The Theater, both standing on the south-west side towards the Field." [1]

At that time plays were forbidden in the city itself, hence one of the reasons, no doubt, for the selection of this spot, which, besides being contiguous with Finsbury Fields, a well-known place of recreation for the citizens, was within easy access of those living within the walls. Civic proclamation could not eradicate the growing love for stage-plays, although it could forbid their exhibition within the boundaries of London itself.

There exists no representation of The Theater, as Burbage's house was called, but there is no doubt that it was built of wood and that it was circular in form. The first goes without saying, because practically everything, with the exception of large public edifices and the palaces of great nobles, was in those days so constructed. The circular form followed naturally the precedent set by the amphitheatres of the Romans, and later by the form which some of the structures for the acting of Moralities and Mysteries took, as may be seen by the representation of one given by Sharp, in his "Coventry Mysteries," where the stage is surrounded by a circular enclosure in which some of the spectators sat, as well as by the shape of the bear- and bull-baiting centres already existing on Bankside. It was open on the top, and was thus little more than a circular enclosure—a small wooden imitation of those vast and splendid amphitheatres

---

[1] So in his 1598 edition. In that of 1603, he makes no mention of the theatres. Mr. Fairman Ordish thinks this a sign of the disapproval with which such places were generally regarded. But I cannot but think it was because by then at least The Theater had ceased to exist there.

whose ruins still exist in Rome and Verona and Arles.
This arrangement did very well for the "activities"
and "shows," which Stow mentions, and which consisted of the baiting of animals, exhibitions of strength
and dexterity, and fencing and mock combat at arms.
When, however, plays were to be given, a stage was
set up in the centre of the arena; so that Burbage was
able to use his new structure for a variety of purposes,
and by surrounding it with a wooden enclosure could
make a charge for admission.

Being a member, as we have seen, of Lord Leicester's
band of players, he was able to arrange for this company to give performances in his house, and that the
venture was successful is proved by the fact that at
his death in 1597, he still owned the property and
bequeathed it to his family.[1]   This event occurred
just as the lease of twenty-one years was on the point
of expiration, and a new one had been prepared,
when Giles Allen, the ground landlord, refused to
execute it. A lawsuit followed and the Burbage family
seem to have been involved in no little trouble with
a landlord who appears to have been of a singularly
grasping character. Burbage's two sons, Cuthbert and
Richard, however, managed to carry on the theatre
for nearly two years after their father's death, at
which time The Theater ceased to exist—a con-
summation at which, it would seem, Allen had aimed.
As the Corporation was also glad to be rid of something of which it never approved, but over which it
had no power, it has been surmised that Allen was
acting under its influence. This seems the more
probable in that the success of the playhouse could
hardly otherwise have been annoying to him, as landlord, from a monetary point of view.

It appears that the principal objection of the

[1] His father-in-law advanced the necessary money for the purchase
of ground and construction of The Theater to the amount of 1,000
marks, about £666. (Fairman Ordish "Early London Theatres.")

Corporation to The Theater was because its "playes doe make assemblies of citizens and their families," and assemblies in those days were regarded with the utmost apprehension by the Guardians of the Peace. Anyhow, such is the reason given in an indictment of Burbage and one John Braynes, who appears to have been his manager, which is among the records of the Clerkenwell Session House.

That there was sometimes good reason for the Corporation's fear of riotous assemblies in such places is proved by the fact that on a certain Sunday in the April of 1580, a "great disorder" had occurred at The Theater; and so serious did the Lord Mayor consider it that he wrote to the Lord Chancellor (who, it seems, had already taken the matter in hand) to inform him "that the players of plays, used at the Theater and other such places, and tumblers and such-like, were a very superfluous sort of men, and of such faculty as the laws had disallowed; that the exercise of the plays was not only a great hindrance to the service of God, but also a great corruption of youth, with unchaste and wicked matters, the occasion of much incontinence, practices of many frays, quarrels, and other disorders, within the City. He therefore begged that order might be taken to prevent such plays, not only within the City, but also in the liberties." [1]

Sir John Branch, who was Lord Mayor in 1580, was equalled in his anti-histrionic zeal by Edward Osborne, who occupied that position three years later, and who is found being addressed by Walsingham thus: "With regard to the letter of the Council on behalf of Her Majesty's players, which the Lord Mayor had interpreted to extend only to holidays and not to other week-days, the Council, considering that without frequent exercise of such plays as were to be presented before Her Majesty her servants

[1] "Remembrancia," 1579–1664.

could not conveniently satisfy her recreation and their own duty, desired that they should be licenced to perform upon week-days and work-days, at convenient times, between this and Shrovetide (Sundays only excepted) 1st December, 1583." [1]

This was a diplomatic counterblast on the part of Sir Francis (a good friend to the players) to confront the Lord Mayor's complaint of "the great inconveniences of the assemblies of people to plays, bearbaiting, fencers, and profane spectacles at The Theater and Curtain and other places," with the authority of the Queen herself, who proved an equally friendly patron to the drama.

Nor was it only civic antagonism to which The Theater was exposed. A year after it had been opened there appeared a book, written by John Northbrooke, entitled "Treatise against Dicing, Dancing, Plays, and Interludes, with other idle Pastimes." [2] It is in the form of a dialogue between Youth and Age; and at one point the former asks: "Doe you speake against those places also, whiche are made uppe and builded for such playes and interludes as the *Theatre* and *Curteine* is, and other such lyke places beside?" To which Age replies: "Yea, truly; for I am persuaded that Satan hath not a more speedie way and fitter schoole to work and teach his desire, to bring men and women into his snare of concupiscence and filthie lustes of wicked whoredome, than those places and plays and theatres are; and therefore necessarie that those places and players shoulde be forbidden, and dissolved, and put downe by authoritie, as the brothell houses and stewes are."

Equally vehement invective flowed from the pulpits, whose occupants used such things as the recurrent

---

[1] "Remembrancia."

[2] It is a black-letter work of 148 pages, dedicated to Sir John Yong, 1577. Another edition appeared in 1579. It was reprinted by the Shakespeare Society, 1843.

plagues to point their attacks and give force to their arguments. There seems, too, to have been an amount of luxury (as luxury was then underſtood) about the decorations of The Theater which irritated the puritanical, whose fulminations the mere faĉt that people enjoyed themselves was quite sufficient to provoke. The faĉt that the playhouse was built of wood and that it coſt what would be equivalent to about a thousand pounds of our money indicates that Burbage muſt have been remarkably lavish both on its ſtability and the beauty of its *décor*. Although, nowadays, such animosity and narrowness of vision seem ſtrange enough, at the same time there is little doubt that the performances in the theatre did give rise to no little trouble, and at a time when the guardianship of the peace was in anything but skilful hands, much abuse crept in. But such things arose rather from other causes than those of dramatic representation, although as being traced to The Theater [1] they were regarded as being due to a play-mad seĉtion of the public. The ordinary price of admission was one penny, but for this only ſtanding room was available. For twopence one could gain access to the galleries around; while further sums were charged for seats in these galleries and for private rooms or boxes. In conneĉtion with these entrance fees, it is intereſting to learn that when Gyles Allen granted his lease to Burbage he expressly reserved for himself and his family the right to occupy, free of charge, one of these boxes during any performance [2]—an early precedent to that exercised by the Dukes of Bedford at Covent Garden Theatre.

From the researches of that remarkable Shakespearian inveſtigator, Halliwell-Phillipps, we are enabled to learn something concerning the dramatic fare

---

[1] A disturbance outside it, June 1584, is described in a letter to Lord Burghley.

[2] Halliwell-Phillipps, "Outlines of the Life of Shakespeare."

placed before the patrons of The Theater. Thus
"The Blacksmith's Daughter," and "Cataline's Conspiracies," are mentioned by Gosson as being "usually
brought in to the Theater." "The Playe of Playes"
(whatever that was), which was performed on February
23, 1581–2; the "History of Cæsar and Pompey,"
and the play of "The Fabii" were also given about
the same time. Then the old pre-Shakespearean play
of "Hamlet" was acted here, to which Lodge, in his
"Wits Miserie," published in 1596, refers when he
writes of one who "looks as pale as the visard of the
ghoſt which cries so miserably at the Theater, like an
oiſter-wife, '*Hamlet, revenge.*'" But by far the moſt
notable piece given at Burbage's playhouse was
Marlowe's glorious "Fauſtus," which, as we shall
see, Henslowe was putting on at "The Rose," any
time between 1594 and 1597.

Besides this classical *repertoire*, the audience were
kept amused during the intervals by what were called
"drolls," a sort of impromptu pleasantry, with which
the names of Richard Tarlton, whose famous "Jeſts"
were firſt published in 1611,[1] and William Kempe of
"The Nine Daies Wonder" (1600) figured prominently, and were apparently as popular favourites
as Mr. George Robey and Mr. Berry (*inter multos
alios*) are to-day. The faſt that their satire, impromptu
and otherwise, was frequently direſted againſt the
civic authority that would gladly have put an end to
them and the playhouse, gave an additional spice to
their witticisms, but hardly helped to soften the
feelings of those in power. Indeed, the latter were
always on the look-out for the leaſt excuse to interfere
with what was becoming daily more and more popular.
When, for inſtance, that diſturbance in June 1584
occurred, to which allusion has been made, the Lord
Mayor aſtually sent two of his Aldermen to Court

[1] On the title page is a rough woodcut of Tarlton, showing his
broken nose which he got "by parting some dogs and bears."

to recommend the suppressing and pulling down of "the Theatre and the Curtein," an incident recorded in a letter from Fleetwood to Lord Burghley.[1] But threatened men live long and some playhouses, The Theater among them, may be said to do the same; for nothing seems to have been done, beyond the fact that Fleetwood sent for the owner of the playhouse (whom Fairman Ordish assumes to have been Burbage, Braynes, or one Hyde, the assignee of the property), who was "a stubborne fellow," and bound him over to appear before the justices. The fact is, as we have seen, the Queen and the Court were too well disposed towards the players to permit the legal courts or the Lord Mayor and Corporation to go to extremities, and in all probability the case was settled; certainly The Theater remained intact and plays and so forth took place there as usual.

It was in the year 1586, one of the most notable in dramatic literature, that Shakespeare came up to London from Stratford and was soon after associated with The Theater, and The Curtain which, as we shall see, stood near by. In what that first association consisted, it is perhaps impossible to tell, but Sir Sidney Lee,[2] the outstanding authority on the subject, does not wholly reject the well-known story which tells how young Shakespeare first found employment by holding the horses of the nobles and gentlemen who had ridden out to see "The History of the Fabii" or the "Life and Death of Dr. Faustus." In any case it was not long before he was offered employment inside the playhouse; perhaps as prompter's attendant, or call-boy. He was ready to put his hand to anything, and good sense and good nature soon had their reward. An actor may have failed or fallen ill at the last moment; a supernumerary may have been required; whatever it was, the chance came, and once given an opportunity, the young

[1] In the Lansdowne MSS.   [2] "Life of William Shakespeare."

Shakespeare's powers were so patent that even a stage-manager could not fail to recognize them. We know that it was first as an actor that he became famous in London, just as it is as a dramatist and a poet that he has since ruled the world; and the glory of The Theater is divided between having been the first of all London playhouses, and the cradle of Shakespeare's genius.

Between the years 1592 and 1594 he was acting at the transpontine theatres, but at the latter date he had, as a member of the Chamberlain's Company, not infrequently performed at The Theater and The Curtain; while he is mentioned by name, with Burbage and Kempe, as receiving remuneration for acting before the Queen at Greenwich, in the December of the same year.

The troubles that had dogged The Theater in its relation with the civic power had recrudescences both in 1592, 1595 and 1597; and although the first seems to have been caused rather by the fact that the place was a rallying point for crowds and, therefore, a source of those broils which arose whenever any number of citizens foregathered in those days, the last had something more directly to do with the playhouse itself, in that, as an order of the Privy Council, issued to the Justices for Middlesex, put it, "lewd matters were handled on the stage." This order was directed against both The Theater and The Curtain, whose proprietors were enjoined "forthwith to plucke downe quite the stages, galleries and roomes that are made for people to stand in, and so to deface the same as they maie not be ymploied agayne to such use."

Such orders were, however, not always intended to be carried out, and this may have been of such a nature; at any rate The Theater was not plucked down; but for other reasons its end was near. Burbage died in 1597, and there followed the trouble between his heirs and the ground landlord, Allen. In the original lease, however, there was a clause permitting the lessees to take away "all such buildings and other things as should be builded"; [1] and Cuthbert and Richard Burbage, finding themselves harassed on all sides, determined to exercise their power. They employed one Peter Street, a builder, to undertake the work of demolition, which was duly carried out about the end of 1598. A lawsuit followed between Allen and the Burbages which does not here concern us, except that in the records of it, printed by Halliwell-Phillipps, will be found an account of the removal of the wood and timber "in the moſt forcible and riotous manner" to Bankside, and the erecͭtion with such materials of "a newe playhowse"; this being none other than The Globe Theatre, famous for its connecͭtion with Shakespeare and his plays, concerning which I shall have something to say later on.

I have been rather diffuse in my account of The Theater, firſt because it inaugurated this form of dramatic headquarters and was, so to put it, the Adam of the world of playhouses; and secondly because much of what I have said with regard to its form and conſtrucͭtion holds good so far as its one contemporary and many of its immediate followers are concerned.

Its significance for us here particularly lies, too, in the facͭt that, with the exception of those ſtrucͭtures in which the baiting of animals took place, it was the pioneer of that vaſt collocation of pleasure haunts with which this book specially deals. Like not a few of these, it came into militant contacͭt with civic authority; it was the *fons et origo* of much unruly conducͭt; it was an offence and a *scandalum* to many who viewed its "shows" with a horror that seems

---

[1] Fairman Ordish, who points out the doubtful legality of this in that the Burbages were acting under the clauses of a lease that had already expired and had not been renewed.

incredible in these days; but it remains the forerunner of the playhouse, which, in spite of mistakes here and there, has done so much to educate the people and to humanize their manners.

The Curtain

Unlike The Theater, the early history of The Curtain is, as was the birth of Yellowpluch, "wropt in a mistry." Its builder, the date of its opening, the cost of the structure, and such-like details, are not forthcoming. Even the Herculean labours of Halliwell-Phillipps in this direction have proved fruitless, and all we definitely know is that this playhouse was the second to be erected in London, and that it stood in close proximity to The Theater, in the precincts of old Holywell Priory, Clerkenwell. Many may reasonably have supposed that its name was evolved from that feature of a playhouse with which the audience is first confronted (that part of the audience, that is to say, that make a rule of arriving early). Not so, however. Indeed, I do not think a curtain was part and parcel of the theatre in these early days, at all. No, the name was simply applied to the playhouse because it was erected on ground known as the *Curteine,* so described in a lease dated 1538, and doubtless perpetuating a point in the fortifications of ancient London formed by the old wall of the city.[1] It probably stood near a road called Holywell Lane, and its name is still perpetuated in Curtain Road, its exact site being marked as Curtain Court, in a plan of Shoreditch which Chassereau produced in 1745.

It would seem that The Curtain arose soon after The Theater, for the two are bracketed together in Northbrooke's Treatise against Dicing, Dancing, Plays, etc., first published in 1577.

---

[1] A curtain, in military phraseology, of course, indicates that portion of a wall extending between two towers.

The reasons which governed the selection of this spot for the building of The Curtain were the same as those that obtained in the case of The Theater; and although two so near each other might be supposed to have affected the prosperity of each, at the same time there were, no doubt, sufficient patrons to fill both, and one may have brought "business" to the other. Besides, the spot was a sort of revelling ground for Londoners; and above all it was beyond the immediate jurisdiction of the authorities.

The uses to which The Curtain was put, and the public that patronized it, were much the same as in the case of The Theater. When plays were not being given, the structure was used for those fencing matches and exhibitions of sword-play which were popular, and which the well-known military *aura* of Finsbury Fields made specially appropriate in this neighbourhood. But one thing differentiates The Curtain from its rival. Here it was that one of Shakespeare's plays was first performed; so that if the one playhouse had the merit of being a pioneer in one direction, the other can claim to have first heard the glorious lines of the great man. That play was inspired by the expedition to Ireland, in 1599, of the Earl of Essex, in whose train the dramatist's friend, Lord Southampton, went as General of Horse. At this time The Theater had ceased to exist, and it is supposed that "Henry V.," the play in question, was performed by the company which Richard Burbage and Shakespeare himself were now running. A direct reference to The Curtain is made in the prologue in that "Wooden O," in which the author questions whether his company could cram

> ". . . . the very casques
> That did affright the air at Agincourt."

Later on, the dramatist indicates the very elementary character of the stage-management, when he writes,

" . . . we shall much disgrace
With four or five most vile and raggéd foils,
Right ill-disposed in brawls ridiculous,
The name of Agincourt . . ."

There was, of course, no attempt at scenery in these
early theatres, and the fact has been too often insisted
upon to need labouring here. Indeed, it is easy to
visualize the circular building filled by a heterogeneous
crowd, with a more or less bare stage in the centre
on which the actors had little to rely on but their own
powers and the beauty of the lines they had to recite.
A return to such archaic methods has been attempted
in our own day—not without the success that often
attends innovation; but we have grown too sophisticated, too used to the gorgeous settings which Sir
Henry Irving initiated and Sir Herbert Tree perpetuated, to much care for mere excellence in acting
or charm of the spoken word, without that elaborate
décor to which we have grown accustomed.

The fortunes of The Curtain seem to have been
on the whole more prosperous than those of The
Theater. Often attacked by the civic authorities, it
was able as continually to weather the storm, and
even in 1601, when a final attempt to bring about its
destruction was made, it was able to escape into a
calm period of prosperity which was to last for nearly
another thirty years. Indeed, so safe did the players
consider themselves that they took to satirizing
people of importance, including, it need hardly be said,
their enemies on the Corporation, which drew down
on them the appeal to the Privy Council of 1601,
that, as I say, proved abortive.[1] That the players
had good grounds for annoyance at the ultra-puri-
tanism of the city fathers seems established; equally
had they some reasonable cause for complaint against

[1] The terms of the complaint are given by Halliwell-Phillipps, in
his "Outlines of the Life of Shakespeare," and are taken from a MS.
Register of the Privy Council.

the cloud of witnesses which rose up against them in the pulpits of churches and in the pages of books and pamphlets. However, they gave as good as they got, no doubt, and their audiences were pleased enough to laugh at stinging invective and covert allusion, and probably did not trouble themselves to listen to the fulminations of clergymen or to read the lucubrations of pamphleteers. One of these counterblasts to authority was Tarlton's "Jigge of a Horse-loade of Fooles," which is said to have been performed at The Curtain.[1]

Mr. Fairman Ordish divides the history of The Curtain into three periods: (i) From 1576 to 1598, when its fortunes were linked with those of The Theater; (ii) from 1599 to 1602, when much agitation went on to get it closed in favour of Edward Alleyn's new playhouse, The Fortune; and (iii) from 1602 to the end of its career about 1627–30.

It was before its final incarnation that The Curtain is said, on good grounds,[2] to have been the playhouse at which "Romeo and Juliet" was first performed in 1597, and where also Ben Jonson's "Every Man in his Humour" was produced in the following year, each being under the *ægis* of the Chamberlain's (Lord Hunsdon's) Company of Players, who were accustomed to give performances both at The Theater and The Curtain; as well as at that Blackfriars Theatre [3] which Burbage had established in 1596.

After the accession of James I., the Chamberlain's Company acted solely at these two new theatres, being succeeded at The Curtain by a company bearing the Queen Consort's name; and in the Calendar of Domestic State Papers there is a licence to this effect.

[1] Tarlton, besides being famous as a droll on his own account, is immortal as having inspired the character of Yorick.

[2] Halliwell-Phillipps was of this opinion, and Fairman-Ordish, who goes carefully into the matter, corroborates it.

[3] See *supra*.

Besides such regular performers, others were apparently able, occasionally, to hire The Curtain, and at least once an amateur performance by young men of the city took place there—in 1615, Wentworth Smith's play: "Hector of Germany" being given there by these neophytes; [1] while later, the newly-formed Prince's Company of Players exhibited their powers in the old house.

The last reference which the combined research of Halliwell-Phillipps and Collier discovered with regard to The Curtain was in a pamphlet entitled "Vox Graculi, or the Jackdaw's Prognostication for 1623"; but Fairman Ordish was able to add to our knowledge the existence of the place at a still later date, *viz.* February the 3rd, 1628, from an entry in the Middlesex County Records, in which it is referred to indirectly as still standing; while he also believed that it remained so late as the general suppression of the theatres which took place between 1642–7, or some twelve to fifteen years later than the generally accepted date of its demolition. If this be the case, it was the longest-lived of these old playhouses; and as such obviously enjoyed a full meed of popularity.

As we shall see, it was destined to pass from being one of the only two such pleasure haunts in London to the position of one amongst many, some of which were fated to outshine it in their architectural characteristics as well as in the fame of their dramatic associations; but The Curtain can always boast the youthful presence of Shakespeare, and the glory of having been the first playhouse in which any of his plays was staged.

[1] Collier's "History of Dramatic Poetry."

CHAPTER II

THE EARLY BANKSIDE THEATRES

The Surrey side of the river has become so closely identified with the fortunes of the theatre during the close of the sixteenth century and the earlier years of the seventeenth, that many people probably imagine that it was there—at The Bear Garden and The Hope, The Rose and The Swan, and above all The Globe—that the Elizabethan drama first found histrionic expression, and will be surprised to find that Shoreditch has a prior claim in this respect. We have seen the reason why. But we have also seen that the proprietors of the two theatres in Holywell, even if they had the advantage of being on a spot long given over to recreation of various kinds and were actually outside the immediate jurisdiction of the civic authorities, were yet close enough to give that authority means of continually attempting their suppression by all sorts of devious arts. When, therefore, in the case of The Theater, these *désagrémens*, coupled with the other more private troubles I have noticed, came to a head, and the Burbages sought some other locality for their theatrical enterprise, they could hardly have selected a safer or more appropriate spot than the borough of Southwark.

For in spite of the jealousy of the City, which was always trying to extend its authority across the bridges, and largely because of the supineness of the Surrey magistrates, who do not seem to have troubled to exercise the authority they had at all, this part of London was in the happy state of doing very much as it wished;

and like the Alsatia, on the northern bank, was bliss-
fully regardless of laws and regulations. On the whole I
should say that it was the moſt amusing part of the
metropolis in Tudor and early Stuart days. One has
but to glance at Agas's well-known map to see,
even in its exiguous outlines and absence of detail, how
many resorts for pleasure and mirth abounded there.
Paris Garden in the weſt, opposite Bridewell (now
Bridge Street, Blackfriars), which Fleetwood once told
Lord Burghley was "the very bower of conspiracy,"
was one of those haunts which under the periphrasis of
"pleasure resorts," connote both illicit pleasures and
not infrequently treasonable plotting. It was as its
name indicates—but as now, with the vaſt *congeries* of
buildings covering it, it is difficult for us to realize—
essentially rural in charaĉter; hidden from the river by
that row of small tenements that ſtretched as far eaſt
as Southwark Bridge, with a wide road which should,
to-day, be an embankment, as in a sense it then was,
between them and the Thames. Behind these houses
were fields and the trees of Paris Garden, which had its
special landing-ſtage from the river, a landing-ſtage
known specifically by that name. A little farther
eaſt there was the circular ereĉtion known as The
Bull Baiting, and beyond in an adjoining field a similar
conſtruĉtion, The Bear Baiting; while further eaſt,
opposite the Tower, was Horsley Down, where a fair
used to be held,[1] and where one of the more innocent
recreations indulged in was the exercising and grazing
of horses, and between it and the river a building
of considerable size embedded in a thickly-wooded
garden which Agas, who generally only puts names to
important ſtruĉtures, is careful to let us know is the
Beere Howse—and quite a super-beer house it must
have been! When it is added that that collocation of

---

[1] There is a picture by Hofnagle at Hatfield House representing
this fair, and dating from some time during the last years of Elizabeth's
reign.

D

low haunts known as The Stews, otherwise brothels, whose rents went to expand the revenues of the Bishop of Winchester, were in close proximity, and known to all, in consequence of the proclamation, made in 1540, to the effect that they should be "whited and painted with signes on the front for a token of the said houses,"[1] nothing more need be said, I think, about the suitability of such a locality for further pleasure haunts in the then relatively novel form of theatres. There were, too, so many places where people, congregating for other reasons, would find a playhouse convenient for the whiling away of some leisure hours, and many of those using such well-known resorts as The Tabard and The Bear might well be calculated upon to increase the audiences. Indeed, this area was, perhaps, the greatest pleasure resort then to be found in London, in consequence of its traditions and the variety of *divertissements* and recreations to be met with. To these the Burbages were to add, if not the most acceptable, at least those whose fame has survived that of their predecessors and contemporaries.

When The Theater, in Shoreditch, was demolished the materials were carried across the river, and therewith was erected that "newe playhouse" which as The Globe was destined to outlive in fame all the theatres of Tudor days. This was done, as we have seen, in the teeth of the landlord, who complained that Burbage and his employees to the number of twelve did, on December 28, 1598, "ryoutouslye assemble themselves together, and then and there armed themselves with dyvers and many unlawfull and offensive weapons, as namelye, swords, daggers, billes, axes, and such like, and soe armed, did then and there repayre to the sayd Theater and . . . attempted to pull

---

[1] It is significant, and characteristic of the habitual failure of legists and reformers to alter human nature, that five years *earlier* "The Stews" were said to be, *as far as possible*, publicly and entirely suppressed!

downe the sayd Theater . . . and having done soe in
most forcible and ryotous manner did take and carrye
away from thence all the wood and timber thereof unto
the Bancksyde in the parishe of St. Marye Overyes,
and there erected a newe playhouse with the sayd timber
and wood."[1]

But early as its existence was among London
theatres The Globe was not the first to be erected in
Southwark, for The Rose had preceded it by some
seven or eight years, and its situation is plainly indicated in Norden's invaluable map, incorporated in his
"Speculum Britanniæ," published in 1593. As I shall
have something further to say of The Rose, I need not
amplify the matter here, as it is convenient to deal with
The Globe first.

The actual position of The Globe has led to some
controversy, Malone[2] asserting that it was in Maid
Lane, while Chalmers is positive that it was situated on
Bankside, "within eighty paces of the river, which has
since receded from its former limits; and that it stood
on the site of John Whatley's windmill, as I have
been assured by an intelligent manager of Barclay's
brew-house, which covers in its ample range part
of Globe Alley."[3] There is hardly any doubt that
Chalmers is right and Malone wrong, and it seems
conclusive that The Globe stood exactly where the
Globe Alley Meeting House was later to exist, and
where Baxter was wont to preach during the years
1676–7.

It was called "The Globe" from its sign, which
represented Hercules bearing a globe on his shoulders,
with the motto, "Totus mundus agit histrionem," beneath. Shakespeare, who, as we have seen, had already
become connected with Burbage, and had obviously
done well for himself, was a shareholder in The Globe,

[1] Quoted in "Shakespeare's England," 2 vols., 1916.
[2] Malone's "Enquiry," p. 84.
[3] Chalmers's "Apology," p. 114.

and here were produced "Richard II.," "Romeo and Juliet," "King Lear," "Othello," "Macbeth," "Love's Labour Loſt," "The Winter's Tale," "The Taming of the Shrew," and "Pericles," as well as "Henry V.," which had firſt been given at The Curtain, and "Henry VIII."

It was during a performance of the laſt piece, on June 29, 1613, that a disaſter occurred. Two small cannon had to be discharged in connection with the performance, and by some means the thatched roof over the galleries caught fire, and totally deſtroyed the building. There are one or two contemporary accounts of the cataſtrophe exiſting. From one, in a letter from Sir Henry Wotton to Sir Edmund Bacon, we learn that "The King's players had a new play, called 'All is True,' representing some principal pieces of the reign of Henry the Eighth, which was set forth with many extraordinary circumſtances of pomp and majeſty, even to the matting on the ſtage, the knights of the order with their Georges and garters, the guards with their embroidered coats and the like. Now King Henry meeting a masque at the Cardinal Wolsey's house, and certain chambers (cannon) being shot off at his entry, some of the paper or other ſtuff wherewith one of them was ſtopped did light on the thatch, where, being thought at firſt but an idle smoak, and their eyes more attentive to the show, it kindled inwardly and ran round like a train, consuming in less than an hour the whole house to the very ground; nothing did perish but wood and ſtraw, and a few forsaken cloaks, and one man had his breeches set on fire."[1]

There are one or two intereſting points in this letter. In the firſt place it indicates that the title of the play was not "Henry VIII.," when given in 1613, and Malone's suggeſtion that it had been revived "with new decorations" and so forth, under the title of "All is True," seems probable; as it was firſt

[1] "Religiæ Wottoniæ," 1685, p. 425.

published in 1604, and could not properly be called a new play, as Wotton calls it.[1]

The spectators, again, had only seen the first act, in the last scene of which the Masque referred to occurs; while that the representation was attended by more than the archaic "dressing," we are accustomed to associate with the exhibition of Elizabethan drama, is proved by Wotton's remarks about the costumes. In another account of the fire, given by Chamberlaine to Sir Ralph Winwood, the details are practically the same, although the writer indicates that it took longer to burn down the theatre than Wotton estimated, and adds that it was a mercy no lives were lost, as there were only two narrow doors by which the audience could escape.

In addition to these prose accounts, a ballad entitled "Sonnet on the Pitiful Burning of The Globe Playhouse in London," was written and widely circulated in manuscript, commemorating the details of the fire.

No time appears to have been lost in rebuilding the playhouse, and we are told that King James and many noblemen and others contributed generously to the cost. It was determined to make it "the fairest in England";[2] and we know that one of its improvements was a tiled roof in place of the thatch of its predecessor.

It is this rebuilt Globe which may be seen very clearly in Visscher's Plan of London dated 1616. It was apparently a brick or cement structure, octagonal in shape, and having some buildings on the top, from one of which a flag is shown flying.[3] There were windows at intervals, from which the necessary light was obtained; and altogether, archaic as it would seem to a modern audience, it was a great improvement on the old structure.

[1] See Dyce's notes on "Henry VIII.," for a confirmation of this.
[2] Chamberlaine to Alice Carleton (June 30, 1614).
[3] This was unfurled during the performances. It bore on it a St. George's Cross. Chalmers's "Apology."

Shakespeare, who had a tenth share in the original house, had a fourteenth in its successor; but his professional career was over by this time, and, with but occasional visits to London, he was living a life of "ease, retirement and the conversation of his friends," as Nicholas Rowe puts it, at Stratford.

The fortunes of The Globe appear to have been of the best, and it remained one of London's leading playhouses, although, as we shall see, many others were about to become its competitors, till April 15, 1644, on which day it was "pulled downe to the ground by Sir Matthew Brand, to make tenements in the room of it."[1]

To be strictly chronological it is necessary here to mention two "private" theatres, as they were called, that came into existence about this time in Blackfriars and its neighbourhood. The first of these was due to the initiative of Richard Farrant, master of the Children of the Chapel at Windsor, and a musician of considerable ability, "a well-known and justly esteemed composer of Church music,"[2] whose anthems have been preserved in the collections made by Bernard and Boyce. At the end of the year 1576, Farrant secured a lease of a house in the precincts of the old Blackfriars Priory, and using the ground floor for himself and his family, converted the second into a small playhouse. He made it publicly known that this was merely for the purpose of affording the children of the Chapel a convenient place for practising, and he took care to give his new venture no more distinctive a name than "the private house in the Blackfriars."

This was done, of course, in order to keep within the stringent laws against playhouses which the City Fathers had promulgated. Farrant died in 1580, and his little theatre ceased its activities four years later.

Although necessarily limited in these, there is no

[1] Quoted in "London Past and Present" from Howes's MS. in Collier's "Life of Shakespeare."
[2] Naumann's "History of Music."

doubt that performances other than those strictly necessary for, as Farrant himself termed, it "the better trayning to do his Majestie service," of his choir-boys; were given here, and together with a similar undertaking established by Sebastian Westcott, master of the boys of St. Paul's, near the Cathedral, which existed till 1608, Farrant's house, small as it was, should properly be regarded as a playhouse. The fact that Westcott's similar undertaking was suppressed in 1590, and remained under the civic ban for several years, indicates that the Corporation had reason to suppose that this was the case.

But it is again on the south side of the river that we shall find the more legitimate expression of Elizabethan drama. About the year 1585, a regular playhouse was erected in Newington Butts, near the spot occupied by Spurgeon's Tabernacle.

Although at one time doubt was thrown on the existence of such a playhouse—and truth to tell there is little enough known as to its history—that it was an actual fact is proved by entries in Henslowe's Diary, wherein is mentioned the performance of plays in Newington during the year 1594, including "Hamlet," "The Taming of the Shrew," and "Andronicus," as well as Marlowe's "Jew of Malta."

It is strange that the name of this playhouse has not survived, as the fact of its existence can hardly be doubted, especially as in 1586, among the acts of the Privy Council, is an explicit reference to "playes at *the theater* and other places about Newington," and Fairman-Ordish has pointed out the natural presumption that this locality, then a very similar holiday resort to Finsbury Fields, where the first theatres were opened, would obviously suggest itself as an appropriate spot for theatrical enterprise. It is, besides, known that when The Fortune Theatre[1] was erected, certain playhouses on the Surrey side of the river

[1] *Vide* supra.

were demolished, and this elusive one may well have been among them.[1]

Philip Henslowe, to whose invaluable diary I have alluded, was the next *impresario* (how amazed he would have been at the word!) to turn his attention to the south bank, and under his *aegis* The Rose came into existence. As in the case of The Curtain, the new playhouse took its name from that of the plot of ground, The Little Rose, on which it was built—Rose Alley still marking the spot. The contract for the erection of the building is dated January 1586–7, and shows (for it is still in existence) that Henslowe was in partnership with a certain John Cholmley in the undertaking, which was estimated to cost £816.

In Norden's map, dated 1593, The Rose can be plainly seen, being marked as "The Play-House," and standing rather to the south-east of The Bear House.

When The Rose was actually erected is not known, but as Henslowe lived close by in The Clink, and contemplated building it in 1586–7, the assumption is that he was already versed in theatrical matters, and did not let much grass grow under his feet before beginning its construction. In his diary will be found all sorts of details concerning the work, by which we find that the theatre was built of wood, although a certain amount of brickwork was used; that the galleries were protected by a thatched roof, and that they were supported on poles. The stage was painted, and the dressing-room, called a tire-house, was roofed in. Entries of plays produced by Lord Strange's company here, and other evidence, show the close connection of this band with Henslowe's management, and the well-known name of Edward Alleyn appears as principal actor; and with him a useful general utility man named William Shakespeare.

Among the dramatists whom Henslowe patronized were Marlowe and Greene, Peele and Nash; and we

[1] "The Henslowe Papers," by W. W. Greg, p. 49.

find record of the performances of the "Jew of Malta," Greene's "Friar Bacon and Friar Bongay," and "Orlando Furioso"; and Peele's "Battle of Alcazar"; while there seems little doubt that "Henry VI." was then very popular, and did good business for Henslowe, as his record of receipts proves. Indeed Nash, in his "Pierce Penilesse," asserts that it had been witnessed by "ten thousand spectators at least." It is interesting to speculate whether it was this remarkable success that caused Greene in his "Groat's Worth of Wit," to exhibit that outburst of jealousy against Shakespeare which has done more than anything to preserve interest in that curious piece of literature.

The one thing that appears to have occasionally interrupted the success of Henslowe's Rose venture was the outbreak of the plague with which Tudor London was so often afflicted. Privy Council warrants are eloquent of these interferences with dramatic performances, and in one we find Lord Strange's servants forbidden "from playinge at the rose on the bankside," although they have permission to do so "for three daies" at Newington Butts; while by another we are told that "the Rose maie be at libertie without anye restrainte so long as it shall be free from infection of sicknes." As time progressed others appear to have taken shares with Henslowe in The Rose. It would, indeed, seem to have been turned into a company, from certain entries in Henslowe's record: one Jeaffes being one of the shareholders for a time, Gabriel Spenser another; and there is some evidence to show that Ben Jonson was to have been one, although he apparently never was. Henslowe was himself manager; he was proprietor of the building, financing the companies acting there and advancing money for the purchase of plays.[1] That it was a profitable speculation, is proved.

[1] Fairman-Ordish from a close study of the very complicated diary of Henslowe.

After 1597, Alleyn resigned his position as a player; and about the same time Ben Jonson appears to have gone over to The Curtain, where his "Every Man in his Humour" (in which Shakespeare had an acting part) was given there in 1598. At the close of the same year the Chamberlain's company established their Globe Theatre on Bankside, although this does not seem to have materially affected the fortunes of The Rose. At the same time this conjunction of circumstances may have resulted in Henslowe's determination to try fortune elsewhere, and the theatre with the eupony-mous name he, in partnership with Alleyn, forthwith set about building. The Rose was now occupied by "Lord Pembrocke's Men" (1600); later the Earl of Worcester's Players performed there; but it would seem that since the Chamberlain's company had been at The Globe, The Rose was not doing its former business. Henslowe and Alleyn had other irons in the fire, for besides the new Fortune Theatre in Golden Lane, Cripplegate, they each had a profitable share in the Bear Garden. Anyhow, Henslowe tried to sell the lease of The Rose in 1602; but was not successful. Even the thorough researches of Mr. Fairman-Ordish were unable to discover any definite history of The Rose after 1603, although he is of opinion that in that year Henslowe discontinued the use of it as a theatre. The building was taken for exhibitions of various kinds, displays of swords-manship, puppet-dancing, and so forth, down to 1620, after which no further mention is to be found of it.

In Norden's map of 1593, there will be observed, close to the "Playhouse," which, as we have seen, was The Rose, another circular building called The Bear-House. It has been questioned whether this was identical with the "Beare-bayting" erection shown in the plans of Agas and Braun and Hogenberg, but it has been doubted, on the ground that these earlier

THE BEAR GARDEN

BANKSIDE

1647

From an enlarged Drawing of an extensive View of London in 1647; 7 Feet 9 Inches by 18 Inches, engraved by Hollar: very scarce, and now in the Possession of Thomas Lloyd Esq.

constructions were admittedly of but a temporary
character. Be that as it may, and the point is not
material to our present purpose, it is certain that
the later Bear-House was used not merely for the
baiting of animals, but also for other less savage
amusements, and among them dramatic representations may well have had a place. If so the fact
that, in course of time, an actual theatre, The Hope,
rose on its site, forms an appropriate sequel to its
earlier activities in this direction; and as The Hope
had a resuscitation in Stuart times as a bear garden,
and each of these incarnations took place on the
spot where the original Bear-baiting of Agas's plan
stood, we get a sort of apostolic succession of
pleasure haunts spreading over a long course of
time.

It appears that the old Bear-baiting building became
so rotten that it collapsed in 1583, and the probability
is that the Bear Garden was then, or soon after, erected
on its site on those circular lines and with much the
same accommodation, although improved, which had
been found by experience to be so generally useful,
not only for the baiting of animals, but for other
shows, and by the erection of a stage for dramatic
displays. There is a record in 1586 that one "Morgan
Pope agrees to pay unto ye parish for the bear garden
and for the ground adjoining to the same where the
dogs are, 6/8$^{d.}$ at Christmas week; and so on after,
6/8 by the year for tithes;" and no doubt this was
the bear-garden in question. The reference to the
ground "where the dogs are" is illustrated in Agas's
map, where a number of dogs are shown chained up
in a double row at the entrance to a range of kennels,
just as they are at the Bull-baiting building almost
adjoining.

I shall have something further to say about these
places as identified with such purposes. Here I
confine myself to their use as sites for theatrical and

other displays which often took place in the same buildings.[1]

It was about the year 1613 that the Bear Garden became converted into The Hope Theatre. As we know, it had been in the hands of Henslowe and Alleyn, who made a profitable thing out of it; but when The Globe Theatre was burnt down (1613) Henslowe, who had bought the place from Alleyn three years earlier, and was always ready to make the most of an opportunity, determined to turn the Bear Garden into a legitimate theatre; but inasmuch as one of the arrangements for the rebuilding was that the stage was to be in a frame and placed on tressels in order that it could be removed when "the game of bears and bulls" was exhibited,[2] it is evident that the manager determined to have two strings to his bow, and still relied on that earlier form of amusement which was so popular that it survived down to the days of William and Mary.

By the description of the new playhouse, given in Collier's "History of Dramatic Poetry,"[3] we find that the foundations were to be of brick, that there were to be two boxes "fit and decent for gentlemen to sit in," and that the covering was to have no supports on the stage (obviously, as the stage was to be removable); while the columns were to be turned, *i.e.* not merely plain fir-poles as hitherto used. This increased luxury gives point to Coryat's remark with regard to the Venetian theatres, which he considered "very beggarly and bare in comparison of our *stately* Playhouses in England; neyther can their Actors compare with us for apparrell, shewes, and musicke."[4]

[1] See "Description of England," by Justus Zinzerling, *circa* 1610: "The theatres (Theatra Comœdorum) in which bears and bulls fight with dogs; also cock-fighting."

[2] In the agreement between Henslowe and one Meade, whom he had taken into partnership, with Katherens, a carpenter, dated Aug. 30, 1613, and quoted by Fairman-Ordish.

[3] Vol. 3, p. 99.   [4] "Crudities," 1611.

The theatre was ready for the Princess Elizabeth's company, which was the first to perform in it, in 1614, when Ben Jonson's "Bartholomew Fair" was given, a play full of allusions likely to be appreciated by the audience and almost certain of success. One of these allusions may be mentioned as it refers to an incident in The Hope's career. One of the characters, Cokes, says: "I think one taylor would go near to beat all this company with a hand bound behind him." Now this refers to John Taylor, the Water Poet, who had engaged in a wit-combat, as it was called, with one Fennor, at The Hope. Taylor himself tells how he had given Fennor ten shillings, as an earnest of his intention to meet him, had advertised the "show" by no fewer than 1000 handbills, and when the day arrived and the house was filled with a great audience, Fennor ran away "and left me a Foole amongst thousands of critical Censurers."[1]

It was in this year that Henslowe died, and the new playhouse, in which Alleyn had a share, was carried on by him. But Meade, the other partner, was a difficult man to get on with, and we find the players complaining to Alleyn about his conduct, which resulted in their dispersal;[2] conduct, by the way, Alleyn himself could well understand, as he was also the victim of Meade's peculiarity, for the latter was essentially the type of the "harbitrary gent," both with friends and foes. Meade was a waterman. Most actors and dramatists at that time carried on other callings (Jonson was a bricklayer, one remembers), hence probably his association with Alleyn, for, as Fairman-Ordish points out, it was to the interest of the water-men plying between the two banks that Bankside should keep up its theatrical reputation; indeed the Company of Watermen had not long before (1613),

[1] Preface to "Taylor's Revenge, etc.," 1615. The brochure was answered by "Fennor's Defence, etc." of the same year.
[2] See "Alleyn Papers," edited by Collier, etc.

on the destruction of The Globe, specifically petitioned
the King "that the players might not be permitted
to have a playhouse in London or in Middlesex,
within four miles of the city on that side of the Thames";
a petition justified by Taylor's "True Cause of the
Waterman's Suit concerning Players."

With the rebuilding of The Globe in 1614, the
fortunes of The Hope may be said to have been finally
blighted, and with the double attacks of internal
dissension (caused by Meade) and external opposition
(caused by the rebuilt Globe), its career as a theatrical
centre ended, and it reverted to being a bear-garden
(as Visscher indicates it in his 1616 plan), and as such
its later career belongs to another chapter, where it
will be found dealt with.

The first notice we have of The Swan is contained
in a communication from the Lord Mayor to the Lord
Treasurer, containing the information that Francis
Langley intended to erect a new playhouse in Southwark, and praying that he might be prevented. The
activity of the civic authorities had in no way abated,
and no opportunity was lost of trying to stop any new
venture of a histrionic kind. It had, in this instance,
at any rate, no effect, and in due course, actually when
is not clear, although it is known to have been shortly
before 1598, The Swan was built and opened. It
stood just south of that well-known pleasure haunt,
Paris Garden, and was, therefore, considerably more
westerly than any of the other Bankside theatres.
A field shown in Braun and Hogenberg's plan indicates
its site; while Visscher, in 1616, exhibits it as by then
ramparted about with other buildings. The fact that
it was adjacent to Paris Garden, which had its special
"stairs" whither boats brought crowds of people,
some on business, some on pleasure, many combining
both, from the north bank, gave it a special advantage,
and there can be little doubt that when people saw the
flag flying, indicative of a performance, numbers of

them made a point of visiting the show. Fairman-Ordish considers that the construction of The Swan was similar to that of The Hope, and he gives certain details of the former which I here transcribe, not merely in order to convey an idea of what a playhouse at this period was like, but also to show what considerable improvements had been made in such things since the construction of The Theater and The Curtain. The Hope was really of later date than The Swan, and was to become its serious rival.   This contract is dated 1613 and was for this new playhouse:

There were to be two staircases without and adjoining the playhouse, similar to those at The Swan; the covering (or Heavens over the stage, as it was called) was to be without supports on the stage, and there were to be gutters of lead for carrying away rain-water. Two boxes in the lower storey were to be provided; and turned columns were to be on the stage. The front of the building was to be of oak; the foundation of bricks, and the whole was to be covered in with a roof of "Englishe tyles."

In addition to this, the representation of the building in Visscher's map shows it to have been a twelve-sided structure, and of a more solid character than its predecessors, giving point to one statement that it was made, not of wood, but of flint. The sign chosen for it, in view of its position close to the river and the trade it brought the watermen, could not have been more appropriate.

The Vestry was soon on the war-path for tithes both from The Swan as well as from The Hope, and a notice to this effect in 1598, establishes the approximate period of the completion of the former.

It was in this very year that one of the best-known foreign visitors to England made his appearance in our midst, noticing our ways and describing our habits, customs and dress. This was Paul Hentzner, who tells us that "without the city are some theatres where English actors represent almost every day Comedies and Tragedies to very numerous audiences; these," he adds, "are concluded with variety of dances, accompanied by excellent music and the excessive applause of those that are present."

That it was customary for still more illustrious visitors to be taken to one or other of the existing theatres, as among the sights it was thought would interest them, is proved by various records of such visits; and in 1610 we find the secretary of Lewis Frederick, Prince of Wirtemberg, writing, "On Monday 30th of April, 1619," that "His Excellency went to The Globe, the usual place for acting plays; the history of the Moor of Venice (Othello) was represented there." By this it is evident that the old Globe still held its supremacy notwithstanding the existence of more up-to-date houses in the neighbourhood.

Between thirty and forty years ago there was discovered, in the University Library at Utrecht, a MS. volume containing a drawing of The Swan Theatre. The value of this is obvious, for it shows us not only what one of these Elizabethan playhouses was like, but curiously confirms the accuracy of the contemporary description on which I have drawn. In the MS. accompanying this invaluable record,[1] which is in Latin, but has been translated, is the following interesting reference to the playhouses of the period:

"There are in London four theatres of noteworthy beauty, which bear diverse names according to their diverse signs. In them a different action is daily presented to the people. The two finest of these are situated to the southward beyond the Thames, named, from the signs they display, the Rose and the Swan. Two others are outside the city towards the north, and are

---

[1] It was published in a notice of Dr. Gaedertz's pamphlet (written on the subject of the sketch) by the late Mr. William Archer, in the "Universal Review" for June 1888.

approached 'per Episcopalem portem'; in the vernacular, 'Biscopgate.' There is also a fifth, of dissimilar structure, devoted to beast-baiting, wherein many bears, bulls, and dogs of stupendous size are kept in separate dens and cages, which, being pitted against each other, afford men a most delightful spectacle. Of all the theatres, however, the largest and most distinguished is that whereof the sign is a Swan (commonly called the Swan Theatre), since it contains three thousand persons, and is built of a concrete of flint stones, and supported by wooden columns, painted in such excellent imitation of marble that it might deceive even the most cunning. Since its form seems to approach that of a Roman structure, I have depicted it above."

One may be allowed to question certain statements in this account of The Swan. First it is highly improbable that it could have held anything like as many as 3000 people; perhaps a nought has slipped in; again all other descriptions of the London playhouses of the period concur in stating that they were constructed, with the exception of those that had a foundation of brick, in wood. Hentzner, a careful observer, expressly says so; although it is difficult to see how the writer could have been mistaken on such a point. But allowing for a traveller's tendency to exaggerate or to be inaccurate, there seems little doubt that The Swan (for the second Globe had not yet come into existence) was far in advance of the other houses in point of decoration, and doubtless, to some extent, in size. This being so, it is disappointing to find that The Swan occupies no outstanding part in the theatrical annals of the day. Indeed its activities would appear rather to have been in the direction of sports, wit-combats and *improvisatoire* exhibitions (one Robert Wilson gave one of these here in 1598), than of the legitimate drama. Thus we find a certain Peter Bromville, noted for "his great skill

E

in feats of activities,"[1] who had performed both before the French king and Queen Elizabeth, choosing The Swan in which to give a public exhibition of his prowess, in the year 1600; again in 1603, William Fennor, whom we have already met, produced "England's Joy"[2] here, which seems rather to have been a spectacular display than a regular drama; while in the following year "a contest for a prize" took place here, during which one Turner received a wound in the eye from which he died. One play is recorded as being given at The Swan, notably Middleton's "A Chaste Maid in Cheapside"; and there is evidence that Ben Jonson acted here: but for the rest, it would seem that The Swan never fulfilled the high expectations of Langley, its builder.

The annexed view is taken from Wilkinson's "Londina Illustrata," and shows The Swan as it appeared in 1614. The latest reference in contemporary literature to the place is in Marmion's "Holland's Leaguer" of 1632, and its decadence is there indicated, for in a description of the three theatres which were to be seen from the grounds of Holland's Leaguer, The Globe, The Hope, and The Swan, the last is referred to as "one other that the lady of the leaguer, or fortress, could almost shake hands with, now fallen to decay, and, like a dying *swanne*, hangs her head and sings her own dirge."[3]

Soon after this was written The Swan was swept away, chiefly, it would seem, because its uses either as a theatre or a place for other recreations had ceased, but also perhaps because a growing puritanism regarded such resorts with ill-favour. When, just ten years later the more famous Globe

---

[1] Note communicated by Halliwell-Phillipps to Mr. Rendle.

[2] It had been promised the year before, but did not take place, and a riot ensued in consequence, "caused by the disappointed would-be spectators."

[3] For an account of "Holland's Leaguer," *vide* supra.

THE SWAN THEATRE

BANKSIDE

1614

From the Long View of London, called, The Antwerp View.

Lately in the possession of the Editor, now of J. T. Pratt, Esq.

was demolished the laſt of the old Bankside Theatres disappeared.

As we shall see, all this area was identified not only with actual playhouses, used indifferently for various exhibitions, but with other places affording popular amusement. But it is its dramatic associations that chiefly diſtinguish it; for it was not only in itself a general recreation ground; not only did many notable playhouses arise on it; but some of those moſt closely associated with such things lived there: Edward Alleyn and Philip Henslowe, and above all Shakespeare, who dwelt near the Bear Garden; and close by might have been found some of those actors who firſt undertook rôles which so many greater men have since made famous, in plays which were then almoſt local in fame, but which are to-day some of the world's moſt precious legacies from those ample and splendid days. The Falcon Tavern was close to Paris Garden, and Shakespeare and his friends were known at the Falcon. There is, indeed, an *aura* of dramatic intereſt over all this part, and if to-day, in the midſt of an unpicturesque environment of modern bricks and mortar, it is difficult to envisage it, we can do so by throwing our minds back into the paſt, and with the help of written records and old plans, can realize something of what it was even before Shakespeare came up from Stratford and touched our dramatic and poetic literature with his golden conjuring-rod. Shakespeare, Ben Jonson, Marlowe, Peele, Greene, Middleton, Dekker, and the reſt, what a conſtellation it is: and it was the beſt work of such men that was produced for the amusement of the Londoner of Elizabeth's day, who in these Bankside pleasure haunts might have torn out Hamlet's myſtery, have partaken of the golden dreams of the Jew of Malta or with Dr. Fauſtus, might have been made immortal by Helen's kiss.

CHAPTER III

SOME SEVENTEENTH-CENTURY THEATRES

I HAVE already spoken of certain playhouses on the north side of the river: The Theater and The Curtain, and those so-called private theatres at Blackfriars in which the protagonists were chiefly the boys attached to the Chapel Royal. With the beginning of the seventeenth century we shall find other theatres coming into existence in London itself. Hitherto, as we have seen, such places of public amusement were forced by civic antagonism to find a *venue* outside the immediate jurisdiction of the authorities, and those that did not were alone able to carry on unmolested by using the euphemism of "private," and by employing children to undertake dramatic characters. As time went on a broader view of such things seems to have obtained and even the leaden-headed old Corporation (as Dickens called it in *his* day) came to recognize that there was something not wholly bad about the drama, and, indeed, something that might be regarded almost as tolerable. The result was that the projectors of playhouses, greatly daring, began to erect them under the very nose of the Lord Mayor, if Clerkenwell can, in those days, be said to have been under the nose of anyone.

For it was in Clerkenwell, at the upper end of what is St. John Street, that the next theatre arose.

It was called The Red Bull,[1] a curious name did we not remember that in early days plays were often

[1] Some interesting data concerning this playhouse, by James Greenstreet, appeared in "The Athenæum," during the year 1885.

given in inn-yards, whose surrounding galleries and ample ground space afforded convenient means for accommodating the spectators, and in all probability The Red Bull had taken the place of such a one and had preserved the sign as its name.

The date of the erection of The Red Bull Theatre has not survived, but Cromwell,[1] who says it was supposed to have been built "in the beginning of the reign of Queen Elizabeth," is, of course, hopelessly wrong, while even Wilkinson,[2] who gives the date, tentatively, as between the years 1570 and 1580, is hardly, I think, more correct. The only record of plays given there, mentions as the *first*, one printed in 1615, and although it may have been acted before then, it would hardly have been written much before 1600, as Heywood, its author, was only born in 1575. I think we may rather place the construction of the building somewhere about the year 1600 (the year, by the way, in which the more famous Fortune Theatre was erected), and a mention of a puppet-play in St. John's Street in 1599, where "the house fell, six persons were killed, and thirty or forty hurt,"[3] may very well not refer to the theatre at all, as in no account of it with which I am familiar is there any record of an event which would almost certainly have been regarded as part and parcel of its history.

There is a fairly early reference to the place in Beaumont and Fletcher's "Knight of the Burning Pestle" (1613), in which it is alluded to by name. That is was a place of importance may be gathered from the fact that it is said, in point of size, at any rate, to have rivalled The Globe and the nearly contemporary Fortune. It is, too, interesting to find, at a rather later date, it being referred to as one of those "publick stages and theatres in this city" upon which

[1] "History of Clerkenwell," 1828.   [2] "Londina Illustrata."
[3] Letter from Chamberlain to Carleton, dated Aug. 23, 1599. "Calendar of State Papers."

"dramatic poesy was so lively expressed and represented, as Rome in the *ange* of her pomp and glory
never saw it better performed . . . in respect of the
action and art, and not the cost and sumptuousness."[1]
In a curious print, published in 1672, the interior of
The Red Bull is shown; by which we see that footlights had come into use there; that the spectators in
the boxes were at the back of the stage, the entrance
to which was below them, and that the rest of the
audience were on the ground floor surrounding the
three other sides of the stage.

In the absence of any detailed account of the Red
Bull Theatre, two contemporary references to it are
welcome. The first is in a play called "Albumazar"
performed at Cambridge in 1614; where one of the
characters, Trinculo (Shakespeare's Trinculo was of
three years earlier), says: "I will confound her with
compliments drawn from the plays I see at The
Fortune and The Red Bull, where I learn all the
words I speak and understand not." The second
allusion is in a memorandum left by Edward Alleyn,
thus: "Oct: 3, 1617, went to the Red Bull, and
received for 'The Younger Brother' but £3. 6. 4."
This last reference is specially interesting, as it may
indicate that Alleyn had a share in the undertaking;
unless it means that the play in question was his
property, and that he had hired it out to "The Players
of the Revells," which was the company who regularly
acted here.

We are able, too, to give the names of at least
four plays which were performed at The Red Bull.
"The Four Prentices," by Thomas Heywood, printed
in 1615, and acted there by the Queen's (Anne of
Denmark's) servants; "Swetman, the Woman Hater,
arraigned by Women," an anonymous play, printed
in 1620, and performed by the late Queen's (who
had died in the previous year) servants; "The Rape

[1] Sir George Buck, writing in 1631.

of Lucrece," by Thomas Heywood, printed in 1638; and "The Seven Champions of Christendome," by John Kirke, which was also acted at The Cockpit and at The Bull in St. John's Street, in the same year.

The renewed wave of puritanism, which began at this period to sweep over this country, had a disastrous effect on the theatres, as may be supposed, for it was even then a time when others than the extreme zealots regarded them with anything but a friendly eye; and we find Randolph, in his "Muses' Looking Glass," performed in 1638, speaking of the denunciation of the playhouses by Flowerdew, a puritanical character in the piece, thus,

> " . . . Lastly, he wished
> The Bull might cross the Thames to the Bear Garden
> And there be soundly baited."

The authorities went further, and an order was sent to the Lord Mayor and magistrates for the "pulling down of all playhouses." Luckily this was not carried into full effect, a temporary closing of some of the theatres being held sufficient to comply with this injunction. The Bull was among these, and like others, opened later, although rather for the exhibition of what were called *drolls* and such-like comic interludes than for regular plays. A collection of such things as were represented here was made by Francis Kirkman, and published in 1672,[1] enriched by the picture of The Bull's interior, to which I have already alluded.

During the Protectorate, we are told that "they used, at Christmas and Bartholomew Fair, to bribe the officer who commanded the guard at Whitehall," *i.e.* to prevent the soldiers dispersing the audience, "and were thereupon connived at to act for a few days at The Red Bull"; while "presently after the Restoration, the King's players acted publicly at The Red

---

[1] It was entitled "The Wits, or Sport upon Sport," 2 parts, 1670-2.

Bull for some time, and then removed to a new-built playhouse in Vere Street, by Clare Market."

It is supposed that it was at The Red Bull that the first female performer appeared on the stage; women's parts being hitherto sustained by men, as is well known from the anecdote that tells how Charles II., angry at once being kept waiting for a play to begin, was mollified by the reply that "The Queen was shaving." There is some reason for supposing The Red Bull to have been the scene of the innovation, from the fact that it was one of that playhouse's special actors, Thomas Jordan, who wrote "A Prologue, to introduce the first woman that came to act on the stage, in the Trajedy of The Moor of Venice."[1]

The subsequent history of The Red Bull is sufficiently vague. From a passage in Prynne's " Histrio-Mastix," 1633, we learn that it had at that time been recently rebuilt, as had The Fortune, and it was then, no doubt, that it was entirely roofed in, and being lighted by candelabra, was able to be used for evening performances.

During the visitations of the plague, The Red Bull was, of course, in common with other public resorts, closed. One of these visitations occurred in 1637, and in "A New Book of Mistakes," published in that year, the fact is thus referred to: "The Red Bull in St. John Streete, who for the present (alack the while !) is not suffred to carrie the flagge in the mainetop," by which we know that, like the theatres on Bankside, a flag was hoisted here during the performances.

As time progressed, and newer playhouses arose, The Red Bull gradually declined in public favour. Trials of skill were held here instead of plays, and a notice of one of these was advertised for Whitsun Monday, May 30, 1664, in which two "scholars,"

[1] " Historia Histrionica, an Historical Account of the English Stage," 1699. This tract, said to have been written by James Wright, was republished in Dodsley's collection.

Benjamin Dobson and William Wright, were to try their skill with "back-sword, single rapier, sword and dagger, rapier and dagger, sword and buckler, half-pike, sword and gauntlet, and single falchion."

About the time when The Red Bull was built, another and far better known playhouse was also in course of erection. This was The Fortune Theatre, which was constructed for Philip Henslowe and Edward Alleyn by Peter Street, the builder, in Golden Lane, Cripplegate. By the contract[1] between these parties, dated January 8, 1599–1600, we are enabled to learn some details as to the size and so forth of the new playhouse.

It was a square structure, probably the first to depart from the circular or octagonal convention, and consisted of three storeys, respectively 12, 11 and 9 feet high. The galleries were 12 feet 6 inches deep with, in each of the upper stories, an additional "jutty" forwards of 10 inches. The stage was 43 feet wide and 27 feet deep. There was a covering over the stage in addition to a roof for the main structure, and this, instead of being, as heretofore, thatched, was tiled. As to the arrangement of the stage, all we know is that it was "contrived and fashioned like unto the stage of the Playhouse called The Globe," which had recently been erected by the same builder. The whole was constructed of wood, lath and plaster.[2] Although the contract price was £440, Henslowe and Alleyn found that it actually cost eighty pounds more. What the original Fortune Theatre looked like may be

[1] It is printed in Malone's "Shakespeare," edited by Boswell.

[2] The Fortune was not peculiar in having three storeys, for Samuel Kiechel, visiting England in 1585, remarks: "There are some peculiar houses which are so constructed that they have about three galleries one above the other." And he adds that the players take from £10 to to £12 at a time, when they act anything new, for which the people have to pay double; that they perform nearly every day in the week; so that, notwithstanding plays are forbidden on Fridays and Sundays, this prohibition is not observed. Rye, "England as Seen by Foreigners."

gathered from the clever reconstruction made on the basis of the builder's contract, which Mr. W. H. Godfrey executed, and which is here reproduced. By this it will be seen that the structure was a great advance on the archaic character of the older play-houses; and in it we get a certain vague likeness to the modern theatre, inasmuch as the proscenium is contained within a rectangular building, and only requires a circular completion of the auditorium to approximate to our modern conception of a theatre.

The records of plays acted here are extremely meagre, but we know that Dekker and Middleton's "The Roaring Girle" (1611), and Yarrington's "Two Lamentable Tragedies," first published ten years earlier, were among them.

One of the fates to which theatres are chiefly exposed is fire, and The Fortune was no exception. On December 9, 1621, flames broke out here, and the place was wholly destroyed. A laconic entry in Alleyn's diary records the event "December 9, 1621. This night att 12 of the Clock the Fortune was burnt"; while Chamberlain, writing to Carleton, six days later, mentions "the destruction by fire of the fairest playhouse in the town, the Fortune in Golding Lane."

Steps were immediately taken to rebuild the theatre, and in the following year it was completed, not in its old shape, but reverting to the circular form, although, as we may see by the illustration in "Londina Illustrata," its front, converted then into tenements, is square and not unlike that of later playhouses.

The history of The Fortune from 1622 to 1649 is a blank, but there is no reason to suppose that it did not do good business,[1] and that plays were regularly produced there. In the latter year, however, when civil disturbances had reached a head and sectarian zeal

[1] Alleyn, we know, derived most of the wealth with which he founded Dulwich College from the proceeds of The Fortune.

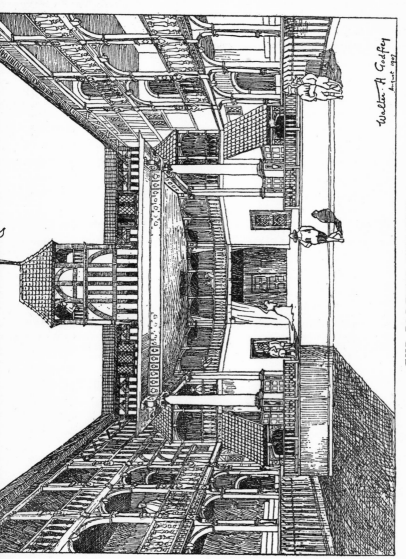

THE FORTUNE THEATRE

1600

From a drawing showing Mr. Walter H. Godfrey's reconstruction.

made a dead set at anything likely to be amusing, the interior of the place was entirely destroyed by a company of soldiers urged on by the puritanical proclivities of a certain class of the populace. After that we may be sure that the place was allowed to fall into ruin. The Protectorate was not a time when theatres flourished, and even when the Restoration occurred and brought back a revulsion in feeling with regard to such things, the playhouse had evidently become too derelict to be worth anyone's while properly reconstructing.[1] Thus we find it, in 1661, being advertised "to be let to be built upon." Its front alone survived this metamorphosis, and even that was converted into shops and dwellings; the back portion of the premises, consisting of the main building, was laid out in what Wilkinson calls "mean tenements"; the garden and surrounding walks and avenues, which were an adjunct to Alleyn's structure, being converted into streets and alleys, one of which, Playhouse Yard, commemorated it.

It is significant that the remainder of the playhouses that arose in the earlier years of the seventeenth century should have been situated, not in far-flung Finsbury Fields or Cripplegate or on the other side of the river, but nearer the centre of what was later to become the centre of fashionable life in London, and in spots which were to become specially identified with theatrical life. One of these, and although it was of the "private" character of those in Blackfriars, it must take its place here, was The Whitefriars Theatre, which was built on the site of the ancient hall belonging to the Whitefriars Monastery, near Dorset Garden, Fleet Street.

It is probable that this area had not then become

---

[1] It was opened temporarily as a theatre after the Restoration, but without success. It had by now become, out of the way, and besides the rivalry of Davenant's and Killigrew's ventures was sufficient alone to kill it.

confirmed in the unsavoury reputation it afterwards gained, as Alsatia, a safe asylum for rogues and proftitutes, although this name is known to have been applied to it before 1623, when it had begun its career as a harbour for all those who sought sanctuary from the law in its various manifeftations, as at a ftill earlier time, ever since the Dissolution, in fact, it had been a recognized refuge for debtors. Here in the disused monaftery lived Henry Grey, 9th Earl of Kent, and the friend of Selden, who died in 1639; here Turner kept his fencing school, one of those minor forms of pleasure haunts which were later to become more abundant throughout the Weft End.

It was, then, in this area (which now resounds to the groaning of machines as they turn out daily papers, and where Carmelite Street alone perpetuates the monaftery's former exiftence) that The Whitefriar's Theatre was conftructed, and proved to be the fore-runner of two famous Caroline playhouses, as we shall see. The actual patent mentioning the Whitefriars for the firft time is dated January 1610, but there seems no doubt that the old hall of the monaftery had been converted to such uses in the previous year. Indeed, plays are said to have been performed hereabouts nearly thirty years earlier, but if this was so, they were probably given in some temporary ftructure or in some part of the disused monaftery, possibly the Hall itself;[1] as no actual theatre is known to have preceded the Whitefriars.

As in the other private theatres I have mentioned, the performers here were children rather than regular actors, and we have record of Barrey's play entitled "Ram Alley"[2] (1611), and Mason's tragedy of "The Turke" (1610), being performed by them here.

---

[1] Just as plays were given in the Halls of the Middle and Inner Temple and elsewhere.

[2] Ram Alley was actually a court in Whitefriars next to 46 Fleet Street. See the author's "Annals of Fleet Street."

After 1610 their place was taken by the then newly formed company called the Second Children of the Queen's Revels, and it is interesting to know that it was for the latter that Beaumont and Fletcher wrote some of their most important plays.[1] One can imagine those full-blooded Elizabethans softened for the nonce by the melody of the lines in "The Faithful Shepherdess," laughing boisterously at the humour of "Wit without Money," or open-eyed at Evadne entering with the dagger in her ensanguined hands, in "The Maid's Tragedy."

As no records later than 1621 are extant with regard to the Whitefriar's Theatre, we may assume that in or about that year it ceased its activities. Before this date, probably in 1617, another private playhouse was opened in Drury Lane. It was known variously as the Phœnix and The Cockpit, the latter name being applied to it from the fact that it occupied the building which had hitherto been used for exhibitions of cock-fighting, a fact which the later name of the site—Cockpit Alley, afterwards Pitt Place—was to commemorate.

Although, like the Whitefriars, it was of a private character, that fact seems to be the only thing in common with the two playhouses. For it would appear to have been a noisy, rowdy place, and if it did not, as Prynne, a very partial authority, says it did, demoralise the whole of Drury Lane, at least it must have done its best to establish an unsatisfactory reputation. Ben Jonson indicates its noisy character in a passage in his Volpone; but a more significant sign of its rowdiness is afforded by the fact that on Shrove Tuesday, March 4, 1616–7, the London apprentices, who claimed a sort of immemorial right on that day to pull down houses of ill-fame, or such places as might be supposed to be a danger to public morals, made a concerted attack on The Phœnix, and very nearly succeeded in demolishing the whole structure. As was not unusual in those

[1] "Shakespeare's England."

days, a ballad forthwith commemorated the prowess
of the band whose destructive instincts were so readily
at hand in the cause of morality.[1] This incident
stopped the performances at The Phœnix for a time, and
after remaining derelict for a period, we find it being
converted into a schoolroom, of all places, in 1647.
I cannot, however, but think that it must have had a
recrudescence as a playhouse before this, as it did
after; for Evelyn, writing on February 5, 1647–8,
remarks that he "saw a tragi-comedy acted in the
Cockpit, after there had been none of these diversions
for many years before the war." One imagines that had
the place been closed for thirty years, the diarist would
have used some other word than "many" to indicate
the fact.

But there seemed an adverse fate pursuing the fortunes of The Phœnix, for on March 24, 1649 (N.S.),
a band of soldiers, set on by sectaries, and probably
fresh from, or proceeding to, their depredations at
The Fortune, broke into the place and demolished it.
But The Phœnix had not been so christened for
nothing, and again it arose from its ashes, and we find
it ten years later the scene of a performance of Davenant's "The Cruelty of the Spaniards in Peru," a
quasi-opera which, we are told, "was represented
daily at the Cock Pit, in Drury Lane, at three in the
afternoon punctually." [2]

Evelyn, not without qualms, went to see it, and in
his diary is this reference: "May 5, 1659—I went to
visit my brother in London, and next day to see a new
Opera, after the Italian way, in recitative music and
scenes, much inferior to the Italian composure (composition) and magnificence; but it was prodigious that
in a time of such public consternation such a vanity
should be kept up or permitted. I being engaged

---

[1] "A Ballade in praise of London 'Prentices, and what they did at
the Cockpit Playhouse in Drury Lane," edited by Collier.
[2] "Annals of the Stage."

with company could not decently resist going to see it,
though my heart smote me for it."

In the following year a company opened here with
more legitimate drama. They had at their head Rhodes,
who had been a prompter at the Blackfriars Theatres,
and who was to do the stage incalculable service by
introducing to it his friend Betterton. Doran says that
at The Phœnix, Rhodes and his merry men, wooed
the willing town; and there seems little doubt that just
as it was at the old Phœnix that the old English actors
said their last say before sectarianism silenced them,
so in the rebuilt house began that new era of the drama,
whose earlier manifestations were to shed a glory on the
days of Charles II.

But Rhodes had powerful competitors. By an Act
passed early in the Merry Monarch's reign, only two
companies were authorized to play, *viz*. that of
Killigrew, known as "The King's Servants," and that
of Davenant, denominated "The Duke's Servants." It
is obvious that to be enrolled in either of these was the
object of every actor, and such outstanding ones as
Hart and Mohun, who had hitherto formed part of
Rhodes's company, seceded to that of Killigrew, while
even Betterton joined the Duke's, and although acting
at The Phœnix, did so no longer under the management of Rhodes.

The days of The Phœnix or Cockpit were, indeed,
numbered, and with the coming of a new theatre in
Lincoln's Inn Fields and another in Drury Lane (on
the site of the present playhouse) its career closed.
It was a link between two eras, and as such, in spite of
a once evil reputation, should be remembered.

Before we pass to the Restoration theatres, as they
may be termed, there is still one other earlier playhouse which requires a short notice. This again was a
so-called "private" theatre, and was erected in Salisbury
Court, Fleet Street, from which circumstance it was
known as The Salisbury Court Theatre, by Richard

Gunnell and William Blagrave, in 1629, on the site of a barn standing at the lower end of the court of Salisbury House, on ground leased to them by the 4th Earl of Dorset, at the rent of £100 a year; practically where the Salisbury Hotel stands to-day. It is the "new faire Play-house . . . the seventeenth which hath been made within the space of three-score years within London and the suburbs" mentioned by Howes in his continuation of Stow.

What its form was exactly it is difficult to say, but it apparently approximated to The Blackfriars and The Phœnix;[1] and it may be regarded as among the "private" houses, if, as I am inclined to think, these were differentiated from the others by being enclosed, and smaller, and having, instead of an open yard for the "groundlings," a pit in which the spectators were accommodated with seats.

Among the plays performed here were Shirley's "Changes, or Love in a Maze," in January, 1632; and Marmion's "Holland's Leaguer," a few days later. The company, known as Prince Charles's Men, was accustomed to perform here, and Fleay[2] assumes that Randolph (Ben Jonson's protégé), who was the manager, produced at this house his "Muses Looking Glasse" towards the close of the year 1632. Later the King's Revels Company returned here and in 1635 gave here, *inter alia*, Brome's "The 'Spargus Garden."

In connection with The Salisbury Court Theatre performances, an unusual incident in quoted by Malone from the MS. book of Sir Henry Herbert, in which that worthy has made the following entry: "I committed Cromes, a broker in Long Lane, on the 16th of February, 1634, to the Marshalsea, for lending a robe with the name of Jesus on it to the players in Salisbury Court."

[1] See Wright's "Historia Histrionica," 1699, where as much is said.
[2] "The London Stage."

It is unnecessary to particularize more fully the names of the plays presented in Salisbury Court, but I may note that outbreaks of the plague were responsible for its being closed at various times; while such Declarations as that of the Parliament of 1642, to the effect that "public sports do not agree with public calamities, nor stage-plays with seasons of humiliation," proved almost more serious to its prosperity. We hear of plays being given *sub rosa* here during the Civil troubles, and once at least the authorities got wind of it, and actually took one of the performers into custody.

When, in 1648, Parliament ordered the suppression of all theatres, and even went so far as to decree that any actor found performing should be publicly whipped and the audience fined, the death-blow was, at least for a time, given to this source of public amusement, and as pleasure haunts the playhouses ceased to exist until the Restoration brought with it a revulsion of feeling that was to swing the pendulum in the opposite direction. Things went even further, and orders were given for the demolition of such places. The Salisbury Court Theatre shared in this drastic *débâcle*, and we read how "The Playhouse in Salisbury Court, in Fleete Street, was pulled down by a company of soldiers, set on by the Sectaries of these sad times, on Saturday, the 24th of March, 1649."[1]

In the meanwhile, one William Beeston had become possessed of the playhouse, and he owned the ruin until, with the return of Charles from exile, he was able to rebuild it. This he did, in 1660, at a cost of £329—from which relatively small sum it would appear that the new structure was merely a wood, lath and plaster one.

We have now arrived at that period when we possess the invaluable record of Pepys, an inveterate playgoer, to illustrate our investigations, and Pepys was

[1] Note by Howes: see Collier's "Life of Shakespeare."

F

often to be found in Salisbury Court; indeed, in March
1660–1, he visited it no fewer than three times. Thus
on the firſt day of the month, he saw "The Bondman,"
by Massinger, aĉted there by Betterton; again the
next day he found the house "as full as could be," a
new play, "The Queen's Masque," better known as
"Love's Miſtress," by Thomas Heywood, being given,
in which the diariſt was chiefly ſtruck by a little boy
who aĉted Cupid, "which is one of the greateſt parts in
it"; while he went again to see the same play at the
same place on March 25, a Sunday; so that the
former regulation againſt sabbath-day performances
had been abrogated.

But these were not the diariſt's firſt visits to Salisbury
Court, for on the preceding February 12 he had gone
there by water, and seen "The Scornful Lady," "now
done by a woman (Mrs. Marshall), which makes the
play much better than ever it did to me," he naïvely
adds. Later in the month (the 23rd, which happened to
be his twenty-eighth birthday) Pepys saw "The Change-
ling," by Middleton and Rowley, there, which, he says,
"takes exceedingly," but what seems chiefly to have
ſtruck him was that "the gallants do begin to be tyred
with the vanity and pride of the theatre aĉtors, who are
indeed grown very proud and rich." In April he sees
"Rule a Wife and have a Wife," by Fletcher, there;
but it did not please him any more than did "Love's
Quarrell," which he witnessed, in company with Creed,
a few days later. One other entry in the Diary refers to
The Salisbury Court Theatre. This was on September
9, 1661, when "'Tis Pity she's a Whore," by John
Ford, was given; "a simple play, and ill aĉted," is
Samuel's comment; but he had compensations, for
"it was my fortune to sit by a moſt pretty and moſt
ingenious lady, which pleased me much."

The greater success of the new playhouse in Lincoln's Inn Fields, where the King's Company aĉted,
as well as of that in Portugal Street, identified with the

Duke's Company, formed serious obstacles to the
continued prosperity of The Salisbury Court Theatre,
and it is significant that after 1661 Pepys does not
record once visiting the latter. It, indeed, gradually
declined in public favour, and in 1662 is said to have
last been used as a regular playhouse. What public
indifference had begun, The Great Fire completed, and
in that holocaust The Salisbury Court Theatre perished,
and was never rebuilt; although a recrudescence of
theatrical prosperity was to attend, if not its exact site,
one quite close by, when, in 1671, The Dorset Gardens
Theatre was designed by Wren and opened under the
nominal management of Davenant's widow.

Before, however, this occurred, other theatres had
come into being, and from Whitefriars we must
transfer ourselves to Lincoln's Inn Fields to find them.

We have seen how, of the two companies of players
authorized by Charles II., that known as "The Duke's"
had installed itself in The Cockpit, or The Phœnix, as
it was called earlier. Here it remained until a new
theatre was ready in Portugal Row or Street, in 1662.
In the meanwhile the King's Company had already
taken possession of another new playhouse, erected on
the site of Gibbon's tennis-court,[1] in Vere Street,
Clare Market, which Killigrew had had reconstructed,
and which was opened on November 8, 1660, with
Shakespeare's "Henry IV." It is obvious that this
theatre was but a temporary one, until the more commodious house in Drury Lane should be ready. As this
new playhouse was completed and ready for use on
April 8, 1663, it will be seen that the Vere Street
venture was of short duration. It was, however, a
success while it lasted, and Pepys, of course, visited it;
first on November 20, 1660, when he saw "The
Beggar's Bush" played, and found it well acted, with

---

[1] I imagine it must have been here that Evelyn saw "The Scornful
Lady" "at a new theater in Lincoln's Inn Fields," on January 16,
1660–1.

Mohun as one of the principals. The diarist must have been easy to please, or the *décor* of the playhouse must have been more elaborate than one might imagine, for he adds: "It is the finest playhouse, I believe, that ever was in England"; which, however, considering the character of its predecessors, does not, after all, necessarily say much.

Again in the following January Pepys witnessed the same play, and what is more interesting "for the first time saw women come upon the stage."

Although the two theatres, that just referred to and that in Portugal Street, were then so near together, the proximity could in no way have affected them adversely, for they alone afforded theatrical amusement to a London ready to patronize, after a long period of repression, any form of amusement. That this was recognized is proved by the building, by Killigrew, of the new house in Drury Lane, which was on far more elaborate lines than anything that had preceded it.

Before saying anything about this new venture, The Duke's Theatre in Lincoln's Inn Fields claims our attention, although its history takes us well into the eighteenth century. It stood on the south side of the Fields, at the back of the present College of Surgeons. As in the case of the Vere Street house, it had been originally a tennis-court, kept by Lisle, and it was Davenant, at the head of the Duke's Company, who converted it into a regular playhouse, after he had for a short time, as we have seen, occupied the old Cockpit.

What the interior of a regular playhouse was like at this period may here conveniently be interpolated. From a print of the period we can see that the stage approximated to those of modern days, and exhibited a remarkable advance on what had served for a proscenium not so many years before. The galleries appear to have been divided into boxes of varying size, and we know that on one occasion Pepys was quite perturbed at being seen in a 1s. 3d. box by some of the clerks in his office who were occupying a 2s. 6d. one; while it is interesting, in view of what obtains to-day, to hear him remarking: "I do not remember that I saw so many, by half, of ordinary 'prentices and mean people in the pit at 2s. 6d. apiece as now." He himself used to pay only 1s., and later 1s. 6d., and then had to crowd in with difficulty.

The roof consisted of sky-lights made of thin glass, but not sufficiently water-tight to prevent heavy rain from getting in; and on one occasion we read of such a storm of hail that "those in the pit were fain to rise, and all the house in disorder"; while on another, the rain came in from the cupola and drenched the audience, who were not protected even in the boxes.

Great advances were made, however, in the matter of scenery and costume, which began to have some relation to the characters personated and the *milieu* in which the play was supposed to be placed. Then, as now, company would go into the dressing-rooms of favourite actors and talk with them during the intervals. There seems to have been some difficulty in adequately lighting the house, for which reason, no doubt, plays were generally performed in the afternoon, usually beginning at three o'clock; although the stage had then to be lighted by many wax candles.

Killigrew was one of those who did much to improve such things, and he was not above sending to Italy not only for singers, but also for painters and others, in order to make both the performances and the setting as complete as possible.

One thing seems curious to us, and that is that the spectators, however high their rank, were accustomed to sit where they could. Once Pepys had to put up with a place in the side balcony, but my Lady Dorset and "a great many great ones" were there too; in spite of the insecurity of the roof as a protection against rain, notable people sat in the pit (which then occupied the whole arena, as it were, of the theatre, and was not, as now, at the back of the ſtalls), and Buckingham and Sedley, Etheredge and Buckhurſt, "and other poets," writes Pepys, were to be seen there, while "a company of fine ladies" was present with them; and were joſtled by the 'prentices and lewd fellows of the diariſt's disdain. In The King's Theatre there was a certain place called The Fops' Corner, to which Dryden alludes in one of his Epilogues, and which, no doubt, was a regular rendezvous for the young bloods of that period, as the ſtalls of The Gaiety were in our own time.

The orcheſtra was placed beneath the ſtage, apparently to the detriment of the acouſtic properties, as Pepys (who was a musician, and therefore critical in such matters) says, it resulted in the trebles being heard very faintly and the basses not at all.

People talked seemingly without reſtraint even during the acting of the play; but then such people were nearly always great wits, like Sedley and Buckingham, and their remarks were not always a bad subſtitute for the fuſtian and bombaſt that were not infrequently presented on the ſtage. People spat freely in the playhouse, and Pepys was once much annoyed at a lady turning round and doing so (he was in a dark place and she could not see him, it is true), until he found her mighty pretty, when he readily forgave her !

The orange girls (Nell Gwynn was one) were a great feature of the theatres. They ſtood with their backs to the ſtage and gave as good as they got from the gallants who occupied what time they did not care to look at the play in bandying jeſts with them. The oranges coſt sixpence each, and the chief seller or miſtress of the orange girls was known as Orange Moll.

Such was, roughly, the kind of interior and so forth of the Lincoln's Inn Theatre, opened by Sir William Davenant, in 1662, "having new scenes and decorations, being the first that were e'er introduced into England." [1]

When we get to that period in our history when Pepys' Diary can be drawn upon, there is a quite natural tendency to bring honest Samuel on to the stage, and to make him act as a sort of chorus. This can be overdone; it has been overdone; and I shall, therefore, refrain from noting the innumerable references the diarist makes to visits to the Lincoln's Inn Theatre, particularly because the reader can so easily refer to those fascinating pages himself, and find far more than he set out to seek. That Pepys' constant play-going made Mrs. Pepys "as mad as the devil," we have his own words to prove, and when I add that there are between seventy and eighty records of visits he paid to this one playhouse in exactly five years (and we know he went to many other places of amusement), many ladies, at least, will think that she had reason to be.

To one of his visits his wife might not, however, have taken any exception. This was on April 9, 1668, when he went "to see Sir W. Davenant's corpse carried out towards Westminster, there to be buried"; for the author-manager had died two days earlier, a fact, however, that did not prevent his theatre carrying on the next day with "The Unfortunate Lovers," by Davenant himself.

The New Theatre had been opened in March or April of 1662 with the "Siege of Rhodes" as the *pièce de résistance.*

This opening was very splendid. The King, who had not hitherto attended a public performance of this character since his Restoration, was present, together with the Duke of York, and a large number of the nobility. Downes, the prompter, was to have taken one of the parts, but the presence of so many august persons seems to have overwhelmed him,

---

[1] Downes's "Roscius Anglicanus."

and he was unable to proceed, and was, besides, to use his own words, "forever spoilt for being an actor."

Among the plays produced during the next few years was "Hamlet," in which Betterton, from hints given him by Davenant, who had seen Taylor, the original performer of the part, made a great hit; "Romeo and Juliet"; "Twelfth Night"; and "Henry VIII." with Harris as Wolsey; so that Shakespeare was popular still. Davenant's "Adventures of Twelve Hours" ran for thirteen days, and his "Rivals" for nine—then considered quite long runs; while Etheredge's "Love in a Tub" was such a success that the company is said to have made by it £1000 within a month.

The theatre went by a variety of names, being known as the Portugal Row Theatre, Sir William Davenant's, Duke of York's, Duke's Old Theatre, New Theatre, and Lincoln's Inn Fields Theatre; from which world of titles no little confusion has arisen.

Its chief entrance was in Portugal Street. Here it was that women are said first to have undertaken theatrical parts;[1] but although Davenant engaged a great many, there was not infrequently a lack of the requisite number, and young men of specially good looks or effeminate appearance still appeared in female parts—the handsome Kynaston being an example, who as "Evadne" in "The Maid's Tragedy," was always sure of a double meed of applause.

Both the Plague and The Great Fire put a stop to theatrical enterprise, and when the Duke's Theatre was shut up in 1666, it remained closed for no fewer than six years, Davenant's company having left it for their new playhouse in Dorset Gardens.

---

[1] The Vere Street Theatre, as we have seen, shares this claim. By the way, a company of French players are said first to have introduced women on the stage at the Blackfriars Theatre, but they were hissed off; though they afterwards did appear at The Red Bull. This was in 1629. (Heckthorn's "Lincoln's Inn Fields.")

On February 26, 1671–2, the Lincoln's Inn play-house was taken as a temporary refuge by Killigrew and the King's Company, who had been burnt out of their Drury Lane house. In the March of 1673–4, this theatre, having been rebuilt, was opened, and with Killigrew's return to it the Lincoln's Inn playhouse was left deserted, to again revert for a time to its former use as a tennis-court. It continued in this use till 1694, when the dictatorial attitude assumed by the patentees of the Drury Lane Theatre caused a secession of the principal performers there, who opened the Tennis-Court again as a playhouse, under the *ægis* of Betterton, Mrs. Barry, Congreve and Mrs. Bracegirdle.

The reconstructed Duke's Theatre, now called in contemporary newsheets The New Theatre in Lincoln's Inn Fields, reopened on April 30, 1695, with a first performance of Congreve's "Love for Love"; and it continued its career for some nine years. Then, in 1704, complaints were made against it as a public nuisance; and it may have been for this reason that Betterton assigned his interest in it to Vanbrugh, who, however, finding the playhouse too small for his purpose, proceeded to build a larger and more convenient one in the Haymarket. Again the Lincoln's Inn house was abandoned, and again it was destined to be resuscitated, this time by Christopher Rich, who demolished it in 1714, and proceeded to rebuild it. Unfortunately he never lived to see it quite completed, dying on November 4 of the same year. However, his son, John, carried on the work, and in the following month opened the place with "The Recruiting Officer."

For some reason—that generally given is that the actors were not equal to those at the Drury Lane Theatre—the thing was a failure, and, indeed, might well have brought disaster on Rich's head, had not that head conceived a brilliant idea. Finding that

he was more than equalled in the legitimate drama
by his competitors, he determined to have recourse
to a different kind of entertainment, and he proceeded
to produce that form of pantomime which will always
be associated with his name, and which under diverse
manifestations has gone on amusing old and young
ever since. Sound and show, as it was said, triumphed
over reason and sense, but Rich could afford to laugh
at the sneers of the superior and the artistic shafts
levelled at him by the great pictorial satirist of the
age. The manager exhibited so much fertility of
invention in what he put before the public, and was
himself so clever in his impersonations, that it is not
to be wondered at that the town flocked to see something which was at once exotic in character and novel
in form. There is no doubt that the legitimate drama
at the other houses suffered considerably through
Rich's innovation. One of his great successes was
"The Necromancer, or the History of Dr. Faustus,"
which was first produced on December 20, 1723.
This production, which had as little to do with Marlowe
as it had with Goethe, inaugurated that Christmas
Pantomime which has ever since held its own, even
in these sophisticated days. But Rich was to have a far
greater triumph, both from an artistic and a monetary
point of view, four years later, when "The Beggar's
Opera" was first given (January 29, 1727–8) and ran
for sixty-one nights in one season. The success of
this play was due to a variety of causes, political ones
being not the least; and people saw Sir Robert in
Macheath, and Sandwich in Jemmy Twitcher; while
the quarrel between Peachum and Lockit but thinly
disguised a *rencontre* that had not long before taken
place between Walpole and Townshend. In a word,
the piece was a topical one, and the charming lyrics
that were introduced made it still more popular with a
people who, if not naturally musical, are naturally fond
of songs and ballads. In our own day we have seen

how, when all its political and topical allusions are
pointless, "The Beggar's Opera" has been able to charm
the town; and in the twentieth century something
like a recrudescence of the popularity it enjoyed in the
eighteenth, when its lyrics were on everyone's lips,
its allusions in everyone's mouth, and its characters and
incidents reproduced on fans and screens, tea-cups
and saucers, has been secured.

The receipts for this play have been preserved,
and we see by them that on the thirty-seventh night
£194 odd was taken, being the highest reached;
while the lowest, two days before it was withdrawn,
was £53 6s. 6d.[1]

The following season began with a play acted by
pigmies, which so much amused the playgoers that
it ran for fifteen nights, and the lowest receipts for a
single performance were £37. It is significant that
when "Macbeth" was given shortly afterwards only
fourteen guineas was taken at one performance.

In those days men of quality were permitted to
have chairs on the stage itself, and in 1721 this
practice led to trouble at an earlier performance of
"Macbeth." A body of young bloods were seated
at the wings, when a certain peer, who had been
drinking heavily, lurched across the stage in the
middle of one of the scenes. Rich came forward and
expostulated, when the peer struck him; whereupon
Rich returned the blow. At this, the young men
jumped up, drew their swords, and a regular riot
ensued, which was only stopped by the arrest of the
ringleaders. It was after this that the players refused
to act until the King had granted them a guard of
soldiers, a custom which continued both at Drury
Lane and Covent Garden.[2]

The Duke's Theatre was closed in 1733 in conse-

[1] It was as the original Polly Peachum that Lavinia Fenton won the
heart of the Duke of Bolton, to whom she was subsequently married.

[2] Heckthorn's "Lincoln's Inn Fields," 1896.

quence of Rich's removal to a new one at Covent Garden. Later, Gifford, who had in the meanwhile been running the Goodman's Fields Theatre,[1] took it, and remained for some seasons, but apparently not with much success, as he returned to his old play-house in the course of a year or so; and in October 1745, when the Young Pretender was threatening invasion, it was used as a temporary barracks, and was apparently found so suitable that eleven years later we find it being occupied permanently in this way. By gradations as an auction-room and a china repository, it merged into commercialism, until, in 1848, it was demolished for the purpose of enlarging the premises of the Royal College of Surgeons.

The Dorset Gardens Theatre

Before saying anything about the Drury Lane Theatre, which Killigrew and his company opened in 1663, it will be convenient to speak of the one in Dorset Gardens, as the activity of that playhouse ceased with the seventeenth century, whereas the annals of Drury Lane are happily not yet closed. Downes, in his "Roscius Anglicanus" (1708), gives the following account of the removal of Davenant's company to Dorset Gardens from Lincoln's Inn. "The new theatre in Dorset Gardens being finished," he writes, "and our company (the Duke's), after Sir William's death, being under the rule and dominion of his widow, the Lady Davenant, Mr. Betterton and Mr. Harris (Mr. Charles Davenant, her son, acting for her), they removed from Lincoln's Inn thither. And on the 9th day of November, 1671, they opened their new theatre with 'Sir Martin Marral,' which continued acting three days together, with a full audience each day, notwithstanding it had been acted thirty days before in Lincoln's Inn Fields, and above four times at Court."

[1] *Vide* supra.

A playhouse at this spot, fronting the river and just to the east of Salisbury Court, had been long in contemplation. Indeed Davenant had secured a licence from Charles I. so far back as 1639 for erecting one here, and two later patents, one dated 1662 and the other 1663, had confirmed this.[1] The Dorset Gardens Theatre took its name from the fact that it stood on the site which had been the grounds of Lord Dorset's residence. It was designed by Wren, and from all accounts must have been the most elaborate structure of the kind yet erected in London; while its interior decorations, scenery, etc., were far in advance of anything hitherto attempted in this direction. What its frontage looked like may be seen from the frontispiece to Settle's "The Empress of Morocco," published in 1673, a drawing for which is in the Pepysian Library. The river front, if less ornate, was impressive. It stood quite close to the water, and had stairs leading down to the river, by which means so many then reached it in days when the Thames was really a highway as well as a pleasure resort. Two stone figures on the land façade represented Tragedy and Comedy, and were the work of Grinling Gibbons.

As we know, Davenant did not live to see his new theatre completed, dying two years before it was opened. In the pages of Downes and Genest may be read many details of the fortunes of the playhouse, the plays produced there, and the actors who portrayed their characters. Success was varied by failure, and we hear of Dryden's "Limberham, or the Kind Keeper," being among those that were damned. It was Dryden's satire against those who conducted houses of ill-fame that wrought this class to fury and urged its members to concerted attack, according to

[1] See the original licence, dated 1639, which is given by Wilkinson in his "Londina Illustrata," vol. 2; although Wilkinson wrongly dates it 1649, at the same time stating that it was issued in the 14th year of Charles's reign !

Langbaine,[1] who quotes these lines in support of his assertion:

> "Dryden, good man, thought keepers to reclaim,
> Writ a kind satire, call'd it *Limberham*.
> This all the herd of keepers straight alarms,
> From Charing Cross to Bow was up in arms;
> They damn'd the play all at one fatal blow,
> And broke the glasse that did their picture show."

For a time, however, success seems to have been the order of the day at the Duke's Theatre, as it was called, and a list of the plays given here and the actors and actresses who presented them, indicates that those who patronized the playhouse had no need to complain of the fare placed before them or the excellence of those who administered it. Thus we find "Œdipus," the joint production of Dryden and Nat. Lee, being given in 1679, with Betterton as the King and Mrs. Betterton as Jocasta, which had a ten nights run—quite satisfactory in those days. Another success was Dryden's "Spanish Friar," as it deserved to be; while with Otway, who is specially identified with the theatre, producing his "Alcibiades" and his "Titus and Berenico," respectively, in 1675–7, and above all his remarkable "Venice Preserved," three years later, the Duke's Theatre floated on a tide of popularity; while lesser plays like those of Lord Orrery ("Mr. Anthony," in 1671, and "Mustapha," in 1673 among them), in the hands of the capable actors performing here, obtained greater success than their merits deserved. Among others whose productions were exhibited here were Shadwell and Crowne, Settle and Mrs. Aphra Behn; and Betterton and Mrs. Barry delighted audiences which crowded the elaborate playhouse, coming by way of Fleet Street and the Strand, or by water.[2]

[1] See Langbaine's "Dramatic Poets."

[2] The Boxes were from 2/6 to 4/-; the Pit from 1/6 to 2/-; the First Gallery 1/- to 1/6; the Upper Gallery from 6d. to 1/-; and these were *raised* prices owing to the expense of the decorations, scenery, etc. See Wilkes's "View of the Stage."

But these halcyon days were not destined to last long; and in spite of an attempt at attracting royal patronage by renaming it the Queen's Theatre in honour of Queen Mary, in 1689, the playhouse was not to have a long life; and in the following year Christopher Rich acquired a dominating interest in it. Five years later Betterton's company seceded from the new manager, and transferred themselves to the new theatre in Lincoln's Inn Fields. After this the Queen's Theatre fell on indifferent days, and in 1699 two Kentish men, William and Richard Joy, here exhibited certain "Tryals of Strength," including the lifting of a weight of 2240 pounds, and the breaking of a rope calculated to bear 3500 pounds weight." In the prologue to Farquhar's "Constant Couple," the incident is thus referred to:

> "Ah, friends! Poor Dorset Gardens house is gone,
>   Quite lost to us ; and, for some strange misdeeds,
>   That strong man, Samson's, pull'd it o'er our heads."

Indeed for several years after its desertion by the legitimate drama, the theatre was the scene of a variety of entertainments which had a vogue, but could hardly be said to uphold its past renown. Conjurors, prize-fighters, *et hoc omne genus*, whose printed puffs and handbills may be found among the ephemeral literature of that day, occupied it from time to time. But in 1703 it had a temporary return of its earlier prosperity, when it was again occupied by actors, to the horror and indignation of the civic authorities, who petitioned that "some effectual course be taken, if possible, to prevent the youth of this city from resorting to playhouses"![1] Apparently this had little effect, however; and in 1706 we find "The deserted Company of Comedians of the Theatre Royal" advertising their opening here with "The Recruiting

[1] See "Fleet Street in Seven Centuries," by Mr. Walter G. Bell, where the author has collected a mass of interesting data about the playhouses in this part of London.

Officer," in which singing and dancing were promised as prominent features. According to Genest seven plays were performed here during a month from this date (October 24). But, after all, it was but a flash in the pan, and henceforth The Queen's Theatre disappears from the list of metropolitan playhouses, although the building over which so much pains had been taken, and even royal appreciation aroused (for Charles II. is known to have taken great interest in its construction), was still standing till the year 1720, as Strype's reference to it proves.

CHAPTER IV

DRURY LANE, COVENT GARDEN, AND THE HAYMARKET

IN the meanwhile Killigrew and his company, after their temporary sojourn in Vere Street, had taken possession of the new playhouse erected for them, at a cost of £1500, in Drury Lane, on the site of the present theatre. This was opened on May 7, 1663, with Beaumont and Fletcher's "Humorous Lieutenant." The house was known alternatively as The Theatre Royal, as we find from a passage in Pepys, who took his wife there the day after it had been opened, and who thus describes it: "The house is made with extraordinary good convenience, and yet hath some faults, as the narrowness of the passages in and out of the pit, and the distance from the stage to the boxes, which I am confident cannot hear; but for all other things is well; only, above all, the musique being below, and most of it sounding under the very stage, there is no hearing of the basses at all, nor very well of the trebles, which sure must be mended." In addition he notes that all the ladies in the pit were "finer and better dressed than they used to be," and he was a little ashamed that his wife and her maid fell short of this, and were, to use his own words, "in such a pickle."

It was here, in the following year (June 1, 1664), that, at a performance of "The Silent Woman," a storm occurred which deluged the pit, and caused that part of the audience to rise in disorder, the Diarist among them; a circumstance which he records as happening again four years later. By which it is evident that, notwithstanding many improvements in theatrical architecture, the builders had failed to overcome the difficulty of combining light with security against the elements.

Some nine years after its opening—to be precise in the January of 1672—The Theatre Royal met the almost invariable fate of playhouses, and was burnt down together with some fifty odd houses in its immediate vicinity. The cause of the fire is not recorded, but its result was the erection of a new house, designed by Wren, which cost £4000, and was opened on March 26, 1674.

As I am anxious to show what the interiors of these older theatres were like, I make no apology for quoting the following passage from Cibber on the subject: "As there are not many spectators," he writes, "who may remember what form the Drury Lane Theatre stood in about forty years ago (*i.e.* about 1700), it were but justice to lay the original figure, which Sir Christopher Wren gave it, and the alterations of it now standing, in a fair light. It must be observed, then, that the area and platform of the old stage projected about four feet forwarder, in a semi-oval figure, parallel to the benches of the pit; and that the former lower doors of entrance for the actors were brought down between the two foremost (and then only) Pilasters; in the place of which doors, now the two stage boxes are fixt. That where the doors of entrance now are, there formerly stood two additional side-wings, in front to a full set of scenes, which had then almost a double effect, in their loftiness and magnificence. By this original form the usual station of the actors, in almost every scene, was advanced at least ten foot nearer to the audience than they now can be." Dryden, in the Prologue he wrote for the opening, modestly calls the new playhouse "plain built . . . a bare convenience only," and speaks of our "mean ungilded stage," and our "homely house"; but this may be taken as mere rhetorical modesty.

That the new house must have proved successful seems pretty certain, and performances were continued here by the King's Company till 1682, when the Duke's Company at the Dorset Gardens Theatre removed from that spot and joined forces with the others. Apropos of this combination, Colley Cibber remarks that "One only Theatre being now in the possession of the whole town, the united patentees imposed their terms upon the actors; for the profits of acting were then divided into twenty shares, ten of which went to the proprietors, and the other moiety to the principal actors, in such subdivisions as their different merits might pretend to . . . which occasioned great contention between the patentees and performers."[1]

Betterton took up the matter, in 1693, and obtaining an interview with the King, was promised relief and support, although in what exact way this was to be afforded does not appear. However, he did procure the royal licence for himself and certain of his fellow malcontents, to act at The Tennis-Court Theatre, Bear Yard, Little Lincoln's Inn Fields, as we have already seen. But again the two companies came together, and in 1704 we find them once more united under Christopher Rich's direction. Again, however, dissensions arose which resulted in the Lord Chamberlain giving an order for the closing of Drury Lane in 1709, but in the same year one Collier, M.P. for Truro, obtained a licence to reopen it, and having ejected Rich, who, however, succeeded in carrying off most of the scenery and costumes, reopened the house on November 23, with Dryden's "Arungzebe," Booth taking the principal part, and Aaron Hill being director. In the meanwhile, a theatre had been opened in the Haymarket (where His Majesty's is now)

---

[1] Cibber's "Apology."

by Vanbrugh,[1] called "The Queen's," and to this
seceded many actors—Betterton, Wilks, Cibber,
Doggett, Mrs. Barry and Mrs. Oldfield among them—
who did not care to be identified with Collier's
speculation. However, in two years' time we find three
of these histrions going into partnership with Collier,
although in the following year one of them, Doggett,
retired from the concern, his place being taken by
Booth.

It is not possible for me here to particularize the
very full annals of such an outstanding playhouse as
Drury Lane, and it will be sufficient to summarize
its history from the close of Queen Anne's reign to
our own times.

In 1714 Sir Richard Steele obtained a life patent in
it, a benefit revoked some five years later, rather from
political motives than from theatrical ones; while
the annals of the theatre for many years reveal that
difficulty of suiting all temperaments, to which the
managers, Highmore in particular, who followed the
triumvirate of Cibber, Wilks and Booth, found themselves exposed, and which was the cause of constant
dissension. But it was not only internal troubles that
upset the peace of mind of the patentees. In 1737
an event occurred of this nature emanating from one
section of the public. It had been usual for the
servants attending those who patronized the theatres
to have free seats in the gallery. In 1737 this
privilege was stopped; with the result that on the
night of March 5, a band of these menials forced
its way into the house and took possession of places
for which payment had not been made. This was
the second attempt at forcible entry, an earlier one
having occurred in the previous month. This being
so, the authorities took a serious view of the case, and
the ringleaders being apprehended, were tried at
Hicks's Hall, and sentenced to hard labour. Again

[1] *Vide* supra.

in 1743 a riot took place for some reason or for none, for such things were not unusual, in the very presence of the King, and was only quelled by the military being called in.[1]

But a far more important landmark in the theatre's history is 1742, in which year Garrick appeared here. He had made his *début* at the Goodman's Fields Theatre in the previous year, and had at once electrified an audience which since Betterton's death had become used to the sing-song diversified with the ranting of less finished players. In 1747 Garrick became a partner with Lacey in the management of Drury Lane, and for nearly thirty years more was destined to delight the public with his inimitable powers— powers ranging from the portrayal of Abel Drugger to the Hamlet in which he had electrified Partridge.

In the year that Garrick left the stage, Sheridan became manager of Drury Lane; and in 1791 the structure which had survived the Gordon Riots, and had been the scene of so many historic triumphs was demolished.[2] In its place arose a new house, designed by Holland, on such grandiose lines, as then con- ceived, that it was regarded as being too large to see or hear in. The old building had been finally closed on June 4, and a humorous advertisement in a paper for the following day noted the event thus: "Last night died Madame Drury, who lived in six reigns, and was 117 years old." The new structure was opened on March 12, 1794; and the fact that Mrs. Siddons, referring to her benefit, remarks in a letter to Dr. Whalley that "there were £60 more in

---

[1] In 1679 a riot took place at the Duke's Theatre, caused by the flaunting splendour of the Duchess of Portsmouth, never popular with the crowd, and some drunken gentlemen who suddenly felt called upon to undertake the roles of *censores morum*.

[2] During Garrick's management, its façade had been wholly altered ; Wren's original work giving place to that of the Adams who besides did other reconstructions and alterations to the building. See Swarbrick's "Robert Adam and his Brothers."

the house than ever known, or was supposed Old Drury could have contained," indicates the relative capacity of the building to that of its predecessor.

It is significant that, on March 12, oratorios were given at Drury Lane to celebrate its inauguration, for the progress that music, not merely as an adjunct to theatrical exhibition, had made in public favour was surprising. The royal patronage of Handel, and the general interest George III. and Queen Charlotte took in the art were largely responsible for this, and, as we shall see, the Concerts of Ancient Music, the Opera, and innumerable private or quasi-private societies, which were started about this time, helped on the good work. Clubs for glee-singing, too, arose, and from the Heir Apparent (who had quite a good voice) downwards all classes of society began to warble ditties martial or sentimental, as the case might be, but also largely amorous and bacchanalian.

The year 1809 was in every way a disastrous one for Drury Lane. In the first place the O.P. Riots, as they were called, played havoc with the place. These disturbances were due to the change in the old prices charged, being resented by the audience, and not only Drury Lane but Covent Garden was destined to be the scene of great tumults when the rioters shouted vengeance at the management, and performed all sorts of antics, including what was called the O.P. Dance in the Pit.

But a far greater disaster was in wait for the play-house, and on the night of February 24, 1809, at about five minutes past eleven, flames broke forth, and in an incredibly short space of time the whole structure was burning furiously. So vivid and far-flung, indeed, was the glare from the burning pile that people so far away as Fulham are said to have been able to tell the time by their watches in the open air.

An important debate was proceeding in the House of Commons, at which Sheridan, one of the principal

DRURY LANE THEATRE
1825

shareholders in the theatre, was taking part; but when the news was brought to him he rose, and with the utmost nonchalance remarked that "whatever might be the extent of the present calamity, he hoped it would not interfere with the public business of the country."[1] However, he soon after left the House and proceeded to the scene of the disaster. As, however, on reaching there he found nothing could be done, he retired to the Piazza Coffee House to be out of the way of the crowd. The story goes that a friend, seeing him calmly taking some refreshment, expressed surprise at his coolness, whereupon Sheridan is said to have remarked that if a man could not take a glass by his own fireside, he should like to know where he could!

No adequate cause has been given for the fire; but when, a short time before, St. James's Palace was partly burned, the Prince Regent received an anonymous letter informing him that other public buildings would share the same fate.[2] The total loss is said to have been £300,000, and the insurance, which only covered £35,000, was immediately attached by the Duke of Bedford, the ground landlord. However, steps were forthwith taken to erect a new house, and Benjamin Wyatt was the architect chosen. The foundation stone was laid on October 29, 1811, and just within a year the place was opened, with a prologue written by Lord Byron (one of the Committee of Management). It was this rebuilding, together with the advertisement issued by the Committee for a Prologue, that inspired "The Rejected Addresses" of James and Horace Smith.

"Hamlet" was the play selected for the reopening, and the theatre was crowded to its utmost capacity by a most enthusiastic audience.[3]

[1] Moore's "Life of Sheridan."
[2] Watkins's "Life of Sheridan."
[3] For full details of the fire and rebuilding see, *inter alia*, Wilkinson's " Londina Illustrata."

Since those now far-off days, many changes, structural and otherwise, have taken place in Drury Lane Theatre; for instance, the portico in Catherine Street was added during Elliston's management, 1819–26; and the colonnade in Russell Street was built in 1831. But notwithstanding these and many other drastic changes, outside and in, Drury Lane remains much in appearance as it was a hundred years ago, and, with the exception of Sadler's Wells, is the oldest existing London playhouse.

Even to summarize the histrionic fare that has been served up at "The Lane," as it is affectionately called by its *habitués*, under the successive managements of Sheridan, Elliston, Rice, Ellen Tree, Lee, Bunn, Hammond, Macready, down to the days of Chatterton, in the 'seventies of the last century, and Sir Augustus Harris, later, would form a small volume in itself. The names of the great actors who have trodden that historic stage are legion, and many of them are household words.

It is sufficient to say that Drury Lane is one of the most important and famous of those pleasure haunts which have provided amusement for many generations and which many generations have loyally patronized.[1]

Covent Garden Theatre

We have seen how, owing to the action of Collier, Christopher Rich, a patentee of Drury Lane, had been practically evicted from that playhouse, and how he had taken a lease of Davenant's old theatre in Portugal Street and had set about building a new one on its site, which, however, he did not live to see finished. This theatre his son, John, completed, and continued to occupy with the roaring successes of his

---

[1] Among innumerable "events" in connection with Drury Lane, I may mention that it was here that Freeman tried to shoot the Prince of Wales (afterwards George II.) in December 1716; and that here Hatfield made an attempt on the life of George III., on May 15, 1800,

pantomimes. In course of time, however, he found it inadequate for the requirements of this then novel kind of entertainment, especially as the town patronized it so consistently, and he cast about for a site on which to erect the more commodious playhouse he had for some time contemplated building. This site he found in Covent Garden, on the west side of Bow Street, and here he determined to construct his new theatre. He selected Mr. Edward Shepherd as his architect, and he drew out plans which, when Rich sought for public subscriptions towards his scheme, proved so acceptable that the work was at once proceeded with; the ground being cleared of some old buildings, traditionally said to have been those of the conventual structure which gives its name to this locality; and the new structure begun in the February of 1731. In the November of the following year the place was finished, although it was not till 1733 that Rich and his company actually took possession of it, an incident perpetuated by Hogarth in his supposed print, entitled "Rich's Glory, or his Triumphant Entry into Covent Garden."[1]

Rich inaugurated his new venture, on December 7, 1733, with "The Way of the World"; but at first little success attended his efforts, and although the charge for both boxes and pit was 5s., only £115 was taken on the opening night. Later in the season Gay's posthumous opera entitled "Achilles" was given, with Quin as Lycomedes.

Rich's reliance on pantomime for the chief success of his new theatre was well founded, as the public showed unmistakably that this kind of entertainment was exactly what suited it. True it patronized Shakespeare and the other leading dramatists; but that was largely because it could get nothing else, and even real drama was better than no show at all.

[1] I say "supposed," because it is of doubtful authenticity. See Dobson's "William Hogarth," pp. 24 and 236.

With such extravaganzas, however, as "Dr. Faustus," which was given in 1736, and at one of the performances of which an accident occurred involving the loss of one life and much injury to certain other players; and particularly "The Dragon of Wantley," a piece by Carey, set to music by Lampe "after the Italian manner," which had an enthusiastic reception for twenty-two nights, when it was stopped by the death of Queen Caroline, Rich reaped a profitable harvest, and London was kept heartily amused at a skit on the opera almost more pungent than "The Beggar's Opera" itself had been.

And so things went on until 1747, when, with Garrick's electrifying of audiences at Drury Lane, and Quin sulking in disgust at Bath, Rich found himself heavily handicapped, with only a very stale pantomime, called "Merlin's Cave; or, Harlequin Skeleton," to charm his patrons.

In this quandary he persuaded Quin to return, and engaged, among others, the incomparable Peg Woffington and the notorious Miss Bellamy to give life to the Covent Garden performances. It is curious, considering the fame she enjoyed during her lifetime—a fame that has survived to our own days—that on one occasion at least the Covent Garden audience does not appear to have hailed Peg Woffington's appearance with enthusiasm. The anecdote is given by Wilkinson thus: "Mrs. Cibber's name was announced in the play-bills to perform the part of Queen Constance in 'King John,' at Covent Garden, in 1750; but being suddenly taken ill Mrs. Woffington came forward to the front of the pit ready dressed for the part of Constance, and offered, with the permission of the public, to take Mrs. Cibber's place for that night. The spectators, instead of meeting her address with approbation, seemed entirely lost in surprise. This unexpected reception so embarrassed her, that she was preparing to retire, when Ryan (the stage manager), who thought they only wanted a hint to rouse them from their insensibility, asked them bluntly whether they would give Mrs. Woffington leave to play Queen Constance. The audience, as if at once awakened from a fit of lethargy, by repeated plaudits strove to make amends for their inattention to the most beautiful woman that ever adorned a theatre."[1]

During Rich's tenancy of Covent Garden, one or two events occurred which properly concern the annals of the house. It was here, for instance, that he and Lambert, the scene painter, initiated the famous Beefsteak Society whose meetings were first held in the scenic-artist's studio in the theatre. That was in 1738; and three years later Handel here produced his "Messiah," which created a sensation in a country where really great music was then for the first time heard.

In November 1761 Rich died; but his patent was still in force, and under its provisions his son-in-law, Beard,[2] carried on the theatre on behalf of Mrs. Rich and her four daughters. Under Beard's management a change came over the character of the Covent Garden performances. Beard was a lover of music, and the pantomime, so dear to Rich's heart, gave place to more artistic fare. Nor was it unsuccessful. For in spite of Garrick's attraction at Drury Lane, Beard was able to fascinate large audiences by the concord of sweet sounds, and under his *ægis* Covent Garden became as famous for its musical entertainments as it had been under Rich for its pantomimic displays; and "Love in a Village," Arne's remark-

[1] "Londina Illustrata."

[2] Beard made his first appearance at Covent Garden in 1736. He was a celebrated tenor and had been one of the singers at Cannons during Handel's residence there under the *ægis* of the Duke of Chandos. He married first (1739) Lady Henrietta Herbert, daughter of Lord Waldegrave, much to the scandal of Lady Mary Wortley Montagu. See her letters; also Hogarth's "Memoirs of the Opera."

able "Artaxerxes," the "Maid of the Mill," etc., were found capable of charming audiences which had probably grown tired of the earlier form of entertainment, and who, led on by the Royal Family and much of the fashionable world, had become bitten with the mania for music, as they had at an earlier time exhibited a passion for pantomime.

Beard carried on for a succession of seasons with the most marked success, and it was only apparently owing to increasing deafness that he determined to relinquish the management. In 1767, he parted with his interest in Covent Garden for £60,000 to Messrs. Colman, Harris, Powell and Rutherford. The new combination did not, however, work harmoniously, and as a result of dissensions, in which forcible entry and violent expulsion had a part, Harris and Powell emerged as the victors. Harris outlived Powell, and in 1781 he contemplated rebuilding the playhouse, a scheme that finally resolved itself into less complete, but yet drastic alterations; and the newly arranged theatre was opened in 1782.[1]

The following year is notable in the annals of Covent Garden, because then John Kemble made here his first appearance; and the Kemble family was destined to be long and closely associated with the fortunes of the playhouse. We hear of further improvements being made in the structure at intervals, during 1785 and 1787; also of other notable *débuts* here: those of Charles Kemble, in 1794; of Mrs. Glover, in 1797; and of Liston, in 1802, for example. In the following year John Kemble became proprietor; and it was during his management, on September 20, 1808, that occurred the disastrous fire which, breaking out at four o'clock in the morning, completely gutted the place, and resulted in the death of between twenty and thirty people, as well as the destruction of £15,000

[1] It was in 1779 that Hackman shot Miss Ray as she was leaving the theatre.

worth of properties alone. The insurances on the structure and contents were said only to have covered a quarter of the loss; and public subscriptions were immediately opened; but nothing could replace the original scores of Arne and Handel, and other objects of real and sentimental value which the flames destroyed.

No time was lost in rebuilding the theatre, and on December 31 of the same year, the foundation stone was laid by the Prince of Wales. The architect of the new house was Sir Robert Smirke, and the building, on a far more ambitious scale than its predecessor, cost no less than £150,000. Its opening, in September, 1809, was the occasion of those famous O.P. Riots, which were brought about by a revision of the prices of admission, and were, in a way, a recrudescence of those earlier disturbances by which the public had marked its disapprobation of an interference with existing tariffs.

The following note attached to an allusion to the O.P. troubles, in the "Rejected Addresses," so succinctly gives an account of them that I insert it here *in extenso*.[1]

"The new Covent Garden opened on the 18th Sept., 1809, when a cry of 'Old Prices' (afterwards diminished to O.P.) burst out from every part of the house. This continued and increased in violence till the 23rd, when rattles, drums, whistles, and cat-calls having completely drowned the voices of the actors, Mr. Kemble, the stage-manager, came forward and said that a committee of gentlemen had undertaken to examine the finances of the concern, and that until they were prepared with their report the theatre would continue closed. 'Name them!' was shouted from all sides. The names were declared, viz., Sir Charles Price, the Solicitor-General, the Recorder of London, the Governor of the Bank, and Mr. Anger-

---

[1] It will be found at the end of "The Rebuilding," a parody of Southey.

ſtein. 'All shareholders!' bawled a wag from the gallery. In a few days the theatre reopened: the public paid no attention to the report of the referees, and the tumult was renewed for several weeks with even increased violence. The proprietors now sent in hired bruisers to *mill* the refractory into subjection. This irritated moſt of their former friends, and amongſt the reſt the annotator (Horace Smith), who accordingly wrote the song 'Heigh-ho says Kemble,' which was caught up by the ballad-singers, and sung under Mr. Kemble's house-windows in Great Russell Street. A dinner was given at the Crown and Anchor Tavern in the Strand, to celebrate the victory obtained by W. Clifford in his action againſt Brandon, the box-keeper, for assaulting him for wearing the letters O.P. in his hat. At this dinner Mr. Kemble attended, and matters were compromised by allowing the advanced price (seven shillings) to the boxes. The writer remembers a former riot at the same theatre (in the year 1792), when the price to the boxes was raised from five shillings to six. That tumult, however, only laſted three nights."

There had been an even earlier exhibition of public indignation in this respect, in 1763, when Walpole writes that the Half Price Riots affected Covent Garden even more than they did Drury Lane; but that both theatres were "demolished on the inside" during the diſturbances.[1] The riot laſted for no fewer than sixty-seven nights, and as a result, the prices of the pit were reduced to 3*s.* 6*d*.[2]

Those who are curious to know what theatrical fare was provided at Covent Garden during the years 1801–12 will find a liſt of the principal pieces produced there, as well as at Drury Lane, in Doran's "Annals of the English Stage," together with a note of the more famous players who took part in

[1] Letters to Conway and Mason, February 28 and March 4, 1763.
[2] The circumstance is perpetuated by the O.P. Club.

them. In the last-named year, Mrs. Siddons here took her farewell benefit; and four years later Macready made his first appearance. From then onward the place had a variety of managers, among them such men as H. Harris in 1818, Charles Kemble in 1823, Osbaldiston in 1835, and Macready himself two years later. From 1839 Madame Vestris and Kemble and Lambert succeeded each other in the post; but the expenses were so heavy and the takings often so inadequate, that for a time the legitimate drama was driven away, a circumstance due, no doubt, to a variety of other smaller theatres which were attracting a public always avid after novelty. During the winter season of 1845–46, Jullien gave a series of Promenade Concerts here, to be followed by the Anti-Corn Law League, which took a lease of the place in the latter year. In 1847, however, there was a recrudescence of its old glory, for in that year a certain Mr. Benedict Albano took it, and, greatly daring, reconstructed it at a cost of £40,000, and opened it as an Italian Opera House. Notwithstanding the repeated assertion that the English people are fond of music, it is a curious thing that opera in this country never seems to be, or to have been, at any rate, a financial success, and Mr. Hammerstein's comparatively recent venture in Kingsway reproduced the fate of the over-optimism of Albano these eighty years ago. Less than a year after his venture was opened there was found to be a deficit of nearly £35,000; in the following year, of over £25,000; but the *impresario* must have had a heavy financial backing, for as an Opera House, Covent Garden continued, although it was occasionally let, I imagine in the off seasons, for other purposes. And this state of things went on till March 5, 1856, when the building was again wholly destroyed by fire after a *bal masqué*, organized by Professor Anderson, had been held there.

In the illustrated papers of the day we can see the theatre in the throes of this its second dissolution, with the firemen reinforced by the still-archaic fire-engines then in use, vainly spurting water into a hopelessly burning structure, in which Edmund Kean had last acted just twenty-three years previously.

But again it was to emerge, phœnix-like, from its ashes, and in the hands of E. M. Barry, a new playhouse arose, this time designed expressly for opera, and was opened in May 1856, with Mr. Gye as presiding deity. Since that day half a century has elapsed, during which opera, with more or less success, has been given here with the Promenade Concerts during the off-seasons, and by this combination the concern has happily prospered. Gala performances on special occasions, such as the visits of foreign sovereigns, and so forth, have also helped to preserve that *aura* of fashionable patronage with which the opera is so largely identified; while the Promenade Concerts have kept it in touch with the less decorative, but equally musical, section of the public.

The Haymarket Theatre

"At the new theatre in the Haymarket, between Little Suffolk Street and James Street, which is now completely finished, will be performed a French Comedy as soon as the rest of the actors arrive from Paris, who are duly expected."

With this announcement in a newsheet for December 15, 1720, the public was made aware of the completion of the little playhouse which one John Potter, a carpenter, had erected at the modest cost of £1500. Just a fortnight later, the house opened with its French comedians, who gave "La Fille à la Morte, ou le Badeaux de Paris." The prices were moderate; 5s. for a box and 2s. 6d. for a seat in the gallery. The theatre, in consequence of its inauguration by a foreign troupe, and perhaps with the hope of being permanently identified with continental players, called itself "The new French Theatre"; but this name soon gave place to that of "The Little Theatre in the Haymarket," to distinguish it from the other house, built by Vanbrugh some years before, which stood where His Majesty's does to-day.[1]

The "Little Theatre," as it will be convenient thus shortly to call it, does not seem greatly to have prospered with its imported talent, and in the following year we find it in the hands of an English amateur company run by Aaron Hill, who gave some performances of "Henry V." here. For a time, indeed, the profession seems to have fought shy of it, and in 1723 we still find amateurs—this time playing "The Female Fop"—in possession. This play was not a success, and the Little Theatre was reduced to giving asylum to entertainments of various kinds, concerts being perhaps the best of them. Then came a season of Italian opera, in 1726, although that was diversified by feats of agility, in which rope-dancing and tumbling, gladiatorial contests, and so forth, were conspicuous features.

In 1733, however, a change came over the fortunes of the place. In that year Theophilus Cibber and others, having quarrelled with the management of Drury Lane, took the Little Theatre, and inaugurated the success it was destined to maintain in its old as well as its rebuilt house down to to-day.

Cibber's company called themselves "The Comedians of His Majesty's Revels," and with this high-sounding title opened at the Haymarket, on September 23, 1733, with Congreve's "Love for Love," in which Theophilus himself, his notorious sister, Mrs. Charke, and Mrs. Pritchard figured.

But although this inaugurated, as I have said, the

[1] As it was so identified with music as to be one of the homes of opera, I shall deal with it in the chapter devoted to Musical Entertainments.

H

fame of the Little Theatre as a legitimate playhouse, that fame was to have occasional vicissitudes, and only a year of Cibber's venture had run when he gave it up, and one Fielding, with what he grandiloquently called "The Great Mogul's Company of Comedians," reigned in his stead. This company acted various dramatic satires, including "Pasquin" and "The Historical Register," which Fielding had written, and which appear to have excited the authorities, for their performance gave rise to the Licensing Act of 1737, by which it was enacted that a licence from the Lord Chamberlain was necessary before any play could be publicly performed. After this the playhouse was closed for a few years, and we next hear of it in 1744, under the management of Macklin, who produced "Othello," with Foote in the name-part and Macklin himself as Iago. But this was but a temporary success, and Macklin was succeeded by the egregious Theophilus Cibber, who returned to his old house after an absence of some ten years, but without a licence, a disability he attempted to overcome by advertising his performances as a concert: "At Cibber's Academy in the Haymarket," to be followed by "an exhibition (gratis) of a rehearsal, in the form of a play, called 'Romeo and Juliet.'" This proved a failure, and Cibber was followed by Foote as manager, equally without a licence, which *he* endeavoured to circumvent by inviting the public to "drink a dish of chocolate with him," and incidentally to witness his diverting "Diversions of a Morning," which proved very much to the taste of the town.

It was during Foote's first management, which closed in 1749, that a hoax was perpetrated by someone (the real culprit has never been unmasked) who issued handbills promising to appear on the stage, and, in addition to performing other marvellous tricks, to get into a common wine bottle, in the presence of the spectators, and to sing songs the while. Needless to say, in a credulous generation such a bait drew crowds to the theatre; and when the conjuror did not appear the audience forthwith showed its fury by wrecking the place and making a bonfire of its contents. This was in 1749, and another riot occurred in the following year when a French company attempted to perform, but for some reason were not permitted to by the rougher element in the audience, which resulted in "several young men of quality" drawing their swords in defence of the actors and actresses.[1]

It is said that when Foote took the "Little Haymarket" in 1747, he continued as manager for thirty years. This is not quite correct, as after the riots, Cibber again appeared on the scene, and made his short career as manager notable by the introduction of Mrs. Abington to the public. But from first to last Foote had, when he gave it up in 1777, been associated with the playhouse intermittently for that period; and in 1767 it had been made a *royal* Theatre for his benefit.

Foote, with all his faults—and it is common knowledge that he was as full of them as he was of wit and repartee—made the Little Theatre in those days. He called himself a popularity-monger, but he reconstructed the playhouse, obtained its royal licence, and joked and elbowed his way to a success that had then few equals. He knew exactly what the public wanted, and he gave it what pleased it. Nor was he alone in attracting audiences. He managed to get together such men as Charles Bannister and John Palmer; Parsons the humorist, and Baddeley, famous and still remembered for his Cake; Shuter, a ready wit, and Quick, who always made George III. laugh. In 1777, Foote retired and sold his licence to the elder Colman for an annuity of £1600 and the right to earn by acting £400 more in any one year. Dr. Johnson once

[1] See Walpole's "Memoirs of the Reign of George II."

wondered what Colman would get by this transaction; but it turned out fortunately for him, as Foote only played three times, and was dead, from a stroke of paralysis, within a year of the bargain being struck.

At first Colman did not meet with much success, but with the introduction here of Henderson, Edwin, and Miss Farren to the public, the tide turned, and the new manager did excellent business; although the *début* here of George Frederick Cooke proved so great a fiasco that that fine actor left London not to return till after an interval of over twenty years.

It is impossible to give with any detail the events which occurred in the Little Theatre under the management of George Colman and his son, who succeeded him in 1795, and who ten years later sold a part of his share in the concern to Messrs. Morris and Winston. During those twenty-eight years the playhouse enjoyed an almost uninterrupted period of success; and with the exception of a disaster due to overcrowding, when George III. and Queen Charlotte visited the house in 1794, without any of those *désagrémens* to which so many theatres have been liable. It did not even get itself burnt down, which alone helps to differentiate it from several of its most notable rivals. Such famous histrions as Miss Farren, Edwin, Henderson, old Kemble, Liston, and Elliston, to name but these, made their *débuts* here during these prosperous years, and here Poole's "Paul Pry" was originally performed; here Kean acted occasionally, and here Polly Fenton had charmed successive audiences.

Towards the end of the younger Colman's management things were not quite so prosperous as they had been: lawsuits arose, and other difficulties beset the *impresario*. It is possible, too, that the town had outgrown the little house. Be this as it may, it was finally closed in October 1820, and although it remained standing after its successor had been built,[1]

[1] See illustration.

it was but in a ruinous condition, and was only too ready for those undertakers of bricks and mortar, the house-breakers.

The New Haymarket Theatre

The exterior of the Haymarket Theatre, as we know it to-day, is essentially the same as emerged from the hands of John Nash's builders in 1821, and as it appeared when the playhouse was opened on July 4 of that year. Internally, however, great changes have taken place in the structure. In those times the pit extended over the whole of the flooring and reached to the footlights—as the old oil-lamps that did duty as such were facetiously called; in which the Haymarket appears to have been behind its compeers, where gas had already been introduced. The general differences in internal appearance from what it now presents cannot be better realized than by a quotation from a contemporary's account of the house.[1]

"In point of architectural beauty," writes this enthusiast, "the Haymarket Theatre is the most elegant in London. The middle doors lead to the boxes, the outer on the right to the box-office, and that on the left to the pit. The gallery entrances are on each side without the portico. The ground-rent of this theatre is about five guineas a foot in front, and three guineas for the back part of the premises. The auditory is remarkable for having the sides straight, and the centre very slightly curved; different in this respect from any other theatre in London. The fronts of the side-boxes, however, project semi-circularly: all are decorated with gold chequered work on a pink ground, and the insides are a crimson colour. There are two circles of boxes, besides half-tiers parallel with the lower gallery. In the front circle are five private boxes, and in the second

[1] This is given in Mr. Cyril Maude's delightful and amusing account of the theatre, in which he scored so many triumphs.

tier eight. The house holds upwards of £300. It is, perhaps, one of the most elegant interiors in London, but for convenience of seeing and hearing, the worst contrived, and so small are the hall and lobby of the boxes, that whilst sitting in the dress-circle the audience are not infrequently annoyed by the sounds of carriages rattling in the street. The prices of admission are: boxes 5s., pit 3s., gallery 2s., upper gallery 1s. Half-price is not taken. The doors open at six, and the performances commence at seven."

Such was the playhouse which opened on July 4, 1821, with Sheridan's "The Rivals" (this had been played just fourteen years previously at the Little Theatre) and an address spoken by Terry. The house was under the management of Morris, Colman's son-in-law, who numbered among his company such well-remembered players as Madame Vestris, William Farren, and Mrs. Waylett, and to which Benjamin Webster was, not long after, to add his brilliant qualities as an actor, and, in 1837, his abilities as an manager.

During the Webster *régime*, an extraordinary galaxy of histrionic talent illuminated the boards of the Haymarket, and Macready, the younger Mathews, Helen Faucit, Tyrone Power, Benjamin Wrench, Mrs. Fitzwilliam, Mr. and Mrs. Charles Kean, Samuel Phelps, Madame Celeste and Mrs. Stirling, were among the more famous of the players; just as Bulwer Lytton, Sheridan Knowles, and Douglas Jerrold were among the playwrights who ministered to the amusement of the public and upheld the prosperity of the theatre. Benjamin Webster, too, did other things for the Haymarket besides providing it with plays and actors of first-class ability. He introduced gas in place of the old and malodorous oil-lamps; he enlarged the proscenium by eleven feet; and in other ways he added to the convenience both of the audience and the actors. Among the most

Drawn & Engraved by Daniel Havell

THE OLD AND NEW HAYMARKET THEATRES

1825

successful of the plays he staged here were Lytton's
"Money," Sheridan Knowles's "Love Chase," and
"Time Works Wonders," by Douglas Jerrold. But
he had at least one marked set-back. For some
recondite reason he advertised his willingness to pay
£500 for a comedy; and Mrs. Gore, the fashionable
writer of the day, secured the prize with her "Quid
pro Quo, or the Day of the Dupes," which, however,
turned out a dismal failure, and was so badly received
that it had to be withdrawn forthwith.

Webster had been managing the Haymarket for
a year when he engaged Macready, at a salary of
£4000 for the season, and the great actor first appeared
as the hero in Lytton's "Sea Captain," that play which
would be as dead as the Dodo had not Thackeray
preserved its incidents in his famous address to
Lytton, termed "Epistles to the Literati," in which
Yellowplush gives both play and author innumerable
hits in his inimitable style of badinage.

Webster's management came to an end in 1853,
when he was succeeded by Buckstone, who had
already been associated with the Haymarket as an
actor since 1837 when Webster engaged him as one
of his leading comedians. His first season lasted
for over five years, which must, as Mr. Maude[1] thinks,
be a record; and he proved a very successful and
capable manager. It was under his *ægis*, in 1861,
that Edwin Booth made his first appearance in London,
playing the part of Sir Charles Overreach in Massinger's "New Way to Pay Old Debts," and proving
equally skilful in such parts as Shylock, Richard III.,
and Richelieu, although he does not appear to have
quite hit the popular taste at that time. There was,
perhaps, another reason for the fact that only very
ardent play-goers would sit through a play produced by
Buckstone. This was the inordinate length of time

[1] "The Haymarket Theatre: some records and reminiscences,"
by Cyril Maude, 1903.

they occupied; and we are told that a piece beginning at seven often went on till well over midnight. Half-pay, which had been introduced, did something to alleviate this, and people were admitted after nine o'clock on these terms; and had plenty for their money; but Buckstone later abolished this old system; so that even that relief was but temporary.

The stories told of Buckstone are as the sands of the sea, and the Haymarket was the scene of many of them. Queen Victoria was a great admirer of the actor, and before the death of the Prince Consort was a regular visitor here. It was customary in those days for the manager to light the royal party to their box with a pair of candles; and Buckstone's adventures in his capacity as usher are responsible for some of the amusing tales that have survived about him.

Successful as he habitually was in his management, it is doubtful if he ever did better, from a monetary point of view, than when he engaged Sothern to play that part of "Lord Dundreary" which has become classic. It created a veritable *furore*, and "An American Cousin," the piece in which the character figures, was on everyone's lips. Night after night the playhouse was packed with an audience tumultuous with enjoyment and laughter, the curious thing being that during the first few performances the play had not been a marked success.

Buckstone continued his management till 1879, and in the following year Mr. and Mrs. Bancroft took the Haymarket, entirely reconstructed it, and began their career of extraordinarily successful management, which is within the memory of many of us, and which closed, too early, five years later. During that short period what memorable plays were given here; what triumphs the Marie Wilton of earlier days and her talented husband (still happily to be seen about, as if Time had forgotten him) earned! Who can forget the original presentment of "Diplomacy," or the tenderness of "Peg Woffington," or "The Rivals," with Lal Brough as Bob Acres; or the beautiful Mrs. Langtry in "She Stoops to Conquer"; or Mrs. Bernard Beere in the lurid "Fedora"!

Once, and perhaps only once, the Haymarket under this splendid *régime* was nearly empty. It was in the January of 1881, when London was blocked up with snow, and seven die-hards fought their way to the stalls, with the rest of the house as deserted as Tadmor in the Wilderness!

On June 20, 1885, the Bancrofts gave their farewell performance, when such a galaxy of histrionic talent supported them in scenes from "Money" and "Masks and Faces," with Sir Henry Irving and Toole and Clement Scott making complimentary speeches, and such a brilliant audience, including various members of the Royal Family, as had not been seen even in the Haymarket of so many glorious triumphs.

After the Bancrofts came Herbert Tree to carry on worthily the traditions of the theatre. Here he introduced some of his most notable productions: "The Red Lamp," with his unforgettable impersonation of "Demetrius"; "The Dancing Girl," with the Duke of Guisebury and his bull-dog; and the rest. Tree continued at the Haymarket till July 15, 1896, when he gave his final performance here; and soon after the theatre was taken by Mr. Frederick Harrison and Mr. Cyril Maude, whose joint careers as managers here, during which such popular successes as "The Second in Command," with an *etcetera* far too long for me to attempt to fill up, brings us to the still successful and delightful Haymarket of our own day, with Sir James Barrie's conjuring name (as I write) illuminating its portal, and indicating that "Peter Pan" indeed bids fair never to grow up out of public favour.

CHAPTER V

THE disputes which occurred at intervals between the King's Company and the Duke's, in the time of Charles II., and which continued down to the days of the earlier Georges, and did harm to both, paved the way for those who saw profit in providing theatrical entertainment for London, and Sir John Vanbrugh built his theatre in the Haymarket (later to be known as The Opera). But, after all, London was growing by leaps and bounds, and Vanbrugh's playhouse could only conveniently be patronized by those living more or less in the West End. This being so, it occurred to one Thomas Odell, a dramatic author, and first licenser of plays under Sir Robert Walpole's Licensing Act, that there was room for a playhouse in the East End, and he took some premises in Great Alie, or Ayliffe Street, Goodman's Fields, for that purpose. It is rather remarkable that in his capacity of licenser of plays he did not think it necessary to obtain a licence for his new venture, which he opened on October 31, 1729. What kind of histrionic fare he administered to the denizens of Whitechapel and the Minories does not appear. It was probably of a very rudimentary, if not rough, character; but in any case it began to scandalize the unco' guid of the neighbourhood, partly, it is but fair to state, because of the gradual increase of houses of ill-fame, which was largely attributed to its influence. So notorious did this become, indeed, that the incumbent of St. Botolph's, in the vicinity, preached a sermon directly aimed against the scandal, and so frightened Odell that he took immediate steps to dispose of his interest in the little playhouse. He found a more daring spirit, ready to brave ecclesiastical fulminations and possibly civic interference, in one Henry Gifford, who, employing Shepherd, the architect of Covent Garden, to design a new house for him, had one built, and on October 20, 1732, opened his "new, beautiful and convenient theatre," as he termed it. As may be supposed, the erection of a new and more elaborate structure only added fuel to the fire of ecclesiastical antagonism, and the denunciations and complaints increased so much that Henry Gifford had nothing for it but to remove his company to the safer purlieus of Lincoln's Inn Fields, whither he betook himself in 1735.

For a time, then, the "Goodman's Fields" Theatre remained vacant, and an advertisement in a contemporary newsheet[1] indicates that it was for sale, and in the hands of Shepherd, the architect, for that purpose. Nothing, however, was done; and not long after we find Gifford returning to his old quarters.

The house having no licence, the performances were, as usual under such circumstances, disguised as concerts "of Vocal and Instrumental Music," at the *late* theatre in Goodman's Fields. It was under such a periphrasis that the theatrical performances sheltered themselves when, on the evening of October 19, 1741, a date never to be forgotten in dramatic annals, David Garrick made his first appearance on any stage here, in the part of Richard III. The fact had been disguised in the following words on the notice bills of the performance: "Between the two parts of the Concert will be presented an Historical Play called *The Life and Death of King Richard the Third*; . . . The part of King Richard by a gentleman (who never

[1] "The London Daily Post and General Advertiser" for September 14, 1738.

appeared on any stage): King Henry, by Mr. Gifford. . . . With an entertainment of Dancing by Mons. Fouret, Madame Duvalt, &c."[1]

Garrick, writing to his brother the next day, says: "Last night I played King Richard the Third, to the surprise of everybody. . . . I shall make very nearly £300 per annum by it, and as it is what I doat upon I am resolved to pursue it." He did!

For the first few nights there was nothing to indicate that a new planet had swum into the histrionic heavens. The receipts did not markedly rise; the reception was not specially enthusiastic; and then suddenly, as such things will happen, the whole of play-going London seems to have been aroused. Drury Lane and Covent Garden were practically deserted for a time by the rank and fashion of the west: "Mr. Garrick," says Davies, "drew after him the inhabitants of the most polite parts of the town. Goodman's Fields were full of the splendour of St. James's and Grosvenor Square. The coaches of the nobility filled up the space from Temple Bar to Whitechapel." This might have seemed exaggeration, had we not other evidence to confirm it, amongst which we find that of Gray writing to Shute, and remarking: "Did I tell you about Mr. Garrick, that the town are horn-mad after! There are a dozen dukes of a night at Goodman's Fields sometimes."

Horace Walpole was always to the fore with any novelty that the town had to show, and we find him, in a letter to Mann,[2] informing his friend that "all the run is now after Garrick, a wine-merchant who is turned player, at Goodman's Fields. He plays all parts, and is a very good mimic.[3] His acting I have

---

[1] Quoted in "London Past and Present."

[2] May 26, 1742. Toynbee's "Letters of Horace Walpole."

[3] Probably Walpole saw him in the part of Bayes, in which he so mimicked Delane, a well-known comedian, as to have seriously injured that actor in the estimation of the town.

seen, and may say to you, who will not tell it again here, I see nothing wonderful in it; but it is heresy to say so: the Duke of Argyll says he is superior to Betterton."

In spite of Walpole's criticism, the whole of London continued to pour eastwards to see the prodigy. Even Pope came from Twickenham, and Garrick tells how he saw the poet watching him "with serious and earnest attention," and how the poet's hands joined in the applause with which Richard was greeted. It need hardly be said that Garrick was not allowed to remain beyond his first season east of Temple Bar, and Drury Lane, with a bait of £600 a year, a hundred more than Quin was receiving, drew him to the west.

After that Goodman's Fields Theatre sinks into the obscurity from which Garrick's budding fame had for a time raised it; and in 1746 the little building was pulled down. At a later date, another small playhouse was erected on its site, and it is said that Braham, the singer, described then as "Master Abrahams," first appeared here in 1787. Thirteen years after this date the place met the not-unusual fate of playhouses and was burnt to the ground. The Zoar dissenting chapel stands on the ground where Garrick and Braham first became acquainted with London audiences.

Although the original Goodman's Fields Theatre was a relatively small one, it must have had some pretensions to decorative elaboration, if we are to judge from the drawing which Capon has left of its painted ceiling, in which are introduced portraits of Shakespeare, Dryden, Congreve, and Betterton, and in which an allegorical central panel is surrounded by an elaborate design.[1]

The other theatre in Goodman's Fields, of an earlier date, known as "Goodman's Fields New

[1] The original drawing, which is in the British Museum, was executed by Capon, in 1786. It is reproduced by Wilkinson, in his "Londina Illustrata."

Wells," was rather in the nature of a dancing and singing centre, much resorted to by sailors than a regular playhouse. It was, needless to say, unlicensed.[1]

Towards the close of the eighteenth and the early years of the nineteenth centuries, a number of playhouses sprang into existence, some of which in their reconstructed form are still with us. A return, too, was made to the south side of the river, and the Transpontine Drama, as it was called, catered for many years to not over-critical or sophisticated audiences.

Of these *The Surrey Theatre* was the oldest, and, although not originally intended for the legitimate drama at all, or, for the matter of that, for any kind of drama, became in time one of the best known. Indeed it was first projected as a circus, in opposition to the more famous one owned by the elder Astley, and was opened for this purpose by Messrs. Hughes and Charles Dibdin, with whom the notorious seventh Earl of Barrymore (Hellgate) was associated, on November 7, 1782. Hughes had earlier run a "Horse Academy" in opposition to Astley's venture of the same character, in 1772. Both these places were open-air arenas, and performances took place in daylight, weather permitting. For some reason these pleasure haunts were shut up by order of the magistrates in the following year—perhaps they had become centres of betting, on which the authorities always looked with suspicion, and there is little doubt that they were often the resort of ne'er-do-wells.

Anyhow, they seem to have given Dibdin an idea: and he projected a resort where horsemanship should be allied with decorative adjuncts, such as reproductions of the jousts and tournaments, tilting at the ring and such-like amusements of earlier days, so that, as it was said, his entertainments might "become objects of popular encouragement and profit." The

[1] See, too, The Garrick, in this part of the city, *supra*.

equeſtrian department was under Hughes's super-
vision, and the ballet-maſter (by which the variety
of the entertainment is indicated) was Grimaldi, the
father of the famous clown. Hughes and Dibdin,
backed by various intereſted people, a Colonel Weſt
being one of their chief supporters, opened their new
venture on November 7, 1782, in a building which is
said to have coſt £15,000. The diverse charaĉter of
the performance can be judged by the words in one of
the preliminary advertisements, which tell us that
"Feats of Horsemanship will be relieved by the efforts
of a number of children educated in the Academy,
who will perform their exercises in music, dancing,
oratory, etc."

But it had only a doubtful success, and even the
exertions of Sir John Lade and particularly of Lord
Barrymore to infuse new life into the concern by the
produĉtion of a sort of pageant called "The Four
Quarters of the World," and the pierrot Delpini, in a
comic pantomime, were powerless againſt internal
dissensions and the withdrawal of the licence. Hughes
and Dibdin quarrelled, and although they appear to
have been reconciled, and to have reopened the place,
only a few weeks elapsed before further dissensions
drove them apart; Hughes, with his equeſtrian
proclivities, having had little sympathy with Dibdin's
love of music.[1] However, the place remained open till
1789, when it was taken over by Palmer and a man
named Read,[2] who produced here a speĉtacular show
called "The Baſtille," which had such a success that
it was performed for seventy-nine nights to crowded
and enthusiaſtic audiences. But it was the swan's song
of the circus, and at the close of the run the place was
shut up; and so remained for four years.

In 1793, we find it being reopened with that kind

[1] Dibdin wanted to get up an entertainment in commemoration of
Arne, and Hughes would have none of it.
[2] Read wrote a "History of the Circus."

of variety entertainment in which Horsemanship and
Rope Dancing were the chief items. Like many of the
circuses, it possessed a stage in addition to its arena,
but the former adjunct appears to have remained
unused. Indeed it was not till 1799 that the building
was wholly reconstructed, by Cabanel, as a theatre in
the proper sense of the word, being reopened with a
play called "Almoran and Hamet." In the following
year it was further improved and embellished, and
with the engagement of actors from Drury Lane and
Covent Garden, may be said to have entered into its
career as a home of "the legitimate." But disaster was
at hand, and in 1805 it was totally destroyed by fire,
involving a heavy loss, as the insurance had been
allowed to lapse. However, in the following year a new
house rose on the ruins of the old one, at a cost of
£14,500.

The career of this for the few following years is
hidden in obscurity, by which we may, I think, surmise
that it was neither markedly successful nor wholly a
failure.

In 1809, things changed with Elliston becoming its
lessee. For a time he enjoyed a remarkable run of luck,
although his expenses were so great that, by the close
of his tenancy in 1814, he appears to have lost considerably by the venture. With an eye on the character
of his transpontine audiences, he produced a series of
burlettas, as they were called, in which with incredible
daring he converted "Macbeth" and "The Beggar's
Opera," "George Barnwell" and "Raising the Wind,"
and other plays, into burlesques of the most audacious
character, but no doubt to the vast amusement of
those who were ready to go anywhere and to witness
any desecration for the sake of a laugh. It was during
the Elliston *régime* that the house became known as
"The Surrey Theatre."

He was followed here by Tom Dibdin, with a short
interregnum during which Dunn took over the place,

reconverted it into a circus, and ran it so badly that Wilkinson says even "the Dog and Duck and the Apollo Gardens would have been reckoned genteel places compared with it." It need hardly be said that the authorities were not long in descending on the building, and Dunn, forced to quit, gutted it of every conceivable movable, and held an auction of what he did not carry away.

With Dibdin's management, which extended from 1816 to 1822, a different state of things obtained. Re-converted into a theatre, it became, in Dibdin's words, and he was after all an authority, if in this instance a partial one, "without exception the best constructed house, both for audience and actors, in or near the metropolis."[1]

Subsequently the place continued a successful career under the successive managements of Davidge and Creswick. But in January 1865, it was again destroyed by fire, and the existing house, now converted into a music-hall, was erected on its site, from the designs of Mr. J. Ellis, and at a cost of £25,000.

Before returning to the other side of the river, and in spite of strict chronology, it will be convenient to say something of another well-known transpontine theatre, which in our own times has become famous as "The Old Vic." The Old Vic, in spite of reconstruction recently carried out, is perhaps the best example we have of the kind of house our forbears were accustomed to patronize. Still somehow hangs about it that odour of the later Georgian times; and we can imagine Lamb hanging over the gallery there, and Hazlitt, there, criticizing the drama of his now distant day.

The house is but a little over a hundred years old, yet so historic have those early years of the nineteenth century become, and so changed are we in our habits

[1] See his Autobiography.

I

and customs, that there is still almost an *aura* of antiquity about the Old Vic, which began life as "*The
Cobourg*," while George III., at least in name, was still
king.

The Cobourg stands on historic foundations, for
when it was projected, the remains of John of Gaunt's
palace in the Savoy were being demolished, and much
of the stone was brought across the Thames for use
as the superstructure of the new theatre. The first
stone was laid on September 14, 1816, by Prince
Leopold of Saxe-Cobourg (the husband of Princess
Charlotte, and later Leopold I., king of the Belgians),
hence the name given to the building which Cabanel,
who, as we have seen, was responsible for the Surrey
Theatre, had designed.

The work of construction went on but slowly.
Money did not come in as quickly as had been hoped;
once, at least, a strike of workmen delayed matters;
but finally, these difficulties being overcome, the
theatre was opened on May 11, 1818, under the *ægis*
of Jones and Dunn, whom we have met with in connection with the Surrey. What the interior looked like
can be seen by Schnebbelie's drawing, reproduced in
"Londina Illustrata," where, too, some interesting, if
rather technical, details concerning the theatre's inception and building will also be found. The drop scene
appropriately represented "Claremont," then occupied
by Prince Leopold.

By a bill of the first night's entertainment we can
see that the management relied rather on spectacular
effect than on legitimate drama; and with "a new
melodramatic spectacle entitled Trial by Battle,"
a "grand Asiatic ballet called Alzora and Nerine";
and a "splendid Harlequinade called Midnight
Revelry," hoped to secure the suffrages of the
neighbourhood.

That it did so seems certain; but in course of time
a change both in the name of the theatre and its

productions took place; and it blossomed into "The Victoria," in honour of the Princess who was to become Queen, and opened, as such, on July 1, 1833, with "Black-Eyed Susan," and T. P. Cooke in his memorable impersonation of William. The success of this was phenomenal, and many who are but dimly acquainted with the dramatic pieces and their impersonators of the past, know at least by name the actor who charmed the town by his William of "Black-Eyed Susan."

For a number of years after this, the Victoria or The Vic, as it was called, was a recognized home of that tempestuous sort of drama which relied for its appeal on awakening the sentiment rather than the intellect of its auditors; and nowhere else was what was known as "The Transpontine Drama" so eloquently expressed as here.

After a time—perhaps its patrons had become tired of too much blood and thunder—the theatre was closed. At length it was determined to make the experiment of giving musical entertainments shorn of the vulgar element of *double entendre*, etc., and a company being formed for that purpose, the house was, in 1881, opened as the Royal Victoria Coffee Hall, where smoking was allowed and all but alcoholic drinks could be obtained.

Since those days another great change has come over the place, and under the direction of Miss Bayliss, an attempt, as successful as it is praiseworthy, to familiarize the people with the standard dramatic works in our language, has been made; and at the Old Vic, as it is affectionately called, one may witness the plays of Shakespeare and other famous writers, at those popular prices which are so out of proportion with the excellence of the fare provided. The prosperity which has attended these efforts is sufficient to show that, just as our forbears flocked to Bankside in his own day to hear the magician's words, so have those words still power to shake with laughter or to move to tears their descendants, and that, in spite of problem-plays and their congeners, Shakespeare no longer, as he was once said to do, spells failure.

Royalty Theatre

Before the close of the eighteenth century, although only shortly before, three theatres arose in London: The Royalty, in far-flung Wellclose Square, in 1787; the Lyceum, in 1790, and the Sans Souci, in 1793; and one could hardly perhaps find three of more dissimilar character. Wellclose Square is known to few people who happen to forget that Thomas Day, the author of "Sandford and Merton," was born there, and it is so far away in Whitechapel that once when G. F. Cooke determined to visit it, he thought it so much at the other end of the world that he started out at eight o'clock in the morning for that purpose.[1]

The theatre which was built there owed its existence to John Wilmot and John Palmer, the actors, backed by the monetary assistance of various friends. The foundation stone was laid on December 26, 1785, and the theatre was named The Royalty. The opening took place on June 20, 1787, with a performance of "As You Like it," followed by the farce of "A Miss in her Teens." It was advertised that the proceeds would go to "the London Hospital"; because it had been found that, being a "minor theatre," it was restricted to pantomimes and such-like lesser enter-tainments, and the patentees of the regular playhouses had memorialized the Lord Chamberlain to withhold his licence. Wilkinson gives a detailed account of the opening night, and the speech Palmer made on the occasion; and by a list of the pieces performed here, which he also prints, one can see that the character of such performances was wholly of the burlesque and pantomime order.

[1] See his "Journal."

Jealousy on the part of the larger theatres was responsible for this and also for Palmer being involved in many grave difficulties connected with his rather ill-starred undertaking; and it was not long before he was obliged to return to the Drury Lane, whence he had seceded in his attempt to introduce legitimate drama to the East End. After that the Royalty was for a time shut up; then various people tried to revive it, and it later blossomed into the East London Theatre, but with little or no success. But in its decadence it could remember that Braham had begun his career as a vocalist here, and that here Clarkson Stanfield had produced scenery before he was known as a great landscape-painter.

In 1820, the theatre was purchased by Peter Moore, M.P., and six years later (April 11, 1826) it was burnt down.

After the Royalty had disappeared, its site was occupied by the so-called *Brunswick Theatre*, which was designed by T. S. Whitwell, and opened on February 25, 1828. It had been run up in seven months, although it is said to have had a façade resembling the famous one of the San Carlos Theatre at Naples. Its proprietors were not long, however, in finding out the jerry-built character of the structure; for, during the progress of a rehearsal, only three days after the place had been opened, it collapsed, killing ten people, among whom was one of the proprietors, Mr. Maurice, and injuring many more; the catastrophe being due to the insecurity of the iron roof and the strain of the great weights attached to it.

The Lyceum

If both the Royalty and its successor, the Brunswick, have little or no history, the same cannot be said of the Lyceum, which, in point of date, came into being three years after the former. For so many years, during our own time, has the Lyceum been a name to conjure with, that it is perhaps better known than any that has existed in London. Although it dates really from the 'nineties of the eighteenth century, at least its site has an earlier history not unconnected with the drama. Here in 1765 the architect James Paine had originally built a structure as an academy or *lyceum* for a society of artists; but when the Royal Academy was started, and he had no further use for the place, he sold it to Garrick, who purchased the lease of the premises with the express purpose of preventing their being converted into a playhouse. Paine's Academy, however, still sometimes held exhibitions here, even many years after Garrick's death, for a notice of one of these, dated 1790, informs us that an exhibition of paintings was to be held "in the Society's old room called the Lyceum, near Exeter Change." But this is the last notice we have of such a connection, and later in the same year the property was purchased by a Mr. Lingham, who combined the occupation of making breeches and a love of music, and who opened the place for musical performances. These entertainments were of a more or less varied character, and consisted chiefly of songs, recitations, and such-like amusements, in which Wewitzer, Gray, Master, and Mrs. Reeve were among the principal performers. The admission to the better seats was 2s. 6d., to the inferior ones, 1s.

What success, if any, attended these diversions, is not recorded; but about four or five years later we find Lingham leasing the building, together with certain adjoining land, to Dr. Arnold, who proceeded to erect one of those theatres-cum-circuses which had so great a vogue at this period. For some reason— probably the neighbouring Drury Lane and Covent Garden had something to do in the matter—the licence which Arnold had secured was revoked; and the theatre, not being any longer available for legitimate dramatic performances, became for a time the home of such composite entertainments as musical concerts, exhibitions of horsemanship (one Handy took it for this purpose in 1795, and called it "The New Circus") and even reverted to its former use as a medium for the exhibition of pictures. Later Astley acquired it, when his Amphitheatre across the water had been burned down; and it was thus a home for all sorts of ventures, good, bad and indifferent. In 1803–4 Winser here exhibited his gas-lighting apparatus, which was destined to create a revolution in street and house illumination; and at one time a foreigner, Philipstal, really made a great deal of money by exhibiting here the first "phantasmagoria" ever shown in this country.

The place was a theatre without a drama; its protagonists were entertainers without being actors. Even so novel a show as the so-called "Ægyptiana," which Mr. Lonsdale, backed by many influential and some eminent men, produced, did not succeed; and while Philipstal's "terrific shadows," as they have been called, were being shown at the smaller theatre, Lonsdale's more classic entertainment was being given simultaneously to nearly empty houses, in the larger. For before this the building had been thus divided.

It is interesting to recall roughly the nature of the entertainments given, not because they can be said to have been theatrical in the proper sense of the word, but because they help to indicate the kind of amusements which were tried, with more or less success, on our unsophisticated forbears. Thus, a clown known as Mr. Bologna at Covent Garden, fired by Philipstal's good fortune, opened the smaller playhouse with a varied form of the phantasmagoria which he termed Phantascopia, and which for a season proved not unprofitable. Undeterred by such horrific names the public not only flocked to Bologna's show, but were also found ready to patronize a company of Germans who had taken the larger building and were giving there an exhibition called Ergascopia, in which the Winser of gas fame seems to have had a part. Then Dibdin appeared with a mixed entertainment, not without melody, we may be sure; and after him Laurent, another clown, opened here in 1805, after he had taken both theatres and converted them into one with the title of "The Theatre of Mirth," where a rather low-class entertainment resulted in its projector's financial failure. There followed, in 1806, Ker Porter's exhibition of a great picture representing the Battle of Agincourt; then an entertainment organized by Palmer which he called "Portraits of the Living and the Dead"; and in 1807 and 1808 Incledon's "Voyage to India," and Dibdin's "Professional Volunteers." It will thus be seen what a strange medley of amusements were provided here, before the Lyceum really became a theatre within our meaning of the word.

It was Mr. J. Arnold, the son of the Doctor, who had, as we have seen, been once associated with the place, who, in 1809, having procured a licence, opened the premises, which he had enlarged and improved, as the English Opera House; and Drury Lane being burnt down in this year, members of that company were allowed to perform here. It was at this period that it received the name of "The Theatre Royal, Lyceum." The success of Arnold's venture seems to be indicated by the fact that in 1816 the house was rebuilt by Beazley. For fourteen years it pursued the even tenor of its way, when, on February 16, 1830, it was totally destroyed by fire.

No time was lost in getting out plans for a new playhouse, Beazley again being the architect, and at a cost of £35,000 a new house arose, rather to the west of the old one, and, Wellington Street being formed about the same time, the opportunity was taken of placing the chief entrance in that thoroughfare (it had been formerly in the Strand, where the pit approach still is), and instead of a very humble façade, that

Corinthian portico which we all know so well was erected. The new house was opened on July 14, 1834, still desperately clinging to opera as its mainstay.

Since then how may notable events have not been connected with the Lyceum? Madame Vestris took it in 1847, and richly re-decorated its interior; the Keeleys here performed to crowded houses, and here Fechter portrayed the classic figures of British drama. But it was in our own days that the Lyceum leaped into fame, in the hands of Irving, who, with the still ever-green Dame Ellen Terry, for season after season entranced London, gave a richer setting than had ever hitherto been attempted to Shakespeare's genius, and created such an *aura* around the theatre that the production there of a new play was a fashionable event, and people fought and struggled in that pit entrance, when neither love nor money could obtain a better seat in the house, on some long-expected first night.

The last of the eighteenth-century theatres which requires some slight notice, was the *Sans Souci*; but inasmuch as, compared with those already dealt with, it was small and unambitious, that notice need be but a short one. The first Sans Souci was erected by Thomas Dibdin, the song-writer, behind a shop he kept in the Strand, near Exeter Change. Dibdin, besides being a song-writer, was one of those men whose facility allows them to turn their hands to anything, and it is said that he not only himself painted and decorated his little playhouse, but wrote the songs and recitations with which he regaled his audience, accompanying himself on a piano of his own invention. He first opened his new venture on February 16, 1793; and it was on its stage that Edmund Kean, as a child, distinguished himself by his recitations.[1]

Here Dibdin seems to have remained with more or less success until we find him, three years later,

[1] "London Past and Present."

migrating to Leicester Square, where he took new premises. These were situated nearly on the site of the Feathers Tavern, which had been a favourite resort of Hogarth, at Nos. 2 and 3, on the east side of Leicester Place. In three months the little playhouse was completed, and was named the Sans Souci, after the earlier one in the Strand. Here Dibdin gave single-handed performances, so that in reality the name of theatre was rather a misnomer. These entertainments were, in a way, pioneers of those with which Mathews, in his "At Homes," later delighted the town, and which were still later to take on new forms in the hands of men like Paul Bedford, Toole, and others. We have met with Dibdin before as a lessee of the Surrey Theatre, when it was a circus, but his connection with the legitimate drama went back to the days of Rich's glory at Covent Garden and Garrick's triumphs at Drury Lane. He will rather be remembered, however, as the laureate of the sailor, whose hopes and fears and manifold experiences he voiced in many a stirring ballad—ballads that were on the lips of everyone who could carol forth a lay, as our later eighteenth-century and earlier nineteenth-century forbears were so fond of doing.

Dibdin carried on his Leicester Square playhouse till 1805, when it was closed, after barely sufficing to keep the wolf from the optimistic but improvident showman's door.

Together with his quite extraordinary inventiveness (he produced the words for 600 songs alone) [1] went a certain irritability which was always leading him into quarrels and difficulties, and to which may probably be traced the causes that made him close his theatre. That his good work on behalf of the British Tar, and of song-writing in general, was recognized, is proved by the fact that, in 1805, he received a Govern-

[1] They were published in the four volumes of his "Professional Life" which he issued in 1803.

ment pension, which was, however, stopped by that meanest of Prime Ministers, George Grenville, but restored by his successor, the Duke of Portland, in 1807. Six years later Dibdin died.

Within half a dozen years after the beginning of the nineteenth century, a number of lesser theatres sprang into existence. Of these the Strand, or Sans Pareil, as it was called, the Regency, the Olympic, and the Adelphi were the principal, and are those alone that need be mentioned, as they represent the class of playhouse which then provided theatrical amusements for the people, and were in the nature of those old-fashioned houses of which some remained within living memory, and of which the Old Vic, so far as its architectural lines are concerned, is, or perhaps I had better say was, as changes are about to take place there, the only survivor.

The Strand Theatre is not to be confounded with the Strand which later stood on the south side of the thoroughfare, four doors west of Surrey Street; and still less with the present playhouse bearing that name at the corner of Catherine Street, although the site of the latter is very much nearer the old original Strand, which stood almost opposite the Adelphi, on ground that had been cleared of some ruinous houses for the purpose of its erection, ground in earlier days forming part of the grounds of old Bedford House. The *Sans Pareil*, as it will be convenient to call it, to differentiate it from the later Strand Theatre, was opened on November 27, 1806, and was the precursor of the Adelphi. It owed its existence to a Mr. John Scott, who had a shop on this site, No. 411 Strand, and who converted it into a playhouse in order to exhibit the histrionic talents of his daughter, who, later, was to make a name for herself both as an actress and a writer. The performances were first of that heterogeneous character associated with the careers of some of the smaller theatres, and a medley of "turns," much akin to those of a music-hall, preceded the legitimate drama here.

A print, published in 1816, shows the exterior of the place as it was when first opened, and in "Londina Illustrata" is a picture of its interior, by which one can see that it was rather like a glorified hall than an actual theatre, although its proscenium was ample enough. In 1814 Scott made large improvements to the building, lengthening it by 26 feet, adding boxes, and giving it a new and quite imposing classic entrance; which additions cost no less than £5000. The venture appears to have been a success, and Miss Scott, who acted in plays she had herself written, was well patronized. Her father carried on the theatre till 1819, when he sold it to Rodwell and Jones, who in the following year opened it as The Adelphi; and as the Adelphi it has since remained.

From the first it was prosperous, largely owing to the success of Moncrieff's play of "Tom and Jerry," founded on Pierce Egan's well-known book, and first produced on November 26, 1821. It so delighted the town, indeed, that it ran for no fewer than three hundred nights, and resulted in a profit of £10,000. With such a send-off the fame of "the little Adelphi" was assured, and after the death of Rodwell, his executors were easily able to dispose of the property to Terry and Yates in 1825. It is interesting to remember that Terry, who was a friend of Sir Walter Scott, was financed by him as well as by Ballantyne. When Terry withdrew from the partnership, Yates was joined by Charles Mathews the elder, and under them the place had another era of success, in which Mathew's famous "At Homes" were for so much. It was during this period, actually in 1840, that a new façade was erected in the Strand. Four years later Madame Celeste became directress of the theatre, and here scored also some of her successes as an actress. She was followed by Benjamin Webster, who in 1858 entirely rebuilt the house from the designs of T. H. Wyatt; and it was under Webster's management that two special successes were scored with "The Dead Heart," by Watts Phillips, and Boucicault's "Colleen Bawn."

Since those times the little theatre has been the scene of many triumphs, and was, for a number of years, identified with the species of melodrama of the better kind which has given its name to a particular form of dramatic performance. That this was no new feature is proved by two lines in the Bon Gaultier Ballads, where, in the parody on "Locksley Hall," we read:

> "Or in the Adelphi sitting, half in rapture, half in tears,
> Saw the glorious melodrama conjure up the shades of years."

Of the many notable actors connected with the Adelphi none stands out so prominently as William Terriss, not only because he was the *beau-ideal* of the popular hero; but because he was foully murdered by a ruffian named Prince, as he was entering the stage door in Maiden Lane, in the December of 1897. It was just ten years before this tragic event that the Adelphi had been again enlarged and wholly reconstructed in accordance with modern ideas.

The other *Strand Theatre* to which I have already alluded as being close to Surrey Street, was originally known as Barker's Panoramic Exhibition, and had a more or less prosperous career until about 1831, when it was taken over by a company which included Lionel Benjamin Rayner, Captain Bell, well known on the Turf, and Mr. Gilbraith, who, during the off seasons, had been giving conjuring performances at the Adelphi. They converted the structure into a regular theatre, and in 1831 opened it as "Punch's Playhouse." When first started, it was not intended that money should be taken at the doors, but that tickets should be sold at an office outside. This, I imagine, was due to the fact that the lessees for long could not procure a licence. In course of time, however, Miss Kelly did succeed in obtaining a temporary one; and in 1836, through great exertions, the playhouse was officially recognized by the Lord Chamberlain; and "burlettas," as they were called, similar to those being given at the Adelphi and the Olympic, were later (1839) produced here under the management of Mr. Hammond. Hammond was followed as manager, after an interval of ten years, by Farren, and in 1855 Holcroft took over the theatre. Three years later the Swanborough family carried it on with marked success, and it was under their management that Marie Wilton (the Lady Bancroft of our day) appeared here. Among other theatrical lights who have delighted London audiences in the past, and who have been at one time or another associated with the Strand Theatre, may be mentioned Mrs. Waylett, Mrs. Stirling, Mrs. Glover, Lydia Thompson, Mrs. Selby and Mrs. Manders, as well as Farren, Compton, Thorne, James, Anderson, and Leigh Murray. Here, too, were produced some of Douglas Jerrold's earlier plays and several of the dramatized versions of Dickens's books.

The Strand Theatre (and exactly when it was so named from its original Punch's Playhouse I do not know) is no longer in existence, having been demolished, as have so many other of the Strand playhouses, in the interests of improvements or other requirements, but its name survives in the new Strand Theatre at the corner of Catherine Street, Aldwych.

Not only is the *Olympic* a thing of the past, but even its name no longer survives among the innumerable playhouses that exist in London. It was situated in Wych Street (and Wych Street, which ran behind, and parallel with, Holywell Street, is as forgotten as Tadmor), being bounded on its north-east side by that Maypole Alley which once perpetuated the famous Maypole in the Strand. It stood on the site of the once-splendid Craven House, the residence of Lord Craven, the devoted friend of Elizabeth, Queen of Bohemia, to whom he once lent it; or, to be more exact, about the middle of the north side of the large, semi-circular piece of ground on which Bush House stands.

Craven House, fallen from its high estate, had long been let out in tenements—Craven Buildings—erected in 1731, in which once lived Mrs. Bracegirdle and Mrs. Pritchard, the actresses, Hayman, the painter, and Dr. Arne. In 1803, these tenements were demolished, and two years later, Philip Astley, having secured a lease of sixty-one years at £100 a year, from Lord Craven, erected on their site what he called his Olympic Pavilion, at a cost of some £2500, which was the minimum sum he had agreed to expend. He is said to have purchased the timbers of an old French man-of-war, captured in one of Nelson's sea-fights, and to have used them in the construction of his pavilion. There is another story to the effect that the wood had once formed part of a vessel on which William IV. had served as "middy," and that it was given to Astley, together with a chandelier, by George III.

The new house was opened on September 8, 1806, and a curious place it must have been, judging from an extant water-colour of it by Winston, which, parenthetically, shows Astley seated in a gig, superintending the labours of his workmen. The place did not prove a success; and in the end Astley lost heavily by it, although he was able to dispose of it to Elliston, for £2800, in 1812. It was its new proprietor who converted it into a regular playhouse, and carried it on, with varying good and bad fortune, till Madame Vestris (she had been preceded by Egerton, in 1822) came and took it in 1832, and did well there for some seven years. In 1839, however, she disposed of it, and in the following year it was opened by George Wild, who was succeeded in turn by Mrs. Brougham and Delafield. In 1848 a Mr. Watts had become manager, and on March 29 of the next year a fire broke out which entirely gutted the little place. That no time was lost in rebuilding it, is proved by the fact that on the following December 26 it was reopened by Watts, who remained in command till 1850, when Farren took the house, but only for three years, after which he was succeeded by Horace Wigan, who produced here "The Ticket-of-Leave Man," with Henry Neville in the chief part, with enormous success. From 1857 till 1863 Robson and Emden carried on the theatre, and later, under Benjamin Webster, it became a popular resort for those who delighted in the finished acting of such as Ada Cavendish, Henry Neville, and Mr. and Mr. Charles Mathews.

A later era was inaugurated by Mrs. Liston, who produced here Halliday's adaptation of "David Copperfield," called "Little Emily"; but a still more marked success was the acting of Ada Cavendish in "The New Magdalen," the play which Wilkie Collins had constructed from his famous novel. Many notable histrions, indeed, have acted at the Olympic, Elliston, Edwin, Charles Kean, Charles Mathews and Keeley among them; and it was here that Tyrone Power made his first appearance in London, in 1841. In our own days the Olympic was carried on successfully, and many remember the little house, so retired, so exiguous, but having something about it that wafted one back to those earlier days when, if not in so elaborate a *décor* or with such a wealth of scenic adornment as we are now used to, the acting left little to be desired. On the site of the little Olympic we have out-Vanbrughed Vanbrugh by erecting Bush House.

CHAPTER VI

LESSER THEATRES OF THE PAST (*continued*)

THE *Regency Theatre*, like several of those which came into existence during the early years of the nineteenth century, was the outcome of an altogether different kind of venture. In this case the site had once been occupied by a Concert Room for Ancient Music, which had been established by the Earl of Sandwich, and much patronized by George III., whose love of music is well known and who on several occasions visited the room in Tottenham Street, Tottenham Court Road. In course of time the little place became too small for the fashionable audiences that were drawn thither, and the "Ancient Concerts" were removed to the more convenient Hanover Square Rooms.

After the departure of the more illustrious patrons of music, the place was taken by one Hyde, who opened it for concerts of a less ambitious character, and the premises became known as Hyde's Rooms. How long Hyde carried on is not certain, but after he had given up the rooms they remained untenanted for some time till Colonel Greville took them, fitted them up in an "elegant" manner, to use a word much beloved at the time, and here instituted his Pic Nic Society. This entertainment was primarily intended to afford opportunity for stage-struck amateurs to air their powers. "Here," says Angelo, "spouting, music, and sing-song were practised in that superior style which suited the more refined ears of the accomplished gentlemen and ladies at the court end. This famed

K

society, too, originated for the purpose of affording an opportunity for amateur performers to enter the lists for the prize of fame: such a coterie may not meet again for a thousand years;"[1] and he gives a long account of the venture, its successes, its troubles (for the large theatres became jealous and took steps to limit its exertions), the lampoons and caricatures, Gillray "letting fly at the mighty covey with his double-barrelled gun," and so forth, to which it was exposed. Here it is only necessary to mention it, as one of those minor pleasure haunts to which one section of society once flocked, and as the precursor of the little theatre with which we are more immediately concerned.

The Pic Nic Society continued here for some years, and then we find the place being taken over by one Saunders (1808), who fitted it up in a very haphazard sort of way, apparently, chiefly for equestrian exhibitions, but also for occasional stage performances. These were patronized by a very low kind of audience, and the character of Saunders's entertainments may be judged from the fact that he was accustomed to parade his entire company through the streets as a means of advertising his performances. It need hardly be said that his venture was not a long or successful one; and two years after he had started it, he disposed of the premises to Mr. Paul, who, in order to gratify the ambition of his wife—an indifferent performer— took the place and converted it into a theatre, adding a portico, and otherwise improving it. Mrs. Paul opened here with "Love in a Village" as a burletta, contrary to Act of Parliament. In the course of a few weeks the place had to be closed, and the unlucky and too-uxorious Paul retired into the Bankruptcy Court.

There followed a variety of people who successively tried their luck with the place, and the first of them, Penley, found it illusive. Later, however, when

[1] Angelo's "Reminiscences," vol. I, p. 288.

a fine but not properly appreciated actor named Cobham performed here, there were signs of success, still it was but a flash in the pan, and the crowded audiences of the first few performances gradually dwindled, and the novelty ceasing, the Regency Theatre was closed and allowed to fall into decay. In 1814 the lease was sold to Beverley, formerly of Covent Garden, for three hundred and ten guineas. According to the conditions of sale the privilege of keeping open all the year, upon a magistrate's licence, was that the theatre should have cost £4000; Wilkinson, who states this, adds: "If the present occupier can possibly make it answer, it must be by reducing the expenses to a very low scale indeed . . . the chief support is from the half price."[1] Wilkinson's book was published in 1825, so that it would seem that by "the present occupier," he indicates Brunton, who is known to have acquired the theatre four years earlier. His daughter, afterwards the celebrated Mrs. Yates, acted here with much success, and was one of the chief attractions of the place, owing largely to which circumstance Brunton was able to carry on the venture till 1831.

In the meanwhile its name had been changed from "The Regency," which had replaced the clumsy "New Theatre, King's Ancient Concert Rooms," of earlier days, to the "Queen's Theatre," in honour of Queen Adelaide. In 1831 the playhouse was taken over by Mr. Macfarren (the father of Sir George Macfarren), and two years later, for some recondite reason, blossomed forth as "The Fitzroy," under which new name it had a temporary popularity. Burlesques by Gilbert à Beckett were given here, and here the great French actor, Frédérick Lemaître, appeared; while Mlle. George played in Voltaire's "Mérope"; probably the only time that play has been given in an English theatre.

[1] "Londina Illustrata."

In 1835 Mrs. Nesbitt is found reopening the house, which now reverted to its name of "The Queen's." But it was not till Marie Wilton took it in our own times, and re-christened it "The Prince of Wales's" that the little playhouse can be said to have achieved real success. The performances, however, at the Prince of Wales's, if they are a dead-letter to the present generation, were things to conjure with at an earlier day, and there began that amazing period of prosperity which the Bancrofts were to crown with the triumphs of the Haymarket.

From the year 1830 to the present time London has witnessed the rise and decline of a large number of playhouses. Some of these no longer exist, others have been changed in name and character from what they originally were, still others are rising about us as I write, and must await the lapse of time before they will have made history, or otherwise. In some cases theatres with similar names have succeeded each other, not necessarily on the same sites. This, as we have seen, is the case with the Strand; it is so, too, with the Prince of Wales's and the Royalty, the Gaiety and the Garrick, to mention but these; and it is with the last that I can conveniently commence what I have to say about these late Georgian and early Victorian houses.

The original *Garrick Theatre* stood in a very different spot from the playhouse which now bears that name. It was, indeed, in the wilds of Goodman's Fields, and was situated in Leman Street. In view of the earlier Goodman's Fields Theatre, the locality was appropriate for a playhouse, and this its projectors may have felt when, in 1830, they set about its construction; certainly the reason for its being christened the Garrick was because the great actor had made his *début* at the old theatre there, as we have seen.

At one time the proprietors of the Garrick were Messrs. Conquest and Gomersall, and it was during their reign here that the structure was burnt down, on

November 4, 1846. It was rebuilt, but as there is no mention of it in the lists of such places of amusement given in the various histories of London published during the middle of the last century, it may be regarded as having become one of those lesser playhouses whose fortunes were various and whose entertainments were of a low or negligible character.

Another minor playhouse which arose in 1830 was the so-called *City Theatre*, in Milton Street (the Grub Street of eighteenth-century literature). It began its career with operatic performances; but that it not long after attempted legitimate drama and, in spite of its distance, attracted the quality, is proved by an extract from "The Mirror," for November 19, 1831, where we read that "a new theatre has here arisen, whose boards have been graced by a Tree and an Ayton; and within these few months its boxes have been graced with the presence of my Lords Brougham and Grey." In spite, however, of talent and high patronage, the City Theatre can never be said to have been a success, and shortly after, it was closed, its premises being converted into a chapel.[1]

A small theatre in the West End, now known as *The Royalty*, in Dean Street, Soho, was originally erected by Miss Kelly, in 1840, primarily as a school for acting, but also for the representation of amateur talent. In course of time it passed into being a regular playhouse, and though limited in space, as such places go now, it has, in our own times, had some marked successes, "Charley's Aunt" for one. It is just one of those little houses that are often available when the more ambitious ones are engaged, and its size makes it favourable for such attempts at theatrical representation as may be questionable successes. It is one of the few survivals of an earlier type of playhouse.

[1] The City of London Theatre, in Norton Folgate, first called after the name of that thoroughfare, was erected for Mrs. Honey the actress, in 1837. It has, however, no special history.

A year after it came into existence, the *Princess's* in Oxford Street was erected from the designs of Nelson, the architect, with Renaissance decorations by Crace, at a cost of £47,000. It began its career, not as a theatre at all, but as the "Queen's Bazaar," with a series of promenade concerts, and was first opened on September 30, 1841. But when Charles Kean took it, a change indeed came over the scene. Never before had the plays of Shakespeare been mounted with such splendour and correctness of detail. Kean was not a supreme actor like his father, but he was a superb stage-manager, and besides could sustain a variety of parts, if not with genius, at least with knowledge and talent. He may be said to have been the first to realize the importance of archæological detail in the theatre, and to have been the direct predecessor of Irving and Tree in this respect. There is now a tendency to go to the other extreme and to imitate the early drama in those limitations of dress and scenery which it exhibited because it did not know any better. If Shakespeare were alive to-day it is probable he would prefer to see "Much Ado about Nothing" as Irving produced it, or "As You Like It" as given by Tree, than with the archaicisms of the Stage Society, with which he might have been familiar, but which he would, one thinks, find too retrograde for his inquiring and projective mind. It is pleasant to remember that Kean's labours in this direction were recognized, in 1862, by the presentation of a service of plate purchased by public subscription.

After the erection in Church Street, Paddington, of what was called the *Marylebone Theatre*, in 1842 (it was enlarged to hold 1200 people in 1854), a species of what were then termed "penny theatres," a decade passed before any important fresh development occurred in this direction; and it was in 1858, a few years after the Marionette Theatre, in Adelaide Street, Strand, had developed out of the Adelaide

Gallery (1852), that the *Britannia Theatre* came into existence in High Street, Hoxton. Close by had formerly existed the Rosemary Branch Equestrian Theatre, but this being burnt down in July 1853, the Britannia was constructed as a substitute in the way of amusement for that neighbourhood. Although that neighbourhood was so far removed from the centre of fashion, the new theatre was built on lines far in advance of anything then existing. Timbs,[1] indeed, describes it in the following terms: "The Britannia (Finch and Paraire, architects) is provided with promenades and refreshment saloons. The auditory is very spacious, and elegantly decorated. The pit is nearly 80 feet wide and 60 feet deep. The stage is 76 feet wide by 50 feet deep; opening at the proscenium 34 feet wide by 37 feet deep. The house is effectively ventilated by openings left in ornamental portions of the ceiling, in immediate communication with the internal area of the roof, and thence with the open air, by means of louvres extending from one extremity of the building to the other. The provisions against fire are well planned, and the extent of the theatre is considerable."

I have quoted this rather dry account of the Britannia because I want to remind the reader that Charles Dickens, than whom no better judge in matters theatrical could be found, once asserted that he found "the Britannia Theatre at Hoxton, for internal arrangements, lighting, atmosphere, far better than Her Majesty's; far superior even to the Royal Italian Opera-House itself; with a gallery at threepence, another gallery at fourpence, a pit at sixpence, boxes and pit-stalls at a shilling, and a few private boxes at half-a-crown." There was, at the time of his visit, an audience of over two thousand present; but he found "the air of this theatre fresh, cool and wholesome."[2]

[1] "The Curiosities of London."
[2] For further details see "Two Views of a Cheap Theatre," in "The Uncommercial Traveller."

The Britannia Theatre is still in existence, and those who would test the truth of Dickens's description, can go to its far-off recesses and judge for themselves.

Another East End playhouse came into existence in the latter half of the 'sixties of the nineteenth century. This was the *Standard Theatre*, in Shoreditch, which rose on the site of an earlier one destroyed by fire in October, 1866. The Standard was larger than any existing playhouse, with the exception of the Opera House, and was the most important of those People's Theatres, of which the Pavilion, in Whitechapel, the Grand, at Islington, the Elephant and Castle, and such-like existing playhouses are examples known to vast numbers to-day.

Among the innumerable playhouses which crowd together in the West End, one or two are reconstructed relics of a former day; and as such, possess a certain historical interest, apart from their intrinsic importance as the homes of various manifestations of the drama.

Of these is the *St. James's Theatre*, in King Street, St. James's, which was first opened so long ago as 1835, and is therefore a nonogenarian among playhouses. It was designed by Samuel Beazley, who built the Lyceum, for Braham, the singer. The place cost £50,000, in addition to the £8000 which was paid for the site. The interior was elaborately decorated by Crace, and when completed the St. James's was one of the most comfortable and luxurious playhouses in London. In 1836 there was produced here Charles Dickens's pre-Pickwickian burletta, "The Strange Gentleman," which was first performed on September 29; while "The Village Coquettes," with incidental music by John Hullah, was given here on the following December 6.

At a later period the theatre was notable for the presentation of French plays; and later still, under Sir George Alexander's management, for that series of amusing and epigrammatic dialogues which Oscar Wilde in his exuberance, and many other more impartial judges, have regarded as plays.

Another smaller theatre still remaining from an earlier time is the *Vaudeville*, in the Strand, which was first opened by C. J. Phillips, in 1870, with Halliday's "Love for Money." Later, under the management of James and Thorne, it was to have many triumphs, culminating in "Our Boys," whose amazing run was only destined to be outdistanced by that of the perennial "Charley's Aunt."

The Vaudeville being in the Strand, conveniently introduces a few words about two other theatres in that thoroughfare which have disappeared, and two whose sites, and incidentally whose appearances, have changed.

Of the former was *Terry's Theatre*, which stood at Nos. 105–6, and which was erected by that excellent actor and good fellow, Edward Terry, in 1887, from the designs of Mr. Walter Emden. A feature about it was that no wood was used in its construction, and the elaborate arrangements made for escape in the event of fire were much discussed at the time of its opening. Here many of Terry's conspicuous successes took place, chief amongst them his ever-rememberable representation of Dick Phenyl, in Sir Arthur Pinero's great play "Sweet Lavender." Terry was a great traveller besides being a great actor, and the theatre was frequently sub-let by him, while he was scouring the globe or giving his own performances elsewhere. In course of time the little playhouse was demolished, and rebuilding has obliterated its memory.

The other departed playhouse was the *Opera Comique*, which, although it had its principal entrance in the Strand, stood, as did the Globe, on the site of Lyon's Inn, and was entered by an underground passage beneath Holywell Street. Like the Globe, too, the whole of the theatre was practically underground, and the stage was reached by a flight of steps from Wych Street. It was, however, although small, elaborately decorated in that rather factitious style which seemed in keeping with the fare it provided—chiefly of the *opéra bouffe* and vaudeville variety. Like the St. James's, it was frequently the home of French plays, too, and those of Sardou, Chivot and Duru were to be seen here.

The old *Gaiety* has long gone the way of all bricks and mortar: the Gaiety of Nellie Farren and Fred Leslie, Edward Terry and Lonnen, and the rest; the Gaiety of "Monte Cristo Junior" and "Little Jack Sheppard" and "Faust up to Date"; where Kate Vaughan's glorious dancing, the humour of Leslie and Terry, the acrobatic wonders of Lonnen, and the inimitable *espièglerie* of the one and only Nellie Farren, delighted the town night after night, and the young bloods of the stalls, resplendent with canes and gardenias, were almost as perennial and as decorative as the performance itself. *Autres temps, autres mœurs,* the very temple of these mysteries has departed; its site is not. Tadmor in the wilderness is not more desolate of fun. There is a new Gaiety, more like a mausoleum than a theatre. Glorious it is without and within; thousands are spent on its productions; its 'girls,' plays and actresses are as the sands of the sea. Everything is *de luxe;* but oh! for a night of the old times, for the poetry of Kate Vaughan's motion, and the piquant, gallery-turned glance of the one and only Nellie!

The old Gaiety began life as the Strand Music Hall, having been built for that purpose in 1864, by F. B. Keeling, in the Saracenic-Gothic style, which had begun then to have a vogue, and of which Burton, of "The Arabian Nights," once told Hollingshead he had in all his travels never seen anything to equal its overwhelming decorations. Four years later it was reconstructed by Mr. C. I. Phipps, and converted into a playhouse proper, being opened on December 21, 1868. Mr. Hollingshead, who had so much to do with the theatre that one cannot think of it without recalling his name, has written an account of the place which stood (for the sake of those who can't recall it, I give these details) on that island site surrounded by Wellington Street and Catherine Street on the west and east, and by a narrow thoroughfare erroneously called Exeter 'Change, but more properly Exeter Arcade, and the Strand, north and south.

It was Mr. Lawson (the father of the late Lord Burnham) who took the old music-hall and converted it into a theatre on the lines of the Théâtre Lyrique at Paris. It was opened by Hollingshead, who represented what was called "The New Theatre Company, Limited," with an operetta in one act, entitled "The Two Harlequins," "On the Cards," a comic drama, and Gilbert's *extravaganza*, "Robert le Diable."

From that time onwards, under the successive managements of Hollingshead and George Edwardes, the Gaiety enjoyed unbroken popularity and success, with that series of amusing comic operas some of which I have already mentioned ; and so it might, one imagines, have gone on doing indefinitely ; but the Aldwych-Kingsway improvements were at hand, and the old Gaiety came within the scheme. The last performance took place there on July 4, 1903 ; and, later, the properties and material were sold off ; details of which sad event will be found in the *Globe* for the following August 12. The enlarged roadway and the offices of the *Morning Post* occupy the site on which the theatre stood.

The new Gaiety is known to all ; but not all know that where it stands ran in former times two little alleys—Angel Court and Helmet Court, in which latter Henry Condall, Shakespeare's fellow-actor, once owned property; so that the site has had an earlier theatrical association. The present structure was designed by Norman Shaw, and its rounded and splendid front looks like some great galleon toiling its way westward through the teeming Strand. What a long way the Gaiety has travelled from its earlier Gothic, and relatively exiguous proportions to this apotheosis of architectural design!

I have incidentally referred to the *Globe Theatre*, when speaking of the Opéra Comique, to which it was adjacent and with whose subterranean character it had a similarity; although, its entrances being from Newcastle Street, Wych Street, and Holywell Street, it did not front on the Strand. It appears that it had been originally intended to erect a large hotel on its site, but the scheme fell through, and in the excavations which had already been made, Mr. Sefton Parry placed the little theatre, which was opened on November 28, 1868. It was only partially submerged, as the dress circle was level with the ground. The building had a domed roof, and was built to seat 1500 people.

On the whole it was one of the more successful of London's playhouses, and began prosperously with H. J. Byron's comedy, "Cyril's Success." But better remembered by some will be the long run here of "Les Cloches de Corneville," and later, the longer ones of "The Private Secretary" and "Charley's Aunt," with the inimitable W. S. Penley as the protagonist in both. It was in an earlier production called "Jo," based on Dickens's "Bleak House," of which, by the way, so many scenes are laid in the immediate neighbourhood, that Jenny Lee scored so great a triumph in the name-part.[1]

Of existing theatres of more modern construction I do not propose to speak, because they do this for themselves, and are known, as is the fare they offer the

[1] I may add to my list of theatres one called *The Holborn*, built in that thoroughfare in 1866, on the site of old Warwick House; and *The Effingham*, behind the Tavern of that name in the Whitechapel Road, erected in the following year, and subsequently rebuilt. Neither has any history, however.

public, to all those who are patrons of the drama. At some distant time they will take their place properly in any historical record of such things; at present they can hardly be said to do so.

The same may be said of the existing music-halls which have so much in common with many theatres, and which, indeed, are with difficulty differentiated from some of them. As we have seen, some of the old theatres began their career with variety entertainments of an approximately analogous character to that of the older kind of music-hall; while the music-hall, as we know it to-day, has so largely departed from the form of its forbears, and also in the nature of its "turns," that it is not easy to associate the two. In past days, the entertainment on the stage was only a part, often a minor part, of the amusement to be found in these haunts; and the lounge was then a special and much-patronized portion of the house. Now there is no lounge; and those who go to these places do so with the specified intention of watching the performance, or at least the performers, on the stage.

Another change has come over such places owing to drastic regulations enforced by the London County Council and other authoritative bodies, with the result that, so far as their structural conditions are concerned, they have undergone as thorough a rehabilitation as they have in what is termed their moral tone.

Nor are they to any extent, as they used so often to be, the nightly scenes of disorder and riot. We have become a chastened people, ready to be policed, by Act of Parliament and the Force, into an almost puritanical respectability; and it so happens that, save when the young bloods of the 'varsities invade the Town, on special occasions such as the Boat Race, and similar symposia, and, in the lightness of their hearts and the emptiness of their heads, attempt to paint it red, order rules supreme, and London at night has become almost as quiet as Paris.

In these days a form of entertainment which is quite modern, but which has taken so firm a hold all over the world that it has come to be established as if it had centuries of precedent behind it, has arisen, in the cinema. Theatres came to us more or less gradually, but cinematographs, to give them their full official title, swarmed. They have, to-day, more or less found their level, but at their inception they descended not only on London, but in every town, one had almost said every village, in the country, with almost alarming frequency. Shops were converted into cinemas; even private houses did not escape; and anything in the nature of a hall or lecture-room which showed signs of decrepitude was snapped up and turned into a picture-palace, as they are, with the popular love of alliteration, alternatively called. One remembers their early manifestations when one was confronted with a blurred and moving something which purported to be the actual representation of some social event or some notable circumstance. You had to take a great deal for granted in those, as they seem to us, prehistoric days. Now everything is different: the cinematograph operator is part and parcel of every ceremony, from Royal processions downward; villages are built and villages are destroyed; railway accidents are engineered and great ships are sunk to provide "settings" for some story of real life; splendid palaces are erected, gorgeous scenes are evolved, marvellous freaks, photographic and otherwise, are arranged, for the production of some drama filched from the fables of the East, or drawn from the decorative ages of the West. Sums which would seem incredible had we not come habitually to think in millions, are spent on the production of some super-cinema; and salaries are earned by the well-known protagonists which would make the ears even of dramatic and operatic stars of the past tingle with astonishment; and great actors and actresses are seduced from the more legitimate practice of their art to show themselves by proxy to millions who would otherwise never have recognized them from ordinary people.

And the cinema has produced such marvels; it has been enabled to overcome technical difficulties so successfully; it has brought so easily (as it seems to those sitting complacent before its moving wonders) the ends of the earth and the days of long ago before our eyes, that can it be wondered at how popular it has become, how vital in importance, how far-reaching in results? Much that is thus exhibited may not be of value or advantage; may even be inſtinct with a detrimental effect on impressionable minds. But as much may be said for many other forms of amusement; as much, indeed, may be said for anything if it be allowed to become an obsession. Taking the cinema, however, on the whole, one would, I think, be right in regarding it as an innovation which has brought pleasure to many, inſtruction to many, and to many a realization of what the world and its hiſtory is and has been, which otherwise they would never have known.

So great, indeed, has been the revolution created by this means, and so marked has been its inſtant acceptance and enduring effect, that if the age of Elizabeth may be said to have been that of the baiting-ring; and that of the Georges, the age of the Ridotto and the Assembly; our own day may well be regarded as that of the cinema, for this has differentiated it from earlier times, when the theatre was as popular, if not as extended as now; and from those earlier times ſtill when rougher and more brutal amusements were those that were chiefly known and thus those that were alone generally popular.

CHAPTER VII

BEAR- AND BULL-BAITING AND OTHER PASTIMES

When the traveller, Paul Hentzner, visited this country in the year 1598, he wrote a diary in which he noted our manners and customs, as well as the principal buildings and other sights of the metropolis. After mentioning the existence "without the city" of some theatres, he proceeds to give a description of another pleasure haunt which at that time rivalled, for it was of far older date, the then more novel spectacles afforded by regular stage-plays. "There is," he writes, "still another place, built in the form of a theatre, which serves for the baiting of Bulls and Bears," by which he indicates the chief centre of that sport, which was situated in Southwark.

The baiting of animals was at that time but a continuation of what had been a popular pastime from time immemorial in this country. Fitzstephen, in 1174, mentions it, even at that early day, as one of the recognized amusements of the people; and it is known that from the sovereign and the Court downwards, all classes, men and women, regarded it as a legitimate and fascinating sport.[1] Herds of bears as well as bulls were kept specially for this purpose,[2] and their baiting by dogs was held to be as legitimate as the hunting of wolves and deer in the open country. Even the jugglers who taught bears to dance and perform other tricks, and who were to be seen, the centre of admiring throngs, at every fair held in London or other places,

[1] Strutt's "Sports and Pastimes."
[2] Erasmus in his "Adagiorum Epitome."

also trained the animals to fight with dogs;[1] and at last so recognized did bear-baiting and bull-baiting become, that it is not surprising to find special structures being erected for this purpose, in place of the peripatetic nature of its earlier manifestations.

In London these centres were to be found in the borough of Southwark, where the as yet unbuilt spaces, as well as the relative civic freedom enjoyed by that outlying part of the city, afforded convenient sites for shows which, although recognized, were yet looked at askance by the authorities, not necessarily in themselves, but because of their power to draw crowds, a circumstance which always gave rise to apprehension.

As we shall see, there were those who were not slow in recognizing the financial profit to be made out of such things, and Henslowe and Allen, the chief *impresarios* of Elizabethan days, divided their energies between the running of bear- and bull-baiting rings and the conduct of theatres. The allusions in Shakespeare's plays to the sport, from which he draws so many forceful analogies, prove its deep-seated foundation in the minds of the people, who must have recognized and hailed with delight, at the Rose and the Globe, allusions to what they could see close by in Paris Garden or "The Bear-Baiting." The neighbouring Bear Garden is probably not identical with "The Bear-Baiting," and was rather a theatre than an arena for the exhibition of animals, but it may have had some connection with it, as its name implies. It appears to have been erected in 1526, and was constructed to hold as many as a thousand spectators; the entrance being one penny for ordinary places, and an extra penny for the better seats.

In 1570 another similar building was erected specially for bull-baiting, and "The Bear-Baiting," which

---

[1] Even in that adjunct to old games called "Baste the Bear" which was but a form of punishment for failure on the part of those taking part, we can see an association with that bear-baiting which for so long maintained its popularity as a popular amusement.

L

had hitherto been used indifferently for the baiting of bulls and bears, was restricted to the latter. Sunday was the most popular day for the spectacles, and it was on a Sunday in the January of 1583 that an accident occurred here, when seven people, including two women, were killed by the collapse of some scaffolding. It need hardly be said that this catastrophe, happening on such a day and in connection with a sport which, in spite of its general popularity, was repugnant to many, gave rise to much outcry; and we may, I think, trace to it the remarks of the Lord Mayor of the day, in reply to an order from the Privy Council recommending the enforcement of the laws for the practice of archery, to the effect that the neglect of this sport was largely due to the growing interest in bear- and bull-baiting.

It is curious to find the civic authorities taking up this attitude what time the Court was never tired of patronizing the sport. Both Elizabeth and James encouraged it, and no sooner had a foreign ambassador or other person of distinction arrived here than he was as regularly carried to Bankside to see a bear or a bull baited, as he would now be taken to the opera or a gala performance at one of the theatres.[1] Indeed such things had an almost official *imprimatur*, and the fulminations of the civic authorities, and the protests of the neighbouring inhabitants who complained of the noise and perpetual tumults occasioned by these shows, were alike disregarded.

The bears were known by special names, and were hailed by the multitude with the joyful recognition now accorded to stage favourites. Sackerson is the best remembered, because Shakespeare has immortalized him,[2] but others were as popular—Ned of Canterbury, Don Jon, Blind Robin, and the rest.

[1] See Hentzner, and the diaries of other foreigners who visited this country at that time. Rye's "England as seen by Foreigners" contains many allusions bearing out this.

[2] See "Merry Wives of Windsor," Act I, Scene 1.

Notwithstanding the complaints of the Corporation, which was otherwise powerless in respect to this part of London, and the fulminations which were launched from many pulpits, the sport went on, and, indeed, when the Swan Theatre was erected, its builder was instructed to make it capable "for players to play in, and for the game of bears and bulls."

In Agas's plan of 1560 we can see the two circular erections, named respectively "The Bull-Baiting" and "The Bear-Baiting," with their adjuncts of long rows of kennels, in which the dogs (who are there shown looking out of their receptacles) were kept ready for the fray; the bears and bulls probably being stabled in the arena itself during the interval of the combats.

When one of these performances was about to take place, the keeper of the bears, or the bear-ward, as he was called, was accustomed to parade the streets as a kind of advertisement of the event, the animal, on these occasions, generally being preceded by minstrels who carried monkeys on their backs, and attracted further attention by their shrill pipings.[1] Of the actual show, Hentzner has left us this account: "The Bulls and Bears . . . are fastened behind, and then worried by great English bull-dogs; but not without great risk to the dogs, from the horns of the one, and the teeth of the other; and it sometimes happens they are killed upon the spot; fresh ones are immediately supplied in the places of those that are wounded, or tired. To this entertainment there often follows that of whipping a blinded Bear, which is performed by five or six men, standing circularly with whips, which they exercise on him without any mercy, as he cannot escape from them because of his chain; he defends himself with all his force and skill, throwing down all who come within his reach, and are not active enough to get out of it, and tearing the whips out of their hands and breaking them;" and he adds that at all these spectacles, "and

[1] Strutt's "Sports and Pastimes."

everywhere else, the English are constantly smoking Tobacco . . . from pipes of clay"; so quickly had Raleigh's initiative been followed by an imitative people!

Although the heyday of bear- and bull-baiting was in the time of the Tudors and of the first Stuart, we find it continuing in the reign of Charles I., and in a work published in 1637, entitled "A New Booke of Mistakes," we read that "The White Bull at the Beare-garden . . . tosseth up dogges like tennis-balls, catching them again upon his hornes." But, soon after, the sport was put a stop to, and in 1642, the Bear-baiting was ordered to be closed by Act of Parliament. That, however, the bears still remained, and probably shows were still given *sub rosa*, is indicated by a passage in Townshend's Annals,[1] which, under date of February 1655, reads thus: "Colonel Pride, by reason of some difference between him and the keeper Godfrey of the Beares in the Bear Garden in Southwark, as a Justice of the Peace, caused all the beares to be fast tied up by the noses, and then valiantly brought some files of musketeers, drew up, and gave fyre; and kill'd six or more beares in the Place (only leaving one white innocent cubb), and also cockes of the game. It is said all the mastives are to be shipt for Jamaica."

With the Restoration, however, both bear- and bull-baiting were resuscitated, and, of course, Pepys was a visitor, although he did not really like such brutality. On August 14, 1666, he took his wife and Mercer to the Beare Garden, "where I had not been, I think, of many years, and saw some good sport of the bulls tossing of the dogs: one into the very boxes; but," he adds, "it is a very rude and nasty pleasure." In the following year he went by himself, on May 27, but it was, in this case, to see a prize-fight between

[1] A manuscript, quoted in Prattendon's Collection, in the Society of Antiquaries. See also Harrison's "England" (New Shakespeare Society)

a butcher and a waterman, who fought with swords, when, as a result of what was regarded as a foul stroke, all the partisans of the combatants engaged in a free fight, during which the diarist was in great fear lest, as he stood in the pit, he "might get some hurt"; however, at last the battle ended, and he escaped.

Three years later, on June 16, 1670, we even find the grave Evelyn going to the Bear Garden, "where was cocke-fighting, dog-fighting, beare- and bull-baiting, it being a famous day for all these butcherly sports or rather barbarous cruelties." The bulls on this occasion did well, says Evelyn, adding that one of them tossed a dog full in a lady's lap, as she sat in one of the boxes at a considerable height from the arena. At last he left, "most heartily weary of the rude and dirty pastime."

Still the pastime continued, and there is extant a warrant,[1] signed by Arlington and dated March 28, 1676, for the payment of £10 "to James Davies, Esq., master of His Majesty's Beares, Bulls and Dogs, for making ready the roomes at the Bear Gardens and Bayteing the Beares before the Spanish Ambassadors, the 7th January last." Bears and other wild animals were, we know, kept at the Tower (indeed they were "a sight" there down to modern days), where, in the days of James I., baiting took place before the King and his court, not only between dogs and bears, but also lions; and it would seem that Davies was their keeper in the time of Charles II.; perhaps, too, they may have been sent to Southwark for such "official" occasions.

But the days of the Bankside Bear Gardens—and there were in all four of them, the two I have mentioned, one at the north end of Bear Garden Lane, and The Hope, better known (as we have seen) as a playhouse were numbered. In the days of William and Mary, baiting of animals was removed to Hockley-in-the-Hole,

[1] In the Additional MSS. British Museum.

where the butchers, who had become the principal patrons of the sport, chiefly congregated. A man named Preston was the keeper, or marshal, as he was not infrequently called, of the bears there, and was eventually killed and almost wholly devoured by one of his charges.[1] He was succeeded by his son, who is said to have written the libel on Pope entitled "Æsop in the Bear Garden." All sorts of amusements of the rougher kind, in addition to the baiting of animals, went on at Hockley-in-the-Hole, where the recognized days for such things were Mondays and Thursdays, as Gay in his "Trivia" reminds us.

As time went on, the more brutal parts of these entertainments seem to have become less pronounced, although, as we should consider them, they still remained sufficiently brutal even in the days of Queen Anne and the earlier Georges. Strutt gives two curious advertisements, which I transcribe, not only because they show us the more diversified form into which the original bear- and bull-baiting had merged, but also because the second one indicates another Bear Garden in Tothill Fields. The first is as follows:

"At the Bear Garden in Hockley-in-the-Hole, near Clerkenwell Green, this present Monday, there is a great match to be fought by two dogs of Smithfield Bars against two dogs of Hampstead, at the Reading Bull, for one guinea to be spent; five lets goes out of hand; which goes fairest and farthest in wins all. The famous Bull of fire-works, which pleased the gentry to admiration. Likewise there are two Bear-dogs to jump three jumps apiece at a Bear, which jumps highest for ten shillings to be spent. Also variety of bull-baiting and bear-baiting; it being a day of general sport by all the old gamesters; and a bull-dog to be drawn up with fire-works. Beginning at three o'clock."

[1] A note by Oldham to one of his poems.

The second runs thus:

"At William Wells' bear garden in Tuttle-fields, Westminster, this present Monday, there will be a green Bull baited; and twenty dogs to fight for a collar; and the dog that runs farthest and fairest wins the collar; with other diversions of bull- and bear-baiting. Beginning at two o'clock."[1]

But it must not be supposed that these brutal delights, such a sad falling off from the time when tournaments and jousts, tilting at the ring and such-like martial sports attracted the people and attuned their minds to the military ardour which gradually declined from the days of Henry VII. downwards, were those alone to which the Londoner of Elizabeth's day and onwards paid attention. There were other sports and pastimes which had not infrequently their recognized headquarters, and which should, therefore, properly be included in any survey of the London pleasure haunts.

One of these was cock-fighting, a form of amusement, or sport, which you will, that survived from Tudor times to the early days of the last century. Indeed, it was of such early origin that Fitzstephen mentions the London schoolboys of his remote day[2] bringing "cocks of the game to their master and all the forenoon delighting themselves in cock-fighting," every Shrove Tuesday; while a milder form of puerile diversion was the hurling of stones at cocks, a sport known as cock-throwing.

It was not, however, till the time of Henry VIII. that cock-fighting could be said to have become a regular organized diversion, for it was in that monarch's reign that the first cockpit was constructed in London. This was erected, some time probably in the 'thirties

[1] In a "Miscellaneous Collection of Bills, etc.," in the Harleian Library.

[2] See, too, Brand's "Observations on Popular Antiquities."

of the sixteenth century, near what is now Birdcage Walk, in St. James's Fields, its approximate site being perpetuated in Cockpit Stairs still existing. This building seems to have been built on quite elaborate lines, and was sufficiently spacious to be used, as it sometimes was in Elizabeth's day, for dramatic performances[1] and other shows. The fact that it existed till 1816 proves at least its architectural stability.

This gave the lead to a number of other structures erected for the same purpose, and cockpits sprang up in various parts of the city, and became exceedingly popular. The three principal ones, in addition to that in St. James's Fields, were in Jewin Street (where much of "Paradise Lost" was written, by the way), Shoe Lane, and St. Giles in the Fields; while the sport was exhibited in Paris Garden, as allusions in the dramatic works of the sixteenth and early seventeenth centuries testify. James I. was an enthusiastic supporter, and Howell includes the diversion among others which were popular, such as tennis-playing, shuffle-board, playing at cudgels, bear- and bull-baiting, at the time (1657) he wrote his "Londinopolis," and which he says was "a sport peculiar to the English." He was but recording for his period what Stow had done for his, and Fitzstephen for his still earlier day.

The cockpit in Jewin Street, after such places had been prohibited by Act of Parliament, and temporarily closed for such uses, was apparently turned into a conventicle, for in 1670, when these were put down by law, there is mention of it as being "a meeting house of one Grimes, with three galleries, many pews, forms and benches."

The cockpit in Shoe Lane is even better remembered, because Pepys visited it, and has left some records

---

[1] These took place, too, in The Cockpit, which stood within the purlieus of Whitehall Palace, a place which afterwards became an official adjunct, where Prime Ministers held their levees, and often transacted State business.

of his experiences there. Thus, on December 21, 1663, he went "to the Shoe Lane, to see a cocke-fighting at a new pit there, a spot I never was at in my life: but Lord! to see the strange variety of people, from Parliament man . . . to the poorest 'prentices, bakers, brewers, butchers, draymen, and what not; and all these fellows one with another cursing and betting. I soon had enough of it. It is strange," he adds, " to see how people of this poor rank, that look as if they had not bread to put in their mouths, shall bet three or four pounds at a time and lose it, and yet bet as much the next battle, so that one of them will lose £10 or £20 at a meeting."

Pepys had good precedent for his visit, for many years before no less solemn a person than Sir Henry Wotton mentions (1633) going there; and that this was not a solitary experience is indicated by his remark that he was "a *rara avis* there." Strutt preserves a story connected with this Shoe Lane cockpit, which is thus given in the authority he quotes.[1] "Sir Thomas Jermin, meaning to make himself merry, and gull all the cockers, sent his man to the pit in Shoe Lane, with a hundred pounds and a dunghill cock, neatly cut and trimmed for the battle; the plot being well layd the fellow got another to throw the cock in, and fight him in Sir Thomas Jermin's name, while he betted his hundred pounds against him, the cock was matched, and hearing Sir Thomas's name, had many betts layd upon his head; but after three or four good brushes, he showed a payre of heeles: every one wondered to see a cock belonging to Sir Thomas cry *craven*, and away came the man with his money doubled."

That there were many other centres for cock-fighting in London at this time is probable; indeed we find Pepys, on one occasion, expecting to see some sport of this kind at Fox Hall, whither he had gone by water,

[1] "Merry Passages and Jests," a MS. temp. James I. in the Harleian MSS.

but being disappointed; while we find him, on April 6, 1668, at "the new Cocke-pite by the King's Gate (Whitehall)," to see what it was like; but again he shows his astonishment at the "mixed rabble of people." On this occasion he witnessed two battles of cocks, "wherein is no great sport," he says, adding, "but to consider how these creatures, without any provocation, do fight and kill one another, and aim only at one another's heads!"

Although the rougher, though hardly more barbarous, sport of bear- and bull-baiting died out with the advent of the eighteenth century, cock-fighting went on gaily; indeed it actually became more popular as time went on; and was at its zenith in the early years of the nineteenth century. The Birdcage Walk pit is shown in one of the illustrations by Rowlandson and Pugin, in Ackermann's "Microcosm of London," dated 1808, where it is called "The Royal Cock-pit," and is seen decorated by the royal arms. There is no doubt that, as the writer of the accompanying letterpress states, this "picture has great merit, and conveys a more perfect idea of the confusion and hustle of a cock-pit, than any description." Hogarth had before, in 1758, published his print of "The Cockpit," which records, with his usual fidelity, the interior of the place in his day. In 1816 this building was demolished, "that behind Gray's Inn having the only vogue," we are told; but if this was the case it did not deter some daring spirits from erecting a new one in Tufton Street hard by; and it was this one, built in 1821, with which Tom and Jerry were, in Pierce Egan's hands, made familiar. Grantley Berkeley was equally well acquainted with the place, and in his reminiscences [1] gives this vignette of it:

"There was an ancient building in Tufton Street, Westminster, called the 'Cockpit Royal,' and the

[1] "My Life and Recollections," by the Hon. Grantley Berkeley, 1865.

royal arms had once been emblazoned over the door.
It was in this building I first witnessed a main of cocks,
and there the grandfather of the present Duke of
Norfolk—notorious for his extraordinary appearance
—attired in that sky-blue dress which, when I was a
boy, I had often seen, with large ruffles at his wrists,
with which, in shooting, he would at times wipe out
the pan of his gun—went to see one of the great
'mains of the day.' " [1]

There was yet another cockpit in this neighbourhood, as is proved by a reference to it in one of Lord
William Pitt Lennox's books,[1] where the author
writes: "Duck Lane, Orchard Street, Westminster
(long since swept and garnished, and named anew)
was the site of the old cockpit, where the above brutal
amusement (dog-fighting) was carried on; here, in
addition to the above, a celebrated African monkey,
Jacko Macacco, showed his prowess by conquering
some of the stoutest breed of dogs this country could
boast of. At first the feats of Jacko were witnessed
only by persons of the lowest grade, but as his victories
increased, and fame blew her trumpet louder and louder
at every conquest, the curiosity of the higher classes
was excited, and the patricians of St. James's, Grosvenor
Square, and Mayfair were soon intermingled in one
undistinguished, incongruous mass with the plebeians
of Tothill Fields, St. Giles's, Chick Lane, West
Smithfield, and the New Cut. The peer and the pickpocket, the duke and the 'duffer,' the earl and the
housebreaker, the country gentleman and the Whitechapel ' cadger,' the squire and the dog's-meat man
actually elbowing each other." [2]
There is no doubt that the change in manners and
customs inaugurated by the accession of Queen

[1] There is, too, an account of the place in "The London Magazine,"
for November 1822.
[2] "Fashion Now and Then."

Victoria gave the death-blow to these and such-like diversions, which during the Regency had had, so far as certain of them were concerned, a recrudescence of a very marked character: a period when prize-fighting and general pugilism first became really systematized.

Pugilism may be said to have had its rise in the wrestling and fisticuffs of earlier times. Stow tells us of "divers days" spent in such sports during the feast of St. Bartholomew, particularly when such exhibitions took place in a large tent at Skinner's Well, near Clerkenwell, and had an official sanction from the officers of the City, inasmuch as the Lord Mayor and Sheriffs were wont to attend the ceremony in their scarlet gowns and gold chains. Later, wrestling and trials of strength between man and man were part of the performances often given at the Bear Gardens, and at the annual fairs at Greenwich and Southwark and elsewhere. But it was not till the eighteenth century that regular pugilism took on that specialized character which it has exhibited ever since; and it was not till the beginning of the following century that there arose those great exponents of the science whose names still survive as outstanding landmarks in its annals: Broughton, Mendoza, Tom Sayers[1] and the rest.

The chief places where prize-fighting took place in those days were the Tennis Court, Windmill Street; the Fives' Court, in St. Martin's Street, Leicester Square; Dan Mendoza's "school" near the Eagle Tavern, City Road, and "Gentleman" Jackson's "academy" at 9 Old Bond Street, much patronized by Lord Byron, whose "corporeal pastor" Jackson was said to be.[2]

---

[1] There is a beautiful colour-print showing the assembled prize-fighters and their patrons, of the day.

[2] He helped Byron in other ways, for Mr. John Murray possesses a screen once belonging to the poet, one side of which is covered by portraits of famous boxers, which were pasted on by Jackson himself.

At an earlier time the famous Figg had an amphi-theatre in Marylebone Gardens, a fact recorded in the lines:

" Long lived the great Figg, by the prize-fighting swains
Sole monarch acknowledged of Marybone's plains."

and was succeeded, close by, by the more famous Broughton. Broughton's establishment was in the Oxford Road, "at the back of the late Mr. Figg's." It was near Adam and Eve Court, opposite Poland Street, and was built in 1742–43. Here, and else-where, Broughton remained the unbeaten champion of the ring for eighteen years, until, indeed, he was defeated in his own premises by Slack, the butcher; after which he retired to Walcot Place, Lambeth, where he died in 1789, aged eighty-four.

There is no doubt that the interest displayed by George, Prince of Wales, and some of his brothers, in pugilism gave it that fashionable character which it enjoyed during their period; and the literature of the time is full of allusions to the combats which took place, not only in the recognized centres, but in spots outside London such as those of which George Borrow has told us. The Prince was a not infrequent spectator at some of these, until the occasion when he saw a man killed, which had so great an effect upon him that he would never afterwards consent to be present at a prize-fight.

As everyone interested in such things, and most people who are not, know, the present headquarters of pugilism is the National Sporting Club, in Covent Garden; which is housed in that picturesque and historic mansion in which Admiral Russell, afterwards Earl of Orford, lived, and which Hogarth has per-petuated in the "Morning" of his "Four Times of the Day." The history of the institution from its inception has been written in an interesting volume;[1]

[1] "The National Sporting Club," by Bettinson and Outram Tristram, 1902.

so there is no need to say more on the subject here; but it may be remarked that nothing has done more to place the science of pugilism on a sound and dignified basis than this famous club, which has done so much to eliminate that *aura* of brutality and vulgarity which once, in spite of notable protagonists, surrounded it.

Other centres of boxing now existing in London are "The Ring," in the Blackfriars Road, once the well-known Surrey Chapel of the Rev. Rowland Hill; and the Holborn Stadium, at 85 High Holborn; while boxing matches also take place occasionally at Olympia and at the Albert Hall, and elsewhere.

In an account of the pleasure haunts of a great city the spots where amusement of any kind had an organized activity must necessarily find a place; and we shall discover such centres of recreation as bowling-greens part and parcel of those pleasure gardens which at one time were so extraordinarily numerous in every part of the metropolis. The antiquity of bowling-greens is shown by the fact that Gosson, in his "Schoole of Abuse," published in 1579, speaks of such haunts with, it must be confessed, some acrimony: "Common Bowling Alleys," he calls them, "or privy Mothes, that eate uppe the credit of many idle Citizens, whose gaynes at home are not able to weighe downe theyr losses abroad, whose Shoppes are so farre from maintaining their play, that their Wives and Children cry out for bread, and go to bedde supperlesse ofte in the yeere"; while Stow makes a very similar complaint, and even in Shakespeare's plays will be found an oblique hit at the tendency to gamble at this seemingly harmless game.[1] Nowadays one would be hard put to it to find a London tavern with a bowling ground, although such may possibly still be existing, as they were but

[1] See "Shakespeare's England," 2 vols., 1916.

a relatively few years ago, in such outlying districts as Chelsea and Hampstead.

A delight in all games has been from time immemorial an adjunct of humanity, and in this country the sports and pastimes of the Londoner of Fitz-Stephen's day were matched by those of Tudor times, when certain games were lawful, especially those connected with a ball or with gymnastic ability, and others unlawful, when associated with cards or dice, or, curiously enough, with swimming.

There has been no break in this continuity of pleasure-seeking in our own time, and just as we have tennis-courts (although in less central parts of the town), so did our forbears; and just as they had their dancing saloons, so we have our night-clubs and other centres of Terpsichorean activity.

Tennis has long been a favourite game in England, but its chief manifestation has been in the lawn tennis, which may be said to be an adaptation of the older form, associated with the nineteenth century, although a passage in Nichols's "Progresses of Queen Elizabeth" indicates that it was not unknown in her day. At an earlier period, however, especially in the times of the Stuarts, tennis courts were to be found in various parts of London, but were, for a variety of reasons, restricted to the use of the wealthier classes.

At one time, under the Tudors, the game was penalized by law as interfering with those military exercises which the authorities had so much at heart; but gradually it became generally popular and unrestricted. Henry, Prince of Wales, was so fond of it that he is said, by some, to have owed his death to his indulgence in it. But it was not till somewhat later that actual tennis-courts were opened to all who could afford the expense of the game.[1] One of the best-

[1] Henry VII. is known to have played; so, of course, did Henry VIII. and Charles II., both of whom had special dresses made for the purpose. See Strutt.

known of these was Gibbons's Tennis Court, in Clare Market, which was afterwards converted by Killigrew into a theatre, and the remains of which were not removed till the early years of the nineteenth century. It was run by one Charles Gibbons, hence its name, and although at the Restoration it was used first as a playhouse, its original title stuck to it, and it is even referred to as a regular tennis-court by Shadwell, in "A True Widow," 1679; so that, in the intervals of dramatic performances, it may still have been used for this purpose.

Another notable tennis-court of the time, and for long after (it remained, indeed, till 1866), was that in James Street, at the back of the Haymarket, to which Phil Porter, one of the bloods of the Restoration, refers in the lines:

> Farewell, my dearest Piccadilly,
> Notorious for good dinners;
> Oh, what a Tennis Court was there!
> Alas! too good for sinners." [1]

This tennis-court was part and parcel of the once-notorious gaming-house known as Shaver's Hall; and there is a tradition that both Charles II. and James, Duke of York, were frequently to be seen walking up the Haymarket on their way to it. On January 4, 1680, the roof of the court collapsed, and from the Hatton Correspondence we learn that "Sir George Etheredge and several others were very dangerously hurt. Sir Charles Sedley had his skull broke, and it is thought it will be mortal." However, Etheredge recovered, and Sedley was to live twenty-two years longer. [2]

Those who wish to play tennis, or lawn tennis, to-day, are able to do so in a variety of places in London: Queen's Club, near Baron's Court; Prince's Racquets

[1] Wit and Drollery: Jovial Poems, 1682.
[2] See the author's "Restoration Rakes."

and Tennis Club, in Knightsbridge; and at Lord's;
while many of the Squares' Gardens have been at laſt
made useful and attractive by the additions of tennis
courts, which have even invaded Lincoln's Inn Fields,
nearly on the spot where Lord William Russell was
executed in 1683. The "Princes" juſt mentioned is
not to be confounded with that famous Prince's Club
whose extensive grounds covered the site now occupied
by Cadogan Square and Lennox Gardens, and to
which, in addition to its cricket ground (where *moi
qui vous parle,* have seen the great W. G. Grace batting
and Spofforth, who ſtill lives on the other side of the
world—"the Demon," as he was called—bowling),
possessed tennis and racquet courts, and a marble
skating rink. It was an ultra-fashionable place, much
patronized by the late King Edward, when Prince of
Wales, and society flocked there as a more mixed
society flocks to Hurlingham and Ranelagh.

The mention of the place reminds me of the intermittent vogue of roller and real ice skating. In the
'seventies of the laſt century it began with the American
Plimpton's invention of the ball-bearing skate, and
rinks arose on all sides, with the insiſtence of the
cinema, but without its power of endurance. Everyone
suddenly began skating, or learning to skate (for there
is not much opportunity for the real thing in this
country), and covered rinks and open-air rinks alike
resounded to that clacket and rolling of wheels which
the generally attendant band could not wholly dominate.
And then, suddenly, the craze died out. A decade or
about that elapsed, and a recrudescence took place;
later another phase of the amusement found such
places as Olympia ready for it; and the new Prince's
went one better by producing what was to all intents
and purposes real ice, on which it was possible
to skate not on wheels, but on the regulation blades.
Nothing in the hiſtory of amusement seems to me
so curious as the way in which the mania for skating

M

has, so to speak, bobbed up and down during the last fifty years; and as a result, although much money muſt have been made, much has also been loſt by those to whom the psychology of a people is a perpetually new problem.

I have incidentally referred to dancing, and to-day dancing has taken to itself a cult which is another remarkable phenomenon. That it was always popular, as it has been in all times and among all nations, is a commonplace. But in older days people danced in the open or wherever place or opportunity allowed. The dances of paſt times were innumerable; and from the galliard, and the volte, a variety of it, the pavane, the bransle, the coranto and the allemande,[1] to the mazurka and the schottishe, the quadrille, polka, the waltz, and so forth, of Victorian days, people have danced their way, if not through life, at leaſt through a considerable portion of it.

In course of time dancing saloons came into being, and high life disported itself at the super-exclusive Almack's, while others patronized such places as the Argyll Rooms, and even less fashionable resorts, many of which degenerated into haunts on which the authorities looked with suspicious eyes and not infrequently with well-founded disfavour.

But dancing rooms, of a less elaborate character, had been of an earlier date than these; and Hickford's Great Dancing Saloon, near the Haymarket Tennis Court, was in exiſtence as early as 1713. Hickford had his auction rooms on the south side of Panton Street, and the principal apartment was frequently put to use as a ball-room; while at leaſt on one occasion the Weſtminſter boys here played Otway's "Orphan" (February 2, 1720–1). The room is referred to by Prior, who wrote the prologue to the play in queſtion.

[1] See for such things and others relating to the amusements of the time Peacham's "Compleat Gentleman," 1622.

Such places as Ranelagh and the Pantheon, Vauxhall and Mrs. Cornelys's Assemblies in Soho Square, also afforded, as we shall see, opportunities for Terpsichorean exercise; but they were of a different character from the saloons of later Georgian and Victorian days, and were chiefly identified with the elaborate masquerades and ridottos of a more decorative period. Many of the early-Victorian dancing centres came, as I have said, on bad times in that they departed gradually from their original intention; and we shall meet in another and more appropriate chapter some of these whose names peep out of the memoirs of the period, but whose annals are not always particularly edifying.

Among other haunts of pleasure, as they may be properly called, I think, were such places as Major Foubert's Riding School, which had once been situated in that Military Yard, behind Leicester House (where the Empire is now), where Henry, Prince of Wales, was accustomed to take horse exercise, but which was afterwards moved to Swallow Street, now represented, not by the present Swallow Street, but by Swallow Passage. Foubert's name is preserved in Foubert's Court, off Regent Street, close by his old equestrian establishment. This academy, as it was called, was a long, low brick building, similar to a shed, or ropewalk, as may be seen by a coloured drawing of it made in 1801 by Tomkins,[1] not long before its demolition. Brayley tells us that when Swallow Street was demolished, the greater part of Foubert's Passage, including the Riding School, which had been converted into livery stables, was also pulled down; and he speaks of only one of the original houses as standing in his day [2] (1829).

There was a semi-official air about Foubert's

[1] In the Crowle Pennant.
[2] "Londiniana." Foubert's Academy is even mentioned in the verse of Prior and Young.

Academy, which was actually established to "lessen the vast expense the nation is at yearly in sending children to France to be taught military exercises," and we find the King, in 1679, contributing £100 towards its formation. The interest Evelyn took in the place is attested by several passages in his "Diary," in which he speaks of visiting it; and one of these entries tells us of some of those who were being trained here, and the sort of exercises through which they were put. "December 18, 1684.—I went with Lord Cornwallis to see the young gallants do their exercise, Mr. Foubert having newly rail'd in a manage and fitted it for the Academy. There were the Dukes of Norfolk and Northumberland, Lord Newburgh and a nephew of the Earl of Feversham. The exercises are: (1) running at the ring; (2) flinging a javelin at a Moor's head; (3) discharging a pistol at a mark; lastly, taking up a gauntlet with the point of a sword; all these performed at full speede." Among people of note who were there as spectators, Evelyn mentions the Prince of Denmark and Lord Lansdown, son of the Earl of Bath.

Evelyn's interest in the place had, no doubt, been originally caused by the fact that, as he himself tells us in 1682, "The Council of the Royal Society (of which he was a member) had it recommended to them to be trustees and visitors, or supervisors, of the Academy which Monsieur Faubert did hope to procure to be built by subscription"; and he adds, "We thought good to give him all the encouragement our recommendation could procure." [1]

Foubert's Academy was in existence in the eighteenth century, and we read of the young Duke of Cumber-

---

[1] In Reresby's Memoirs is a curious passage telling how Foubert went to the writer and tried to enlist his interest to protect Count Koningsmarck in connection with the murder of Thynne of Longleat, not without a hint at a substantial bribe. Young Koningsmarck, the son, was one of Foubert's pupils.

land (of Culloden fame) having his first riding lesson here in 1731.[1] The founder himself had been dead many years then, as Luttrell mentions his being killed in the wars during the year 1693.[2] His name is there spelt Fobert; Evelyn calls him Faubert, but the more general way was the Foubert which still survives in Foubert's (or, as Rogers tells us it was always called in his youth, "Major Foubert's") Passage or Place, in Regent Street.

Apart from its special uses as a training school and military academy, Foubert's was as much a haunt of the men about town of Charles II.'s day as Tattersall's has been since; and I daresay horses changed hands at the former and bets were laid and taken, much as they are, *mutatis mutandis*, in the famous establishment at Knightsbridge to-day.

Tattersall's should certainly be included among our pleasure haunts, especially as it has had a long and notable history and may be said to be the headquarters of the Turf, just as the Jockey Club is its official head. We have become so used to Tattersall's in its present *local* that it is sometimes forgotten that this is but a modern home, and that it began its prosperous career off Grosvenor Place, just behind St. George's Hospital, by which it was entered by a narrow lane. Although it has always been a private institution solely identified with the name of the family which has owned it since Richard Tattersall started it in 1766, it has become something akin to a national institution. Everyone has heard of it, most people know it, and in a nation of sportsmen—for has it not been said that "*L'equitation est pour les Anglais, ce qu'est le musique pour les Italiens?*" [3]—this is appropriate, for it focusses within itself the best traditions of the sporting element in this country.

[1] See Doran's "London in the Jacobite Times."
[2] "Brief Relation of State Affairs," by Narcissus Luttrell, vol. 3.
[3] Grosley, in his "Londres," 3 vols., 1774.

The premises at Hyde Park Corner were acquired on a ninety-nine years' lease in 1766, and a few years after, some say in 1773, but I am inclined to think rather before then, Richard Tattersall opened his new venture. By the time of his death in 1795 he had so firmly established a reputation for integrity, and had placed his institution on so firm a basis, that when his son Edmund inherited it, he found himself in possession of a very lucrative and popular concern.[1] Goede, speaking of the routine of a young blood of fashion at the time he visited England, remarks: "He repairs to Tattersall's, where he meets all his friends seriously engaged in studying the pedigree or merits of the horses to be sold, or in discussing the invaluable properties of a pointer, setter, courser, or other sporting dog";[2] and the writer of the note illustrating Rowlandson and Pugin's picture of the place in Ackermann's "Microcosm of London," describes it as "the grand mart for everything connected with the sports of the field, the business of the turf, and equestrian recreations"; and he says, "the days of sale are every Monday and Thursday during the winter season, and on Mondays only in the summer. On the morning when there is no sale," he adds, "this Repository is a fashionable lounge for sporting gentlemen. The horses, etc., are then examined, their merits or defects considered, and sporting intelligence from all parts of the country detailed and disseminated."

In 1865 the lease of the Hyde Park Corner premises expired, and Tattersall's migrated to what was then called Middle Row, Knightsbridge, which had been secured a year or two earlier, and on which the necessary buildings were begun in 1864,[3] essentially, except

---

[1] He died in 1810. Dighton drew his portrait; and a good-looking man he must have been.

[2] "The Stranger in England," 3 vols., 1807.

[3] It was, of course, in the earlier Tattersalls that Sir John Lade performed his feat of driving a coach and four round the yard and out again into Grosvenor Place.

for certain later alterations and reconstructions, as we know it to-day.

The earlier Tattersall's, next to which Richard Tattersall had his private house, was, as I have said, entered by a narrow lane, at the end of which stood the Turf Tavern, opposite the entrance to the Repository, as Tattersall's was called. It consisted of a circular-shaped enclosure surrounded by a gravel path bounding a grass plot, on which the horses for sale were exhibited. In the centre stood a tree. Beyond the gateway was the subscription-room, designed by George Tattersall, the author of "Sporting Architecture." On the right a passage led to a courtyard, surrounded on three sides by a covered way, at the end of which stood the auctioneer's rostrum. Adjoining were the stables, containing ninety-seven stalls and thirteen loose-boxes. In the middle of the enclosure stood the domed and pillared structure, which seems at that time to have been used as an elaborate sort of pump, and above it was placed a bust of George, Prince of Wales, a frequent *habitué* here.

Elsewhere in the building was a room where the Jockey Club for a number of years had its headquarters, and in these rooms congregated at various times such a number of notable and notorious men, from Richard Vernon, "the father of the turf," and "Old Q" and Selwyn, Barrymore and Lade, downwards, as make an eighteenth-century comparison picture to that which now hangs in the Subscription Room of its successor, in which the well-known figures of the late King Edward, Admiral Rous, the Duke of Beaufort, Lord Falmouth, George Payne, *et multos alios*, are prominent.[1]

[1] For a full account of Tattersall's see the author's "Knightsbridge and Belgravia," 1909.

CHAPTER VIII

THE STEWS, GAMBLING HELLS, ETC.

In all great cities there has existed, at all times, a certain class of establishment about which few people are ignorant but concerning which it was at one time the fashion to keep a discreet silence. The law takes cognisance of such and the police keep a wary eye on their doings; but as they are as old as civilization, and as human nature is what it is, it is as impossible entirely to eradicate them as it would be to curb the passions, and to regulate everyone's actions to those regarded by the authorities as becoming and seemly. That such places are pleasure haunts no one but a hypocrite would attempt to deny; that they are, as so many other forms of pleasure are, often productive of disastrous consequences, is another commonplace. But there they are and have been, just as they have been and are in every city in the world, and as such, fall to be considered in a book dealing with pleasure haunts and not merely with haunts of licit pleasure.

In these days when, as Montaigne remarks, *tout se sçait*, there is no necessity to mince words, as there would have been had I been writing thirty or forty or more years ago, and I need hardly say that it is the brothels, or houses of ill-fame, or whatever name (and they have had many) one cares to call them by, that I here indicate, and about which I shall say not more than is necessary.

One need not go back beyond Tudor days to find such places occupying a recognized place in civic life. In those times Southwark, as being without the immediate jurisdiction of the Lord Mayor and Corporation, was a hotbed of them, as it had been since the days of the Plantagenets. They were then and for centuries later known as Stews, and there is an ordinance of the city which provides: "That no boatman shall have his boat moored and standing over the water after sunset; but they shall have all their boats moored on this (the city) side of the water, that so thieves and other misdoers may not be carried by them under pain of imprisonment: nor may they carry any man or woman, either denizens or strangers, unto the stews (of Southwark) except in the daytime under pain of imprisonment."

This last phrase might have seemed somewhat cryptic, and to have inferred that the authorities were not averse from the stews being patronized before dark, were it not obvious that it was inserted in order not unduly to hamper the trade of the boatmen, who could hardly be responsible for the reasons for which their services were engaged during the daytime.

The notoriety of Southwark for general lawlessness, and especially as a spot selected by brothelkeepers, continued through the centuries, and in the reign of Henry VIII. Bankside was popularly known as "The Stewes Bank"; while there are extant certain "ordinances touching the governance of the stewhoulders in Southwarke under the direction of the bishope of Winchester, instituted in the tyme of Henry the Second."[1]

Stow, in his survey of this part of the city, after referring to the Bear Gardens here, adds: "Next on this banke was sometime the Bordello or Stewes, a place so called, of certain stew-houses privileged there, for the repaire of incontinent men to the like women"; and he proceeds to detail the privilege

[1] Harleian MSS., 293, ff. 62–7.

with its curious conditions, of which he prints the following:

"That no stew-holder or his wife should let or staye any single woman to goe and come freely at all times when they listed.

"No stew-holder to keepe any woman to borde, but she to borde abroad at her pleasure.

"To take no more for the woman's chamber in the weeke than fourteene pence.

"Not to keep open his dores upon the holy dayes.

"Not to keep any single woman in his house on the holy dayes, but the Bayliffe to see them voyded out of the Lordship.

"No single woman to be kept against her wille that would leave her sinne.

"No stew-holder to receive any woman of religion, or any man's wife.

"No single woman to take money to lie with any man, but shee lie with him all night till the morrow.

"No man to be drawn or enticed into any stew-house.

"The Constables, Balife, and others every weeke to search every stew-house.

"No stew-holder to keepe any woman that hath the perilous infirmitie of burning, nor to sell bread, ale, flesh, fish, wood, coale, or any victuals.

We may be surprised to find that such places were under the direction of the Bishops of Winchester; but it is equal matter for astonishment that Sir William Walworth, the Lord Mayor in Richard II.'s reign, *owned* some, that they were farmed by "Froes of Flaunders," and that Walter Tighler (in whom we identify Wat Tyler) "and other rebelles of Kent" spoyled them,"[1] which fact, by the way, may have given an added strength to Walworth's hand when

[1] Stow's "Survey of London": edited by Kingsford.

he struck down Wat Tyler as he spoke to the King. It appears that, in the reign of Henry VII., these houses were for a time inhibited, according to Fabian, who, however, adds that it was not long before they were reopened, at least some of them, for of the original eighteen, six were not allowed to carry on their trade. These places were known by certain signs painted on the walls, such as a Boar's Head, Cross Keys, a Gun, a Castle, a Crane, a Bell, a Swanne, and even a Cardinal's Hat.

In Henry VIII.'s reign, "this row of stewes in Southwark," says Stow, "was put downe by the King's commandment, which was proclaymed by sounde of Trumpet, no more to be privileged, and used as a common Brothel, but the inhabitants of the same to keepe good and honest rule as in other places of this realme."

Although Southwark had an unenviable notoriety in this respect, it need hardly be said that it was not the only quarter of the city where such places existed, but as being for a time recognized by the authorities and as forming a collocation of houses of ill-fame, they were naturally more publicly known than others which hid themselves discreetly and separately elsewhere. We can still draw on old Stow for the indication of at least another, situated in Queenhithe, where he speaks of an alley called Stew Lane "of a stewe or hotte house there kept."

As time went on, the keepers of such places sought different quarters, and Whetstone Park, that curious little lane at the north of Lincoln's Inn Fields, was for long notorious in this respect. Whetstone, the original constructor of the houses forming the "Park," was a tobacconist and a vestryman of St. Giles's,[1]

---

[1] They were built on the site of the ancient Spencer House, for whose history see Heckthorn's "Lincoln's Inn Fields," etc. A certain number of the houses were built by a Mr. Phillips, and were called, in consequence, Phillip's Rents.

turned speculative builder, and as he seems to have been rather concerned in obtaining high rents than in having good tenants, the houses were soon snatched up by those whose remunerative trade made the former a matter of indifference to them.

Among the posthumous works of Samuel Butler, published in 1715, will be found a poem entitled "The Court Burlesqued," and in it occur these lines, which show what a reputation the place had gained at least before 1680, the year in which the author died:

> "And makes a brothel of a palace
> Where harlots ply, as many tell us,
> Like brimstones in a Whetstone ale-house."

These brimstones or inflammable and generally violent women, for to them was the slang term applied, were to be found haunting the purlieus of Lincoln's Inn Fields, ready to snare any man they came across into their adjacent quarters. Macaulay tells us, indeed, as much in his survey of the manners and customs of the town during the Caroline period: "When the lord of a Lincolnshire or Shropshire manor appeared in Fleet Street," he writes, "he was as easily distinguished from the resident population as a Turk or a Lascar. His dress, his gait, his accent, the manner in which he gazed at the shops, stumbled into the gutter, ran against the porters, and stood under the waterspouts, marked him out as an excellent subject for the operations of swindlers and banterers. Bullies jostled him into the kennel. Hackney coachmen splashed him from head to foot. . . . Painted women, the refuse of Lewknor Lane and Whetstone Park, passed themselves on him as countesses and maids of honour."

That the habits of the inhabitants was not lost on those apprentices of the period who were fond of disguising much of their own frequent misdoings under the guise of *censores morum* of the delinquencies of others, is proved by an entry in Pepys's Diary, where we read, under date of March 24, 1668–9,[1] of "great talk of the tumult at the other end of the town, about Moorefields, among the 'prentices, taking the liberty of these holidays to pull down brothels. . . . So Creed and I to Lincoln's Inn Fields, thinking to have gone into the fields to have seen the 'prentices; but here we found these fields full of soldiers, all in a body, and my Lord Craven commanding of them, and riding up and down to give orders, like a madman. And some young men we saw brought by soldiers to the guard at White Hall, and overheard others that ſtood by say, that it was only for pulling down the brothels; and none of the byſtanders finding fault with them, but rather of the soldiers for hindering them. And we heard a Juſtice of the Peace this morning say to the King that he had been endeavouring to suppress this tumult, but could not. To which the King made answer: 'Why, why do they go to them then?' and that was all."

As was usual in those times, such occurrences gave rise to a flood of pamphlets on the subjeʧ, some of which are curious enough. Thus we find "The Wh—s Petition to the London Prentices," followed by "The Citizens' Reply to the Wh—s Petition, and Prentices' Answer"; and finally, "The Poor Wh—s Petition to the Illuſtrious Lady of Pleasure, the Countess of Caſtlemayne!"[2]

It need hardly be said that the presence of these houses, apart from the moral effeʧ they appear to have had on the London apprentices, was generally to make this quarter one of lawlessness and riotry, and there is the record of some gay young men coming between 11 and 12 at night to the ale-house kept by

---

[1] It was the custom of the 'prentices to employ their holidays, particularly that which fell on Shrove Tuesday, to search for ladies of easy ethics and get them imprisoned during Lent. In a "Satyre against Separatists," published in 1675, it is alluded to.

[2] They were, with others, published in 1668, and were reprinted in 1870.

one Petty here, and "hammering so loudly on the door and not gaining admittance, proceeding to break the windows, that the furious landlord at laſt emerged, musket in hand, and pursuing them into Great Queen Street, shot one of them dead."[1] This was turning the tables on such diſturbers of the peace, for at an earlier time, notably on February 26, 1670–1, three of Charles II.'s sons, in a drunken frolic, had here killed a beadle, an incident recorded in a poem on the subjeƈt, beginning:

> "Near Holborn lies a Park of great renown,
> The place I do suppose is not unknown,
> For brevity's sake the name I shall not tell,
> Because most genteel readers know it well." [2]

In plays by Wycherley, Shadwell, Crowne and Dryden, references are to be found to Whetſtone Park, all showing, if additional evidence were needed, the charaƈter of the place and its inhabitants. In Ned Ward's "London Spy," however, it is spoken of as being "ploughed up," and Bedlam is indicated as taking its place. As Ward's book appeared at intervals in parts during 1698 to 1700, we may take this date as approximately marking the period when Whetſtone Park became more or less innocuous.

We have seen that Macaulay brackets with this locality that of Lewknor Lane. Lewknor's Lane, to give it its correƈt title, afterwards became Charles Street, now re-chriſtened Macklin Street, running out of Drury Lane on the eaſt side, nearly opposite Short's Gardens. It was so named after Sir Lewis Lewknor, one of James I.'s Maſters of the Ceremonies, who resided close by in Drury Lane, and became known as such before the end of Charles I.'s reign, by which time the eſtate had begun to be covered with small houses and tenements. From that period

---

[1] Quoted from "The Proteſtant Domestic Intelligence," for February 14, 1680, in "Notes and Queries," for December 30, 1893.

[2] "The Three Dukes killing the Beadle," etc., "State Poems," 1697.

onwards the place enjoyed an evil reputation, and as such is to be found mentioned in contemporary literature and plays. For instance, in Dryden's "Wild Gallant," published in 1663, an old procuress says that she lodges at the Cat and Fiddle in Lucknor's (*sic*) Lane; while the wild gallant himself, bemoaning his undoing, exclaims, "Plague! had you no place in the Town to name but Lucknor's Lane for lodging?" Butler, too, speaks of

> "The nymphs of chaste Diana's train
> The same with those of Lewknor's Lane";

and what in these days will be more familiar, owing to the recrudescence of the play, a reference to the place is to be found in "The Beggar's Opera," where Drawer, in reply to Macheath's question as to whether the porter has gone for the girls he wants, remarks: "I expect him back every minute. But you know, sir, you sent him as far as Hockley-in-the-Hole for three of the ladies, for one in Vinegar Yard, and for the rest of them somewhere about Lewknor's Lane."

It was here that Jonathan Wild, among his other activities, kept a house of ill-fame which was presided over by one Jane Sprackley. Indeed, from the time of the Stuarts, when Sir Roger L'Estrange speaks of it as "a rendezvous and nursery for lewd women, first resorted to by the Roundheads," onwards, Lewknor's (it seems sometimes in the eighteenth century to have been called Lutenor's) Lane preserved a notoriety in this respect hardly equalled by any other quarter in London.

The Vinegar Yard, a little collocation of buildings in a court off Short's Gardens, referred to by Drawer, and whose name, by the way, is but a corruption of Vine Garden Yard, or Vineyard, was another haunt of such characters, as was Short's Gardens itself, and, as we have seen, Hockley-in-the-Hole, which from time immemorial had been associated with the rougher element of the population and for long preserved its lawless and immoral character.

From a passage in D'Urfey's "Pills to Purge Melancholy" (1719), we get a list of other centres of what at a later date would have been called "cyprian" activity; and the author mentions "the Sisterhood of Nightingale Lane, Ratcliffe Highway, Tower Ditch, Rosemary Lane, Hutton Wall, Saffron Hill, besides the Wetstone Park, Lutenor's Lane" (as he thus spells them), which I have already noticed, "and other places adjacent for the general encouragement and advancement of their occupation." Most of these centres can be only said to have been the haunts of the lower order of London *hetairæ*, because their general character was such as to make them more or less safe asylums for such light ladies. Nightingale Lane, in East Smithfield, and Saffron Hill, whose evil reputation, even down to Victorian days, is known to every reader of "Oliver Twist," were matched in the still farther east by Ratcliffe Highway and Tower Ditch, favourite and convenient haunts for sailors, who fell an easy prey to those ever on the look-out for such unsophisticated victims; and many a one has been lucky only to lose his money in the innumerable low brothels and taverns which at one time existed in these quarters.

It is known that the magistrates, Sir John Fielding prominent among them, were continually taking steps to combat the activities of the women of the streets and the bullies of whom they were often enough the victims and tools. In Hogarth's "Harlot's Progress" (plate 3) we see one of these magistrates, Sir John Godson, a well-known "harlot-hunting justice," paying one of his domiciliary visits, with a view to ordering the offender off to the Bridewell, where we find her in the following picture. But they did even more than this, and a passage in Malcolm's "Anecdotes"[1]

1 "Anecdotes of the Manners and Customs of London during the Eighteenth Century," by James Peller Malcolm, 1808.

indicates the author's view of the uselessness of such drastic methods as were then in force: "A futile plan has long been in use," he writes, "intended to lessen the number of women of the town, and particularly in 1762, when the Society for the Reformation of Manners followed an old and unprofitable example, by sending some of their constables through the streets to apprehend those miserable young persons; 40 were taken to Bridewell, eleven were whipped, one sent to the Magdalen,[1] and the remainder are said to have been returned to their friends. Such has been the practice at long intervals ever since, perhaps with some variations in the punishment inflicted, and I am afraid an omission of inquiring for their friends. One need only pass through the Strand and Fleet Street late in the evening, to perceive how ineffectual this method of reformation has been." [2]

From the time when a noted procuress of Charles I.'s reign rented the old moated house in Paris Garden, known as Holland's Leaguer, this class of woman has been perennial, and this early exemplification of her trade has had, as we shall see, many notorious followers, and her headquarters many successors. What we know about Madame or Donna Hollandia or Holland, as she is alternatively called, is from a very rare tract entitled "Hollands Leaguer, or An Historical Discourse of the Life and Actions of Donna Britannica Hollandia, the Arch-mistress of the wicked women of Eutopia." This was written by Shakerley Marmion, who produced a play also called "Hollands Leaguer," in which the place is shown to have been nothing but a brothel whose appearance is indicated by the wood-cut on the title of the pamphlet.

---

[1] The Magdalen Hospital, founded in 1758, for the reformation of penitent prostitutes, first in Prescot Street, Goodman's Fields, later in St. George's Fields. Dr. Dodd used to preach here.

[2] See, too, on this subject, Steele in Nos. 190 and 266, of "The Spectator."

N

From a description of Madame Hollandia herself, we are told that, having been evicted from a former residence and only just having escaped being sent to Newgate, she seeks a new *venue* for the conduct of her "profession," and finds it in "a place fit for her purpose, beeing wonderous commodiously planted for all accommodations," and which, besides, "was renowned for nothing so much as for the memory of that famous Amazon, Long-Margarita,[1] who had there for many yeeres kept a famous *infamous* house of open hospitality." This place she takes, as being specially convenient for her purpose, in that it was in close proximity to those theatres, the Globe and the Hope, to which so many gallants of the city resorted, as we have seen in a former chapter, and here she for a time carried on her business prosperously enough, as the particulars given in Marmion's tract testify. At length, however, she attracted the notice of the authorities, and a party of peace officers were sent to dispossess her of her stronghold and bring her before the magistrates. On account of the organized resistance she made, and was actually still making, apparently, when the tract was published, her mansion was besieged or *beleagured*; hence the name given it by Marmion, a name by which it was afterwards known. Holland Street, at the south-east corner of Blackfriar's Bridge, perpetuates its name and runs over its site.

That there were many contemporary characters similar to Madame Hollandia goes without saying, and many immediate successors, but these names have been, perhaps mercifully, forgotten and their precise *habitats* are unknown, except that certain quarters of the town

---

[1] Longa Margarita, known popularly as Long Meg, was no doubt one of the stew-holders in this part, to whom reference has already been made. The remainder of Marmion's tract is occupied with a list of those girls who were kept here by Madame Hollandia, her servants—including a bully called Cerberus and so forth.

were recognized haunts of such procuresses. In the earlier years of the eighteenth century, however, largely owing to the painted moralities of Hogarth, we are able to identify three outstanding women of this class. One of these was Mother Douglas, who appears in the artist's "Enthusiasm Displayed,"[1] as well as in Plate XI of "Industry and Idleness," and in "The March to Finchley"; and who had her headquarters in the Piazza at Covent Garden. Besides this pictorial immortality Mother Douglas enters into dramatic literature, as the Mrs. Cole of Foote's play, "The Mirror," 1765; and also as the Mrs. Snarewell in Joseph Reid's "The Register Office."[2] She is said to have become *dévote* in her old age, after having made a fortune by trafficking in her own and other women's virtue!

Close by Mother Douglas's in the Piazza were the even better known headquarters of Moll or Mary King, who succeeded to Tom King's Coffee House, and carried it on in a very different manner from what the name would suggest; although, to be sure, Tom King's was a sufficiently notorious place in itself: "What rake is ignorant of King's Coffee House?" asks Fielding in his prologue to "The Covent Garden Tragedy" of 1732. Indeed the character of the place is clear enough from Hogarth's "Morning," where some disorderly young bloods are seen emerging from it in company with their prostitutes who are looked at askance by the solemn lady going to early service at the neighbouring church.

Covent Garden, deserted by the *haut-ton*, which had departed to the newer glories of Grosvenor, Cavendish and Hanover Squares, was taken possession of by such

[1] She was supposed to be the convulsed woman in the foreground; but in Hogarth's revised version of the print, entitled "Credulity, Superstition, and Fanaticism," Mary Tofts, the Rabbit Woman of Godalming, is substituted.

[2] Perhaps the Mrs. Cole of Cleland's "Memoirs of Fanny Hill," is intended for the same woman.

people as Mother Douglas and Moll King, and became for a time as notorious a centre for such traffic as Whetstone Park and Lewknor's Lane. But two of the most noted procuresses of the day, Mother Needham and Mother Bentley, did not live there. In fact they catered for a more select *clientèle*, and had their haunts in the quarters of fashion.

Mother Needham resided in Park Place, St. James's Street; and that she at last attracted the attention of the authorities is shown by an entry in Fog's "Weekly Journal," for May 1, 1731, where we read that "the noted Mother Needham, convicted (April 20, 1731) for keeping a disorderly house in Park Place, St. James's, was fined 1/-, to stand twice in the Pillory—viz., once in St. James's Street over against the end of Park Place, and once in the New Palace Yard, Westminster, and to find sureties for her Good Behaviour for three years." A further entry in the "Grub Street Journal" states that "yesterday (May 6) the noted Mother Needham stood in the Pillory in Park Place, near St. James's Street, and was roughly handled by the populace. She was so very ill that she lay along her face, and so evaded the law which requires that her face should be exposed." Before she could undergo the second part of the sentence, she died.

Her name enters into the literature as well as the less creditable social annals, of the period, for Pope mentions her in "The Dunciad"; and a footnote to the two lines he gives her there, states that "she was a matron of great fame, and very religious in her way; whose constant prayer it was, that she might get enough by her profession to leave it off in time, and make her peace with God. This, however, was not granted to her, as she died from the effects of her exposure in the pillory."

One of her most constant patrons was Colonel Francis Charteris, and in Plate I of "The Harlot's Progress," Hogarth has drawn her enticing a young country girl for the redoubtable Colonel, who ſtands in the background awaiting the result. She enters, too, into that scurrilous publication called "Don Francisco's Descent to the Infernal Regions," in which she is one of the interlocutors; while "Mother Needham's Lament," published after her death, is ſtill more directly concerned with her notorious career.

The *habitat* of Mother Bentley is not known, but Hogarth has also preserved her features in the shrieking beldam (in the sixth plate of "The Harlot's Progress") who sits in the left-hand corner of the picture with a bottle of gin by her side.

During this period, and for many years preceding it, there were a number of places in the purlieus of Covent Garden whither not only men, but women of fashion were accuſtomed to come. Bagnios, as they were called, were opened in London on the model of such places in Paris and elsewhere, and although some of the former were not oſtensibly intended for such purposes, they often degenerated into them, and imitations of the name covered what were neither more nor less than centres of proſtitution.

The Bagnio proper was practically what the Turkish Bath is now, and in Charles II.'s time a certain Sir William Jennings obtained a patent from the King "for the making of all public Bagnios and Baths, either for sweating, bathing, washing, etc." One of the moſt important of these places was that known as the Duke's Bagnio in Long Acre, later re-chriſtened the King's[1] and then the Queen's. It was built in 1682, and was enlarged and reconſtructed in 1694. It is described as "a ſtately edifice, of an oval figure, in length 45 feet, and in breadth 35. 'Tis covered at the top with a high and large cupola, in which there are several round glasses fixt to let in light, which are much larger and no fewer in number than those of the Royal

[1] There is a broadside of this bagnio, then called The Kings, with a description and print of the bath, dated 1686.

Bagnio."[1] At the beginning of the eighteenth century, the charges were "5/- some, and 2/6 other, rooms."

The Royal Bagnio, referred to here, was in Bath Street, Newgate Street, and was erected in 1679, by some Turkish merchants. Hatton's description of it is worth transcribing, as it indicates at least the architectural features of such places: "The Royal Bagnio, situate on the north side of Newgate Street," he writes, "is a very spacious and commodious place for sweating, hot-bathing, and cupping; they tell me it is the only true Bagnio after the Turkish model, and with 18 degrees of heat. . . . Here is one very spacious room with a cupola roof, besides other lesser; the walls are neatly set with Dutch tiles. The charge of the house for sweating, rubbing, shaving, cupping, and bathing, is 4 shillings each person. There are nine servants who attend. The days for ladies are Wednesdays and Saturdays, and for gentlemen, Mondays, Tuesdays, Thursdays and Fridays."

This Bagnio remained till relatively recent times, when it was in use as an ordinary bath, being called the Old Royal Baths. It was demolished in 1876 to make room for offices.[2] Its name survived in the Bagnio Court, which in 1843 became Bath Street, until, in 1869, all the houses on the east side were demolished to make way for the new Post Office buildings.

There is every reason to suppose that places like the Dukes and the Royal Bagnios were legitimately carried on only for the purposes they professed; but many lesser ones arose which, under this cover, were convenient centres for other things; and they became as notorious as did certain of the taverns about Covent Garden and elsewhere, whose reputation was anything

1 Description of the Duke's Bagnio, by Sam. Haworth, M.D., 1683. There was another of these establishments at No. 63 St. James's Street, known variously as Peyraults, Pieraults, or Peros, Bagnio, which was established about 1699. It was a very fashionable lounge, and the charge for a cold bath was 2s. 6d. and for a warm one 5s.

2 "London Past and Present."

but a good one. Tom (or Moll) King's, as we have
seen, was of these; the White Lion in Drury Lane
was another, whither not only Jack Sheppard was wont
to resort, but where even women of fashion were
sometimes to be found. The Rose, in Russell Court,
and the Star Tavern had also a bad reputation; and
it was at the latter that Casanova describes sending
for a number of girls, none of whom pleased him.[1]

It would seem, indeed, that many of the houses of
ill-fame came to term themselves by the convenient
name of Bagnios.[2] Mother Douglas's was so called;
so was that of a certain Mrs. Gould, notable for its
special elegance; and Mrs. Stanhope, known as "Hell-
Fire" Stanhope, because she was the mistress of Sir
Francis Dashwood, the president of that fuligenous
society, also kept one where the decorations and female
habitués were of the most alluring character. Two
other resorts of this kind were known as the St. James's
and the Key Bagnios.

It was not only in the West End that such places
existed. In Goodman's Fields, the suggestively named
Leman Street and its neighbourhood was a hotbed of
such resorts; indeed Sir John Hawkins speaks of the
Goodman's Fields Theatre as being surrounded "by a
halo of bagnios"; and the generally universal character
of the locality is referred to by Foote in his play called
"Taste," published in 1752, and is more particularly
described at a later date by Malcolm, who speaks of
it as being "formerly inhabited by silk-throwsters,
ribbon-weavers, and others, whose trades employed the
industrious . . . but now there is a bunch of grapes
hanging to almost every door, besides an adjacent
bagnio or two."[3]

[1] Casanova's "Memoirs."
[2] At one of the taverns in Bow Street, the knives and forks were
chained to the tables; and at another, a notice was put up that "Here
you may get drunk for a penny; dead drunk for twopence; and get
straw for nothing."
[3] "Londinium Redivivum."

At an earlier period, notably in 1731, a Committee had been appointed for the suppression "of night-houses, night-cellars, and other disorderly houses," and had bound over to "the Quarter Sessions no fewer than fifty-eight persons charged with keeping houses of the above description, and had committed sixteen to prison for the same offence; besides twenty-four who were indicted, and their neighbours bound to prosecute them, and twenty-six houses which were utterly suppressed and their landlords absconded."[1]

In course of time, and greatly daring, those who ran such places began to give them a still less equivocal name, and Seraglios, as they were called, came into existence; the first of such centres being opened by the notorious Mrs. Goadby, in Berwick Street, Soho, where those who wished were received after the closing of the theatres, and the young ladies who formed the household worked or played the guitar, and demeaned themselves in quite a respectable way during the daytime—a sort of "Maison Tellier" catering for a higher class of patrons.

Indeed Mrs. Goadby—the Great Goadby, as she was termed—seems to have run her establishment on as well-regulated lines as the nature of her "business" allowed. Everything was well done; the furniture was good, the viands were good, the household was—well, if not good, at least well looked after, and such lights o' love as ranged the street and infested the taverns would have had no better chance of being received into her house than they would of being received at Court.

It need hardly be said that she had competitors, and the names of Mrs. Weatherby and Mrs. Margeram, who lived opposite each other in the same street, and often shared the same *clientèle*, were among them, as were Mrs. Banks, of Curzon Street, Mrs. Bradshaw, in Queen Anne's Street, and Mrs. Mitchell, who,

[1] "London during the Eighteenth Century," by Malcolm.

however, never seems to have risen beyond a rather *bourgeoise* ambition.

Of all the spots in London once identified with this traffic, King's Place, Pall Mall, was, perhaps, the most notorious, because there congregated a whole nest of such houses. In a work entitled "Nocturnal Revels, or the History of King's Place and other Modern Nunneries," published in two volumes, in 1779, there is a description of these haunts where such women as Charlotte Hayes[1] (a sort of successor to Mrs. Goadby), Mrs. Adams, Madame Dubéry, Mrs. Prendergast, Mrs. Windson and Mrs. Mathews, were actively engaged, and at which a certain notorious negress named Harriot was to be met with in one or other of these houses.

As might be expected in such a work as "Nocturnal Revels," not only are the procuresses named, but also those who made use of their services, and men like "Old Q," George Selwyn and Samuel Foote are thus introduced into its unedifying pages.[2] "Old Q," indeed, was an inveterate patron of such establishments, and his name is to be found, with those of Lord Falmouth, the Duke of Dorset, and others, among the frequenters of another place of the kind, that kept by a Mrs. Nelson, in Wardour Street. This woman, by the way, at last came in contact with the law for having enticed two young ladies from a boarding-school at which she had got herself engaged as a French governess for that very purpose. In consequence of the publicity thrown on this incident, she was obliged to fly and lie low for a time; but she is found, at a later period, opening a similar place in Bolton Street, Piccadilly.

During the time of the Regency there was no

[1] Charlotte Hayes once sent a sort of circular to her regular clients to the effect that a dozen girls would execute, on her premises, the celebrated Ceremonies of Venus as practised in Otaïte!

[2] A French version, called "Les Sérails de Londres," appeared in 1801.

diminution of such establishments, and one of them, that run by a Miss Collett, in Tavistock Court, was a then well-known one to men about town. But a still more notorious one was the White House, in Soho Square, which was made the subject of two distinct novels (if they can be so termed) bearing the title of "The Annals of the Whitehouse."

The White House (which now forms part of Messrs. Crosse and Blackwell's premises) was originally the mansion of the Bellasyses, Lords Falconberg, one of whom married Cromwell's daughter Mary; and later became successively the residence of the famous seaman, Sir Cloudesley Shovel, and Ripperda, the Spanish Minister. Such historic memories have become obliterated by the later reputation of the mansion. When it was transformed into its new uses, its interior was decorated in the most lavish, and, indeed, weird, manner. One room was all gold, another all silver, yet another all bronze, and each was known from the prevailing style of its decorations; all were fitted with mirrors let into the walls; other apartments were called The Painted Chamber, The Grotto, The Coal Hole, and in one, The Skeleton Room, a skeleton was made by a mechanical contrivance to issue from a cupboard! All sorts of contrivances were used for the incitement and gratification of the visitors to this house of iniquity; and it stands forth as perhaps the most complete example of a class of resort of which many others existed at this period.

The Miss Collett whom I have mentioned as beginning her career in Tavistock Court, Covent Garden, moved later to Portland Place, and afterwards to Bedford Street, Russell Square, where death put an end to her activities. She was succeeded by her niece, Mrs. Mitchell, who carried on the same kind of business successfully in various places, among others at No. 22 (afterwards 44) Waterloo Road, and finally in St. Mary's Square, Kensington, where she died. Later still, a Mrs. James, who had been a maid in the

THE WHITE HOUSE

Soho Square

1854

household of Lord Clanricarde, opened an establishment at No. 7 Carlisle Street, Soho, where she did so
well that she was able to do what Mother Needham
always hoped to—retire with an ample fortune which,
at her residence at Notting Hill, she exhibited to her
friends in the form of pictures and on her own person
in the form of jewellery. Then there was Mrs. Emma
Lee, whose real name was Richardson, who was to be
found at No. 50 Margaret Street, Regent Street; Mrs.
Phillips, at No. 11 Upper Belgrave Place, Pimlico;
Mrs. Sarah Potter, *alias* Stewart, at various addresses;
and many others. But the most outstanding was undoubtedly Mrs. Theresa Berkeley, of 28 Charlotte
Street, Portland Place, who, with the assistance of
various *hetairæ* of the day, most of whom were known
to *habitués* by special nick-names, carried on a very
lucrative business, in which the famous "Berkeley
Horse," which she invented in 1828, and other appli-
ances of a similar character, were for much in her
success. She wrote her "Memoirs," in which a picture
of the machine is reproduced. At her death, in 1836,
one of her executors, Dr. Vance, presented it to the
Society of Arts—a strange sort of present for so solemn
and learned a body!

A brochure published in 1863, entitled "Mysteries
of Flagellation," was called forth through the arrest
of the Mrs. Potter mentioned above, for flogging a
girl; and in that pamphlet, "The White House," "the
den of Mother Commins," and "the Elysium in
Brydges Street," are referred to. Mrs. Potter first
carried on her business in Wardour Street, although
she was actually apprehended at No. 3 Albion Terrace,
King's Road, Chelsea, whither she had removed some
months earlier. After her release from prison, she went
to Howland Street for a time; but she seems to have
found it safer continually to change her address, as we
find her successively at Castle Street, Leicester Square;
the Old Kent Road, and finally in Lavinia Grove,
King's Cross, where she died in 1873.

In a translation of Mirabeau's well-known "Le Rideau Levé," which a Mrs. Mary Wilson of Old Bond Street published in 1824, that lady states, writing from Hall Place, St. John's Wood, that she has given up her establishment in Tonbridge Place, New Road, St. Pancras, and has retired in favour of Mrs. Theresa Berkeley, "to whom she can most confidently recommend her patrons." Later we find a work on a similar subject, printed at the expense of Mrs. Berkeley, "for the benefit of Mrs. Wilson," who had fallen on bad days—a sort of *quid pro quo* for Mrs. Wilson's earlier testimonial, one supposes.

During the earlier years of the nineteenth century there was a notorious society which was accustomed to meet at the White Swan public-house of one James Cook, which was situated in Vere Street, Clare Market, whence the members were known as the Vere Street Côterie. When the authorities found out the nature of the place, they made a descent upon it, and Cook, the landlord, was thrown into prison. He does not appear actually to have participated in the doings that went on in his premises, although he no doubt made a very good thing in a monetary way by his compliance. When in Newgate, he came into contact with an attorney named Woolley, who introduced himself on pretence of bringing him through his difficulties. Another lawyer, named Holloway, really does seem to have tried to help the man, and towards that end wrote a book on the subject, which was published in 1813. In this is a description of the house, its various apartments and arrangements, which cannot be particularized more clearly than by stating that it was practically on the lines of an ordinary brothel of the period, although women were notable by their absence.

The Vere Street Society was dissolved in July 1810; and in a contemporary newspaper we read that "about 11 o'clock last Sunday evening three separate parties of the patrol, attended by constables, were detached

from Bow Street upon this service, and such was the
secrecy observed, that the object of their pursuit was
unknown, even at that moment, to all but the con-
fidential agents of Mr. Read, who headed the respective
parties. The enterprise was completely successful."
The result was that twenty-three were captured and
taken to the Watch-House of St. Clement's Danes,
whence they were conveyed in hackney coaches to
Bow Street for examination, "amidst an enraged multitude, the majority of whom were females," and who
were so violent that it was with the utmost difficulty
the prisoners could be saved from destruction. At the
Middlesex Sessions, on Saturday, September 22, seven
were tried and found guilty, and sentenced to various
terms of imprisonment from three years downwards,
and to stand in the pillory in the Haymarket, opposite
Panton Street. Another contemporary account records
the terrible experiences of the côterie at the hands of
the mob.

There was a similar house in Clement's Lane, near
St. Clement's Danes Church, which was subjected to
a raid about the same time, and where many delin-
quents, taken in *flagrante delicto*, were apprehended and
duly punished.

The brothels of a more ordinary character in the
region of the Haymarket, Panton Street, etc., were
well known in early Victorian days. The house of the
notorious Kate Hamilton was one[1] such, and a characteristic specimen of its class, whose red-lamps were a
sign of the trade carried on—a trade which the Early

[1] Ossington Castle, as it was called, in Orange Street, was another,
and yet other places where "life" could be seen were "Jack Coney's,"
"Jack Jehu's," "Harry Mott's," in Foley Street, The Café Turc,
and the Doughty Rooms, in Bloomsbury. Shops, purporting to be
purely commercial, were often used as cloaks for such places, and if
we are to believe the tale called "The Fruit Shop," published in 1765,
Betty's famous fruit *dépôt* in St. James's Street was not innocent of
these uses; it was certainly a place of assignation and gossip, as students
of the eighteenth-century social life of London are aware.

Closing Act of 1872 did much to lessen, if not entirely, as nothing will entirely, eradicate.

There used to be published little guides to such haunts, where their situations, the names of those who ran them, and such-like data, were given for the use of the unsophisticated, and which were, it need hardly be said, sold *sub rosa*, and were obtainable, often enough, in quite other places than book-shops.

As may be supposed there is a large literature connected with this subject, in which may, no doubt, be found the names and *habitats* of other women of this character not included above; but the reader will probably consider that enough has been said about this phase of pleasure haunts without seeking in such works for further details, which, although they have an undoubted value as exhibiting certain aspects of social life during various periods, are not such as one cares unduly to dwell upon.[1]

Such places as the Cider Cellars, at No. 20 Maiden Lane, which Porson used to frequent, and which was "The Back Kitchen" of "Pendennis," Evans's, in Covent Garden, the original of Thackeray's "Cave of Harmony" and the Cole Hole, in Fountain Court, Strand, Offley's Symposium, in Henrietta Street, Covent Garden, one of Edmund Kean's haunts, as well as some not dissimilar resorts in the East End, "The Holy Land," and so forth, come rather under the heading of taverns, and in some cases clubs, than of such centres of pleasure as are included in this volume.[2]

[1] Mr. Ashbee's "Index Librorum Prohibitorum, Absconditorum," etc.; the "Memoirs of Fanny Hill," by Cleland; "The Rambler or Fashionable Emporium," 1822, wherein is a series of papers on "London Hells Exposed;" the memoirs of Harriette Wilson, and so forth, may be consulted by those interested.

[2] See Daniel's "Merrie England," for a list of such-like resorts, as well as Pierce Egan's "Life in London"; "The English Spy," etc. At the Cider Cellars "grilled bones, poached eggs, gin punch, and singing, not of the most refined order, were the attractions"; ("Fashion Then and Now," by Lord W. Pitt Lennox).

Nor were the gambling hells and gaming houses of the past anything but clubs where anyone with money in his pockets was more than welcome. From the Shaver's Hall of early days, and from Crockfords— or Fishmongers' Hall, as it was called—downwards there was a large number of such places in the neighbourhood of St. James's Street and Pall Mall, most of which were fitted up in an elaborate style, and where "pigeons" were rooked in the most "elegant" surroundings. At the beginning of the nineteenth century there were alone some twenty-four of such haunts within a few minutes' "walk" of each other, and as the curious may like to know exactly where they were situated, I append a list as a conclusion to this chapter. Nos. 1, 2, and 50 St. James's Street; Nos. 5, 6, 8, and 10 King Street; Nos. 6, 7, 15, 16, and 28 Bury Street; No. 12 Park Place; No. 9 Bennett Street; No. 4 Pickering Place; No. 77 Jermyn Street; No. 3 Cleveland Row; No. 16 Waterloo Place; Nos. 6, 32, 33, 55, 58, and 71 Pall Mall; No. 8 Oxenden Street; and No. 13 Leicester Street.

CHAPTER IX

PARIS GARDEN, SPRING GARDENS AND VAUXHALL

ALTHOUGH the Londoner is not supposed, owing to the vagaries of climate and a form of home life almost peculiar to himself, to participate in open-air amusements to the extent that continental nations, not so much shackled by such conditions, are accustomed to do, it is remarkable that through the ages there have been in the metropolis a succession of out-of-door pleasure haunts, ranging from the Paris Garden of Tudor days, and coming by gradations through the Spring Gardens and Mulberry Gardens of Caroline times, and the Ranelagh and Vauxhall of the Georges, to yesterday, so to say, when the Earl's Court Exhibitions, the White City, and the existing Wembley: varied permutations of the same instinct on the part of the Londoner to take his pleasure out of doors when he can. Nearly all these places, from the earliest to the latest, possessed ample means for defying the elements; but in spite of the perennial grumbler at the weather, so many days and nights permitted, as they still permit, the pleasure-seeker to find it under the stars, that such shelters were often enough to be found deserted, and it is probable that those in Elizabeth's day who went to Paris Garden, or those in the times of the Georges who haunted Ranelagh and Vauxhall, only crowded into the buildings when they could not walk in the grounds; and if the famous Rotunda at Ranelagh was often filled when the weather was fine, not so much desire for shelter as the desire to be fashionable and to see those who regarded it as "the thing" to remain under cover, was probably the cause. The popularity of the lesser pleasure-gardens, the tea-gardens, the wells, and such-like places during the late seventeenth and eighteenth centuries, further attest the fact of that delight in the open-air; and the result is that if there are very many pleasure haunts within four walls to be noticed, there are almost as many in the open air; and it is with these that I deal in this and the following chapters.

I begin with Paris Garden because there seems little doubt that under this generic title (for it connoted a manor or liberty in Bankside, Southwark) there was a pleasure-garden of that name apart from the theatre with which I have already dealt. From contemporary maps,[1] we see a collocation of houses, surrounded on the south sides by gardens, and these gardens we know to have been full of trees and retired spots. That Paris Garden was not a systematized haunt of pleasure, such as places like Ranelagh and Vauxhall were to become, is clear; but it seems equally certain that those landing at this spot (for there was a regular Paris Garden landing-stage on the river) to go to the bear- and bull-baiting, or the theatres that congregated here, or to the less-reputable haunts close by, made this spot a centre of amusement, where refreshments could be obtained, and where the gardens afforded pleasant recreation.

That many who did this came for the purpose of privacy, sometimes to concoct plots and conspiracies, is known; and Fleetwood, writing in 1578, describes the place as being notorious for the secret meetings of foreign envoys and their agents. It was essentially a spot suitable at night time for stratagems, for it was so dark that unless, as a contemporary writes, you were lynx-eyed, you could hardly see anyone. But if the grounds were thus "the very bower of conspiracy," as they were described, the houses attached to them were, no doubt, gay enough, and must have done a good

[1] Those of Agas, Braun and Hogenberg, etc.

business in supplying not only visitors to the place, but also those who were going on longer journeys, into the country, of which Paris Garden may be described as the first stage.

There seems every reason to suppose that the proper name of the place was Parish Garden,[1] as, indeed, it is often found spelt in early records, and that, although this name was applied to the whole district, it had also a more special and limited meaning as denoting this particular site within it.

Although we are without precise details as to the constitution of Paris Garden, we may, I think, visualize it as a forerunner of that cloud of tea-gardens and such-like pleasure haunts which at a later time spread all over London, and which had their more direct forerunners in the Spring Gardens and Mulberry Gardens of Caroline times.

These two places may be described as the seventeenth-century equivalents of the Ranelagh and Vauxhall of a later day. There were two distinct Spring Gardens, one at Charing Cross, the other, and rather later one, at Lambeth, which was to become, in course of time, the Vauxhall of the eighteenth and earlier nineteenth century. The exact position of the earlier Spring Garden is shown in Morden and Lea's map of 1682. It was situated immediately behind Wallingford House, now the Admiralty, and could be entered by an alley from Whitehall, or the passage from Trafalgar Square which to-day bears its name. When exactly it came into being is not recorded, but it is mentioned in documents bearing the date of 1610 and 1611, although at that time it would appear rather to have been part and parcel of the royal appanage of St.

[1] According, however, to Taylor the Water Poet:

"How it the name of Paris Garden gained—
The name it was from a Royall boy,
Brave Ilion's firebrand. . . .
From Paris, Paris Garden hath its name."

James's Park than a place of public resort, and may be identical with the garden, described by Hentzner, in 1598, in which was a "jet d'eau, with a sun-dial, at which, while strangers are looking, a quantity of water forced by a wheel, which the gardener turns at a distance, through a number of little pipes, plentifully sprinkles those that are standing round." If the word "strangers" indicates the patrons of the place, and not merely such as were by royal permission allowed to visit the garden, this would help to prove that the Spring Garden, as such, actually had an Elizabethan origin. The conclusion is that the Spring Garden was part and parcel of the royal domain, that it was looked after by the royal keepers, but that the public were allowed access to it, just as they are to-day in the case of a portion of the gardens of Kensington Palace. This is confirmed by the fact that in 1629 William Walker constructed a great bowling-green here for Charles I., with turf brought from Blackheath, and also erected a new garden house for the King to rest in.

That the Spring Garden became a very fashionable and favourite resort is proved by the many contemporary allusions to it, and the heyday of its popularity was during the reign of Charles II. At an earlier day it would appear inferentially that the public who were admitted to the bowling-green had not always behaved with becoming restraint; for in 1634 we read that "the Bowling-Green in the Spring Garden was, by the King's command, put down for one day, but by the intercession of the Queen it was reprieved for this year; but hereafter it shall be no common bowling-place." Nor was this all, for we are further informed that "there was kept in it an ordinary of six shillings a meal (when the King's proclamation allows but two elsewhere), continual bibbing and drinking wine all day under the trees; two or three quarrels every week. It was grown scandalous and insufferable; besides my Lord Digby, being reprehended for striking Will

Crofts in the King's garden, he answered that he took
it for a common bowling-place, where all paid money for
their coming in."[1]

For a time the Charing Cross Spring Garden
was closed to the public. But bowls were so favourite a
diversion at this time (Charles I. was, as we all know,
greatly addicted to the game) that a new Spring Garden
was formed, and the writer of the account just quoted
thus mentions it: "Since the Spring Garden was put
down, we have, by a servant of the Lord Chamberlain's,
a new Spring Garden erected in the fields behind the
Muse, where is built a fair house, and two bowling-
greens made, to entertain gamesters and bowlers at an
excessive rate; for I believe it has cost him £4000—a
dear undertaking for a gentleman barber. My Lord
Chamberlain much frequents that place, where they
bowl great matches."[2]

The Muse here mentioned was the Royal Mews,
which stood where the National Gallery is now; and
the fields behind, to-day covered with houses, are shown
in Faithorne's map of 1658 as a large open space to the
east of the Haymarket. It seems probable that this
venture was not a success, for we hear nothing more
about it; and no doubt when the original Spring Garden
was again thrown open, people went back to their
accustomed haunt. That this must have been before
1649 is proved by an entry in Evelyn's "Diary," where
we read that the diarist treated certain ladies of his
relations there. However, later, in 1654, Cromwell
again shut up the old Spring Garden, and Evelyn had
to go to the Mulberry Garden instead. Four years later,
however, Spring Garden was again available, and the
diarist, after having been to see a coach race in Hyde
Park, on May 20, 1658, "collationed," as he calls it,
there.

In a work entitled "A Character of England," pub-

1 "Strafford Papers." Garrard to Lord Strafford.   2 *Ibid.*

lished in the following year, and attributed to Evelyn himself,[1] there is an interesting description of the place and the habits of its frequenters, which is worth transcribing: "The manner is as the company returns (from Hyde Park), to alight at the Spring Garden so called, in order to the Parke, as our Thuilleries is to the Course; the enclosure is not disagreeable, for the solemnness of the grove, the warbling of the birds, and as it opens into the spacious walks at St. James's; but the company walk in it at such a rate, you would think that all the ladies were so many Atalantas contending with their wooers. . . . But as fast as they ran they stay there so long as if they wanted not time to finish the race; for it is usual here to find some of the young company till midnight; and the thickets of the garden seem to be contrived to all advantages of gallantry, after they have been refreshed with a collation, which is here seldom omitted, at a certain cabaret, in the middle of this paradise, where the forbidden fruits are certain trifling tarts, neats' tongues, salacious meats, and bad Rhenish; for which the gallants pay sauce, as indeed they do at all such houses throughout England." From other sources one gathers that the Spring Garden was one of those places which were fashionable and which were affected by the society of Caroline times, much as St. James's Park was by the Georgians, and Hyde Park in the reign of Victoria: it was a place to gossip and stroll in; a place where acquaintances would be met, a place for assignations, and for exhibiting fine figures and fine clothes by both sexes.

In course of time, however, a rival arose at Lambeth. People have always shown themselves pleased to go distances to enjoy what close to their own homes comes after a time to seem jejune; and so there is nothing to wonder at that so relatively distant a place as Lambeth should have come gradually to outrival so central a spot

[1] It is included in his "Miscellaneous Works," published in 1825.

as Charing Cross. Besides which, in those days, the river was made use of. It was, indeed, in itself a pleasure haunt, and people took boat on it as much for the mere enjoyment of floating on its surface, as from necessity caused by the scarcity of bridges. As Lambeth could be reached in this way, a double source of enjoyment was possible when paying it a visit, and a new Spring Garden came into being there—the Spring Garden which was to become the Foxhall of Pepys, was to blossom into the Vauxhall of Georgian times, and was destined to survive within living memory. When the new Spring Garden was opened, it did not actually ruin the existing one, which carried on for a time as the *Old* Spring Garden, until it was closed and the ground built over. The approximate date of the opening of the new venture was in 1661, and on July 2 of that year Evelyn went to see it, and found it "a pretty contrived plantation." Pepys was a constant visitor to the Charing Cross Spring Garden, as he was to the *two* Spring Gardens[1] which existed simultaneously at Vauxhall at this time. These were known as the Old and New Spring Gardens, and the former has thus often been confounded with the *old* Spring Gardens, at Charing Cross. Pepys preferred the newer of these latter two, as is shown by an entry in his "Diary" for May 29, 1662, where he writes: "Thence home and with my wife and the two maids and the boy took boat, and to Fox-hall, where I had not been a great while. To the old Spring Garden, and there walked long, and the wenches gathered pinks. Here we staid, and seeing that we could not have anything to eat but very dear, and with long stay, we went forth again without any notice taken of us, and so we might have done if we had had anything. Thence to the New one, where I never was before,

[1] Monconys, the French traveller, describes "Les Jardins du Printemps," at Lambeth, in 1663, but it is not clear if he indicates the old one or the new. See Wroth's "Pleasure Gardens of London in the Eighteenth Century."

which much exceeds the other; and here we walked, and the boy crept through the hedge, and gathered abundance of roses, and after a long walk, passed out of doors as we did in the other place, and so to an ordinary house that was an ordinary house, and here we had cakes and powdered beef and ale, and so home again by water, with much pleasure." It is not only Pepys who complains of the exorbitant charges made for refreshments at these pleasure haunts, and there is no doubt that it was owing to this that they gradually fell into disfavour. However, the New Spring Garden, being a novelty, was able to fleece people who required sustenance there, and was a delightful rendezvous for those who merely wanted to enjoy its sylvan delights. Pepys liked doing the latter, and on June 7, 1665, we find him "walking an hour or two at Foxhall," as he now calls it, "with great pleasure." In the following month, while the Plague was raging, he went again "To Foxhall, where to the Spring-garden," but found no one there, "the town being so empty of anybody to come thither." He returned by coach, and between Whitehall and his house he only met two other coaches and two carts! Two years later it was very different, "I by water to Foxhall, and there walked in Spring Gardens," he writes, on May 28, 1667. "A great deal of company, and the weather and garden pleasant: and it is very pleasant and cheap going thither, for a man may go to spend what he will, or nothing, all is one. But to hear the nightingale and other birds, and hear fiddles, and there a harp, and here a Jew's trump, and here laughing, and there fine people walking, is mighty diverting." Pepys, who always had an eye for a pretty woman, was recompensed on this occasion by the sight of two, who were being pursued by "some idle gentlemen," but, as they were in evident distress, he was much amazed at the pertinacity of their followers, until the ladies at last escaped "and took boat and away." In the following month, he went there again with

Creed, by water, but his chief object appears to have been to see some cock-fighting, which, however, was over before he arrived; so he and his friend walked for a time up and down Spring Garden, in reflective mood, musing on "the bad management of things now, compared with what it was in the late rebellious times when men, some for fear, some for religion, minded their business, which none now do, by being void of both." One fears there were no pretty ladies about on this occasion, at any rate.

How long the Vauxhall Spring Garden[1] existed as such, is a little difficult to determine. Wycherley, in his "Gentleman Dancing Master," speaks of it then as among the fashionable haunts; and indeed they continued to be advertised under this name till late in the seventeenth century. Its reputation began to suffer from the doings of such mad gallants as "Young Newport" and Harry Killigrew, who were probably the two Pepys saw pursuing the ladies, as they were accustomed to do this sort of thing, and would force themselves into the little arbours where any pretty faces attracted their attention, and would almost seize the owners of them, who were "perhaps civil ladies," as Pepys conjectures. Something of the same sort occurred, one remembers, when Jos Sedley took Emmy and Becky to the place when it had become the Vauxhall of later Georgian days.

During the latter part of the seventeenth century the Vauxhall Spring Garden became rather notorious as a place of assignation, and as such is to be found referred to in contemporary plays as being a haunt "where both sexes meet, and mutually serve one another as guides to lose their way, and the windings and

[1] The title was a favourite one, at a rather later date; there was one between Ebury Street and Belgrave Terrace; another at Knightsbridge where William Street joins Lowndes Square; one at Stepney, a little north of the Mile End Road, abutting on Globe Road; and one at Stoke Newington; but they were smaller places than the two mentioned in the text.

turnings in the little wildernesses are so intricate, that the moſt experienced mothers have often loſt themselves in looking for their daughters."[1]

By 1711, when Swift went with Lady Kerry and Mrs. Pratt to hear the nightingales there, the place had become known as Vauxhall, *tout court*, and as such Swift speaks of it, although that the old title of Spring Garden was ſtill alternatively applied to it, is proved by its being referred to under that name by Addison, in 1712, when he carries Sir Roger de Coverley there, on the well-known occasion when the knight, considering "the fragrancy of the walks and bowers, with the choirs of birds that sung upon the trees, and the loose tribes of people that walked under their shades, . . . could not but look upon the place as a kind of Mahometan Paradise."[2]

We may, I think, take it that the Spring Garden had loſt its hold on the better class of patrons shortly before it was to have a recrudescence as Vauxhall Gardens under Jonathan Tyers, in 1728. True, a guide to London for two years earlier mentions it as one of the sights of the town; but guide-books, especially of that period, are not notably reliable in such matters, and the writer of this one was probably rather remembering what the place had been than what it was. Indeed, it had become disreputable; and might easily have shared the fate of many another pleasure haunt, had not a man like Tyers come forward to give it a new lease of life, and to eſtablish it on so firm a basis that it was deſtined to exiſt for another hundred and thirty years of pleasurable aĉtivity. Its palingenesis was, indeed, so marked that under this new form it claims a place apart, as, although Vauxhall Gardens was the immediate successor of Spring Garden, it was in all essentials a new place. Before dealing with it, I interpolate a few words about another seventeenth-century resort, to which I have

[1] "Amusements," by Tom Brown, 1700.
[2] *The Spectator*, for May 20, 1712. No. 383.

already referred—the Mulberry Garden, which, with the two or three Spring Gardens, formed the chief of those open-air resorts in which our seventeenth-century forbears found amusement.

The Mulberry Garden,[1] at least by name, enters into our dramatic literature, for Sedley took it as the title of his well-known play, and it is constantly found referred to in the works of other contemporary playwrights.

In the year 1609, James I., anxious to establish a silk industry in this country (something in the same nature was tried in the reign of Queen Anne—equally without success), caused a garden of mulberry trees to be planted on the spot now approximately occupied by Buckingham Palace. Nearly a thousand pounds was expended in the "embanking of a piece of ground and in planting mulberry trees near the palace of Westminster [2];" and for a time great hopes were entertained of the success of the venture. Charles I. took special interest in the project, and in 1629 he granted to Lord Aston "the custody and keeping of the Mulberry Garden near St. James's . . . and of the mulberries and silkworms there." There were buildings, including a dwelling-house, on the site, and three years later Lord Goring purchased these, and the post of keeper, from Lord Aston for £800; whence the name of Goring House by which the residence was for a time known. Lord Goring created a mansion out of what had been but a small abode, and spent no less than £12,000 in doing so. In course of time Speaker Lenthall is found occupying the place, and it was then, apparently, that a large portion of the grounds was separated from the house and garden immediately

[1] There was a Mulberry Garden in Clerkenwell, opened in 1742, which must not, of course, be confounded with its Pimlico prototype. There was yet another at Chelsea, but the latter had nothing to do with amusements.

[2] "Calendar of State Papers."

surrounding it, and turned into a pleasure resort on the lines of the Spring Garden at Charing Cross.

After the Restoration (to follow the fortunes of the residence itself) Lord Goring, who had been living out of London, returned to it; but when he died, two years later, his successor in the title sold the property to Lord Arlington, and it became known as Arlington House, a place which, in spite of Goring's expenditure, Evelyn found "ill-built, but capable of being made a very pretty villa." In 1674 it was destroyed by fire, and about the same time the Mulberry Garden adjoining ceased to be a place of public amusement.

The Garden, therefore, which chiefly interests us here, had but a relatively short career, but during that period it not only became fashionable, but, as I have said, so well known that the dramatists of the period, who but infrequently mention Spring Garden, are full of allusions to it; while it need hardly be said that both Evelyn and Pepys were acquainted with it. It is, indeed, the former who has left the earliest reference we have to it. Writing on May 10, 1654, he says: "My Lady Gerard treated us at Mulberry Garden, now ye only place of refreshment about ye towne for persons of ye best quality to be exceedingly cheated at; Cromwell and his partizans having shut up and seized on Spring Garden, which till now had been ye usual rendezvous for the ladys and gallants at this season."

Ludlow also mentions the place, characteristically, in order to record that Charles II. once, "at a debauch in the Mulberry Garden," drank some healths, a thing he had himself issued an order forbidding.[1] Pepys, on July 10, 1660, a day notable for him because on it, he says: "I put on my new silk shirt, the first that I ever wore in my life," went there to "a great wedding of Nan Hartlib to Mynheer Roder,

[1] Ludlow's "Memoirs."

which was kept at Goring House." By this the actual residence may be indicated, but I am inclined to think that the garden had been hired for the occasion. However, if this was so, Pepys had forgotten it eight years later, for on May 20, 1668, he speaks of going "to the Mulberry Garden, where I never was before; and find it a very silly place, worse than Spring Garden, and but little company, only a wilderness here, which is somewhat pretty."[1] However, on the following August 23, being in the Park, he met his friends Mr. and Mrs. Pierce with three more, and carried them all to the Mulberry Garden, where he "spent 18s. on them, and there left them." The last visit Pepys appears to have paid to the Garden was on April 5, 1669, when he went with Sheres, "who is to treat us with a Spanish Olio, by a cook of his acquaintance that is there: and without any other company, he did do it, and mighty nobly; and the Olio was indeed a very noble dish, such as I never saw better, or any more of. . . ." So pleased was the diarist with his experience that later in the day, "meeting The: Turner, Talbot, W. Batelier and his sister, in a coach, we anon took them with us to the Mulberry Garden; and there, after a walk, to supper upon what was left at noon; and very good; only Mr. Sheres being taken suddenly ill for a while, did spoil our mirth; and by and by was well again, and we mighty merry."

Dryden, as well as such men as Sedley, Etheridge, Wycherley and Shadwell, who all introduce the place into their plays, was a visitor here. The arbours and cross walks, and the dining-room, where cheese-cakes were sold, as well as such more substantial fare as the Olio Pepys partook of with such gusto, were evidently much appreciated, as even so late in the garden's

---

1 Pepys had seen Sedley's play "The Mulberry Garden," then first represented two days before, and this, no doubt, induced him to pay the place a visit.

career as 1671, Shadwell[1] speaks of it being very full "of gentlemen and ladies that made love together till twelve o'clock at night."

The last reference we get to the Mulberry Garden is in the nature of a sad retrospect, when Dr. King, in his "Art of Cookery," published in 1709, exclaims:

"A princely palace on that space does rise,
　Where Sedley's noble muse found Mulberries."[2]

Before the close of the seventeenth century a few Wells and Spas and such-like resorts had begun to come into existence: The London Spa, in 1685; Cuper's Gardens in 1691; the Lambeth Wells, St. Chad's Well and Pancras Well, in 1697. But it was not till the days of the Georges that such places had a pronounced vogue, and, as we shall see, it was the eighteenth century that was to witness both the rise and decline of the many which were at that time dotted over the map of London.

Before dealing with these, four outstanding places of public amusement have to be considered: Vauxhall Gardens, Ranelagh, Mr. Cornelys's Assemblies, and the Pantheon, together with Almack's, as the *ne plus ultra* of fashion in this direction.

Vauxhall Gardens

We have already seen how Vauxhall Gardens had their origin in the Spring Garden[3] which succeeded at this spot the earlier Spring Garden at Charing Cross. It was in the year 1728 that Vauxhall entered into its long career of success as a haunt of pleasure. In that year Jonathan Tyers took a lease of the old Spring

---

[1] In "The Humorists," 1671.
[2] Quoted in Malcolm's "Londinium Redivivum," vol. 4.
[3] As a matter of fact the title of Spring Garden survived till 1785, although the place is found generally referred to in contemporary letters as Vauxhall. Even, however, till the last, the annual licence was taken out in the old name.

Garden for thirty years at £250 per annum. Having done this, he set about reconstructing and improving the place, and on June 7, 1732, he opened it with one of those ridotto alfrescos which were then so popular. This one was exceptionally brilliant, and the Prince of Wales was one of the company, the majority of whom wore dominoes and masks. The admission was one guinea, and the fête lasted from nine o'clock in the evening till four o'clock the next morning. It was exceedingly select, only about four hundred of the *haut-ton* being present; and so successful was it that during the same season several others on similar lines were given.

It is quite obvious that such intermittent entertainments would not have been sufficient alone to repay Tyers, and there is every reason to suppose that the ordinary admission to the gardens during other times was much less than the guinea demanded for such exceptional fêtes. In 1737, indeed, we know that it had been fixed at one shilling and that silver badges were issued to season-ticket holders. In course of time, when Hogarth became associated with Tyers in the beautifying of the gardens, that great artist designed some of these badges,[1] one of which, in gold, inscribed with the words "*in perpetuam beneficii memoriam*," the grateful Tyers presented to his coadjutor, thus making him free of the gardens during his lifetime.[2]

Tyers was unceasing in his attempts to increase the beauty of the gardens and to add to their amenities and the comfort and amusement of his patrons. For several of the rooms Hogarth painted pictures; and it was the fact of the painter living in South Lambeth soon after his marriage that was responsible for his making Tyers's acquaintance, and thus being engaged by him in this work. It has been said that Francis

---

[1] Richard Yeo, the medallist, designed others.
[2] There is a good collection of these badges in the British Museum; and some of them are reproduced in Wilkinson's "Londina Illustrata."

Hayman first suggested adorning the buildings with pictorial subjects;[1] and he certainly contributed some of these, among others a later series of the "Four Times of the Day" which Hogarth had popularized. One of Hogarth's pictures here represented, curiously enough, Henry VIII. and Anne Boleyn, in which it is said the portraits of Frederick, Prince of Wales, and his mistress, Miss Vane, were recognizable.[2]

Nor were pictures the only artistic objects with which Tyers decorated Vauxhall. Cheere, the statuary, was engaged to place in the gardens some of those leaden figures which are to be found in the grounds of so many country mansions, and through Cheere, Roubiliac was introduced to Tyers, and for him produced that statue of Handel which Walpole says "fixed" the sculptor's fame, and for which he received £300. Roubiliac is said also to have executed a figure of Milton for Vauxhall; but concerning this nothing seems to be definitely known.

In representations of Vauxhall at a rather later date, an orchestra is always a prominent object. The first of these was erected soon after Tyers took over the place, and an organ was part and parcel of it; in course of time, however, notably in 1758, a more elaborate structure in the Gothic style, which Horace Walpole was making popular just then, replaced the less imposing building; and whereas originally only instrumental music had been given, Tyers added the vocal strains of such famous singers of the day as Mrs. Arne, Rheinhold, and Thomas Lowe, the last of whom was to be a sort of musical standing-dish here for nearly twenty years.

Each season began in April or May, and was inaugurated by a special entertainment in the form of a Ridotto or similar species of amusement. Until

---

[1] See "Sketch of the Spring Gardens, Vauxhall: in a Letter to a Noble Lord."

[2] Austin Dobson's "Life of Hogarth."

his death in 1751, Frederick, Prince of Wales, was a friendly patron of Tyers, and was frequently to be seen arriving with a gay company by water from Kew. For his convenience Tyers caused what was called "The Prince's Pavilion" to be constructed opposite the orchestra, whence Prince Fritz could listen to the strains of the band or the voices of Mrs. Arne and the rest, and then take supper. The well-known view of the gardens as they were in 1751, executed by Wale, gives so good an idea of the elaborate character of the place at this period, with its great semi-circular arcade, its pavilion, its extensive walks, and umbrageous alleys, that further description is unnecessary. Its rather unpromising entrance in the foreground immediately abutted on Kennington Lane, and the record of the notable people who have driven along there and been set down at that little porched doorway would fill a volume. When the royal prince came by water, he disembarked close by, and either walked or was carried by chair up the Lane to the Vauxhall entrance. Those arriving from London would drive over Westminster Bridge, and along the Kennington Road.

If there was a select air about an opening day or such special occasion, at Vauxhall, that air was not general, for there is no doubt that it was no more exclusive than any place could be whose entrance fee was one shilling. But that did not prevent the upper classes from visiting it, and there was, probably, no more motley crowd to be found anywhere in the London of that day. Great people came as to a kind of picnic here, and were amused to find themselves among the merchants and cits. Fenchurch Street and the Minories contributed their quota, as did the Temple and Grosvenor Square, "even Bishops," writes a contemporary, "have been seen in this Recess without injuring their character."

To a decorative, but *au fond* very unsophisticated

period, the charms of Vauxhall appealed in a way we can hardly understand. The fact is, I think, that those who had few opportunities for seeing anything exciting outside their ordinary daily experience, naturally found it pleasant to walk in what someone called "a realization of Elizium," to listen to music and singing, and to have a chance of rubbing elbows with their more gorgeously dressed betters; while the latter liked something that was only to be reached by a considerable drive, or, better still, by water, where they had an opportunity of meeting their friends and acquaintances, and of showing off the glory of a new brocade or lutestring or of flourishing a clouded cane or fingering an amber snuff-box.

In any case, Vauxhall not only became the fashion, but with surprising pertinacity remained the fashion for several generations. It entered into fashionable conversation, it found its way into our literature; its buildings and groves were reproduced on fans and knick-knacks; every foreigner went to it as surely as he went to the Abbey or the Tower. It became, in a word, part and parcel of the daily life of the citizen, the varied amusement of the *haut-ton*, with Ranelagh and the Pantheon and Mrs. Cornelys's Assemblies, as winter resorts; the objective of those who, like Grosley, came to our shores to note our manners and to describe our sights. The novels of Fielding and Smollett and Richardson, the letters of Walpole and Gray and Lady Mary, are full of references to it, and Goldsmith and Johnson knew it, if from less frequent visits, at least probably quite as well as did Horace Walpole or Gilly Williams or George Selwyn.

A contemporary account[1] of Vauxhall tells us that "this is a place where are those Spring Gardens, laid out in so grand a taste that they are frequented in the three summer months by most of the nobility

[1] In "England's Gazetteer," 1751.

P

and gentry then in and near London; and are often honoured with some of the royal family, who are here entertained with the sweet song of numbers of nightingales, in concert with the best band of musick in England. Here are fine pavilions, shady groves, and most delightful walks, illuminated by above one thousand lamps so disposed that they all take fire together, almost as quick as lightning, and dart such a sudden blaze as is perfectly surprising. Here are, among others, two curious statues of Apollo, the god, and Mr. Handel the master of musick; and in the centre of the area, where the walks terminate, is erected the temple for the musicians, which is encompassed all round with handsome seats, decorated with pleasant paintings, on subjects most happily adapted to the season, place and company."

Those thousand lamps (at a later day there were to be many more) must have had quite an exciting effect on those who entered the gardens for the first time, and many, both in real life and fiction, confess themselves dazzled by them when they passed into the Elysian enclosure. Indeed, these lamps, glimmering among the trees and hedges and casting a fairy-like glamour over the mysterious alcoves and *bocages*, possessed such a cumulative power of impressing, what time the music rose and fell, or the clear soprano or rich alto rang out, that those who became lyric over such things may well be forgiven for indulging their enthusiasm; even Goldsmith makes his "Citizen of the World," the usually unimpressionable Chinese philosopher, grow enthusiastic over the scene.

There was a certain system in the form of the amusements provided at Vauxhall. First the orchestra claimed attention with its simple airs and sentimental ditties; then at nine o'clock the cascade began playing, and away went the crowd to watch that for a time—a very short time apparently—after which a return was made to the music; and the adjacent supper-boxes began to fill up, and on one of these occasions, the most conspicuous box was occupied by Lady Caroline Petersham, Lord Orford, lured away from an adjoining one, Harry Vane, Miss Ashe, and Mr. Horace Walpole; with Betty, the flower-girl from St. James Street, in attendance with hampers of strawberries and cherries.

If there is one passage in Walpole's letters that has been quoted more often than another, it is this one where he describes how they minced chicken in a china bowl, and made themselves so noticeable with laughter and noise that they at last had the whole concourse round their box, some of whom came into the adjoining booths to hob-nob with Harry Vane filling bumpers and drinking their healths. This was in June 1750; and they did not get home till three o'clock in the morning.

This merry party appears to have brought its own supper, certainly the fruit was from Betty's shop; and many people did the like; but refreshments of all sorts, ranging from chickens at 2*s*. 6*d*. to Shrewsbury cakes at 2*d*., were to be had here, and could be washed down by champagne at 8*s*., burgundy at 6*s*., Frontiniac at 6*s*. or claret or hock at 5*s*. a bottle; while punch could be made with ingredients supplied or might be bought at 8*s*. a quart, in that arrack variety which at a later day was to prove so fatal to Jos. Sedley. And then there was that marvellously cut ham, which was so thin that it was said you could read a newspaper through it, and of which a certain famous carver undertook to cover the whole superficial area of the gardens from a single joint.

Among the many documents *pour servir* for the history of Vauxhall at this period—and they are as the sands of the sea in number—*The Connoisseur* has some of the most illuminative notes on the place, its amusements and *habitués*. The writer is generally rather satirical and unmeasured in his strictures: he calls the waterfall which so many gazed and gaped with wonder at, "a tin cascade"; and he is specially indignant at the diminutive size of the 2s. 6d. chickens, which he affirms were little bigger than sparrows.[1]

The great period of Vauxhall was from 1750 to 1790, and during those forty years, when Horace Walpole and his set frequented it, and Fielding's "Amelia" went there and was dazzled by its splendour, and Fanny Burney's "Evelina" knew it, and Beau Tibbs, and even the great Doctor himself condescended to quote its protagonist, it relied simply on its essential attractions, without having recourse to any of those *réclames* which other centres of recreation often called in to aid their flickering or waning popularity. Boswell calls it, with good reason, "that excellent place of public amusement . . . peculiarly adapted to the taste of the English nation; there being a mixture of curious show,—gay exhibition,—music, vocal and instrumental, not too refined for the general ear; for all which only a shilling is paid, and, though last, not least, good eating and drinking for those who choose to purchase that regale."

The notices of Vauxhall Gardens in the daily Press never indicated any special features, but restricted themselves to intimating the ordinary performances.

Tyers was so certain of his public, it would seem, that there was no necessity to lure them to a place to which they went on their own volition. On occasion, indeed, the company on its way thither must have created no little confusion. If they arrived by boat they found the landing-stages crowded, other boats and wherries jostling them in all directions; if they drove, then the road became almost impassable owing to the obstructions which frequently occurred; sometimes people never reached the doors at all; and those that did must have been an unconscionable time getting there. But nothing interfered with what Matthew Arnold would have termed their blood-thirsty seeking

[1] *The Connoisseur* for May 15, 1755.

after enjoyment; and Lydia Melford and Evelina and Amelia forgot the *désagrémens* to which they had been subjected in a sort of rapt enthusiasm at what they had seen in Mr. Tyers's paradise.

Ten years after Vauxhall had re-opened its doors under Tyers's *ægis*, Ranelagh came into existence, but this opposition did not materially affect the prosperity of the older place, although Ranelagh was destined for a little while to cast it into the shade and to outrival it in fame and popularity as time went on. Vauxhall possessed two great advantages, and they were such as Horace Walpole for one recognized:[1] people could go to it by water, and, although Ranelagh had its wonderful rotunda, the gardens at Vauxhall were far superior; thus it happened that the latter became chiefly a summer resort, while the former relied principally on the winter to bring it patronage. As we shall see, Ranelagh was open throughout the year, but it was when people could not enjoy out-of-door recreation that it was chiefly patronized.

Although Walpole was a frequent visitor to Vauxhall, he affects not greatly to be allured by it: "The trees at Vauxhall and the purling basins of goldfish never inspire me," he tells Henry Fox, in 1746; but such a hold had the place taken on fashionable life that one cannot open a volume of his letters or those of his contemporaries without coming across some allusion to it and the Ranelagh which was to prove its one competitor in its special direction. Even the solemn Gray went there: "My evenings have been chiefly spent at Ranelagh and Vauxhall," he tells Wharton;[2] and every foreigner of distinction from the King of Denmark downwards was taken there, as a matter of course, to see some special ridotto or other entertainment got up in his honour. Indeed

---

[1] "Walpole's Letters," edited by Mrs. Paget Toynbee, vol. 1, p. 228.

[2] See "Gray's Letters," edited by D. C. Tovey.

all the world of fashion, and much of the world of a lower strata, crowded those twelve acres of pleasure grounds, walking along the gravel paths, losing themselves in the less discreet alleys and labyrinths, the Dark Walk and the Long Alleys, as they were named; standing or sitting before the Gothic orchestra, listening to the music; or dining in the adjacent alcoves, as we see them in that famous colour print after Rowlandson's drawing; or, if they were country cousins, wondering open-mouthed at the Cascade, or the gilded figure of Aurora, or one or other of those innumerable decorative objects, which looked better at night-time than in the daylight, which showed too often their very trumpery character.[1]

It need hardly be said that a place thus open to all classes, and with opportunities in its retired fastnesses for all sorts of questionable happenings, was soon taken advantage of by the rakes and dare-devils of the period. Men like Hell-gate Barrymore were to be found here with their boon companions, and masquerades enabled more illustrious personages to mix themselves, unknown, with the crowd, and to play all sorts of pranks. Loose characters began to frequent those dark alleys, and to such an extent that, in 1763, Tyers had to have them railed off. Sometimes bands of young drunken fellows, bent on mischief, paraded the grounds insulting the ladies and resenting the interference of their protectors; one such to the number of fifty, in 1764, tore up the railings Tyers had been at pains to erect, and played havoc in the wildernesses; even irrupting into the private boxes where parties were seated peacefully

[1] To one Frenchman at least Vauxhall did not appear so gay as the Londoner himself found it; for although he speaks of it as being "un spectacle charmant, agréablement disposé," and so forth, he adds, "Tous les bâtimens auquels on a donné le nom de Vauxhall dans Paris, ne sont qu'une esquisse médiocre de ce beau lieu; mas la gaieté, la folie les embélissent, et celui de Londres est *morne, silencieux*," etc. ("De Londres et de ses Environs," Anonymous, 1788.)

eating their suppers surrounded by the pictorial representations of plays and sylvan amusements. Fire-eaters like Fighting Fitzgerald and Sir H. Bate Dudley (a parson, by the way) and Captain Crofts occasionally diversified the regular entertainments by picking quarrels and having hand-to-hand fights;[1] Barrymore would appear with his rowdy set, and the prize-fighter, Hooper, "The Tinman," who generally accompanied him on such occasions, dressed as a clergyman; and a pretext for a quarrel with some unoffending visitor generally resulted in a row in which numbers of those present took sides.[2] Or young bloods, fresh from some tavern carouse, would appear in the gardens, take liberties with attractive young ladies, in spite of the presence of their male friends, and not infrequently got well chastised for their impertinences.

But in spite of such occasional disturbances, an evening spent at Vauxhall must have been a pleasant one, especially at a period when people of all classes were as much addicted to music, particularly in its vocal form, as a large class was to drink. It was a time when glee-singing was rampant, when hardly a social meeting could take place without some one singing a favourite ditty, generally of an amorous or sentimental character, when glee-clubs were amazingly numerous, and when the Prince of Wales (who had a good voice and an hereditary love of music) obliged with a song with a condescension that for a time went far to militate against his generally rakish, even raffish, propensities.

Vauxhall was the very centre of song and minstrelsy; it was a veritable nest of singing birds, from its own special nightingales to those imported human ones who trilled forth the roulades of some Italian

[1] See "The Vauxhall Affray, or the Macaronis Defeated," 1773.
[2] An incident of this kind is given in Robinson's "Life of Lord Barrymore."

opera, or gave voice to those nautical and national ditties which breathed a spirit of patriotism in a nation not yet grown self-conscious.[1]

In fine weather, as I have said, the Gothic orchestra was surrounded by a gratified crowd; in less clement seasons that same crowd could repair to the Great Room, or New Music Room, as it was indifferently called, but which the wits nicknamed, because of the shape of its roof, the Umbrella. The concerts began about five or six and lasted till nine or ten; and they usually consisted of sixteen pieces, songs and sonatas and concertos alternating; the whole being preceded by an overture on the organ. Certain well-known composers supplied such music as was required for special purposes, or as a variety to older compositions; and the strains of Dr. Arne, and Dr. Morgan who was the regular organist to the Gardens, were heard between sonatas and concertos by Corelli, Veracini, Scarlatti, and the rest. Sometimes an instrumental solo was given, and a certain Valentine Snow, the royal serjeant trumpeter, was a great success in this capacity, about 1745. So great an authority as Dr. Burney has recorded that "Snow's silver sounds in the open air, by having room to expand, never arrived at the ears of the audience in a manner too powerful or piercing."

The songs given were legion, and in the *London Magazine* for the period may be found the words of new ones and often the music; while collections of "Vauxhall Songs," notably "The Warbler," were sufficiently numerous to attest the popularity of this portion of the entertainment.[2]

The death of Jonathan Tyers in 1767, after he had amassed a large fortune by his conduct of Vauxhall,

1 People in the private boxes sometimes "obliged," and the orchestra, by request, accompanied them. Lord Sandwich—Jemny Twitcher—once, at least, did so.
2 See Wroth's "Pleasure Gardens."

did not materially affect the fortunes of the place. It had become too firmly established in public favour, even for the disappearance of one who had been for so much in its prosperity, to be jeopardized by such an event; and it continued under the *ægis* of his two sons, Tom and Jonathan, in its successful career. Tom Tyers, whom old Johnson liked so much, although he wrote many songs for the Gardens, never took a large share in the conduct of the place, and in 1785 he sold his interest in it to Jonathan, who carried it on till 1792. Under the new management the gardens continued much in the same way as before, but the concert hours were made later, and in 1783 they began at eight and ended at eleven.

It was during this period that those occasional disturbances I have referred to chiefly happened, although they were by no means solely confined to this time, instances of earlier rowdyism and later being on record. One reason for their outbreak was the fact that the last night of the season was made a special occasion for a kind of small riot, when the hot-heads broke the lamps and did as much damage as the management thought it wise to permit; when more was done, the authorities took action, as we may see by the following extract from one of the daily news-sheets — for September 1774: "Upwards of fifteen foolish Bucks who had amused themselves by breaking the lamps at Vauxhall, were put into the cage there by the proprietors, to answer for the damage done. They broke almost every lamp about the orchestra, and pulled the door leading up to it off its hinges."

Some years before this, notably on May 10, 1769, one of the greatest entertainments Vauxhall had ever witnessed was given. It was a ridotto al fresco, and it is said that no fewer than ten thousand people were present. The thousand lamps of earlier days had been multiplied by five; a special place for dancing under a vast awning had been formed. Walpole was there with Conway, but the crowd going to it was so great that "it was half an hour after nine that we got half-way from Westminster Bridge," he tells Montagu. After scrambling under horses, through wells, over posts and rails, they at last reached the gardens; but after they had walked twice round, they were "rejoiced to come away." The difficulty of getting back equalled that in going, and, says Horace, "we found three strings of coaches all along the road, who did not move half a foot in half an hour."[1]

In the days of the Georges the opportunities of hearing good music and well-known singers were not so great as they have since become, and as the proprietor of Vauxhall made a point of engaging much of the best talent available in this direction, we can, I think, trace to this the fact that Vauxhall remained so long a fashionable as well as a popular resort. Mr. Wroth, in his exhaustive account of the gardens, gives a list of some of the principal singers who were accustomed to appear there; and in this list we find such familiar names as those of Mrs. Baddeley, the actress; Mrs. Weichsell, a great favourite at Vauxhall and the lady who is singing in Rowlandson's picture; Miss Wewitzer; Mrs. Wrighten; Mrs. Kennedy, and Mrs. Martyr; all singing between 1768 and 1789. Vernon, the tenor, had succeeded Lowe in 1764, and Arrowsmith, another tenor and pupil of Michael Arne, came later, and sang till 1785, when his place was taken by Incledon, who was a special favourite here till he left in 1790. In 1774 Hook had taken Morgan's place at the organ, and was destined to fill it till so late as 1820; in 1783 Barthelemon conducted the regular orchestra; while an additional band of drums, fifes, clarionets, and horns perambulated the gardens after the regular orchestra had ceased its activities for the evening.

[1] Letter to George Montagu, May 11, 1769.

VAUXHALL GARDENS
MME. WEISCHELL SINGING
ABOUT 1780

A kind of apotheosis of Vauxhall's career was reached in 1786, when it celebrated its jubilee, on May 29. Why this date was selected I do not know, as the place had been running its prosperous career since June 7, 1732, and was, therefore, just upon fifty-four years old at the date of the Jubilee. There is extant a beautiful admittance card, signed by Jonathan Tyers, and stamped with his seal, in which one detects the hand of that famous engraver Grignion. To whom, one wonders, did that magic bit of pasteboard belong? Amelia may have owned it, or Lydia; on the other hand, it may have been in the pocket of my Lord Barrymore or Mr. James Boswell, or Bate Dudley, or "Old Q." It is idle speculating; but there it is, that voucher which enabled its possessor to pass into what our forbears called "an elizium."

That "elizium," a few years later, was to raise its ordinary entrance fee to two shillings, and to make those grand galas and ridottos and masquerades, which formerly had been but rare occurrences, a regular feature of its attractions. One such ball was given on May 31, 1792, and Vauxhall was crowded with people in every conceivable kind of costume, amongst which the actor, Munden, representing a deaf old man, had a *succès fou*.

During the following thirty years, Vauxhall kept up its reputation for its musical programmes as well as for its ridottos and masquerades; and those whose names I have already given as being outstanding performers, were succeeded by others not less capable and popular: Darley and Mrs. Franklin; Mr. Mountain and Mrs. Bland, who, with Charles Dignum, were special favourites here. On the title-page of one of those collections of Vauxhall Songs, which Messrs. Bland and Weller published, is a charming little vignette of the orchestra, and the selection is of songs sung by "Mr. Dignum, Mr. Denman, Mrs. Franklin, the two Miss Howells and Mrs. Mountain."

But as time went on it was found that something more than balls and music, an intermittent cascade and ham of supernatural thinness, was required to interest the patrons of Vauxhall, and incidentally to keep pace with its rival, Ranelagh, which had been, as it were, re-inforced by two other popular pleasure haunts, Marylebone Gardens and Cuper's Gardens. All these places had already added firework displays to their other attractions, and Vauxhall fell into line with them in this respect in 1798. That it did not do so before, is a proof of its conservatism and also of the sure grasp it had already on the popular taste. Fireworks were, however, in the air at that moment; and famous anniversaries and other notable events began to be regularly celebrated by rockets and squibs, and catherine-wheels and cascades of golden fire. The earlier years of the new century, when Nelson was clearing the sea of our enemies and Wellington was sweeping the French out of Spain, were pregnant with happenings that obviously demanded pyrotechnic display, and Vauxhall, which had come rather late into the race, made up for it by an activity which was all its own.

This was the period when Emmy Sedley and Becky Sharp were accompanied thither by George Osborne and Jos Sedley, with an obsequious Dobbin very much in the background; and the picture Thackeray draws for us of the place, and the experiences of "our visitors," with the fatal effects of that famous rack punch, might have been predicated of hundreds of other Vauxhall evenings and of hundreds of other middle-class families who went there in much the same way and often with many similar *désagrémens*.

Other circumstances happened, too, on this famous occasion recalling earlier days; and when Jos volunteers to sing a song, and the crowd, attracted by his doings, surges into the arbour where the party is sitting, we get a companion piece, *mutatis mutandis*, to that when Horace Walpole and the rest helped Lady Caroline Petersham to mince her chickens and Harry Vane drank the health of the onlookers.

Just, too, as there was a difference between the fashionable company in the mid-eighteenth century and its rather *bourgeois* counterpart at the beginning of the nineteenth, so Vauxhall itself was passing from being a fashionable haunt to being merely a popular one. All sorts of fresh attractions were added to those which had sufficed for an earlier generation; and whereas ordinary fireworks had once been able to excite an unsophisticated crowd, the human element was now introduced, and Madame Saqui came over from Paris, and, bedizened in elaborate costumes and waving feathers, disported herself on a tight-rope, and appeared, through the medium of blue-flames and bursting rockets, more sylph-like and ethereal than she really was. This performance inaugurated what was for long to be a regular feature of the Vauxhall of later Georgian times.

Nor was this change in the nature of the programme the only thing that differentiated the place from its earlier character. Much of its once-sylvan charm was taken from it by the demolition of many of the trees and the erection of a vaulted colonnade supported by cast-iron pillars. When rain descended, as it seems so often to have done on "Vauxhall nights," this was a convenience; but it helped to expose that artificiality which the old groves and umbrageous trees had done so much to conceal; by 1805 all the trees of the earlier Tyers period had disappeared.

However, the place still had power to attract the native and to impress the foreigner. One of the latter, who has left us his impressions of London at this period, can thus write of it: "Vauxhall is, to a stranger, the most imposing, as well as most delightful of all the London spectacles. He enters with astonishment the brilliantly decorated arcades, which form a promenade in the illuminated gardens. A Gothic temple stands in the centre, appropriated to the music, which is both vocal and instrumental. A spacious rotunda joins on this light, elegant fabric, and leads through a suite of apartments. Elegantly convenient supper-boxes surround the whole, where the guests repose without losing any part of the magnificent scene that surrounds them. Splendid fire-works, illusive transparencies, and martial music, intersperse among the trees, and ornament the seducing scene."[1]

Changes had by now come over the management of the gardens; the younger Jonathan Tyers had died in 1792, and his son-in-law, Bryan Barrett, carried the place on till 1809, to be followed by *his* son, George Barrett, till Vauxhall was sold by the Barrett family to a syndicate composed of Bish (who had kept the lottery ticket office), Gye and Hughes, in 1821.

This circumstance inaugurated the last period of Vauxhall's existence; and with it the name became changed to the Royal Gardens, Vauxhall, with the approval of George IV., who in his earlier days had much frequented the place. Under the new title it first opened on June 3, 1822, with Darley singing the song entitled "The Prince and the People," in which one verse (quoted by Mr. Wroth), considering the general conduct of His Royal Highness, seems to reach the high-water mark of sarcasm:

> "Endow'd with each virtue, the dignified youth,
>   Ere Reason enlighten'd his mind,
>   Burst forth on the world in example and truth,
>   The boast and delight of mankind."

It must have needed the smiling face of Darley (as he looks at us from the print showing him singing the song), and the "20,000 additional lamps" with which the gardens were now lighted, to blind the auditory to the almost comic inappropriateness of these lines.

1 "The Stranger in England," by C. H. G. Goede, 3 vols., 1807.

A ground-plan of Vauxhall as it appeared in 1826 shows how buildings had gradually ousted the more sylvan characteristics of an earlier day; and if one compares it with Wale's view taken in 1751, it will be seen what changes had taken place there. One new feature was a theatre, which occupied the space once thickly covered by trees; two octagon temples have also been added; and a new supper-room and ice-house adjoin the Rotunda and Picture-Room; while the Fire-work Tower, the Smugglers' Cave, and other buildings are dotted about in parts where previously trees and hedges were paramount.

Notwithstanding such changes, however, the main features remained practically unaltered, and the lamp-surrounded orchestra, so familiar in Pugin's drawing and in Cruikshank's etching,[1] was but an amplification of that earlier one in which we have seen Mrs. Weichsell singing, with the Prince and Perdita standing by, and Dr. Johnson supping in an adjoining box.

One of the chief alterations, in that it indicated a change in public taste, was the substitution of a stage for rope-dancing, for the cascade which had been, indeed, abolished in 1816; and in an age notable for its love of panoramic and such-like displays it is significant that what was called by the horrific title of Heptaplasiesoptron[2] was established in the room where Hayman's pictures had once been a sufficient attraction.

A list of some of the "shows"—for Vauxhall had by now really become a home for such things—exhibited here, includes the once well-known Ramo Samee, the Indian sword-swallower, shadow pantomimes, and Grey's Fantoccini; while in place of the

[1] In the "Sketches by Boz" where Dickens gives an amusing account of "Vauxhall by Day"—with the gilt very much off!

[2] It is described by Wroth as "plates of glass ingeniously distributed. Manifold reflections were produced of revolving pillars, palm-trees, turning serpents, coloured lamps and a fountain."

soft airs of Arne and Bishop, comic songs became the rage, and men like Mallinson and Williams were their popular exponents. But better singers than these appeared here, and when the management engaged Braham and Miss Stephens and Madame Vestris, who created a *furore* with "Cherry Ripe," the entrance fee was raised to four shillings, and was willingly paid. Other attractions were the representation of the Battle of Waterloo, in 1827, in which a thousand horse and foot soldiers took part; later the Polar Regions was one of the shows, and later still "Venice" with "imitation water"; while Ducrow and his horses was another popular feature. Such a hold had Vauxhall on public taste that when, in 1833, a return was made to a one-shilling entrance, no fewer than 27,000 people crowded the gardens on a single day.

This year 1833 was a red-letter one in the annals of Vauxhall, for on August 19 took place the benefit of C. H. Simpson, who for thirty-six years had acted as Master of the Ceremonies here. On that night Robert Cruikshank made a drawing of the great man, who was one of the institutions of the place. There he stands in his well-known attitude of greeting strangers, and behind him rises an immense representation in coloured lamps of the man whom Thackeray has described as "the gentle Simpson, that kind smiling idiot."

From this period onwards a new attraction was added by those innumerable balloon ascents at which people never seemed tired of "assisting." One of the best-known aeronauts of the day was Charles Green, and apparently the first ascent he made from the gardens was on November 7, 1836, when, with two others, he went up at 1.30 p.m., and after an eighteen hours' journey descended in Nassau, in a balloon afterwards bearing that name; another venture in the following year was attended by tragedy, for a para-chute was attached to the balloon and one of Green's companions, Cocking, in attempting to descend by this, was killed; in 1850, the daring Green actually ascended in his balloon on horseback!

In that year what Vauxhall had become is indicated in Doyle's well-known drawing among his "Manners and Customs of ye Englishe." There is the orchestra, with a very opulently endowed lady singing; there are the colonnades and the lamps; and the inevitable balloon in the distance; but there, too, are people dancing in a very *déréglé* manner; and others sitting and drinking; a company composed of the citizen and his family—the "snobs," as they were called; all with a raffish air that seems æons away from the time when the fashionable *habitués* haunted the place; when royalty patronized it, and when even the sensitive Gray and the exclusive Walpole were to be seen in its umbrageous walks.

Indeed Vauxhall was steadily deteriorating. It had been closed in 1840, when the proprietorship of Gye and Hughes came to an end; but was again opened in the following year, with Alfred Bunn as manager, and it was here that he and "Alfred Crowquill" published their "Vauxhall Papers"—now scarce enough; although sixteen parts were issued, each being published every other day during the week. Perhaps Bunn was too much taken up with his literary efforts to pay proper attention to the conduct of the place; but whatever the cause, the gardens were put up to auction on September 9, 1841. Although they were bought in at £20,000, some of the accessories were disposed of, and among them twenty-four of Hayman's pictures, which were given away, so to speak, at sums ranging from 30s. to £9 odd each.

After this Vauxhall was carried on for a time, and some efforts were made to add to its attractions: Musard was engaged, in 1845, to give promenade concerts here; gas lamps (and more of them) were substituted for the old oil ones; carnivals were organized,

Q

and so forth. But the end was not far off. In 1853 its licence was opposed on the grounds that its *bals masquées*, which had become a feature, and a very rowdy one, lasting from 11 till 5 or 6 the next morning, were not only a nuisance to the neighbourhood, but were frequented by a variety of disreputable people of both sexes. Sunday opening was tried in order to allow people to walk in the gardens, but without, of course, any other amusements, and gala entertainments were given. But nothing could bring back the past popularity of Vauxhall, and on July 25, 1859, it was finally closed, the firework display concluding with the rather pathetic device of "Farewell for Ever."

Everything was then sold off, the contents realizing but £800; and the whole place was soon levelled to the ground. On its site a church (St. Peter's, Vauxhall), houses and thoroughfares were formed between Goding Street, which marks the western boundary of its grounds, and St. Oswald's Place on the east.

Thus, after an existence of one hundred and twenty-seven years, or, if we include its earler form as Spring Garden, nearly two hundred years, the Vauxhall of many memories disappeared. With the exception of Ranelagh, no single place has bulked so largely in the social life of pleasure in England. In its first simple form as the Spring Garden it witnessed the more decorative and free period of Caroline times; and the change through the days of Anne to the Georgian era; as Vauxhall Gardens it was to see the whole remaining epoch pass away, and was to last well into a period within living memory.[1] The paths which Pepys and Evelyn, and Buckingham and Sedley and their merry men trod, were to be trodden by the Chesterfields and Walpoles, the Lepels and Bellendens of a later day;

[1] Lady Dorothy Nevill records going there, and mentions that once during a rainy season the management sent out men with huge umbrellas on which the attractions of the place as an open-air pleasure resort were vividly set forth!

the hardly less real figures of Amelia and Lydia, of Beau Tibbs and the Chinese Philosopher were to precede those of another Amelia, and Becky, and Jos, and Dobbin. Dickens and Thackeray knew the place which Dryden and Wycherley and Congreve had known. George, Prince of Wales, was there to follow in the footsteps of his grandfather; and it was not till his grand-niece had been on the throne twenty-two years that the end came to this scene of so much amusement, so much intrigue, so much gay and irresponsible frivolity. The philosopher wandering about the squalid streets that mark the site of Vauxhall can evoke many memories and can draw the usual moral.

CHAPTER X

VAUXHALL had been in existence just ten years when the residence of Lord Ranelagh at Chelsea came into the market. Lord Ranelagh had himself built the mansion, which stood just east of Chelsea Hospital, about the year 1690, and had lived in it till his death in 1712. It remained some twenty years in the Ranelagh family, when it was sold, to be precise, in 1733, and Lacy, then the patentee of Drury Lane Theatre, made arrangements to convert it into a place of entertainment somewhat similar to the already flourishing Vauxhall. For some reason, nothing was actually done, however, till 1741, when William Jones, the architect, was commissioned to erect an amphitheatre (as it was first called) in the grounds, a building which, indeed, was to become that famous rotunda whose shape somehow bulks in the background of all the social annals of the day, and forms, as it were, the characteristic hallmark of the fashionable life of over half a century.

We are told that the capital necessary for the starting of the concern was contributed by certain shareholders who held between them thirty-six shares of £1000 each, the largest holder being that Sir Thomas Robinson, who from his immense height was known as "Long Sir Thomas," but whom a later writer calls more poetically Ranelagh's Maypole and Garland of Delights. Robinson, who lived in a house in Prospect Place, close to Ranelagh, was its first manager, a post he held till his death in 1777.

228

It was on April 5, 1742, that Ranelagh was first opened, and this date is, in the annals of English fashion, one of the most important on record. Then it was that that amazing Rotunda, which Canaletto and Bowles have perpetuated for all time, was first seen by an astonished London; then that those grounds were first trodden by thousands who hitherto only knew of their beauties by hearsay.

It is from Horace Walpole that we get the most illuminating side-lights on the new place of amusement; for only a fortnight had elapsed after its opening before he paid it the first of numberless visits. Writing to Mann, on April 22, 1742, he says: "I have been breakfasting this morning at Ranelagh Garden: they have built an immense amphitheatre, with balconies full of little ale-houses: it is in rivalry to Vauxhall and costs about twelve thousand pounds. The building is not finished, but they get great sums by people going to see it and breakfasting in the house: there were yesterday no less than three hundred and eighty persons, at eighteen pence a-piece."

But although the place, in its unfinished state, was thus thrown open to the public, its more formal inauguration did not take place till the following month, on the twenty-sixth of which Walpole tells Mann that: "Two nights ago Ranelagh Gardens were opened at Chelsea; the Prince, Princess, Duke, much nobility, and much mob besides, were there. There is a vast amphitheatre, finely gilt, painted and illuminated, into which everybody that loves eating, drinking, staring, or crowding, is admitted for twelvepence. The building and disposition of the gardens cost sixteen thousand pounds. Twice a week there are to be ridottos, at guinea tickets, for which you are to have supper and music."

At first Horace "did not find the joy of it," and preferred Vauxhall; but in the following July he was there again, to a masquerade; and he hears that "the King is fond of it and has pressed people to go"; so that from the first it started under illustrious patronage. Yet Horace was not pleased: "I told you," he writes to Mann, on July 14, "that I was going to the masquerade at Ranelagh Gardens, last week: it was miserable; there were but an hundred men, six women, and two shepherdesses. The King liked it, and that he might not be known, they had dressed him a box with red damask! Lady Pomfret and her daughters were there, all dressed alike, that they might not be known."

For a man who found the place miserable, Horace went often enough—but he was full of affectation, and is continually belittling what he secretly enjoyed. Later in July he took his father there: "It was pretty full," he writes, " and all its fulness flocked round us; we walked with a train at our heels, like two chairmen going to a fight; but they were extremely civil, and did not crowd him (Sir Robert), or say the least imperti-nences—I think he grows popular already!"

It only required the place to become really fashion-able for Walpole to like it well enough, and by 1744 he is found going there constantly, as he himself confesses to Conway. In June he was at a subscription-ball there with the Pomfrets and the Carterets, and he is able to write that by then "Ranelagh has totally beaten Vaux-hall. Nobody goes anywhere else—everybody goes there;" and he tells how Lord Chesterfield had grown so fond of it that he has ordered all his letters to be directed thither: . . . the floor," he proceeds, "is all of beaten princes—that you can't set your foot without treading on a Prince of Wales or Duke of Cumberland. The company is universal: there is from his Grace of Grafton down to children out of the Foundling Hospital —from my Lady Townshend to the kitten—from my Lord Sandys to your humble cousin."

As at Vauxhall, so at Ranelagh, the arrival on our shores of illustrious foreigners was a signal for some special masquerade or ridotto alfresco.   In 1746 the Prince of Hesse went to one arranged in his honour,

A View of the Rotunda House & Gardens at Ranelagh with an exact representation of the Jubilee Ball as it appeared May 24 Djaring the Birth Day of his Royal Highness George Prince of Wales.

Vüe de la Maison=Rotunde, les Jardins de Ranelagh, et du Bal public donné le 24.me May 1759, pur dela Naifance de son altefse Royale George, Prince de Galle.

Printed for Robert Sayer, Fleet Street, London.

RANELAGH GARDENS
THE MASQUERADE
24 MAY 1751

in a round which comprised gala performances at
Covent Garden and the Opera, and a ridotto at the
Haymarket.

The growing popularity of the place, combined with
the presence of so many illustrious people, resulted in
the usual overcrowding, and Walpole's moan at the
time it took him to reach Vauxhall on one occasion is
matched by his remark to George Montagu in May
1748, that "t'other night in a string of coaches we had
a stop of six and thirty minutes," on their way to
Ranelagh.

Walpole's friend, Gray, at first seems equally to have
thought the gardens insipid, and even went so far as to
tell Chute on one occasion (July 1745) that "they do
not succeed"; but this was wrong, for they succeeded
from the first, and in the following year the poet was
continually going to them or to Vauxhall, and found
them as pleasant as Goldsmith and Reynolds and the
learned Mr. Carter did, and as Dr. Johnson did at a
later date, when he said that its *"coup d'œil* was the finest
thing he had ever seen; and gave an expansion and gay
sensation to his mind such as he never experienced
anywhere else."[1]

Perhaps the best general description of the place is
to be found in a work of fiction rather than in the
innumerable references to it in the letters and diaries
of the period, and if Lydia Melford's words seem
rather overcharged, we must remember that she is
describing the natural sensations of a young girl first
introduced to a place which far more sophisticated
people found ravishing: "Ranelagh," she exclaims,
"looks like the enchanted palace of a genio, adorned
with the most exquisite performances of painting
carving and gilding, enlightened with a thousand
golden lamps that emulate the noonday sun; crowded
with the great, the rich, the gay, the happy and the
fair; glittering with cloth of gold and silver lace,

[1] Boswell's *Johnson*, under date of 1777.

embroidery, and precious stones. While these exulting sons and daughters of felicity tread this round of pleasure, or regale in different parties, and separate lodges, with fine imperial tea and other delicious refreshments, their ears are entertained with the most ravishing delights of music, both instrumental and vocal."

Old Matthew Brambles's verdict was very different, one remembers. He found that one-half the company were following one another's tails, in an eternal circle, like so many blind asses in an olive-mill, where they can neither discourse, distinguish, nor be distinguished; while the other half are drinking hot water, under the denomination of tea, till nine or ten o'clock at night, to keep them awake for the rest of the evening.[1]

Whether or no the tea was of the innocuous variety indicated by the old cynic, at least the general kind of refreshments were no more notable for their extent or variety than were those at Vauxhall. An entrance fee of 2s. 6d., which included a "regale" of tea, coffee and bread and butter, was not likely to ensure any great strength in the liquids or special abundance in the solid portion of the fare. Foote nick-named the place "the Bread and Butter Manufactory," for apparently nothing else, except on special occasions, was procurable; and even Vauxhall had its chickens (small as they were) and its ham of sylph-like proportions. The entrance fee had earlier been varied from 1s. to 2s., raised to 3s. on nights when fireworks were let off; while half-guinea and guinea tickets were issued for the masquerades, people being admitted during the day-time to view the place at 1s. each.

Although Ranelagh was sometimes advertised as

---

[1] See Smollett's "Humphrey Clinker." Smollett, who lived near by at Monmouth House, knew Ranelagh well; and here gives the two points of view of old and young, regarding it.

being open every evening, it was usually only on Mondays, Wednesdays and Fridays that evening concerts were given. These concerts began at about 7 o'clock, and during the intervals the audience walked in the gardens, or perambulated round the Rotunda.

The gardens were not so rural or extensive as those at Vauxhall, but they had the advantage of a small canal, in the middle of which was a Chinese House and a Venetian Temple. On each side of the canal was a long formal alley with trees. But those rural characteristics which made Vauxhall so pleasant and attractive during fine weather were absent. Where, however, Ranelagh more than competed successfully with its rival, was in that great Rotunda, 150 feet in diameter, which proved an ideal lounge during rainy or cold days and nights, and in the winter time afforded a splendid place for dancing and the frequent masquerades and ridottos that were given there.

The Rotunda was no less than 555 feet in circumference. The roof was supported in the centre by a square erection with pillars, and in the space between these the orchestra was originally placed; later, however, it was moved, and a huge fireplace was constructed, thus enabling the building to be used, as I have said, during the winter and colder months. Around the vast area were ranged two tiers of fifty-two boxes, each capable of holding as many as eight people, and provided with lamps and other decorations, including what were termed "droll pictures." The lower tier was level with the ground, and its boxes were open to the arena, thus having the appearance of alcoves. Seats and tables were placed about the centre of the floor, and between them and the alcoves was ample space for the fashionable *habitués* to promenade round in the way which Matthew Bramble so rudely describes. The whole of the interior of the Rotunda was elaborately painted and gilded, and from the ceiling, which was tinted in olive-green and across which a rainbow flashed its varied colours, hung a number of chandeliers suspended by long ropes from the roof. Entrance to the place was by four Doric doorways, and sixty windows above afforded ample light.

After the removal of the orchestra from the centre it was placed in a specially constructed stand at one side of the Rotunda, and behind it an organ, built by Byfield, was set up in 1746.

What the exterior of the Rotunda looked like may be seen from a contemporary picture, which shows it as the background to a crowd of masqueraders celebrating the anniversary of the birthday of George, Prince of Wales, on May 24, 1751.[1] It had an encircling arcade and gallery, which gave a redeeming touch to what would otherwise have been monotonous enough; enthusiasts at the time likened it to the Pantheon at Rome, but it was (except in the fact that it was circular) no more like the Pantheon than the Pantheon is like the Albert Hall.

It would seem that walking round the Rotunda constituted one of the pleasures of the visitor; and this constant "ring of folly," as the satirists called it, was continually being made fun of by both native and foreign critics, some of whom did not hesitate to describe Ranelagh, in this manifestation of its entertainment, as the most insipid place it was possible to imagine, while others found the music bad, the tea bad, the bread and butter bad. It is notoriously difficult to please all tastes, and that such judgments were those of a small minority, is proved by the fact that all London crowded to Ranelagh year after year with unflagging zeal and apparently insatiable appetite.

After it had been properly heated by the great

---

[1] So it is inscribed, but George, Prince of Wales (afterwards George III.), was born on June 4. Perhaps the masquerade was an anticipatory one.

central ſtove the Rotunda was often used during the winter for dances and such-like entertainments; but the grounds were not regularly opened till from about Eaſter to the close of the summer.

Although on the whole Ranelagh appears to have been more ſeleƈt than Vauxhall, diſturbances were not entirely unknown there, although they were not exaƈtly of the charaƈter familiar elsewhere at that time. Once Dr. John Hill was caned there by an infuriated gentleman for some reason or other, and a contemporary print, with an extraƈt from the *Covent Garden Journal*, perpetuates the incident. This was in 1752; twelve years later, some footmen were charged before Sir John Fielding with "hissing several of the nobility relative to their not giving or suffering vails to be taken." Four of the ringleaders were apprehended, and the throwing of brick-bats and breaking of windows was also laid to their account.

But such things were obviously of rare occurrence, and we find no syſtematic rowdyism here, as we do at Vauxhall or Marylebone Gardens. The faƈt is, Ranelagh, if not always ultra-fashionable in its company, was always well-behaved and discreet. It was the thing to be so, and those who came from other quarters than the quarters of the *haut-ton*, took on the air of their betters, and conduƈted themselves in so seemly a way that Rogers, the poet, who knew the place during the laſt quarter of the eighteenth century, could write of it, that "all was so orderly and ſtill that you could hear the whishing sound of the ladies' trains as the immense assembly walked round and round the room."

But this does not necessarily indicate that Ranelagh was a dull place; it was, indeed, far from that, and the innumerable entertainments that were given here, and of which Walpole is the beſt and moſt consiſtent hiſtorian, prove it to have been quite otherwise. One of these was of a very special charaƈter, and Horace devotes pages of a long letter to Mann in describing it. As it is symptomatic of others, it is worth while quoting at least a portion of his account:

"The next day," he writes on May 3, 1749, "was what was called 'a jubilee-masquerade in the Venetian manner,' at Ranelagh: it had nothing Venetian in it, but was by far the best understood and prettiest spectacle I ever saw: nothing in a fairy tale ever surpassed it. One of the proprietors, who is a German, and belongs to the court, had got my Lady Yarmouth to persuade the King to order it. It began at three o'clock, and, about five, people of fashion began to go. When you entered, you found the whole garden filled with masks, and spread with tents, which remained all night *very commodely*. In one quarter was a May-pole dressed with garlands, and people dancing round it to a tabor and pipe and rustic music, all masked, as were all the various bands of music that were disposed in different parts of the garden; some like huntsmen with French horns, some like peasants, and a troop of harlequins and scaramouches in the little open temple on the mount. On the canal was a sort of gondola, adorned with flags and streamers, and filled with music, rowing about. All round the outside of the amphitheatre were shops, filled with Dresden china, japan, etc., and all the shopkeepers in masks. The amphitheatre was illuminated; and in the middle was a circular bower, composed of all kinds of firs in tubs, from twenty to thirty feet high: under them orange-trees, with small lamps in each orange, and below them all sorts of the finest auriculas in pots; and festoons of natural flowers hanging from tree to tree. Between the arches, too, were firs, and smaller ones in the balconies above. There were booths for tea and wine, gaming-tables and dancing, and about two thousand persons. In short, it pleased me more than anything I ever saw."

In course of time firework displays became a feature

here. "At Ranelagh," remarks Walpole in 1761, "all is fireworks and sky-rockets";[1] but more wonderful still, we find the young Queen Charlotte (if one can ever think of her as young) being described by Horace as "so gay that two nights ago she carried the king to Ranelagh"; but for once the letter-writer had been misinformed, and in a subsequent letter corrects his assertion. He was more accurate when, in 1768, he tells that the King of Denmark, then on a visit to this country, was to give a masquerade there "to all the world." Foreigners, indeed, *pace* the critics I have quoted earlier, generally showed a marked predilection for the place: "Ranelagh, they tell me, is full of foreign dukes," writes Walpole to Lord Strafford, in 1771. "There is a Duc de la Trémouille, a Duc d'Aremberg, and other grandees." Grosley, one of the most observant of foreign visitors, gives a long description of the place, and concludes by saying: "Imagine to yourself the saloon, amphitheatre, boxes and galleries, all filled with company, and, on the ground floor, a multitude of persons walking in every direction; the murmuring of this crowd drowned by a continual symphony; the whole illuminated with a milder gleam than that of day; you will easily conceive that there are few objects more striking."

At this time it was the custom for people of fashion to frequent Ranelagh in what was called "undress," and Grosley, commenting on this, says that "as it brings them near a level with the citizens' wives, the uniformity of appearance gives that air of freedom and ease to the whole assembly, which is the constant concomitant of equality." Another curious habit was to arrive abnormally late there. "The present folly is late hours," writes Walpole to Mann, in June 1777.

[1] In a subsequent letter, June 10, 1765, he tells Montagu that "a thousand sky-rockets launched into the air at Ranelagh or Marybone," illuminated his Strawberry Hill Garden, "and give it an air of Haroun Alraschid's paradise."

"It is the fashion to go to Ranelagh two hours after it is over"; and in 1782 he indicates that this custom then still held its ground.

That in the matter of costume a change was to come over the laws of etiquette as applied to Ranelagh, is proved by the remark of another visitor, who tells us that "Ranelagh . . . is famed for the splendour of its decorations, and the superior elegance of the company who frequent it, all, by the fiat of fashion, *full* dressed."[1]

The fact is that various as the attractions of Ranelagh were, the main object of the visitors seems to have been mutual inspection; and one writer speaks of the Rotunda being erected "to feast the eyes of the belles and beaux, who crowd thither to become spectators to one another."[2] A more satirical version of the same idea is to be found in "Harlequin at Ranelagh," in the *London Magazine* for 1774, where, after referring to the habit of arriving late, the writer adds that the visitors "stare about them for half an hour, laugh at the other fools who are drenching and scalding themselves with coffee and tea: despise all they have seen, and then they trail home again to sup."

Although the place was on the whole more select than Vauxhall, it probably appeared to be so rather from the fact that better order prevailed, than because there was much to choose between the company that patronized either place.

In "Ranelagh House—a Satire,"[3] published in 1747, one can get a good idea of the mixed character of the gatherings, which a scarce little work, entitled "A Sunday Ramble," issued thirty years later, confirms.

But although promenading round the Rotunda,

[1] Goede, "The Stranger in England."
[2] "Tour through Great Britain," by Defoe, continued by Richardson, 4 vols., 1778.
[3] It was written by Joseph Warton, when a young man at Oxford, and is in prose " in the manner of Monsieur Le Sage."

walking in the gardens, talking scandal and "quizzing" one another, with other amusements less reputable, may have been the *raison d'être* of Ranelagh's long popularity, its managers did not by any means neglect such other attractions as they thought likely to enhance the *agrémens* of the place. As we have seen, constant masquerades, ridottos, and similar forms of amusement were organized, with great success. Firework displays also added to the fairy-like scenes to which the grounds and the various buildings on them were such appropriate backgrounds. But music of the best kind was also provided, and it was this that formed the staple of the attractions for many years, and was probably one of the chief causes of the long prosperity Ranelagh enjoyed.

During the earlier period of its career, such then well-known performers as Beard, the actor and singer, and Guilia Frasi, the Italian vocalist, were engaged under the general directorship of Michael Festing, the conductor, whom Dr. Burney, who was to become the organist here at a later date, speaks of as a very successful leader of the orchestra, in which Caporale, the 'cellist, specially distinguished himself. Other favourites at this time were Abram Brown, Parry, the Welsh harpist, Mrs. Storer, Miss Young, and Miss Formantel, whose "Ten Favourite Songs" were published by Oswald in 1758. Besides these individual attractions, choruses from various well-known operas were a feature of the entertainments, and Arne's "Acis and Galatea" was among the favourites; while, later, Bonnell Thornton's success with his "Burlesque Ode on St. Cecilia's Day,"[1] whose humour so pleased Dr. Johnson (not a sound musical critic, however), which had been adapted by Dr. Burney for "the saltbox, marrow bones, cleavers, hum-strum, and hurdygurdy," shows that the taste of the frequenters of Ranelagh was at least catholic, if not unimpeachable.

[1] See Drake's "Essays on the Rambler," vol. 2, p. 326.

Indeed, it is remarkable how those who could listen to the airs of Arne and Handel (who wrote music for the fireworks!) with appreciation, and could wonder at the little Mozart playing his own compositions on the organ and harpsichord, could also enjoy "Skeggs playing on the broomstick as bassoon," and all the noisy parody of Thornton's burlesque ode. It is obvious that the managers of Ranelagh had little difficulty in providing for a taste which was so all-embracing, and it does them great credit that they should have been at pains to secure the services of such masters as Handel and young Mozart, and should have engaged the famous tenor Tenducci, whose notes, "neither man's nor woman's," threw Miss Lydia Melford into such an ecstasy that she thought herself in Paradise while he was singing.

Perhaps no more interesting musical performance ever took place here than that given by the eight-year-old Mozart. One imagines him with his father and sister, as they appear in De Carmontell's picture, which Delafosse engraved in this very year (1764): Papa Leopold playing on the violin, Marianne singing, and the diminutive Wolfgang Amadeus sitting sedately at the harpsichord, his tiny feet far from the ground, his gaze steadfastly fixed on the music before him; while the gentle notes of one of his youthful compositions floated out to the wonder-struck crowd.

At a later date Dibdin was to be heard here singing his breezy, rollicking solos, or collaborating with Mrs. Baddeley, Bannister, and Mrs. Thompson in those part-songs which had such a vogue. Other performers, in the early 'sixties of the eighteenth century, at Ranelagh were Champness and Hudson, Miss Thomas and Miss Brent, Dearle and Miss Wright and the elder Fawcett; all of whose names are a dead letter to us, but had then the power of drawing crowds to Chelsea, and of delighting not only the Lydias of the day, but more sophisticated critics.

In the fashionable annals of Ranelagh, with its masquerades and its fireworks, its ever-circling crowd in the Rotunda, and those who loitered in the Chinese Pavilion and the Venetian Temple, we are apt to overlook the services the place rendered to music; and in the gay crowd which flutters through the pages of Walpole's Letters—the Lepels, and Bellendens, the Petershams and the Gunnings, little Miss Ashe and foolish Miss Sparre, Prince Fritz and Culloden Cumberland, Lord March and Lord Chesterfield, Dr. Johnson (with Mr. Boswell at his heels) and Dr. Goldsmith (in Filby's plum-coloured suit, or, more surprisingly, in a domino), the fact that it helped for many a long year to keep the musical flag flying in this country.

It might be wondered how these concerts were arranged; how those who were promenading round the Rotunda were made aware of attractions elsewhere; and some reminiscences of the time tell us:

"An evening at Ranelagh," we read, "was accounted by the noblest and fairest of England's sons and daughters one of the most agreeable interludes in a life, whether of business or pleasure. Drawn round a stack of solid chimneys, which formed a centre to the pile, and in some degree supported it, the Rotunda was distributed internally into two circles, both of them filled up with boxes, on either side of a broad avenue; and both exhibiting, at measured intervals, their orchestras for the accommodation of musicians; for music and dancing were the sports of the hour, of which the latter was pursued exclusively within an open space round which the inner circle ran; where, gazed at by crowds of well-dressed people of all ranks, the beau and the belle of their day showed off their graceful figures in a minuet. Meanwhile, serenaded by a dozen bands, groups of pedestrians promenaded round and round each charmed ring, till the sound of a bell gave notice that some favourite singer

R

was about to perform; or weariness, or the recognition of friends in one of the side boxes, drew them away to some new and more agreeable occupation. Neither were such as preferred the cool airs of heaven to the heated atmosphere of the Rotunda without their resources. From the branches of the trees that shaded every walk, festoons of coloured lamps hung down; and beneath their canopy, bright eyes made answer to the tale which is seldom told with more effect than in the intervals of music and dancing. . . ."

"The hour of assembly," continues the writer, "was from eight to nine o'clock, that of departure about eleven or twelve, while land and water alike furnished a highway to such as made 'Pleasure's Temple' their point of attraction. They whose habits induced them to adhere to the solid earth, passed from Piccadilly or St. James's Park through open fields, and were set down opposite to the Chelsea Bun House. . . . Meanwhile the bosom of the Thames was covered with barges and wherries, all of them laden with the most distinguished fashionables of the day; and all steering their course from Westminster stairs, the ordinary point of embarkation, to a quay or landing place below the Rotunda, to which an avenue of syca-mores communicated."[1]

The proximity of the Thames to Ranelagh was a great feature in its popularity,[2] and the management on at least one occasion made the river itself an acces-sory to its entertainments. This was in 1775, when the Ranelagh Regatta and Ball took place on June 23. A beautiful admission ticket to this combined fête, designed by Cipriani and Bartolozzi, is extant, and shows Father Thames with attendant deities, acting

[1] These reminiscences are included in Gleig's "Traditions of Chelsea College."

[2] In Rocque's Plan of London, 1746, the relative position of the gardens, immediately abutting on the east side of Chelsea Hospital, is well shown, as well as the formation of the gardens themselves.

as umpire to a race rowed by cupids. "Early in the afternoon of that day," we are told, "the whole river from London Bridge to Millbank was covered with pleasure boats, and scaffold erections were to be seen on the banks, and even on the top of Westminster Hall. Gambling tables lined the approaches to Westminster Bridge: men went about selling indifferent liquor, Regatta songs and Regatta cards. The river banks now resembled a great fair, and the Thames itself a floating town. Wild calculations fixed the number of the spectators at 200,000, or 'at least' three millions! At 7.30 a cannon signalled the start of the racing-boats, and about 8.30, when the prizes had been awarded, the whole procession began to move 'in a picturesque irregularity towards Ranelagh.' The Director's barge, with its band playing and gold Regatta ensign flying, led the way, and the fortunate persons who had ball-tickets landed at Ranelagh Stairs at nine o'clock. Dancing took place in the Temple of Neptune, a temporary octagon erection in the grounds. Mrs. Cornelys had been given seven hundred guineas (it is said) to supply the supper, and it is lamentable to reflect that the supper was 'indifferent, and the wine very scarce.' Among the illustrious present were the Duke of Gloucester, the Duke of Northumberland, the Duchess of Devonshire, Lord North, Sir Joshua Reynolds, David Garrick and Samuel Foote."[1] Horace Walpole went to see the show on the river; but did not proceed to make one of the company which he tells Lady Ossory, "is now stewing in Ranelagh." "There were such crowds in the streets," he moans, "that I could scarce pass home. I feel as glad to be returned as I did from the Coronation, and I think I will go to no more sights."

Although we are told by Angelo that of all the public places known at that time or since, Ranelagh

[1] Wroth.

had most decidedly the preference (he says, too, that he had often seen a line of carriages extending from Tattersall's to Chelsea), there appears to have been a falling off of public interest in the place between 1775 and 1790; and so far from being "the *élite* of fashion," as he calls it, it appears to have suffered a temporary eclipse. Why this was so is among the mysteries, for after the latter date the place again became popular; and a recrudescence of the masquerades seems to have given it a new lease of life; while the more elaborate character of the firework displays, often under the direction of the elder Angelo, as well as of such experts as Caillot, Rossi, and Tessier, helped to draw a class which delighted in such entertainments.

I think it likely that its revived glory was due to royal patronage, for we know that George, Prince of Wales, and the Duke of Clarence (with Mrs. Jordan on his arm) were to be occasionally seen there at those masquerades which again became a feature of the place, two of which were given during the season of 1792. In this year, too, a new feature of attraction was introduced in the form of an exhibition called "Mount Etna," an early example of that kind of "show" which was to become so generally popular soon after. From a contemporary account of this, we learn that a special building was erected for its reception, and a scene was executed for it by G. Marinari, "painter to the Opera." "Mount Etna with Vulcan's Forge and attendant Cyclops, as described in the 'Æneid' of Virgil," so the advertisement assured the public, was shown; what time an *olla podrida* of music taken from the works of Gluck, Haydn, Handel and Giardini, was played; the whole ending "with a tremendous explosion."[1]

Among other "shows" which had now evidently

---

[1] As Wroth points out, the idea seems to have been taken from Torre's "Forge of Vulcan," which had been exhibited in Marylebone Gardens some twenty years earlier.

been found necessary to attract the public to Ranelagh, we find, in 1793, that remarkable person the Chevalier D'eon exhibiting his, or her, fencing capabilities with M. Sainville; the Prince of Wales and Mrs. Fitz-herbert being interested spectators. Incledon and Madame Mara, too, electrified audiences by the beauty of their singing, in 1798; and in 1802, a Mr. Thomas Todd, garbed in a weird and wonderful diving-suit of his own contrivance, was advertised to descend into a reservoir specially prepared for him, and did so, but owing to some miscalculations only remained beneath the surface for a few minutes.

It was on June 2 of this year that a great ball given by Boodles' Club took place here, at which the ladies were all presented with sprigs of laurel, which they wore during the evening fastened on to the dresses of white and silver which they all wore by arrangement. In the intervals of the dances they amused themselves by drawing prizes in a Lottery Booth erected for the purpose, a lottery in which one imagines there were no blanks. The habit of giving entertainments at Ranelagh received a great impetus from this venture of Boodles' Club; and later in the year we find the Picnic Society, of which Colonel Greville was the protagonist,[1] holding "an afternoon breakfast" here, at which the French aeronaut Garnerin made a balloon ascent accompanied by a Captain Snowden. A ball given by the Spanish Ambassador was another of the outstanding enter-tainments of this character with which Ranelagh was identified about this time; but that held in commemora-tion of the Installation of the Knights of the Bath, on June 1, 1803, was still more splendid, and seems to have been its crowning effort in this direction. It was, too, the last of any consequence. For the place had been gradually declining for some time, and such

---

[1] For an account of it see Angelo's "Reminiscences." We have met with it, too, earlier in the present volume.

entertainments as these did little more than give it an artificially prolonged existence, and by their splendour helped to show how monotonous in comparison had become its attractions. It was a case of gradual inanition, with flashes of energy that died down almost immediately after they had been called into being; and it was only a little over a month after this last great ball had been held that the Rotunda was opened for the last time, on July 8, 1803.

Two months later the Rotunda and the other buildings in the gardens were demolished, and their contents sold by auction—the organ at which Dr. Burney had for long presided and whose key-board had been touched by Mozart's youthful fingers, going to Tetbury Church, in Gloucestershire, where it remained till 1863. A portion of the grounds was soon after absorbed in those of an adjoining owner; but were later purchased by Chelsea Hospital, and now form part of the gardens surrounding Wren's creation. Jesse, writing in 1871, remarks that "a single avenue of trees, formerly illuminated by a thousand lamps, and over-canopying the wit, the rank, and the beauty, of the last century, now forms an almost solitary memento of the departed glories of Ranelagh." [1]

Ranelagh, as I have attempted to indicate, was something more than a mere place of amusement and recreation. Almost from its beginning it became an institution. One can no more visualize the social life of the eighteenth century in London without it, than one can think of the Regency without Carlton House or the days of Charles II. without Whitehall Palace. It resumed in itself all the characteristic features of a decorative period. Its name enters into the letters and diaries of the time with a frequency that alone indicates the large space it occupied in the fashionable life of that day. The great novelists of

[1] "London: its Celebrated Characters, etc.," 3 vols., 1871.

the Georgian era seldom fail to take their characters
to it; and the great artists of the period were not less
tired of reproducing its amazing Rotunda, its alcoves
and pavilions, its tree-lined alleys and its exiguous
canals, than were the topographers and compilers
of guide-books of expatiating on its manifold attractions
and what seemed to them its amazing wonders.

Vauxhall was older and long outlived its rival;
and Vauxhall bulks largely in the social life and contemporary annals of a period of nearly two centuries;
but somehow the fame of Ranelagh, with its sixty
years of activity, has outsoared that of its rival; and if
we had to sum up in one word the characteristics of
the social life of eighteenth-century London, with its
patches and pomander boxes, its lace ruffles and its
lute-string gowns, its airs of the *ancien régime;* with its
curtseyings and its bowings, its atmosphere of *haut-ton,*
its vapours and its gaddings, its superficiality and its
manifold adornments, its glitter and its glamour,
that word would be Ranelagh—the Ranelagh whose
very site is now forgotten; but where, on moon-lit
nights, surely, a ghostly company assemble, and gallant
gentlemen and stately ladies dance a minuet to the
gentle harmonies tinkling from a harpsichord or,
masked and hooded, emulate Venetian carnival while
the airs of Scarlatti and Geminiani float on the summer
air, and cause some old Chelsea pensioner to turn rest-
lessly in his sleep. . . .

The Pantheon

In the *Macaroni and Theatrical Magazine* for
January 1773, appears the following short but pregnant notice: "Pantheons: The *Nobilitys,* Oxford
Road; the *Mobility's* Spawfields." Concerning the
latter of these I shall have something to say in another
chapter; the former was that famous and fashionable
centre of amusement which, if it does not bulk so
largely in the annals of the period as do Ranelagh

and Vauxhall, is yet continually entering into contemporary letters and literature, as it entered into the
gay life of the best part of George III.'s long reign.

In a remarkable mezzotint by R. Earlom, we get,
if not a complete view of the interior of the Pantheon,
at least something which suggestively indicates its
classic character and vast proportions, and which
recalls something of those Roman buildings on which
so many of our architectural landmarks have been
modelled; while the figures that sit or stand beneath the
massive columns, introduce the authentic eighteenth-
century note into what would otherwise have been
a wholly classic convention.

In my account of Mrs. Cornelys's assemblies in
Soho Square, I have shown how the prosperity of
those fashionable gatherings was largely interfered
with by the erection of this Pantheon, which, in an
age avid for novelty, proved for a time a magnet that
drew all fashionable London to its classic haunts.
"This most elegant and superb building which would
have done honour to Greece at its most splendid
period of taste," to quote the somewhat hyperbolic
expressions used by Wilkinson, in his "Londina
Illustrata," was erected from the designs of James
Wyatt, and was opened on April 28, 1772. It had
taken some two years to construct, and Walpole,
writing to Mann, in May 1770, remarks : "What do
you think of a winter Ranelagh erecting in Oxford
Road, at an expense of sixty thousand pounds?"
The architectural features of the place appealed to
Walpole as much as its fashionable *aura* was subsequently to do, and in the following year he tells
how he took the French Ambassador to see the work
in progress: "It amazed me myself," he writes,
"Imagine Baalbec in all its glory! The pillars are of
giallo antico. The ceilings, even of the passages, are
of the most beautiful stuccos in the best taste of the
grotesque. The ceilings of the ballrooms, and the

panels painted like Raphael's *loggia* in the Vatican. A dome like the Pantheon glazed. It is to cost fifty thousand pounds. Monsieur de Guisnes said to me, "Ce n'est qu'à Londres qu'on peut faire tout cela;"[1] and in the following January, referring to Lady Stafford's correspondence with Mann, he says, "If she does not tell you that the Pantheon is more beautiful than the Temple of the Sun, read no more of her letters."

A few months after the formal opening in April, a great masquerade was held here, and Walpole, describing what he elsewhere calls "the most beautiful building in England," speaks of it as so glorious a vision, that he thought he was in the old Pantheon, or in the Temple of Delphi or Ephesus amidst a crowd of various nations. "All the friezes and niches," he proceeds, "were edged with alternate lamps of green and purple glass, that shed a most heathen light, and the dome was illuminated by a heaven of oiled paper well painted with gods and goddesses;" and he sums up that Mr. Wyatt, the architect, has so much taste that he thinks he must be descended from Sir Thomas, "even Henry VIII. had so much taste that, were he alive, he would visit the Pantheon."

In these rather general descriptions of the place, it might be supposed that Walpole was over-enthusiastic (although that is a fault not generally to be found with him) had we not a consensus of similar praise from all sorts of writers of the period. One of these was in general so adversely critical about any building in London, that when we find him among those giving unstinted praise to the interior of the Pantheon, we may be pretty sure that it deserved it. I refer to Ralph, who, in his "Critical Review of the Public Buildings of London," thus speaks of Wyatt's achievement: "Much taste and invention is displayed in the building called the Pantheon. Its exterior has nothing to demand

[1] Letter to Mann, dated March 30, 1771.

our attention; on the contrary, the entrance from Oxford Street may be justly esteemed a deformity in itself, and an incumbrance to the street. But the inside is adorned with every embellishment that modern luxury can wish for. The principal room is truly magnificent: it is lighted by a centrical dome of considerable magnitude; the galleries are supported by columns formed of a new-discovered composition, which rivals the finest marble in colour and hardness. The roof is supported by an upper range of them. The stated diversions of this place are a concert once a fortnight with a ball after it; to which anyone is admitted who purchases the tickets necessary for that purpose. Masquerades are occasionally held here, when the building is finely illuminated, and has been allowed to exhibit a more splendid scene of this kind than is, perhaps, to be beheld in any other country."[1]

Dr. Johnson was one of the earlier illustrious visitors to the Pantheon. He went there in company with Boswell; but they did not think it so striking as Ranelagh, although, to be sure, as the Doctor himself remarked, they did not see it under equally favourable conditions. Gibbon was another frequenter of the place, and Goldsmith and Fanny Burney both knew it well, and introduced it into their works. "I'm in love with the town, and that serves to raise me above some of our neighbouring rustics," exclaims Mrs. Hardcastle in "She Stoops to Conquer," "but who can have a manner, that has never seen the Pantheon . . .?" while in "Evelina" and "Cecilia," Miss Burney refers to the place to which she had often been a delighted visitor.

During the earlier portion of its career the Pantheon was chiefly notable for its masquerades. It had been created largely for that purpose, and no doubt its

[1] This description is to be found in the enlarged work, published in 1783, based on Ralph's earlier publication of 1734.

projectors realized how it might be made, in virtue of its size and elaborate architectural details, in this respect a successful competitor to the more restricted space which Mrs. Cornelys then had at her disposal in Soho Square. That they were correct in their judgment is proved by the undoubted popularity of the place, a popularity that for nearly twenty years remained unabated. The more obvious reason, as given by Wyatt himself, was to make it "a town Ranelagh." He once told Farington that it cost £25,500, so that Walpole's estimate far exceeded the actual outlay. On another occasion he said that the expenditure was defrayed by subscribers at £500 each; that he had two shares which he sold after a year or two at £900 each; and that by admission during the building to those anxious to see the new wonder, he made no less than £3000.[1]

Although these masquerades proved at first so profitable to the Pantheon, there can be little doubt that a too-insistent reliance on them brought about its undoing, as had been to some extent the case with Mrs. Cornelys's efforts in the same direction. At first, when a more or less select company patronized them, things went well; but, as we have seen, anyone who liked to pay the price of admission had the *entrée* there; and in course of time the attendance grew as mixed as it was at Vauxhall or Ranelagh. An air of fashion pervaded the place, but it was not sufficient to leaven the mass; and even fashionable people were ready enough to take part in scenes which began to be talked about, and which a writer in the *Westminster Magazine*, so early as 1774, reprehends in no measured terms. "In short," he concludes, after describing a masquerade at which he was a spectator, "I am so thoroughly sick of masquerading from what I beheld there, that I do seriously decry them as subversive of virtue and every noble and domestic point of honour." I think it is probable that these strong criticisms were

[1] "The Farington Diary."

evoked by the great entertainments given by Boodles' Club at the Pantheon on May 3, of which Gibbon thus writes to Holroyd on the following day. "Last night was the triumph of Boodles. Our masquerade cost two thousand guineas; a sum that might have fertilized a province (I speak in your own style), vanished in a few hours, but not without leaving behind it the fame of the most splendid and elegant fête that was perhaps ever given in a seat of the arts and opulence. It would be as difficult to describe the magnificance of the scene, as it would be easy to record the humour of the night. The one was above, the other below all relation. I left the Pantheon about five this morning."

Walpole only gives us an anticipatory note on another similar entertainment in the following year: "You have," he writes to Mann, "not more masquerades in carnival than we have; there is one at the Pantheon to-night (May 17, 1775), another on Monday; and in June is to be a pompous one on the water at Ranelagh. This and the first are given by the club called the Sçavoir Vivre,[1] who till now have only shone by excess of gambling. The leader is that fashionable orator, Lord Lyttelton, of whom I need not tell *you* more. I have done with these diversions, and enjoy myself here (at Strawberry Hill)."

Four years later, however, he gives a long description of yet another masquerade, but one that was not such a marked success, as were those organized by Boodles. Writing to Conway on June 16, 1779, he says: "The town has wound up the season perfectly in character by a fête at the Pantheon by subscription. Le Texier managed it; but it turned out sadly;" and he proceeds to give the reason: "The company was first shut into the galleries to look down on the supper, then let to descend to it. Afterwards they were led into the subterranean apartment, which was laid with

[1] By this name Boodles was at first known.

mould, and planted with trees, and crammed with nosegays: but the fresh earth, and the dead leaves, and the effluvia of breaths made such a stench and moisture, that they were suffocated; and when they remounted, the legs and wings of chickens and remnants of ham (for the supper was not removed) poisoned them more. A Druid in an arbour distributed verses to the ladies; then the Baccelli and the dancers of the opera danced; and then danced the company; and then, it being morning, and the candles burnt out, the windows were opened; and then the stewed-danced assembly were such shocking figures, that they fled like ghosts as they looked."

This seems to have been the last of such entertainments, which, the novelty having worn off, had lost their attraction, and had, besides, become so adversely criticized that few cared to be seen at them.

In the meanwhile the management had made a departure by engaging the then-celebrated singer, Ajugari, at the enormous fee of a hundred pounds a night merely to sing two songs. People were as mad to hear the foreigner sing and to neglect native talent as they have always been; and at a day when La Faustina, Cuzzoni, Farinelli and Senesino, and the rest were carrying all before them, and Italian opera had spelt the neglect of the English musical drama, the success of the Ajugari was instant. Notwithstanding the large sum paid to her, Wilkinson attributes the gradual decline of the Pantheon, not to such heavy expenses, which were accompanied by a corresponding influx of visitors, but to the fact that, later, the management tried to run the place on cheaper lines, when the takings fell off. They engaged another singer, one Georgi, who, however, proved so *difficile* that she could hardly have been remunerative.

The most notable musical circumstance connected with the Pantheon was undoubtedly that great concert given, in 1788, in commemoration of Handel, when

George III., Queen Charlotte and a distinguished company, were present. Among them was Fanny Burney, whose royal mistress, as she tells us, had most graciously given her a ticket for the use of Miss Port, who accompanied her, under the care of Dr. Burney, to the concert.

In 1789 an event happened which gave the Pantheon an opportunity to regain in the realms of music what it had forfeited in those of masquerade. In that year the Opera House was burnt to the ground, and the Pantheon, which had been used for some time for all sorts of heterogeneous exhibitions—Clagget's musical apparatus, Lunardi and his cat, among them, was thereupon taken, and reconstructed by Wyatt[1] as a temporary home for opera. O'Reilly, the proprietor of the destroyed Opera House, obtained a licence, and the Pantheon was duly opened for its new purpose. "The Pantheon has opened," writes Walpole to Mary Berry, on February 18, 1791, "and is small, they say, but pretty and simple; all the rest ill-conducted, and from the singers to the scene-shifters imperfect; the dances long and bad, and the whole performance so dilatory and tedious, that it lasted from eight to half an hour past twelve."

The opposition carried on by the Haymarket, and the rivalry countenanced by the King and the Prince of Wales respectively, are also noticed by Walpole: "*Dieu et mon Droit* supporting the Pantheon, and *Ich Dien* countenancing the Haymarket;" later we learn that "the Pantheon remains master of the field of battle." This is hardly to be wondered at, for a very strong orchestra, in which figured such notable exponents as Giardini, La Motte, Cramer, Fischer, Crosdil, and Cervetto, played here in addition to the best Italian and French vocalists.

Indeed there seems reason to suppose that the place might have had as much success in its musical career

[1] He did this at a cost of 5000 guineas (Wilkinson).

as it had had with more decorative but sometimes less harmonious entertainments, had not a catastrophe for a while stayed its activities in this direction. On January 14, 1792, it was burned to the ground, through a fire which broke out in one of the buildings added to it when it was converted into an opera-house. Everything, except the Oxford Street façade, was destroyed, and the loss was estimated at £60,000, only a fourth of which was covered by insurance. It is a curious fact that Wyatt, the architect, who was travelling to London in a post-chaise, saw the glare of the conflagration while crossing Salisbury Plain.[1] In the Crace Collection are two views taken respectively by H. Wigstead and Winston, of the ruins of the place as they appeared after the fire, as well as a print showing the new building which arose on its site three years later; while Turner painted a picture of the scene which was exhibited at the Royal Academy.

Wyatt was again called in to undertake the work of reconstruction, and he produced a hybrid sort of building which had none of the classic beauties of its predecessor, nor even a theatre such as had been evolved as a temporary opera-house in 1789. It was, indeed, to quote one critic, "but a fancy sort of large room for music, masquerades, etc.," and a contemporary description tells us that "a gallery went round three sides of the room, to which there were two staircases; under the gallery were small recesses of boxes, similar to those at Ranelagh, for supper parties of about a dozen, each box being enclosed with a painted curtain till the supper was announced, when they all ascended. Masquerades, at one guinea, including supper and wine, and at half a guinea, with tea and coffee, and a very few concerts, were occasionally given here till 1810."

[1] This is recorded by Angelo, in his "Reminiscences," where will also be found an interesting account of the fire, given by an eye-witness—Townshend, the well-known Bow Street Runner.

In Ackermann's "Microcosm of London," 1808, will be found a coloured plate by Rowlandson and Pugin, showing the Pantheon as it then was,[1] with a masquerade in progress. Rowlandson (who was responsible for the figures) generally contrives to impart an air of rowdyness to his pictures, but that he was, here, not doing more in this direction than was warranted by the facts, seems proved by the following extract from the accompanying letter-press:

"Since the Pantheon was rebuilt," we read, "it has been principally used for exhibitions and occasionally for masquerades, of which the plate is a very spirited representation. It is composed, as these scenes usually are, of a motley crowd of peers and pickpockets, honourables and dishonourables, Jew brokers and demireps, quidnuncs and quack doctors. These entertainments are said not to accord with the English character; and we should have been inclined to impute this want of congeniality to a fund of good sense, which renders our countrymen insensible to such entertainments, if we were not daily witnesses of their pursuing amusements less rational and infinitely more frivolous."

In course of time both concerts and masquerades were discontinued, and in 1810 Messrs. Gedge and Bonnor took the Pantheon at £1000 a year as the headquarters of their "National Institution for improving the manufactures of the United Kingdom, and arts connected therewith, etc." The idea was to hold here an exhibition of every species of manufacture and every machine in use, together with the assemblage of all sorts of objects directly or indirectly associated with such matters. Wilkinson, commenting on the vastness of the scheme, remarks: "This prospectus held forth such plans that, instead of the Pantheon, it would have required a space as large as Salisbury

---

[1] The entrance in Oxford Street had not been affected by the fire, and remained as Wyatt had originally designed it.

Plain to have carried it into execution. The thing was impracticable." So the would-be organizers evidently found, for shortly after the issue of their grandiose prospectus, they let the Pantheon to Colonel Greville, who had removed his Pic Nic entertainment to the Argyle Rooms, and thought he could transfer the licence he had obtained for music on a limited scale for that place to the Pantheon. In conjunction with one Cundy, a wine-merchant, he converted the latter once more into a very fine theatre, having no fewer than one hundred and seventy-three boxes alone. They opened the building on February 12, 1812, as "The Pantheon Theatre," at opera prices, with a series of Italian burlettas and ballets. But in spite of an extraordinary number of notable singers and dancers, including Radicati, Cauvini, Collini, Fischer, Morelli, Bertini, and Miss Stephens (her first appearance), it did not take; and it was closed on the following March 19. The cost of the new theatre had been no less than £50,000, much of which was subscribed by friends and admirers of Greville, and too-optimistic believers in his business capacity. Cundy appears to have tried to carry on the place for a time, and in 1813 another attempt was made to establish it as an English Opera House; but the regular Opera House authorities became alarmed, and an information was laid against Cundy for carrying on the place without a proper licence; he was fined, and the Pantheon closed. On December 27, however, it was again opened for what was then the last refuge of the theatrically destitute, ballets and pantomimes, with popular prices: boxes at 5s., pit at 3s., and gallery at 2s.

The failure of this is proved by the fact that in the following year the place was put up to auction under a distraint for rent, which had not been paid for three years. The sale took place at Dalphin's Riding School, in Swallow Street, and everything in the place, even to nails and the floor of the pit, was sold. Later another

S

application on behalf of Cundy, through the Duke of Norfolk, was presented to the House of Lords for leave to act regular drama here, and granted; but no more was heard of the matter. The fact was the place was too unwieldy for such purposes, and in 1815 Elliston is supposed to have had a lucky escape when negotiations into which he had entered to take it were broken off.

After remaining closed for a number of years, it was reconstructed in 1834 by Sidney Smirke at a cost of £30,000, and opened as a bazaar, and as such[1] had more or less success till 1867, when it passed into the hands of Messrs. Gilbey & Co., whose business headquarters it still remains.

Few of the pleasure haunts of London have passed through so many metamorphoses as the Pantheon in Oxford Street. At one time it took its place as one of the four outstanding centres of fashionable amusement, and as such, notwithstanding its later less successful career, it will always remain a landmark in the social annals of the period. To what strange uses it was sometimes put is shown by the one-time presence here of Lunardi's balloon, which was suspended from the ceiling, to the wonder and admiration of an unsophisticated generation. This happened in 1785, and F. G. Byron's print of it is interesting, not only as recording the event, but also as showing, in some detail, the architectural features of the original building, whose ceiling, as can be seen in the picture, was an exact copy of that of the Pantheon at Rome.

Mrs. Cornelys's Assemblies

On the east side of Soho Square, just south of the point where Sutton Street joins it, once stood a mansion built of red-brick, and erected some time during the seventeenth century, although the date, 1669, which

[1] There is a description of the Pantheon Bazaar in Timbs's "Curiosities of London."

appeared on the leaden cisterns with which it was provided, did not indicate the date of its construction, but of the creation of the title of Earl of Carlisle, the nobleman who owned it. Carlisle House, as it was called, was an elaborate residence, whose staircase had been painted by that Henry Cooke who did some decorations at Ranelagh House, and who repaired Raphael's cartoons at the order of William III.[1] The mansion occupied the site on part of which the Roman Catholic Chapel now stands, and its banqueting-hall was connected with the main building by a passage known as "The Chinese Bridge." In course of time the Carlisle family migrated elsewhere, and the house was taken by that extraordinary person whose name fills so large a space in a certain portion of eighteenth-century social life.

Mrs. Theresa Cornelys came to this country from her native Germany in or about the year 1756 or 1757. What she did on her arrival is not clear, although it is known that she used occasionally to sing under the name of Pomepeiati; probably she occupied herself with studying the manners and customs of the Londoner of the day, with a special eye to the requirements of fashionable life, in the intervals of her engagements as a vocalist. She saw that both at Vauxhall and Ranelagh the entertainments most in vogue were those masquerades at which society amused itself by imitating the amusements which live for us in the canvasses of Guardi and Longhi. She was also probably not unobservant of climatic conditions. Be this as it may, she determined to cater for a want that was obviously urgent, and in a position which, unlike both Vauxhall and Ranelagh, was central, for at that time Soho Square, if no longer exactly fashionable, was at least "well-inhabited," and was within an easy coach or sedan drive from quarters where the *haut-ton* resided. Whether she had money of her own, or

[1] See Walpole's "Anecdotes of Painting."

whether she obtained financial aid in London, is not known, but in the year 1760 she took Carlisle House, and having decorated and furnished it, she threw it open for balls, concerts and masquerades, such as were not uncommon then, but which few have ever carried to such perfection or with such success, at least for a time, as Mrs. Cornelys.

How it was that a stranger could obtain such instant notoriety as did Mrs. Cornelys, might seem strange, did we not remember that she was a German and no doubt had friends at Court. Count Kilmansegge, who was visiting England at this moment, tells us in his Diary how, on December 31, 1761, he received from the Duke of Richmond a ticket "for the ball this evening in Soho Square"; and on the following January 28, he writes: "I went to a ball which takes place every fortnight in a house in Soho Square."

It is thus evident that from the very first Mrs. Cornelys's venture was a success. But although she had already collected a host of fashionable supporters, she did not disdain the uses of advertisement, and the newspapers of the day (to say nothing of the many circulars and handbills she issued to her regular subscribers and others) prove how indefatigable she was in making her name known far and wide, and in constantly keeping it well before the public. Nor did she neglect other means of increasing her popularity; and we read, on February 18, 1763, that "on Saturday last Mrs. Cornelys gave a ball at Carlisle House to the upper servants of persons of fashion, as a token of the sense she has of her obligations to the nobility and gentry for their generous subscriptions to her assembly." Indeed, "the Heidegger[1] of the age," as Walpole once called her, knew her business *au fond*, and lost no opportunity of extending it. For an annual subscription "the votaries of fashion of both sexes," as

[1] The well-known theatrical manager and *impresario*, who was born in or about 1659 and died in 1749.

THE PROMENADE AT CARLISLE HOUSE.

MRS. CORNELYS'S ASSEMBLY

CARLISLE HOUSE

1781

it was phrased, had the *entrée* to Carlisle House, and might also lend their tickets to friends on the condition that they wrote "the name of the person on the back of the said ticket to whom they have lent it, to prevent any mistake." It is quite obvious that this rather loose privilege resulted in all sorts of people obtaining admission, and if the assemblies were amusing, it has never been pretended that they were not mixed. Indeed it is well known that many of these entertainments were of a decidedly questionable character; hard drinking and anything but modest songs, "which no lady need leave save those who are too immodest to stay," as one of Mrs. Cornelys's advertisements ingeniously phrased it, were *de rigueur* in many of the assemblies, where it was not infrequently the custom at the close to open the windows and to fling the remains of the repast provided to the crowd below, who were accustomed to gather in anticipation of such culinary *largesse*.

One of the leaders of society at this time who did much to extend the popularity of Mrs. Cornelys's assemblies was Miss Conway, daughter of the Marquis of Hertford, and niece of General Conway (Walpole's friend), who had then recently been married to the Earl of Grandison; another lady who was frequently to be seen here was Miss Elizabeth Chudleigh, famous for the daring character of her attire, or rather want of it, who became the wife of Captain Hervey, and bigamously married the Duke of Kingston. But it is impossible to particularize those who visited Soho Square, as they did Ranelagh and Vauxhall Gardens and, indeed, any place where pleasure was to be achieved, for a large section of the society of the day did this, and Walpole, who had his finger on its pulse, and was of, and in, it, tells us all about its vagaries.

That opposition began to be rampant, even before the coming of the Pantheon, is proved by the fact that Mrs. Cornelys thought it worth her while publicly to deny any implied criticism on her part against one of the new ventures which threatened her popularity and continued success; and the following notice appeared in the daily Press: "Whereas it has been industriously reported, to the disadvantage of Mrs. Cornelys, that she has expressed herself dissatisfied with a subscription now on foot to build a large room in opposition to her, she esteems it her duty, in this public manner, to declare that she never once entertained a thought so unjust and so unreasonable."

The "large room" referred to was no other than the famous Almack's, as we see by the following letter from Walpole to George Montagu, dated December 16, 1764, by which, too, we perceive that Mrs. Cornelys was already doing her best to kill the opposition she affects to disregard. "Mrs. Cornelis (*sic*), apprehending the future assembly at Almack's, has enlarged her vast room, and hung it with blue satin, and another with yellow satin; but Almack's room, which is to be ninety feet long, proposes to swallow up both hers, as easily as Moses's rod gobbled down those of the magicians." Beyond merely re-hanging her rooms, Mrs. Cornelys spent a large sum of money, £2000 it is said, in the following year, in the purchase of new furniture and the making of all sorts of alterations and improvements to her rooms. In one of these apartments she added "the most curious, singular and superb ceiling that ever was executed or even thought of"; she also constructed "a new gallery for the dancing of cotillons and allemandes, and a suite of new rooms adjoining"; while, as there had been complaints of the great heat in the rooms, she arranged "tea below and ventilators above."

All these improvements were duly advertised by means of skilfully-worded paragraphs in the weekly newsheets. But, in truth, as yet Mrs. Cornelys really hardly needed excessive *réclame;* she had many and powerful patrons, and although they had to pay an extra guinea subscription for the improvements she had made, they paid cheerfully enough, and were ready to go to any entertainment she chose to provide. One of these, on February 26, 1770, may be recorded in Walpole's words, for although the extract is a long one, it is both amusing and illuminative, as being the description of an eye-witness of the scene:

"Our civil war has been lulled asleep by a Subscription Masquerade, for which the House of Commons literally adjourned yesterday," he tells Mann. "Instead of Fairfaxes and Cromwells, we have had a crowd of Henry the Eighths, Wolseys, Vandykes, and Harlequins; and because Wilkes was not mask enough, we had a man dressed like him, with a visor in imitation of his squint, and a Cap of Liberty on a pole. In short, sixteen or eighteen young lords have given the town a masquerade; and politics, for the last fortnight, were forced to give way to habit-makers. The ball was last night at Soho; and, if possible, was more magnificent than the King of Denmark's. The Bishops opposed: he of London formally remonstrated with the King, who did not approve it, but could not help him. The consequence was that four divine vessels belonging to the holy fathers, alias their wives, were at this masquerade. A fair widow who once bore my whole name, and now bears half of it, was there, and with one of those whom the newspapers call *great personages*—he dressed like Edward IV.; she like Elizabeth Woodville, in grey and pearls, with a black veil. Methinks it was not very difficult to find out the meaning of those masks.[1]

"As one of my ancient passions formerly was masquerades, I had a large trunk of dresses by me. I dressed out a thousand young Conways and Cholmondeleys, and went with more pleasure to see them

[1] "Maria Walpole, Countess Dowager of Waldegrave, married William, Duke of Gloucester. Edward IV. married the widow of Lord Gray." Walpole's own foot-note.

pleased than when I formerly delighted in that diversion myself. It has cost me a great headache, and I shall probably never go to another. A symptom appeared of the change that has happened in the people.

"The mob was beyond all belief: they held flambeaux to the windows of every coach, and demanded to have the masks pulled off and put on at their pleasure, but with extreme good humour and civility. I was with my Lady Hertford and two of her daughters in her coach: the mob took me for Lord Hertford, and huzza'd and blessed me! One fellow cried out, 'Are you for Wilkes?' Another said, 'D—n you, you fool, what has Wilkes to do with a masquerade?'"

Among the company were Lady Waldegrave, Lady Pembroke, the Duchess of Hamilton, Mrs. Crewe, Mrs. Hodges, and Lady Almeria Carpenter. The characters assumed were very eccentric. Sir R. Phillips appeared as a "double man," half-miller, half-chimney-sweeper. The Earl of Carlisle figured as a running footman; Mr. James, the painter, as Midas. The Duke of Devonshire was "very fine but in no particular character"; and Lord Edgecumb, in the character of an old woman, was "full as lovely as his lady." The ladies were superbly dressed; and we are told that "The Countess Dowager of Waldegrave wore a dress richly trimmed with beads and pearls, in the character of Jane Shore." The newspaper-writer could apparently think of no one else as an appropriate companion of Edward IV.; although, as we have seen, the lady really represented Anne Woodville.

Among other notable people at this masquerade we read of the Duchess of Bolton being very captivating in the character of Diana; Lady Stanhope very striking as Melpomene; Lady Augusta Stuart as a Vestal, and her sister, Lady Caroline, as a Fille de Patmos, "showed that true elegance may be expressed without gold and diamonds"; while Lady Pomfret as a Greek Sultana, with the two Miss Fredericks as attendants, "made a complete group." Of all those present, however, the most noticeable was Miss Monckton, Lord Galway's daughter, who appeared as an Indian Sultana in a robe of cloth of gold. "The seams of her habit were embroidered with precious stones, and she had a magnificent cluster of diamonds on her head: the jewels she wore were valued at £60,000."

These extracts will serve to give an idea of the elaborate character of those entertainments which Mrs. Cornelys, in the days of her glory, organized, and which remain as landmarks in the higher social annals of the period. She had, indeed, made of her house a fairy palace, as Walpole remarks, and her assemblies, which had at first rather scandalized many strait-laced people, at length "drew in both righteous and ungodly." But there is little doubt that what went on in her rooms gave good cause for scandal; and although critics who are not "in" things are frequently far more severe than if they were, still there is plenty of evidence to show that when the *Oxford Magazine* and the *London and County Magazine* fulminated against Mrs. Cornelys and her assemblies—characterized, they said, by indecency and mockery of solemn feelings and principles—they had good grounds for their diatribes.

It is not, however, probable that in such an age such things would necessarily have brought trouble upon her. We have seen that although the bench of Bishops disapproved, their wives went to Soho Square, and the King, who had been appealed to, confessed himself powerless to interfere. It is not likely, then, that any other power—save an Act of Parliament, would have met the case, and as Parliament actually adjourned for one of the masquerades, it was hardly likely to take any such steps in the matter. But what could not be affected by royal, ecclesiastical, or even governmental interference, was destined to be brought about by commercial rivalry.

In 1771 there occurred a good deal of friction over the conduct of the opera in the Haymarket. It was managed by Mr. Hobart, a brother of Lord Buckinghamshire, and he greatly annoyed the singer Guadagni by preferring the vocal powers of his mistress, Zamperini, to those of Guadagni's sister. Society became divided over the quarrel, and certain great ladies—the Duchess of Northumberland, Lady Harrington and others—supporting the claims of Guadagni, arranged for him and his sister to sing at Mrs. Cornelys's rooms, where a sort of rival opera was instituted, although it went by the humbler name of Harmonic Meetings. Apparently the Guadagni enthusiasts were in the majority, for the Haymarket began to be almost deserted, and other places of vocal and theatrical entertainment became alarmed and annoyed at this poaching on their preserves, especially as Mrs. Cornelys had no licence for this kind of thing. That she was conscious of the risk she ran is shown by the fact that in order to circumvent the Act she affected to take no money for the entertainments at which Guadagni sang, and, indeed, had the daring publicly to advertise that the subscriptions she received were really only to provide coal for the poor—a double stroke by which she hoped to avoid legal proceedings, and also to curry favour with the mob, a point she had always, with good reason, been particularly anxious about. Then she had the assurance to state that even her masquerades were for the benefit of trade; by which she hoped to secure the sympathy of the commercial classes.

Hobart, however, was not to be taken in by such specious and transparent devices, and he laid an information against her before the Justices,[1] and she

---

[1] See Letter from Walpole to Mann, dated February 22, 1771.

was convicted by Sir John Fielding for allowing dramatic entertainments to be performed on her premises without a licence. Misfortunes seldom come singly; and the unfortunate Mrs. Cornelys, besides receiving this setback, was faced almost at the same moment by the opening of the Pantheon, or Winter Ranelagh, as it was called, which as a novelty began to draw away even those who had been most persistent in their attendance at Carlisle House. Active enemies were now, too, emboldened to make an overt attack on Mrs. Cornelys directly legal attention had been directed to her entertainments: as she had broken the law in one respect, it was felt that she was quite capable of doing so in another—and about this other, the nature of some of her assemblies left little doubt. Bills of indictment were presented to the Grand Jury asserting of the lady: "that she does keep and maintain a common disorderly house, and does permit and suffer divers loose, idle, and disorderly persons, as well men as women, to be and remain during the whole night, rioting and otherwise misbehaving themselves."

This was the beginning of the end, and in the following November Mrs. Cornelys's name appeared in *The Gazette*. A few weeks later the contents of Carlisle House—"all the rich and elegant furniture, decorations, china, etc., thereunto belonging, too well known and universally admired for their aptness and taste to require any public and extraordinary description thereof"—were advertised for sale by auction. As may be imagined, the event created a stir, and the public anxiety to see the interior of Carlisle House and its contents was such that a notice appeared that "to prevent improper crowds, and the great damage that might happen therefrom (and the badness of the season), by admitting indifferent and disinterested people, must be an excuse to the public for the Assignees ordering the Catalogues to be sold at 5/- each, which will admit two to see the house," etc.[1]

This might well have seemed the end of this enterprising lady's activities; but it was not so, and lo! two years later we find society being informed that "the assemblies at Carlisle House will commence soon, under the conduct and direction of a new manager." This new manager was none other than our old friend herself; indeed a little later her name is actually revealed as the protagonist of the resuscitated pleasure haunt. In the following year she is found giving what she called "A Rural Masquerade."[2]

But her day was nearly although not quite over. She still fought bravely against changed conditions, but she saw her old *clientèle* seduced away by the ampler and fresher attractions of the Pantheon and Almack's; and in August another sale of her effects was advertised by Christie. Yet, *mirabile dictu*, after another two years she reappeared, a veritable human cork on the social lake, and, heralded by a long notice in *Lloyd's Evening Post*, she stands forth as the "only begetter" of a great Masked Ball, to be held on February 19, 1776. What success this met with is unrecorded, but for a time, under "Masquerade Intelligence" in the weekly prints, her name intermittently appears, and indicates that she was still struggling indomitably to regain her once almost unrivalled position. Some of these entertainments were characteristically given in aid of the "Infant Orphan Girls of Marylebone and Westminster," for Mrs. Cornelys knew, and no one better, the commercial advantages to be reaped from charitable

[1] In the *Westminster Magazine*, for January 1773, is a humorous article on this entitled "Cupid turned Auctioneer, or Mrs. Cornelys's Sale at Carlisle House."

[2] The British Museum possesses a large collection of brochures, etc., appertaining to Mrs. Cornelys and her ventures. They were collected by Mr. Fillingham. In 1847, Mr. Mackinley of Soho Square printed a private account of Mrs. Cornelys's entertainments.

undertakings. But those who did go—and there was a sad falling off in their number—to her entertainments, were of a very different class from such as once wandered about her satin-hung rooms; and where the Duke of Gloucester had appeared as Edward IV., and the King of Denmark had deigned to be amused, vulgar brawls and even robberies took place, and bullies and demireps trod the floors once graced by the *haute fleur* of English society.

In 1778 Carlisle House was again advertised for sale or "to be hired as usual"; and a daring spirit—one Mr. Hoffmann, a well-known confectioner in the city—took the place, and tried to run it on something like the old lines, but with little or no success. Its future as the headquarters of a so-called "School of Eloquence," a debating club with this somewhat daring name; as the scene of scientific lectures "illustrated by apparatus"; and, in June 1782, as one of the places where the dwarf, Count Boruwlaski, gave two concerts; with a sad finale in Chancery, hardly concerns us. What time its legal guardians were again advertising it for sale, Mrs. Cornelys had retired to the then rural fastnesses of Knightsbridge Grove,[1] where she tried to recapture something of her early successes by giving entertainments of a somewhat similar character. But apparently few people cared for the rather expensive pleasure of her company, and in 1785 she gave up this too. What she did during the next ten years is among the mysteries; but at the close of the decade, she amazingly reappears in Knightsbridge as a "Purveyor of Asses' Milk," and not only this, but again "fitted up a suite of rooms for the reception of visitors to breakfast in public,"

---

[1] Knightsbridge Grove was really a large detached mansion, at the northern end of Porter's Lane, which ran rather to the east of Sloane Square up to Knightsbridge. I imagine the Rural Castle, shown in Bauerkeller's Plan, dated 1842, to have been identical with this Grove, or to have stood on its site.

and attempted other schemes to attract a rather regardless public. A contemporary newspaper tells us that:
"The once celebrated Mrs. Cornellys (*sic*) has taken
the house at Knightsbridge lately occupied by the
dealer in asses' milk—and the grounds are now about
to be laid out in a very superior style as a female
archery." These archery grounds, which were situated
behind Knightsbridge Grove, are shown, by plans,
to have been long in existence after Mrs. Cornelys's
day, and may be noted as another variety of the
innumerable pleasure haunts of a period when
archery was as popular as tennis is now.

This final incarnation of the indomitable lady did
not last long, and misfortune, which never ceased to
dog her footsteps after the year 1772, at last landed
her a prisoner in The Fleet, where on August 19,
1797, she closed her energetic and, in a sense, remarkable career.

There is perhaps no single name, which was not
illustrious, which enters so largely into contemporary
memoirs and letters or newspaper advertisement as
does that of Mrs. Cornelys. Murphy refers to her
in the epilogue of his "Zobeide"; Combe castigates
her in his "Diabolady" (1777); while the large and
curious collection of pamphlets, programmes, prints,
paper cuttings, etc., connected with her enterprises,
forms an interesting and illuminative *dossier* on the
amusements of our ancestors in general and on the
career of this energetic caterer to public entertainment
in particular.

CHAPTER XI

DIORAMAS, PANORAMAS AND OTHER "SHOWS"

WE have seen in a former chapter how through the ages there has been the same delight on the part of the people to congregate in those haunts where they could amuse themselves by taking part in the entertainment and, so to speak, becoming protagonists. We have also seen how equally fond they have been of patronizing theatres and music-halls where the nature of the entertainments required a certain amount of mental co-operation.

In this chapter I want to point out such forms of entertainment which required nothing but an ordinarily intelligent appreciation; where, in a word, the eye was pleased without the brain being unduly exerted; although I am far from saying that those who patronized such things were either stupid or unready to use their brains. But such things were essentially "sights"; and it remained for the spectators to draw intelligent inference from them or not as they might choose. In a word, they were that sort of "shows" which were at once capable of amusing old and young. I refer to that cloud of dioramas, panoramas, *panopticans*, *poluphusikons*, *et hoc omne genus*, which at one time had such a vogue, and for which certain lesser kinds of museums and so forth had prepared the way.

The examination of *lusæ naturæ* had for long been popular with the Londoner, before the exhibition of such things, and analogous ones, had become systematized by those who saw in such "shows" a form of making money. At the great annual fairs held in

Smithfield, at Southwark, and elsewhere, the crowds flocked to see anything in the way of a freak, with just the same zest and eagerness as they have done ever since. In former times, however, such things were almost entirely confined to the booths of fairs, and if some daring spirit wished to astonish the multitude, and incidentally make money, by some hazardous acrobatic feat, he did so *coram populo* in the open, and not, as was afterwards possible through enlarged conceptions, in building, within four walls.

In some lines which Henry Peacham, the author of "The Complete Gentleman," wrote, and which are prefixed to Coryat's "Crudities" (1611), the author glances at this delight of the people to flock to shows of all kinds:

> "Why doe the rude vulgar so hastily post in a madnesse
> To gaze at trifles, and toyes not worthy the viewing?
> And thinke them happy, when may be shew'd for a penny
> The Fleete-streete Mandrakes, that heavenly motion of Eltham
> Westminster Monuments, and Guildhall huge Corinæus," etc.

Peacham might have been more astonished still had he lived till the eighteenth century, and seen not merely the rude vulgar, but half the fashion of London, and no little of the intellect, with the burly Doctor amongst it, flocking to Cock Lane to hear the rappings of the very elusive ghost there. But even in his less sophisticated times he must have known that the bearded lady and the two-headed calf would be always capable of exciting interest and opening the eyes of amazed wonder.

We need not go so far back as his day, however, to trace the apostolic continuity of such things. It will be early enough to begin with the close of the seventeenth century, when we find a museum, with a coffee-house connected with it, being opened by one Salter, a barber, who inaugurated his enterprise in the year 1695, at the corner of Lawrence Street, Chelsea, whence he migrated to another dwelling on the west side of Danvers Street, and finally (and here he begins to interest us) to what is now No. 18 Cheyne Walk. At first the coffee-house rather overwhelmed the curiosities, although when Steele went to visit it, in 1709—a visit of which he has left a long description in No. 34 of *The Tatler*—his eye was "diverted by ten thousand gimcracks round the room and on the ceiling"; and how satirical he was about mine host's collection and description of his treasures, is evidenced by his remark that "he shows you a straw hat which I know to be made by Madge Peskad, within three miles of Bedford: 'It is Pontius Pilate's wife's chamber-maid's sister's hat.' "

However much rubbish he may have accumulated, and however largely he may have drawn on his imagination in his descriptions of his rareties, there is no doubt that Salter was no fool, and was besides a man who could count on trusty and important friends. His very title of Don Saltero was bestowed on him by one of these—Rear-Admiral Sir John Munden, who was living at Chelsea, after an active life, and, like many old sailors, had plenty of time on his hands, and perhaps no little credulity in his head. Another contributor to the museum was the father of Thomas Pennant, who presented the Don with a *"lignified hog,"* and who remembered seeing Richard Cromwell here. Sir John Cope was yet another visitor, and even Benjamin Franklin once made an expedition to see Saltero's curiosities. These were but a few of the patrons and but a thousandth part of the visitors who began to look upon Don Saltero's as one of the minor sights of London.

Saltero produced a printed catalogue of his collection, and those interested in what he had to exhibit, can there read for themselves a list of such a curious collocation of objects as surely has seldom before or since been brought together: from several pieces of the true Cross to a piece of a nun's skin; from a petrified mush-

T

room to the candle with which the Pope cursed the
heretics; from lace made from human hair to "the
Basilisk supposed to kill with his eyes." There were,
besides, many really interesting objects; but on the
whole the collection largely partook of that heterogeneous character which was likely to appeal to the
credulous. That the Don took every means in his
power to advertise his wares, is proved by entries in
contemporary newsheets where his *knackatory*, as one
paper calls it, was sometimes the subject not only of
prose but of poetical description.

Saltero claimed descent from the Tradescants, and
besides keeping a museum and a coffee-house, varied his
labours by writing verses and extracting teeth. Sloane,
whose valet Saltero had once been, when his collections
were moved from Bloomsbury to Chelsea, presented
some of his superfluities to his whilom servant; Smollett
added something, besides giving the museum an advertisement by referring to it in "Peregrine Pickle";
Theobald, the scholar, and Thoresby, the antiquary,
besides all sorts of less notable people, are known to
have visited the place, over whose door hung a green-
and-gold signboard; some to drink coffee, then something of a novelty in this country; some to wander,
open-mouthed, through the museum; the majority to
take the opportunity of doing both.

Don Saltero died in 1728, after which event his
daughter, a Mrs. Hall, carried on the place, until
about the time of George III.'s accession, when the
property passed into other hands. In 1799 the "collection," so vaunted by its first owner, so attractive to
Londoners as well as country cousins, was sold by
auction for £50! It is interesting to know that some
years later certain of the ornaments which had decorated
the Don's smoking-room were offered to Charles Lamb
by one of his fellow clerks in the East India Office.
"Don Saltero's," notwithstanding these changes, continued as a tavern for another half-century or more;

but in 1867 it was pulled down and a private house
was erected on its site.[1]

The Tradescant from whom, as we have seen,
Saltero claimed descent, was John of that name, who
lived in South Lambeth, in a building afterwards
known as Turret House, on whose site the Nine Elms
Brewery stands. Here he collected a vast accumulation
of curiosities of all sorts, which at his death, in 1637
(he was buried in St. Mary's, Lambeth, where there
is an altar-tomb to his memory), he left to Elias
Ashmole, the antiquary.[2] His museum was one of the
first of such private shows, and was frequently visited
by royal personages (Charles I. and Henrietta among
them) and by many people of distinction, and others.
Evelyn records going to see the collection on September 17, 1657; in which, he says, "the chief rarities
were, in my opinion, the ancient Roman, Indian, and
other nations' armour, shields, and weapons; some
habits of curiously-colour'd and wrought feathers . . .
and other innumerable things there were, printed in
his catalogue by Mr. Ashmole, to whom after the
death of the widow, they are bequeath'd, and by him
design'd as a gift to Oxford."

That this was a very different sort of collection
from that which Don Saltero assembled, is obvious,
and the latter had little right to claim a sort of succession to Tradescant, but it is interesting to record it
here as one of those haunts where pleasure and instruction went hand in hand, and which may be said
to have been one of the earliest examples of a *virtuoso*
throwing open his museum, more or less, for public
investigation.

Museums in themselves can hardly be described as

[1] For further details see Bryan's "Chelsea," Beaver's "Memorials of
Old Chelsea," and Mr. Reginald Blunt's fascinating "In Cheyne Walk
and Thereabout."

[2] They form part of the Ashmolean Museum, where may be seen
portraits of the Tradescant family, by Dobson.

haunts of pleasure *per se;* there is an air of too much powder being in the jam for that. At the same time they properly take their place among those forms of recreation of which such varied manifestations exist.

London has long been noted for such places, and it is only necessary briefly to mention the principal ones, because they are known to most people; and to do more would be here impossible.

The British Museum dates from the death, in 1753, of Sir Hans Sloane, who in his will offered the whole of his collections to the nation for the nominal sum of £20,000. The offer was accepted, and old Montague House, Bloomsbury, was secured for the accommodation of Sloane's accumulations, some £13,000 being expended on necessary reconstructions. It was first opened to the public on January 15, 1759, for only three hours a day; and then previous application for a ticket was necessary. The visitors were conducted round as they are in show-houses, only some sixty being admitted in a day; and even in 1808 this number was not more than doubled. Two years later, however, less drastic regulations came into force, and "any person of decent appearance who may apply between the hours of ten and two" was to be admitted without a ticket. A separate department for antiquities was established in consequence of the acquisition made of such things in 1801 and 1805; and this new building was opened in 1807. Nine years later the Elgin Marbles were exhibited for the first time, *in a wooden shed* erected for the purpose; and it was only in 1821, when George III.'s vast library was acquired, that the need for a new structure was found to be urgent. Sir Robert Smirke was commissioned to design the new (King's) Library, a portion of the scheme for rebuilding the whole place; although it was not till another twenty-four years had elapsed that old Montague House was demolished, and the Museum, approximately as we know it, completed; the great portico not being finished till 1847; while the Reading Room was not opened till juſt ten years later.

The Natural Hiſtory branch of the Museum, at South Kensington, ſtands, as do other ſtruĉtures of a like charaĉter, on the site of the Great Exhibition of 1862 buildings. It was designed by Alfred Waterhouse, and opened in 1880. Behind it ſtands the Imperial Inſtitute, the wonderful achievement of Thomas Col-cutt, the firſt ſtone of which was laid by Queen Viĉtoria, in 1887. It was opened some four years later, and apart from what is to be seen inside, is one of the fineſt buildings in London.

The Viĉtoria and Albert Museum, close by, is another landmark in this quarter where the memory of the Great Exhibition of 1851 seems to dwell. It was designed by Sir Aſton Webb, and opened in 1909. But as the South Kensington Museum, or the Brompton Boilers, as it was irreverently called, it has had a much longer hiſtory. It had, indeed, its genesis in that Museum of ornamental art which was eſtab-lished at Marlborough House, between the time of Queen Adelaide's death, in 1849, and the coming there of Edward, Prince of Wales, in 1861. It was opened by Queen Viĉtoria, in 1857; but was then but an inchoate mass of buildings, more permanent ones only being begun after the opening. The larger part of the original iron buildings was taken down in 1868 and re-ereĉted at Bethnal Green, where the Museum, which is but little known to those living in the Weſt, was opened in 1872, and where, besides certain peripatetic exhibitions (the National Portrait Gallery was once housed there), there is a permanent colleĉtion of much intereſt and value.

There are in London a variety of other lesser museums, of which one or two are so little known that they ought not to be overlooked in these pages. I would specially mention the Soane Museum, in Lin-coln's Inn Fields, because there may be seen a remark-

able collection of objects of all ages and in all *genres*,
sculpture, pictures, furniture, books, etc., practically
as they were in the time of their collector, whose
house was bequeathed to the nation to be kept in its
pristine state for all time.

Another little-known exhibition is the Geffrye
Museum in the Kingsland Road, whose furniture,
showing its gradual development in design and crafts-
manship, is to be seen, in the heart of the cabinet-
making district of London.

The Picture Galleries are equally pleasure haunts,
as may be realized by the numbers who are habitually
to be found in those places. Of them the National
Gallery is, of course, the most important; for in the
wealth of art it displays and the arrangement of the
pictures, it is second to none in the world, and, indeed,
in its comprehensiveness is perhaps unrivalled. It
originated in the purchase by the Government of the
Angerstein Collection, which was originally exhibited
in Pall Mall, in a house which stood on part of the
site of the Reform Club. The National Gallery (since
those days enlarged and reconstructed) was designed
by W. Wilkins, and occupied six years (1832–38) in
building; new rooms and wings being added in 1860,
1876, 1884, and so on.

The National Portrait Gallery, next door, was erected
from the designs of Ewan Christian, and here, after
wandering about in various places—29 Great George
Street; South Kensington; and Bethnal Green—the
remarkable collection of portraits of illustrious persons
which it contains, at last came to rest in a building
less unworthy of them than had been those temporary
abodes in which they for a time sought shelter.[1]

The other great national art repository is the Tate
Gallery, which occupies the site of Millbank Prison,
and which came into existence in 1897. It was given

[1] For an account of these galleries, and the almost unknown
Diploma Gallery, see the author's "Walks among London's Pictures."

to the nation by Sir Henry Tate, and was designed by Sidney R. J. Smith. So large was the wealth of British Art that awaited room here, that in 1899 it was found necessary to enlarge the Gallery.

Lastly there is that wondrous treasure-house, the Wallace Collection, occupying Hertford House, once the residence of the Marquis of Hertford, who continued the great assemblage of pictures and other works of art left by his father, and later of Sir Richard Wallace, who completed the great collection, and by whom it was left to the nation.

But this is in the nature of digression, which has led us into certain haunts which may by some be considered hardly as coming within the scope of this book. In any case it has carried us far away from Chelsea, to which I would return in order to say something about what was certainly a pleasure haunt, even if not one of the character of others dealt with in this chapter. The old Chelsea Bun House, which I here indicate, is *sui generis*, and has nothing in common with those pleasure gardens which are considered in another chapter.

In the British Museum there is a print entitled: "A Perspective View of Richard Hand's Bun House at Chelsey, who has the Honour to serve the Royal Family." It was situated in Grosvenor Row, and, as can be seen from the print, had a covered front 52 feet in length, supported by pillars extending half-way across the pavement, rather like the Pantiles, at Tunbridge Wells. Under that canopy walked, one day in the year 1712, a dark, rather formidable-looking man, in the clergyman's dress of the period; it was none other than Dr. Swift, come to buy a bun for a penny. He often walked past the Bun House when he was living in Church Lane hard by, and probably this was not a solitary instance of his regaling himself on what he describes in a letter to Stella as "r-r-r-r-r-r-rare Chelsea Buns."

Indeed the buns were famous far and wide for their "delicate flavour, lightness, and richness," and, apart from general prosaic description, rather wonderingly found themselves the subject of verse, in which they are apostrophized as

> O flour of the ovens ! a zephyr in paste !
> Fragrant as honey, and sweeter in taste!"

No wonder these things became a by-word with all classes; no wonder Sir Richard Phillips tells us he never passed the shop without filling his pockets with its delicacies; no wonder Royalty patronized Mr. Hand, who, on one occasion, told Phillips "with exultation, that George II. had often been a customer of the shop; that the present King, when Prince George, and often during his reign, had stopped and purchased his buns; and that the Queen and all the Princes and Princesses had been among his occasional customers."

Indeed the passion for the Chelsea buns became so widely spread that Bryan, in his account of this district, writes: "From my own personal observation I should say, provided the weather was favourable, there were generally, on Good Fridays,[1] nearly 200,000 people collected in the immediate neighbourhood." It was a fair to all intents and purposes. In the "Five Fields"[2] there were drinking-booths, swings, ginger-bread stalls, nine-pins being played, gaming, and "all the other vicious entertainments, which disgraced the metropolis in former times"; while as late as 1829, 240,000 buns are said to have been sold on Good Friday!

There is no doubt that the Bun House was a pleasure haunt; the objective which made a jaunt out of London worth while. In addition, too, to the buns, there was a

[1] In Smith's "Book for a Rainy Day" is given an advertisement dated March 27, 1793, in which Mrs. Hand makes known her determination not to sell Hot Cross Buns in future, owing to the vast concourse which assembled on Good Fridays.

[2] Where Belgrave Square and its surrounding streets and squares are now.

kind of museum in the house, which Sir Richard Phillips[1] describes as being intended to rival Don Saltero's. But if the examples of its exhibits which he gives were the most prominent he could think of, it must have been but a poor show compared with that in Cheyne Walk. "The bottle-conjuror in a toy of his own age; portraits of Duke William (of Cumberland) and other noted personages; a model of a British soldier in the stiff costume of the same age; and some grotto-works," may, indeed, as he says, "serve to indicate the taste of a former owner"; but are not otherwise particularly exhilarating or interesting. After having afforded an ample competency to four generations of the Hand family, the Bun House was demolished, and the materials and contents sold by auction on April 18, 1839; the objects in the museum going for a few shillings each.

Close by, indeed only separated by one house, another establishment of somewhat the same character arose, called the Old Oakley Bunhouse, where 52 Pimlico Road is now; but it never seems to have had any special popularity; certainly it never approached in this respect "the old original."

The Chelsea Bun House, at least in its capacity as a quasi-museum, justifies its inclusion in this place; but a contemporary museum, in another part of the town, more properly deserved the name. I refer to Sir Ashton Lever's collection of objects of natural history, to which its owner gave the rather horrific name of the Holophusicon, but which the mere man called the Leverian Museum, in Leicester Square.

Sir Ashton Lever, the eldest son of Sir Darcey Lever, of Alkrington, near Manchester, had been interested in natural history from his youth, and in the course of years had assembled a remarkable collection of natural curiosities. It having occurred to him that he might turn his hobby to a profitable

[1] "A Walk from London to Kew," 1817.

account, he hired Leicester House, and converted it
into a museum, in 1771; and some years after opened
it to the public. He is said to have expended no less
than £50,000 on the project, but to have received in
return, from visitors, only £13,000. In course of time
he was obliged to petition Parliament to allow him to
organize a lottery for his museum, and in one of the
affidavits necessary, his manager, Thomas Waring,
stated that the collection "had occupied twelve years
in forming; and that there were upwards of twenty-six
thousand articles. That the money received for admission, from February 1775 to February 1784, amounted
to about £13,000, out of which £660 had been paid
for house rent and taxes." The collection was then
valued at £53,000. As a result Lever was authorized
to issue 36,000 guinea tickets, of which one was to
entitle the holder to the whole museum. Only 8000
tickets were, however, sold, and the winner was a
Mr. Parkinson. Dr. Johnson had favoured a scheme
for the purchase of the collection by the nation; but
this came to nothing.[1]

During Lever's ownership, his museum was open,
in two galleries extending the whole length of Leicester
House, every day from ten to four, admission being
5s. 3d. each person.[2] When, however, Parkinson became
possessed of it, he removed it to the Rotunda, in Albion
Place, at the south end of Blackfriars Bridge, which
he had built for its reception, and where it was for a
time exhibited as the "Museum Leverianum." It was,
however, never a success; and in 1806 the entire
contents were sold by auction, the sale occupying no
fewer than sixty-five days, there being 7879 lots,
among which were the curiosities collected by Captain
Cook during his voyages.

Sir Ashton Lever had died suddenly at Manchester,

[1] See Smith's "Book for a Rainy Day," with valuable notes by Mr.
Wilfred Whitten.
[2] Advertisement in the *Morning Post*, for November 16, 1778.

in 1788; and so was spared the grief of seeing his beloved accumulations dispersed far and wide. Those who seek pleasure under very different conditions from such as the Holophusicon afforded, do so approximately on the spot where the latter was once displayed, when they visit the Empire Music Hall.

Next door to Lever's Museum stood Savile House, and this was let out for entertainments and exhibitions; and it was here that were shown, during the course of many years, those remarkable examples of Miss Linwood's needlework pictures, one of which may, to-day, be seen in the Victoria and Albert Museum. At first Miss Linwood had shown her work at the Hanover Square Rooms, but it is with Leicester Square that she is chiefly identified. In 1830 the charge for admission was two shillings, sixpence being demanded for a catalogue; and that this exhibition was then regarded as one of the "sights" of London, is proved by its being prominently included in the list of such things given in Coghlan's "The Cicerone, or Fashionable Guide to all places of Public Amusement," for that year. In that curious and scarce little publication is a list of those panoramas, dioramas, and the rest which so greatly appealed to our forbears during the earlier years of the last century. Of these Barker's, later *Burford's Panorama* is perhaps the best remembered; and it appropriately takes its place here, as it was also in Leicester Square for a time; although, later, it was removed to 169 Strand, where it remained till 1831, when the premises it there occupied were converted by Rayner into the Strand Theatre.[1] The Panorama was at the north-east corner of Leicester Square, and occupied the site of the Feathers Inn (so called because of the residence of Frederick, Prince of Wales, at Leicester House, close by), forming, indeed, a portion of the Sans Souci

[1] Diprose's "Account of St. Clement's Danes." The author speaks of the Panorama being removed from the Strand to Leicester Square.

Theatre, erected by Dibdin in 1793. Robert Barker had apparently earlier exhibited his Panorama at No. 28 Haymarket, where, in March 1789, was first shown his great painting of Edinburgh, originally exhibited in that city. Notwithstanding the doubts of Sir Joshua Reynolds, its success in London was immediate, for nothing quite like it had been seen before. After three years Burford appears to have migrated to No. 28 Castle Street, Leicester Square, where he opened his new premises with a panorama of "London and Westminster, comprehending the three bridges, from the top of the late Albion Mill." But it was in 1793 that he came into Leicester Square itself, although he for a time kept open the exhibition in Castle Street. The new building consisted of three circles, the largest being 90 feet in diameter and 40 feet in height, and it was opened with a "View of the Grand Fleet moored off Spithead in the year 1791." Three years later, the subject was "The Glorious First of June," in the preparation of which technical details were supplied by various naval officers who had taken part in Lord Howe's victory. "Since then," says Tom Taylor, "every war by sea and land, every scene of interesting incident or discovery, every locality of special natural beauty, every great public ceremonial, has been illustrated in this ingenious pictorial invention, till the other day, when the Panorama buildings disappeared in the architectural changes of the neighbourhood."[1]

A list which Taylor gives of the various exhibitions from 1823 to 1858, prove the correctness of his remarks; they range from the Coronation of George IV., and a view of Pompeii, in the former year, to one of Delhi and Sierre Leone, in the latter, and there appear, indeed, to have been few places or events of importance or interest which did not receive pictorial treatment at the hands of the versatile showman.

[1] "Leicester Square, its Associations and its Worthies."

It was, indeed, Barker who was the protagonist of Burford's, for he ran it till his death in 1806, when he was succeeded by his son, on whose retirement his pupil, John Burford, carried it on, to be followed by *his* son, Robert Burford, who died in 1861. At some time before this it might have seemed that the Panorama had been transferred again to the Strand, for in 1830 it is described as being there, "open daily from ten till dusk, with popular views. Admittance, one shilling."[1] Yet Tallis[2] shows it still in Leicester Square with the words Rome and Malta over the doorway, views of which places were exhibited there in 1839. As a matter of fact Burford was running the two simultaneously, as Barker had previously done, that in Leicester Square being still under the old name; that in the Strand under the new.

Leicester Square, which has ever been a home of amusement and pleasure haunts, once contained one of the latter in its very centre, for that formerly derelict spot, which was converted into its present bust-studded enclosure, and where Shakespeare stands in rather an alien environment, was once filled by the great Globe which Wyld, the Royal geographer, evolved, and which was for long an object of interest to sightseers.

It was in the Great Exhibition year of 1851, that this immense structure, designed by Abrahams, and filling up practically the whole of the centre of the Square, came into existence. The Globe was sixty feet in diameter, and was surrounded by four large rooms for exhibition purposes. The world was figured in relief on the inside, and could be viewed from galleries of varying elevation; while the spectator was examining it, hourly descriptive lectures were given; so that it was as much educational as pictorial. For ten years this structure existed, what time it was the home

[1] Coghlan's "Cicerone," 1830.
[2] "London Street Views," *circa* 1839.

of all sorts of historical, ethnological, and other exhibitions; there were dioramas of the gold-fields, with collections of Australian gold and casts of monster nuggets; there was a vast model of Sebastopol; there was Marshall's series of forty-nine tableaux illustrating the progressive steps from Blackwall to Balaclava; indeed anything that for the time bulked largely in the public eye was reconstructed and pictorially illustrated inside Wyld's Great Globe; and always was there the learned gentleman who lectured on the the subject in hand.

At one time the Globe threatened to become the centre of a still more systematized form of educational enterprise, and some daring spirits even projected a "Cosmos Institute," which was to be "a universal ethnological museum and centre of instruction and intercommunication for all classes and races"; but this, rather mercifully, one thinks, came to nothing; Leicester Square, with such a solemn institution in its midst, would hardly have known itself.

In 1861 Wyld had to take down his structure according to an agreement with the Tulks, the ground landlords, who had the right to re-purchase, and with whom a condition had been made that at the end of ten years the ground should be restored free of buildings.

In the little guide to which I have already referred, the Diorama in the Regent's Park, the Cosmorama in Regent Street, and the Appollonicon in St. Martin's Lane, are given as among those forms of public amusement with which the budding nineteenth century diverted itself. The first was situated on the east side of Park Square, Regent's Park, was designed by Morgan and Pugin, and erected in the remarkably short space of time of four months, at a cost of £10,000. It was constructed to hold the Diorama, invented by Bouton and Daguerre, which had already been exhibited in Paris, and was first opened on October 6, 1823.

WYLD'S GREAT GLOBE
LEICESTER SQUARE
1851

Timbs gives a very full and technical description of the details of this novelty, which I spare the reader, who, if he desires, can find it set forth in an easily procurable work.[1] It is sufficient to say that it consisted of two immense pictures, 80 feet long by 40 high, "painted in solid and in transparence, arranged so as to exhibit changes of light and shade, and a variety of natural phenomena." The spectators sat in a circular chamber which revolved on a pivot, so as to bring each scene successively in view. The first picture exhibited was the interior of Canterbury Cathedral, and a companion picture represented the valley of Sarnen.

Like all novelties, the Diorama at first had a great success, and on the Easter Monday of 1824 the receipts exceeded £200, which was then regarded as remarkable. Every year new pictures were exhibited, and as the venture went on for some fifteen years, it could hardly be called a failure; yet it was, commercially if not artistically; and in 1848, the building was sold, although it was still carried on as a Diorama. In the following year, however, this came to an end, and the sixteen pictures on their cylinders were disposed of for £3000, for use probably in some of the many other exhibitions of the kind which were then, for a time at least, so popular.[2]

The Cosmorama was at Nos. 207 and 209 Regent Street, and was open from ten to four, admittance being one shilling. It was but a rather outstanding form of many such at this period. For instance, one was in the Lowther Arcade (where Messrs. Coutts's Bank is now), where the "Magic Cave," as it was called, produced for a time £1500 a year at sixpence admission. In 1828, too, a similar "show" was at the Queen's Bazaar, in Oxford Street. Curiously enough, it was here that, at an exhibition of a picture repre-

---

[1] "The Curiosities of London," by John Timbs.
[2] The Regent's Park Baptist Chapel, built by John Thomas, the architect, for Sir Morton Peto, stands on the site of the Diorama.

senting " The Destruction of York Minster by Fire,"
on May 28, the scenery caught fire and the place
was entirely burnt out. Even into St. James's
Street has the Diorama penetrated, for at the Bazaar
there which Crockford built, and which has been put
in turn to so many uses, "five large scenes" depicting
the second Funeral of Napoleon were exhibited in
1841. Notwithstanding that these pictures were
painted by members of "The Board of Arts for the
Ceremony," whatever that body may have been, and
the exhibition accompanied by funeral music composed
by Auber, it was not a success. Eight years later another
somewhat similar exhibition was opened at "The
Gallery of Illustration," as it was called, being really
the large room in Nash's old house in Lower Regent
Street, consisting of a series of thirty-one dioramic
pictures of the overland route from Southampton to
Calcutta; the scenery of which was painted by T.
Grieve and W. Telbin, the figures by Absolon, and
the animals by Herring and Harrison Weir. This is
said to have been on the whole one of the most successful of such things ever shown in this country, and no
fewer than a quarter of a million people visited it on
the 1600 to 1700 times it was opened to the public.

But, after all, these things were such as were
exhibited in existing buildings, and unlike the Barker's
and Burford's Panorama, or the Diorama in the
Regent's Park, could not boast homes of their own.
Of the latter, the largest was *The Colosseum*, also in
the Regent's Park, an immense circular building
which Decimus Burton designed for Mr. Horner, a
land-surveyor, which was built in 1824–26. It was
a most ambitious structure, in form not unlike the
Pantheon at Rome, and its chief internal object of
interest was the vast panoramic view of London from
the top of St. Paul's, which Horner projected and
began, and Mr. E. T. Parris completed. The structure
measured 126 feet in diameter and was covered by a
dome; on its west side was a Doric portico whose

columns were exactly the same size as those of the
Pantheon. Besides the Panorama there was a Hall of
Mirrors, a Gothic aviary (they revelled in sham
Gothic at this period), and Stalactite Caves; while
the grounds were filled with artificial ruins, and the
scenery of Mont Blanc, which could be viewed from
the windows of a Swiss Châlet, in which "the illusion
is not a little enhanced by the prospect consisting of
terrific rocks and caverns," as Coghlan, who writes
in a rapture about the whole place, tells us;[1] and he
says elsewhere that "this undertaking is one of the
most gigantic enterprises for public gratification
that has ever been attempted in this country."

Whether the original proprietors found that its
success was commensurate with this immense outlay
or not, it is certain that they took early steps to dispose
of it, for in 1831 Messrs. Braham and Yates purchased
it for £40,000; and carried it on for some years. In
1843, however, it was sold again, this time to a Mr.
D. Montague, at the reduced price of 23,000 guineas;
and it was probably under the *ægis* of the new proprietor that a vast panorama of Paris was added to its
attractions, and one of the Lisbon earthquake was
shown in an adjoining building.[2]

After this the place remained closed for a time, when
Dr. Bachhoffner opened it in 1857, at the charge of
one shilling a head—it had formerly cost two shillings
to see part and five shillings to view the whole. The
Doctor carried it on for six years, when Mr. George
Buckland took it, in 1863; but it must have been even
then in a moribund state, for we hear of it being
closed in the same year. And so it remained empty,
till it was pulled down in 1875, and houses were
erected on its site. That others besides the enthusiastic
Coghlan admired at least its appearance, is proved
by the fact that Samuel Rogers once asserted that it was

[1] "The Cicerone or Fashionable Guide," etc.
[2] See the "Description of the Colosseum—re-opened in 1845,"
dated 1848.

U

"finer than anything among the remains of architectural art in Italy"; which, with all due deference to Decimus Burton, must, one thinks, have been "*said* sarcastic."

In our own time there was a slight recrudescence of the Panorama fever; and, near St. James's Park Station in a building, generally known as "Niagara," afterwards converted into one of London's many skating rinks, was one of these representing, if I remember aright, "The Charge of the Light Brigade at Balaclava." There were others, too, but they all had a more or less short and undistinguished career, and they served to show that the public, even if for a short time it could be galvanized into taking an interest in such things, did so inasmuch as they were novelties, and for no other reason.

I mentioned earlier "The Appollonicon," which is given as one of the shows of the London of 1830. This was a musical instrument "performing by its mechanical powers the most celebrated Overtures, Songs, Duets, Glees, etc."; and which was exhibited at No. 101 St. Martin's Lane, from one till four daily at an admittance charge of one shilling.

Mechanical devices do not greatly excite this generation, which has grown used to them in their most extended manifestations; but our less sophisticated forbears were much intrigued even by a mechanical organ; in which direction Imhoff and Mukle and others were destined further to surprise them. What they would have said to pianolas and such marvellous contrivances, baffles imagination.

But there are some forms of amusement in which we, to-day, are as much intrigued as were our fathers, and one of these is that perennial form of mystification which was once wondered at in the Egyptian Hall, and to-day attracts its equally fascinated crowds in Langham Place.

At one time *The Egyptian Hall* was as much a feature of this part of Piccadilly as was the St. James's

Restaurant (the "Jimmy's" of our youth) and the adjoining St. James's Hall. It was erected, in 1812, for Mr. William Bullock, of Liverpool, for the reception of the museum he had assembled,[1] and was designed with a frontage covered with Egyptian hieroglyphics by the architect, P. F. Robinson. It is said to have cost £30,000, and, like so many of the exhibitions at this period, it was intended to combine amusement with instruction. A contemporary account of the place will indicate its character: "This museum contains curiosities not only from Africa, but from North and South America, amphibious animals in great variety, with fishes, insects, shells, zoophytes, minerals, etc., *ad infinitum*, besides the Pantherion intended to display the whole of the known quadrupeds, in a state of preservation hitherto unattempted. For this purpose the visitor is introduced through a basaltic cavern, similar to the Giant's Causeway, or Fingal's Cave, in the Isle of Staffa, to an Indian hut. This hut is situated in a tropical forest, in which most of the quadrupeds described by naturalists are to be seen, with models from nature of the trees and other vegetable productions of the torrid climes."[2]

Some success attended the exhibition, but it was nothing to the excitement caused when Napoleon's travelling carriage, captured at Waterloo, was purchased by Bullock, and shown here, no fewer than 800,000 people paying for admission to see it.[3] Bullock's Museum continued till 1819, when it was sold for nearly £10,000, which was but a third of its original cost.

After its departure the Egyptian Hall was used for a variety of entertainments and exhibitions, among the latter of which may be noted Belzoni's

[1] Till 1805, this had been exhibited at Astley's Amphitheatre.
[2] Hughson's "Walks in London," 2 vols., 1817.
[3] It was afterwards in Madame Tussaud's. Before Bullock bought it, it had been kept at Carlton House, and afterwards at the King's Mews, where the National Gallery is now.

Model of the Pyramids,[1] in 1821; Haydon's "Mock Election," which George IV. eventually purchased for 800 guineas, in 1828; The Siamese Twins, in the following year;[2] Catlin's North American Gallery, in 1841; Sir George Hayter's picture of "The First Reformed Parliament," in 1843; and in 1845, The Eureka, a machine for composing Latin hexameters, of all things.

In the following year one of the most notable shows took place here, when General Tom Thumb exhibited himself. In another room, at the same time, were hanging two of Haydon's vast classical canvases, "The Burning of Rome" and "The Banishment of Aristides," and readers of the painter's Diary will remember his anger at what he calls "an insanity, a *rabies*, a madness, a *furor*": and how, later, he writes : "Tom Thumb had 12,000 last week, B. R. Haydon 133½ (the ½ a little girl). Exquisite taste of the English people."[3] Nor was the Egyptian Hall without its panoramas, and, in 1848, the first *moving* specimen of them, "Banvard's" "Mississippi," was shown here; to be followed, in 1850, by Frémont's "Overland Route to California," and Bonomi's "Nile."

Among the entertainments were those given by Albert Smith, who described his famous "Ascent of Mont Blanc" to crowded audiences, in 1852, and afterwards his Chinese travels, although not with a like success. Many years after, in 1866 to be precise, Artemus Ward made many laugh over his adventures among the Mormons. Later still picture exhibitions, including that of Lord Dudley's magnificent collection, were held here, and had been anticipated, in 1820, when Géricault's "Wreck of the *Medusa*," now in the Louvre, was exhibited here.

1 With this was shown the marvellous sarcophagus which Sir John Soane eventually purchased, and which is now to be seen in his Museum in Lincoln's Inn Fields.

2 They appeared here again in 1869.

3 "Diary of Benjamin Robert Haydon."

To modern generations, however, the Egyptian Hall was solely identified with the marvels of Messrs. Maskelyne and Cook's contriving, when the Hall of Mystery (which had been originally designed by J. B. Papworth) drew its crowded audiences. For many years the Egyptian Hall was one of the regulation places to which youngsters "home for the holidays" were taken by children of an older growth, only too pleased for the excuse of being mystified and delighted themselves.

In course of time the Egyptian Hall, whose well-known façade had been for so long a feature of Piccadilly (it is shown in one of Boys's exquisite lithographs) was demolished, and new buildings (it stood just opposite Bond Street) erected on its site; and Messrs. Maskelyne and Cook's wonders, later to become Maskelyne and Devant's, removed to Langham Place, where they have now been so long and successfully established; a spot to which those German Reid's entertainments, dear also to childhood, went after they, too, had once occupied the old Egyptian Hall.

I have incidentally mentioned "*Madame Tussaud's;*" and Madame Tussaud's cannot be overlooked in any account of the London pleasure haunts, for it has taken a permanent position among these, and appears to be as popular now as it was in its earlier days.[1]

Waxwork exhibitions have always been a source of amusement to the public, and in earlier days the figures of the kings and other illustrious ones, in this medium, shown at the Abbey, were among the recognized sights of the metropolis. They had their origin in the ancient custom of making a wax effigy of an illustrious deceased person, dressed in state robes, and placing it over the tomb as a temporary monument. Many of them were both elaborate and costly, and were often made by

---

[1] Since this was written, Madame Tussaud's has been burnt out. Little escaped the fire, which gutted the place on the night of March 18, 1925. No doubt it will re-open in course of time, but the unrivalled collection of Napoleonic relics are gone forever. I have left unaltered what I had written before the catastrophe occurred.

artists in this direction, that of La Belle Stuart (the Countess de Grammont) being contrived by Mr. Goldsmith. We know that in the seventeenth century it was customary for the vergers of the Abbey to show these effigies "to the meaner sort of peoples, who then flock thither from all the corners of the town, and pay their twopence to see 'The Play of the Dead Volks,' as I have heard a Devonshire clown most improperly call it."[1] It became the custom at the death of a monarch to add a waxwork representation of him to the collection, and among the rather dilapidated examples which still exist may be seen a well-known one of Charles II., cheek by jowl with those of Lord Chatham and Lord Nelson, which appear to have been added because it was found a more or less profitable and popular method of increasing the sums collected by such means. The regular exhibition of these figures was discontinued in 1830, since when they could only be seen by special permission.

Whether or not this show gave the hint for private enterprise is a moot question; but it is certain that Mrs. Salmon, whose remarkable handiwork was as famous in the eighteenth century[2] as Madame Tussaud's was in the nineteenth and is now, made the thing popular to a remarkable degree. Mrs. Salmon had first opened her "show" in Aldersgate, and later moved it to a house "near the Horn Tavern" (now Anderton's Hotel) in Fleet Street. The sign over the door was appropriately a "Golden Salmon," and within could be seen, according to one of her handbills: "Mrs. Salmon's wax-work—Royal Court of England—the Moving Wax-work—140 figures as big as life. All made by Mrs. Salmon, who sells all sorts of moulds and glass eyes, and teaches the full art, etc."

This energetic and clever lady died at the age of

---

[1] Dr. Pope, in his "Life of Seth. Ward," 1697.

[2] There are several references to it in *The Spectator*, as well, of course, as in contemporary newspapers, in the form of advertisements, etc.

ninety, in 1760, and the collection was then purchased
by a surgeon, living in Chancery Lane, named Clark,
who continued to exhibit it, as did his widow. In 1788,
new premises were taken at 189 Fleet Street, where
Praed's Bank was to be later, and in 1795, when this
house was demolished, Mr. Clark moved to that
historic building, No. 17 Fleet Street, where the
Fountain Tavern was then situated; and it seems
probable that this tavern continued to occupy one
portion of the premises and the wax-works the other.

A description of the wax-works, by one who remembered them,[1] tells us that they were shown by lamp-
light, and were placed in upstairs rooms. In the first,
royal personages of the court of George III. (including
the King and Queen Charlotte) with Mr. Pitt and Mr.
Fox as political supporters, were to be seen, as well as
General Wolfe, Dr. Johnson, the Duke of Devonshire,
Abercromby and Nelson. There, too, was that unfortunate person, Theodore, King of Corsica, who is buried
in St. Anne's, Soho, and for whom Horace Walpole
wrote his well-known epitaph. In another room were
exhibited such a heterogeneous collection as Dr. Dodd
and General Pichegru, Kemble and John Wilkes, Mrs.
Siddons and Dick Turpin and "Old Q"; while in yet
a third apartment was a large pastoral scene with shep-
herds and shepherdesses "making violent love," says
"Aleph," "in a mode scarcely proper, according to our
politer notions."

After Mr. Clark's death in 1812, the whole set of
figures was sold to a Mr. James Templeman for under
£50; and they were then moved to a house at the corner
of Water Lane, where Tompion, the celebrated watch-
maker, had once had his shop. In 1827 thieves broke
in, and besides stealing some money, despoiled the
figures of the more decorative portion of their dresses,
and added insult to injury by smashing most of their
heads. However, they were repaired, and continued to

---

[1] "Aleph," who wrote his reminiscences in the City Press during
the 1850's.

be exhibited till 1831, when they were sold for what they would fetch, under a distraint for rent.

I may mention a sort of rival to Mrs. Salmon's wax-works, which was also situated in Fleet Street. This was *Rackstrow's Museum of Anatomy and Curiosities*, which was shown in a fine old house built before the Great Fire and situated four doors west of Chancery Lane.[1] It must have been rather an educational haunt, however, than a pleasure resort, for its aim was to tell people all about themselves and their internal organs, and one of its handbills informs us that "the circulation of the blood in imitated . . . also the action of the Heart and motion of the Lungs . . . the whole making a most wonderful and beautiful appearance." But this was not all, for Bamford, the giant, and Coan, the dwarf, were shown in effigy; as were the mummy of Pharaoh's daughter, the skeleton of a whale over 70 feet long—and a wax-work model of his Majesty, King George the Second! Rackstrow died in his Fleet Street abode in 1772, and his museum was then sold by auction. The London Museum, and Edward Donovan's Collection of Natural History which followed here, did not prove a success.

Fleet Street was once notable for its exhibitions of all sorts, from the "new motion of the City of Nineveh, with Jonah and the whale, at Fleet Bridge,"[2] and "The Fleet Street Mandrakes," which were to be seen for a penny, to the moving pictures, fire-eaters, "monstrous creatures" of Queen Anne's time, and the famous "Naumachia, or Battle of the Nile," which received "the applause of overflowing audiences," in that of George III.[3]

From Fleet Street to the Marylebone Road is a long way, but we have arrived there at last, in front of that

---

[1] "Fleet Street in Seven Centuries," by Walter Bell.

[2] Mentioned thus by Ben Jonson in his "Every Man in his Humour."

[3] For a list of these minor exhibitions, "raree-shows," and so forth, see Noble's "Memorials of Temple Bar," 1869.

large red-brick building in which Madame Tussaud's amazing collection is housed. From its original home is a longer way still, for it was inaugurated in Paris, in the Boulevard du Temple, in 1780, and was first exhibited in London in 1802, at that home for the derelict, the Lyceum Theatre. Where most of us remember it in our youth was, however, in the Baker Street Bazaar, where it was one of London's "sights" for many years. It was in 1884 that the present building was erected by Mr. W. H. Williams, from the designs of Mr. F. W. Hunt, for the reception of the figures whose numbers had far outgrown their earlier home in the Baker Street, which Thackeray so cordially disliked and which Mr. Sherlock Holmes and Mr. Pitt have made famous. One of the architectural features of the new building was the white marble staircase which came from Baron Albert Grant's great palace at Kensington, when that structure was demolished to make way for Kensington Court, in 1882.[1] But apart from such things and the wax figures, which, as everyone knows, range from the earliest days down to the last famous statesman or murderer (the Chamber of Horrors is an awful place, though not, I think, so blood-curdling as some of the things in the Musée Grèvin), the collection of historic objects here is remarkable, and the Napoleonic legend receives its apotheosis in the rooms where the relics of the great man, collected from all parts, reconstruct in some way for us that amazing career. Madame Tussaud, who was a niece of a certain M. Curtius, a modeller in wax, and who, indeed, taught his niece the art, was born in Berne in 1760, and died in London in 1850. There is a legend that she is buried in Wargrave Churchyard, but I, who happen to know that place well, have never been able to discover her grave.

[1] Grant's mansion was called Kensington House, and was built on the site of two picturesque old residences known as Colby House and Kensington House, and on part of a wretched quarter called Jenning's Buildings.

CHAPTER XII

ALMACK'S

ALTHOUGH in its later incarnation Almack's assumed a character unlike that of any such association which can be named, its origin and intention were at first not widely different from those of such places as the Pantheon and Mrs. Cornelys's assemblies; and if at the beginning of the nineteenth century it became famous for its ultra-exclusiveness, its earlier years were not specially notable in this respect. It was, indeed, started with an idea of being a profitable form of catering to the general desire for amusement; and from being a private enterprise it developed into a tribunal from whose fiats there was no appeal, and which, indeed, for many years ruled social and fashionable London with a rod of iron, exercising a tyranny beside which that of Czars and Sultans seemed a mild and benevolent sway.

We have already seen how Mrs. Cornelys started her assemblies in 1761, and we have also seen how, from their early days, these *réunions* earned a bad name and were looked at askance by many who, from their birth and position, would naturally have had the right of *entrée* to them.

One of those to recognize that profit could be made out of an establishment that should be select and decent, was one Macall, a Scotsman, who had married a lady's-maid of the Duchess of Hamilton, and had come to London to make his fortune. Owing to the unpopularity of the Scots at that time, in London—an unpopularity largely owing to Lord Bute's maladministration

—Macall inverted his name and duly blossomed forth as Almack. By the year 1763 he had already started that successful club which at first went by his name, but was soon after to become far more famous as Brooks's.

That club had been inaugurated under very distinguished patronage, and the Dukes of Roxburghe and Portland, Lord Strathmore, Mr. Crewe, and the "Man of the People" himself, were closely interested in its welfare. Counting, then, on such co-operation in a different direction, Almack looked about for a site on which to erect the Assembly Rooms he had in his mind; and this site he found in King Street, St. James's. No more ideal position could have been secured than that in a street linking up London's most fashionable thoroughfare with its most aristocratic square.

In 1764 the erection of the new rooms began on a site just east of Pall Mall Place, Robert Mylne being the builder employed. One of the earliest people to mention the new scheme, in a letter, is Mrs. Harris, who, writing on April 5, 1764, to her son, afterwards Earl of Malmesbury, remarks that "Almack is going to build most magnificent rooms behind his house (*i.e.* his club-house in Pall Mall), one much larger than at Carlisle House."

This reference to Mrs. Cornelys's establishment is significant, for, as a matter of fact, her rooms were the one centre on which society was then dependent for its indoor amusements, anywhere within proximity to its abodes, Ranelagh being so far away. A contest for supremacy was bound to occur when Almack's new structure should be ready for use: he relying for success on his larger rooms, more central position and, above all, on the novelty; she banking on a strong and loyal *clientèle*, on her known excellence of management, and the beauty of her rooms and, perhaps, also on the fact that there was an air of rakishness about her assemblies which was very attractive to some, and not apparently

displeasing even to the wives of great Church dignitaries. But Almack, besides the advantages he had,
exhibited his acumen by what was really a masterly
stroke : he placed the conduct of his rooms in the hands
of a committee of ladies of high rank, and made it an
immutable rule that the only chance of admission was
by vouchers or by the personal introduction of one of
these patronesses. This was, indeed, to kill two birds
with one stone; for it not only gave some of the most
influential members of society a personal and almost
despotic influence in the management of the place, but
it also furnished an added zest to those anxious to get
in, when it was recognized that the difficulty of admission was only to be equalled by the *kudos* to be gained
by being admitted.

On February 12, 1765, Almack's opened its doors;
but in spite of the presence of a royal Duke, and much
preliminary *réclame*, not under the most favourable
conditions; certainly with little promise of the unequi-
vocal success the venture was destined to achieve.
Walpole was not present, but he managed, as usual, to
learn all about it at once; and only two days later
we find him telling Lord Hertford that: "The new
Assembly Rooms at Almack's was opened the night
before last, and they say is very magnificent, but it was
empty; half the town is ill with colds and many were
afraid to go, as the house is scarcely built yet. Almack
advertised that it was built with hot bricks and boiling
water; think what a rage there must be for public
places if this notice, instead of terrifying, could draw
everybody thither. They tell me the ceilings were
dripping with wet; but can you believe me when I
assure you that the Duke of Cumberland was there?
nay, had a levée in the morning and went to the opera
before the Assembly. There is a vast flight of steps, and
he was forced to rest two or three times. When he
dies of it—and how should he not?—it will sound very
silly, when Hercules or Theseus ask him what he died

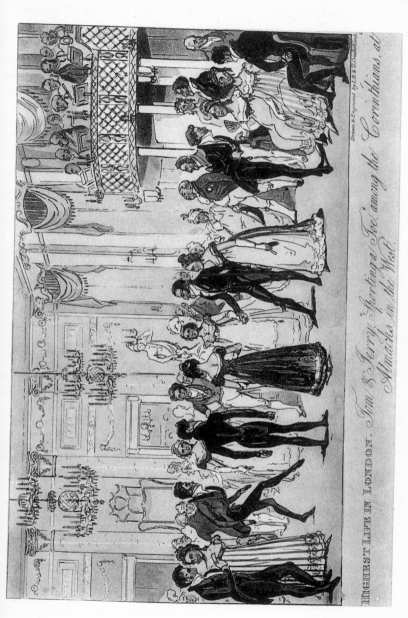

HIGHEST LIFE IN LONDON. *Tom & Jerry "Sporting a Toe," among the Corinthians, at Almacks in the West.*

Drawn & Engraved by I.R & G.Cruikshank.

ALMACK'S ASSEMBLY ROOMS

ABOUT 1810

of, to reply, ' I caught my death on a damp ſtaircase at a new club-room.' "[1]

We get more precise details of the new Assembly Rooms from a letter of Gilly Williams to George Selwyn, dated February 22, 1765.[2] "There is now opened at Almack's," says the writer, "in three very elegant new-built rooms, a ten-guinea subscription, for which you have a ball and a supper once a week for twelve weeks. You may imagine by the sum, the company is chosen; though, refined as it is, it will be scarce able to put old Soho out of countenance. The men's tickets are not transferable, so, if the ladies do not like us, they have no opportunity of changing us, but muſt see the same persons for ever."

The success of Almack's, notwithſtanding its rather ill-omened inauguration, was inſtant and undoubted. In a letter, written in the following March, Gilly Williams is able to ſtate that "it flourishes beyond description," and he adds, "If you had such a thing in Paris, you would fill half a quire of flourished paper with the description of it. Almack's Scotch face, in a bag-wig, waiting at supper, would divert you, as would his lady in a sack, making tea and curtseying to the duchesses."

Nor was Almack's prosperity confined to the early days of its career, when, as a novelty, it might be expected to attract a society avid for anything new. The letters of the period are full of references to its ever-increasing popularity, and three years after its opening Selwyn is able to tell Lord Carlisle that it was "very full," and to give the names of some of the illuſtrious ones who frequented it; the Duke of Cumberland (not, of course, the "Butcher of Culloden," whom we have seen at its opening, but the dissipated younger brother of George III), the famous Duchess of Gordon and the beautiful Lady Almeria Carpenter,

---

[1] The Duke did actually die on the following October 31.
[2] It is quoted in Jesse's "George Selwyn and his Contemporaries."

among them. The Lady Sarah, with whom Selwyn says the Duke was dancing cotillions, was Lady Sarah Lennox, for whom the King had sighed in vain. The Duchess of Gordon, one of Pitt's few intimate friends and "one of the empresses of fashion," as Walpole calls her, stood in relation to the Tory party in somewhat the same position as the Duchess of Devonshire did to the Whigs.

Selwyn's letter is otherwise interesting, as it mentions "a new blue damask room" at Almack's, which was intended for cards, but was used on ball nights for dancing; and I think it probable that it was the creation of this that induced Mrs. Cornelys to hang one of *her* apartments with blue satin, as a sort of counter-blast.

In February, Selwyn has another reference to Almack's: "Lady Sarah," he says, "is in town, and I suppose very happy with the thoughts of a mascarade which we are to have next Monday seven-night, unless in the interim some violent opposition comes from the Bishops." This last paragraph was prophetic; and ten days later (February 26) Selwyn informs Lord Carlisle that "the Bishops have, as I apprehended that they would, put a stop to our masquerade, for which I am sorry, principally upon Lady Sarah's account. I shall go this morning and condole with her upon it." Almack appears to have been more amenable to ecclesiastical interference than Mrs. Cornelys; but we may depend upon it, he had his reasons; and there is no doubt that such bending to authority, as well as other characteristics which differentiated his assemblies from those at Carlisle House, had no little to do with the fact that whereas the latter gradually depreciated and finally came to an ignominious end, his remained for years the most select and aristocratic establishment that London has ever possessed. It stood, besides, almost from the beginning, on a peculiar and unique footing. Its later incarnation as an assembly rooms for

dances of the most select kind has given its name
a merely Terpsichorean signification; but it must be
remembered that during its earlier day it was, in
addition to being a centre for dancing, something in
the nature of a ladies' club, as we know it; and it was
out of this club that arose that later Almack's, whose
laws were as those of the Medes and Persians, whose
lady patronesses wielded a power unique in its far-
reaching effect on society, and from whose *obiter dicta*
the most eminent and the most beautiful were powerless
to appeal.

Mrs. Boscawen, writing to Mrs. Delany in 1770,
gives a minute account of the *modus vivendi* of this
institution:

"The female club I told you of is removed from
their quarters, Lady Pembroke objecting to a tavern;
it meets, therefore, for the present at certain rooms
at Almack's, who for another year is to provide a
private house. It is much the subject of conversation,
I believe, and the other night I heard many particulars
relating to it. The first fourteen who imagined and
planned it settled its rules and *constitutions:* these were
formed upon the model of one of the clubs at Almack's.
There are seventy-five chosen (the whole number is
to be two hundred). The ladies nominate and *choose*
the gentlemen, and *vice versa*, so that no lady can
exclude a lady, or gentleman a gentleman! The
Duchess of Bedford was at first black-balled, but is
since admitted. Duchess of Marlborough and Grafton
are also chosen. Lady Hertford wrote to beg admittance and has obtained it; also Lady Holderness, Lady
Rochford, and Lady Harrington are black-balled, as
is Lord March and Mr. Boothby, and one or two more
who think themselves pretty gentlemen *du premier
ordre*, but it is plain the ladies are not of their opinion.
Lady Molyneux has accepted, but the Duchess of
Beaufort declined, *as her health never permits her to
sup abroad.* When any of the ladies are to dine with

the society they are to send word before, but supper comes, of course, and is to be served always at eleven. Play will be *deep* and *constant* probably."[1]

From this it will be seen that the club, which had not been formed originally in connection with Almack's, became in course of time merged in his institution; and it certainly helped to give it that distinctive character with which it was for so long identified.

Almack, who had, as we have seen, secured selectness by his arrangement for a committee of ladies to superintend the conduct of his assemblies, was now doubly protecting himself by identifying the new club with his already flourishing concern. At the same time, he did not disdain advertisement, notwithstanding he had the patronage of half the nobility at his back. One of his notices, in *The Advertiser* for November 12, 1768, reads as follows:

"Mr. Almack humbly begs leave to acquaint the nobility and gentry, subscribers to the Assembly in King Street, St. James's, that the first meeting will be Thursday, 24th inst. N.B.—Tickets are ready to be delivered at the Assembly Room."

Two years later Horace Walpole tells George Montagu of "the mixed club" established here, of which Mrs. Boscawen has already given us details. "There is," he says, "a new Institution that begins to make, and if it proceeds will make, considerable noise. It is a club of both sexes to be erected at Almack's, on the model of that of men at White's. Mrs. Fitzroy, Lady Pembroke, Mrs. Meynell, Lady Molyneux, Miss Pelham and Miss Lloyd are the foundresses. I am ashamed to say I am of so young and fashionable society; but as they are people I live with, I choose to be idle rather than morose."

For a time Almack's continued to flourish exceedingly, and Mrs. Cornelys in Soho was already hard

[1] See " Autobiography and Correspondence of Mrs. Delany."

put to it to ſtem the tide that was carrying so many
of her whilom supporters from Carlisle House to
King Street. But in the year 1772, the opening of
the Pantheon was a serious blow to both, and although
Almack's, from its peculiar charaɗter, was able to
ſtand againſt an opposition that ruined Mrs. Cornelys's
less seleɗt gatherings, there is no doubt that even
Almack's felt the ſtrain put upon it of contending
with the splendid and classic abode of pleasure that
had arisen in Oxford Street.

I cannot but think it is significant that Walpole,
after the notice of Almack's juſt quoted, hardly makes
a single further reference to the place; and the
"Almack's" of which he does occasionally speak
is the club of that name in Pall Mall, and not the
Assembly Rooms in King Street. As a matter of
faɗt, Almack's, although it was an undoubted success,
really never made such a name for itself during the
earlier years of its exiſtence as it was deſtined to do
at the beginning, and for many years, of the following,
century. It was then that its recrudescence took place;
then that it assumed that special charaɗter which has
since attached to its name.

In this second phase of its career, great changes
took place in its conſtitution: the mixed club, as such,
gradually died out, juſt as did the extensive gambling
with which it had become associated, and there
emerged solely that assembly for dancing, similar in
a way to Almack's original conception, but with this
marked change, that it became praɗtically a close
borough for the *haut-ton* of the period, and was so
zealously guarded by its lady patronesses, that to
enter its almoſt sacred portals was regarded as the
higheſt diſtinɗtion that a man or a woman in society
could achieve.

In the memoirs and diaries and letters of the time,
as well as in those *romans à clef* which had such a
vogue at this period, in the pages of Gronow and the

x

verse of Luttrell, will be found ample evidence of the immutable rules laid down for the governance of Almack's, and the high hand—rather the clenched fist —with which they were carried out. The laws of the Medes and Persians found themselves figuring in a nineteenth-century revival, and it is safe to say that no personal authority, no special endowments, no mere wealth or influence, outside the magic circle were of the least avail if those who possessed these attributes attempted by a hair's-breadth to break through or circumvent the iron-bound rules of the Committee.[1]

Of all the authorities for the history of Almack's during the first two decades of the nineteenth century, Gronow is the most complete and the most illuminating. Without the record of his personal knowledge of the place, one might almost appear to be exaggerating its selectness, and the unlimited power of those who were responsible for its conduct.

Writing of 1814, he says: "Good society at the period to which I refer was, to use a familiar expression, wonderfully 'select.' At the present time (1862) one can hardly conceive the importance which was attached to getting admission to Almack's, the seventh heaven of the fashionable world. Of the three hundred officers of the Foot Guards, not more than half a dozen were honoured with vouchers of admission to this exclusive temple of the *beau monde*, the gates of which were guarded by lady patronesses, whose smiles or frowns consigned men and women to happiness or despair. These lady patronesses were the Ladies Castlereagh, Jersey, Cowper, and Sefton, Mrs. Drummond Burrell, now Lady Willoughby, the Princess Esterhazy, and the Countess Lieven;"—a female oligarchy which, as the Hon. Grantley Berkeley remarks, was "less in number but equal in power to the Venetian Council of Ten."

[1] I have based much of this chapter on a long account of Almack's which forms the second part of my "Memorials of St. James's Street."

"Many diplomatic arts," proceeds Gronow, "much finesse, and a host of intrigues, were set in motion to get an invitation to Almack's. Very often persons whose rank and fortunes entitled them to the *entrée* anywhere were excluded by the cliqueism of the lady patronesses; for the female government of Almack's was a pure despotism, and subject to all the caprices of despotic rule: it is needless to add that, like every other despotism, it was not innocent of abuses. The fair ladies who ruled supreme over this little dancing and gossiping world issued a solemn proclamation that no gentleman should appear at the assemblies without being dressed in knee-breeches, white cravat, and *chapeau bras*. On one occasion the Duke of Wellington was about to ascend the staircase of the ball-room, dressed in black trousers, when the vigilant Mr. Willis, the guardian of the establishment, stepped forward and said 'Your Grace cannot be admitted in trousers,' whereupon the Duke, who had a great respect for orders and regulations, walked away." It reminds one of the horror of the Court Chamberlain who discovered Dumouriez on the verge of entering the royal presence with bows instead of buckles on his shoes!

It was, indeed, as a contributor to the *New Monthly Magazine* wrote some years later, after mentioning that the nights of assembly were confined to every Wednesday during the season: "Selection with a vengeance, the very quintessence of aristocracy. Three-fourths of the nobility knock in vain for admission. Into this *sanctum sanctorum*, of course, the sons of commerce never think of entering on the sacred Wednesday evenings."

Of the eight patronesses whose names I have already given, according to Gronow, the most popular was Lady Cowper, who later became Lady Palmerston; Lady Sefton was kind and the Countess Lieven haughty, Lady Jersey sometimes made herself "simply

ridiculous" with her tragedy-queen airs and her not
infrequently ill-bred manners; and Lady Castlereagh
and Mrs. Drummond Burrell were altogether too
grandes dames to be anything but exclusive and
picturesque figure-heads.

Gronow once owned a water-colour sketch which
had belonged to Brummell, depicting a ball at
Almack's, in 1815, which is reproduced in his
book, and of which he thus speaks, incidentally
indicating some of the chief *habitués* of the
place:

"The personages delineated are well worthy of
notice, both from the position they held in the fashionable world, and from their being represented with
great truth and accuracy. The great George Brummell
stands in a *dégagé* attitude, with his fingers in his
waistcoat pocket. . . . He is talking earnestly to
the charming Duchess of Rutland. The man in a
black coat who is preparing to waltz with Princess
Esterhazy, so long ambassadress of Austria in London,
is the Comte de St. Antonio, afterwards Duke of
Canizzaro . . . a great lady-killer, who married an
English heiress, Miss Johnson. The original sketch
from which these figures are taken included also
portraits of Charles, Marquis of Queensberry, Baron
Neumann, the late Sir George Warrender (who was
styled by his friends Sir George Provender, being
famed for his good dinners), and the handsome
Comte St. Aldegonde, at this period aide-de-camp to
Louis Philippe, then Duke of Orleans."

In 1814, we are told the dances at Almack's were
Scotch-reels and the old English country-dance; and
the orchestra was under the direction of the then
celebrated Scotch violinist, Niel Gow. In the following year Lady Jersey brought back with her from
Paris the quadrille, and there is an extant print showing
the performers of the first quadrille ever danced in
this country. Those portrayed are Lord and Lady

Worcester, Lady Jersey and Clanronald Macdonald.[1]
Gronow, however, states that he recollected the persons
who formed the *very* first quadrille that was ever
danced at Almack's, and he gives their names as Lady
Jersey, Lady Harriett Butler, Lady Susan Ryder, and
Miss Montgomery; the men being the Count St.
Aldegonde, Mr. Montgomery, Mr. Montague, and
Charles Standish.

About this time, too, the waltz was introduced
into England; but it was at first looked at askance,
and few ventured to dance it at Almack's; later,
however, society became reconciled to it, and Lord
Palmerston was to be seen whirling round the rooms
with the Countess Lieven, and Baron Neumann
"perpetually turning," with the Princess Esterhazy;
until the time when people went mad over waltzing,
and practised their steps in the morning "with
unparalleled assiduity," in readiness for the evening
performance.

Raikes places the introduction of the waltz into
this country fully two years before Gronow does; the
matter is not here of special importance, and at least
the credit of having imported it remains with the
Countess Lieven, although the discrepancy as to the
date of its introduction is further accentuated by the
fact that another authority asserts that it came to our
shores first in 1816.[2] "What scenes have we witnessed
in those days at Almack's," writes Raikes, "what fear
and trembling in the *débutantes* at the commencement
of a waltz, what giddiness and confusion at the end."[3]
The writer opines that it was probably the latter circumstance which accounted for the violent opposition
that arose against the waltz; readers of Byron's and

[1] Although the title of this plate, as given in Gronow's "Reminiscences," is "the First Quadrille at Almack's," it looks as if it was a
Scotch reel that was being performed rather than a quadrille. There are
only four persons taking part in it.
[2] The writer of the volume on "Dancing," in the Badminton Library.
[3] "Journal of Thomas Raikes."

Sheridan's well-known lines will account for it on other grounds. There is, in truth, no doubt that many looked upon it as highly immoral: "the anti-waltzing party took alarm, cried it down," adds Raikes, "mothers forbade it; and every ball-room became the scene of feud and contention."

But at Almack's it held its own, and Baron Tripp, a great dancer, and Baron Neumann, Count St. Aldegonde, M. Bourblanc, and many other votaries, went on dancing it in spite of prejudice and adverse criticism; even the Emperor Alexander was seen waltzing round the rooms of Almack's, as recorded by Lady Brownlow, in her "Reminiscences"; and Lord William Pitt Lennox[1] tells us of other illustrious exponents there, among them being Prince Leopold of Saxe-Cobourg, who married the Princess Charlotte; Prince Esterhazy, the Dukes of Beaufort and Devonshire, Count D'Orsay and Lords Londonderry, Anglesey and Donegal.

But the dances at Almack's were not always unattended by mishaps, and Gronow records one such that might have had a tragic ending. Lord Graves, as notable for his bulk as for his skill in dancing, had, on one occasion, Lady Harriett Butler as his partner in a quadrille.[2] The lady astonished the company by the grace with which she executed the *entrechats*, as they were called. Lord Graves, anxious to emulate her, in attempting the difficult figure fell heavily to the ground, when Sir John Burke, who had been an amused spectator, remarked to him, "What could induce you at your age and in your state to make so great a fool of yourself as to attempt an *entrechat*?" Whereupon the offended peer replied, "If you think

1 "Fashion Then and Now." 2 vols., 1878.

2 By the way, the writer of a work on the Court of George IV. "falls foul of the quadrille, although "not prude enough to be offended with waltzing," but it would seem not because he or she thought it immodest, but because of the apparent difficulty in figuring gracefully in it!

I am too old to dance, I consider myself not too old to blow your brains out for your impertinence; so the sooner you find a second the better!" Lord Sefton, who was standing by and overhead the remarks, said, "Tut, tut, man, the sooner you shake hands the better; for the fact is the world will condemn you both if you fight on such slight grounds; and you, Graves, won't have a leg to stand on"; whereupon the parties shook hands, and thus a duel was averted.

If dancing was the ostensible object of Almack's existence, the place was useful in other ways, and, as a contemporary writer says, formed "a matrimonial bazaar, where mothers met to carry on affairs of state; and often has the table, spread with tepid lemonade, weak tea, tasteless *orgeat*, stale cakes, and thin slices of bread and butter—the only refreshment allowed—been the scene of tender proposals." But, after all, this it had in common with many other centres where men and women foregathered, and this hardly differentiates the place from a hundred others. What did, were its exclusiveness and its iron-bound rules. For instance, one of these ordained that no one should enter after eleven o'clock p.m. Often and often this rule resulted in people who were but a few minutes late being turned away. The Great Duke was again one of the offenders; and Ticknor describes what happened. He had dined with Lord and Lady Downshire and afterwards went on to Almack's with the party. On their way they called at Lady Mornington's, where they found the Duke, who, being asked if he was going to Almack's, replied that "he thought he should look in by and by," on which his mother remarked that "he had better go in good time, as Lady Jersey (the presiding Patroness of that evening) would make no allowance for him." However, he was not ready to start, and the Downshire party went on without him. Some time later in the evening Ticknor was talking to Lady Jersey when he heard one of the attendants say to her: "The Duke of Wellington is at the door, and desires to be admitted." "What time is it?" asked Lady Jersey. " Seven minutes after eleven, your Ladyship." She paused a moment, and then said distinctly and with emphasis: "Give Lady Jersey's compliments to the Duke of Wellington, and say she is very glad that the first enforcement of the rule of exclusion is such that hereafter no one can complain of its application. He cannot be admitted." [1]

On another occasion, however, presumably when a less despotic patroness was presiding, the Duke was admitted after eleven, the rule being waived specially in his favour. Once a certain peer managed to get in by a trick—although it was generally very difficult to evade the lynx-eyed Mr. Willis and his myrmidons. Owing to an accident to his carriage, the gentleman in question arrived too late, but instead of attempting to enter, which he well knew would be next to useless, he waited outside until some people with whom he was acquainted came out; thereupon he went up to their carriage and pretended to say "good-night" to them, as another man who had accompanied them out was doing. On their departure he followed the friend in, the latter truthfully telling the servants that they had been seeing some ladies to their carriage.

Lady Jersey exercised her right in respect of non-admittance, and also in that of withholding tickets for the assemblies, with a stringency greater than that of any of the other lady patronesses. So notorious was she in this respect, indeed, that a young Guard's officer who had been publicly refused a card actually challenged Lord Jersey to a duel, to which Lord Jersey replied that if all those who did not receive tickets from his wife were to call him to account for want of courtesy on her part, he should have to make up his mind to become a target for young officers, and he therefore declined the honour of the proposed meeting. [2]

[1] Ticknor's Diary.   [2] Gronow.

Tom Moore, who went everywhere and knew everybody, was a frequent visitor at Almack's, and in his
Diary are many records of evenings spent there. Thus,
in May 1819, he writes: "Went to Almack's and
staid till three in the morning. Lord Morpeth said
to me, 'You and I live at Almack's'; "again in April
1822, he notes another visit, but adds that although
there was a "very pretty show of women," the place
was "not quite what it used to be." Yet he continued
to go, and once, on the following June 4, records with
complacency the fact that Lady Jersey and Lady
Tankerville "were sending various messengers after
me through the room"; a circumstance on which he
was bantered some days later by the Duchess of
Sussex, who told him that she had heard someone say,
"See them now; it is all on account of his reputation;
for they do not care one pin about him."

Sometimes quasi-fancy-dress dances were given
here, and in May 1826 the poet tells of witnessing
a fancy quadrille entitled "Paysannes Provençales,"
danced, much to his satisfaction; although he had expected to see one called "The Twelve Months," which
had, however, been given up owing to the death of the
sister of "one of the twelve months." Some days later
this was actually performed, and here is Moore's
description of it: "*June* 31.—Went away (from a dinner
at Lord King's) . . . to Almack's; was there early;
waited till the Seasons arrived; got into their wake as
they passed up the room, and saw them dance their
quadrille; the twelve without any gentlemen. Rather
disappointed in the effect; their head-dresses (gold
baskets full of fruit, flowers, etc.) too heavy; Miss
Sheridan the handsomest of any; most of the others
pretty, Miss Brand, the Misses Forester, Miss Acton,
Miss Beauclerc, etc. As soon as I had seen them dance,
came away."

There are various other references to the assemblies
at Almack's in that delightful store-house of anecdote

and information which Moore[1] has left us; and we are told there that the young girls of the period "dated their ages and standing by their seasons at Almack's"; one of them, Miss Macdonald, considering herself an old woman from its being her second season!

Lord Lamington has remarked that "Almack's was the portal to that select circle of intellect and grace which constituted the charm of society";[2] and there is little doubt that for a considerable period it was. But as time went on, the glamour of the place gradually wore off, and the essential tyranny which ruled it became the more apparent. Fashion is ever fickle; and people will only submit to despotism while novelty reconciles them; as the novelty passes away, the shackles begin to gird. This is, I think, what gradually happened in regard to Almack's. Ticknor, who was again in this country in 1835, to some extent found this the case: "Almack's was very brilliant, as it always is," he notes, "and the arrangements for ease and comfort were perfect; no ceremony, no supper; no regulation, no managing; brilliantly lighted halls, very fine music, plenty of dancing. It struck me, however, that there were fewer of the leading nobility and fashion there than formerly, and that the general cast of the company was younger."

Modification of the rules had obviously occurred, when a visitor could write that there was no regulation and no managing; and, indeed, in one important particular we know that there had been a change in the rules, for Ticknor on this very occasion records that he and his party arrived "just before the doors were closed at midnight." A foot-note to Luttrell's "Advice to Julia" tells us, indeed, that it was very lately settled that even *after* half-past eleven the whole string of coaches then formed in the street[3] might deposit its

1 "Memoirs, Journal, and Correspondence of Thomas Moore." Edited by Lord John Russell. 8 vols., 1856.
2 "The Days of the Dandies."
3 It may be remembered that until 1830 King Street was practically a cul-de-sac, having only a foot-way into St. James's Street.

contents in the ballroom. "By this equitable construction," the writer adds, "many were admitted *after*
midnight; but now (1827) the hour of limitation has
been enlarged till twelve o'clock and the privilege of
string abolished."

That a certain decadence, which Ticknor adumbrates,
was creeping over Almack's, is still more insisted on by
a writer in the *Quarterly Review* for 1840, who draws
from it the conclusion that "the palmy days of exclusiveness are gone by in England," and he adds, "though
it is obviously impossible to prevent any given number
of persons from congregating and re-establishing an
oligarchy, we are quite sure that the attempt would be
ineffectual and that the sense of their importance would
extend little beyond the set."

The end of Almack's synchronized roughly with
the beginning of Queen Victoria's reign; and it is not
difficult to account for this. Conditions of society were
undergoing a drastic change. With the accession of a
young female sovereign an entirely new era was
inaugurated, and the fact that a woman occupied the
throne made it impossible for powerful ladies of the
aristocracy to sustain that leadership of fashion, which
hardly clashed with the royal prerogative while easy-
going monarchs like George IV. and William IV.
governed the land. Again, the once-formidable
patronesses of Almack's were either growing old or
tired of their power, or, as in the case of the Princess
Esterhazy and the Countess Lieven, had left the country.
But although Almack's may he said for these reasons
to have become *démodé*, it never became mixed in the
sense that other haunts of amusement became. Towards
the end people obtained admission who would have
had little chance of doing so during its hey-day; but
they were people who cast no discredit on it; people
who were received in general society, and who had
only formerly been made *peris* to the King Street
paradise because the guardians of that stronghold were
ultra-select, and made a habit of being despotic.

There is quite a literature connected with Almack's besides the fact that its name enters incidentally into almost all the memoirs and diaries and letters of the period during which it flourished. From Carlyle, who sighed for the "gum flowers of Almack's to be made living roses in a new Eden" (whatever he meant by that), to Tom Moore, with his complacent references, and Ticknor, with his observation, everyone has had a word to say about the place who has had a word to say about the social life of the first forty years of the nineteenth century.

But in addition to such passing *memorabilia*, Almack's has entered into the fiction of the time, and a novel (and a very stupid novel it is *per se*) appeared in 1827, bearing its name. It is, as is usual with such things, a *roman à clef*, in which actual people are but thinly disguised under fictitious names, a key to which was once supplied by no less an authority than Mr. Disraeli. The book, in which, if there be a plot, I, who have laboured through its three volumes, fail to detect one, consists of a number of "scenes" of fashionable life in town and country. Homer has sung of the search for the Golden Fleece; Malory has written concerning the quest for the Holy Grail; the author of "Almack's" shows us the pursuit for tickets to subscription dances! The work is, indeed, one long account of the mad endeavours and the intrigues to obtain admission to Almack's; the despair incident to failure; the beatitude attending on success.

In the following year "Almack's Revisited" appeared, also in three volumes, and as the *Literary Gazette* regarded it as superior to its forerunner; it may be better worth reading; although I have never had the courage to embark on the undertaking.

In addition to these works, one remembers that in "Vivian Grey," when its writer wished to draw a lady of ultra-fashionable proclivities, he called her Lady Almack; that Jeames de la Pluche, Esquire, in the days of his glory was to be seen "worling round in walce at Halmax with Lady Hann, or lazaly ſtepping a kidrill with Lady Jane"; while Tom and Jerry, who went everywhere, are to be found "amidſt a crowd of high-bred personages, with the Duke of Clarence himself looking at them dancing at Almack's." And finally in Luttrell's "Advice to Julia," that delightfully witty poem on the fashions and fads of the day, Almack's is conſtantly referred to, and the once-outſtanding place it occupied in the social annals of the day, is summarized in the four lines which tell:

> "If once to Almack's you belong,
> Like monarchs, you can do no wrong;
> But banished thence on Wednesday night,
> By Jove, you can do nothing right."

The later hiſtory of the place intereſts us here, for although it came in time to have little in common with the ultra-seleƈt assemblies in the days of its glory, as Willis's Rooms it for long occupied a recognized position. Years before the discontinuance of Almack's it had been managed, under the Lady Patronesses, by Willis, who was a nephew of Almack himself; and thus after the death of the latter and the extinƈtion of the earlier assemblies it was carried on by him and came to bear his name. It was for long used indifferently for dances, leƈtures, readings, and concerts.[1] Here in 1839 Maſter Bassie, one of the infant prodigies of the day, appeared in what is described as "an extraordinary *mnemonic* performance," when but thirteen years of age. Five years later Charles Kemble gave here his "Readings from Shakespeare"; and in 1851

---

[1] By permission of the Lady Patronesses concerts had been given in earlier days here, and in 1808 to 1810, Mrs. Billington and Braham and Signor Naldi gave a series of concerts in opposition to those of Madame Catalini at the Hanover Square Rooms. Here, too, M. Fierville held his subscription balls, for which Bartolozzi engraved the beautiful little benefit tickets. I possess a "Gentleman's Ticket" for the "Amicable Assembly" held here on May 16, 1822, which was in the nature of a musical *réunion* apparently.

Thackeray delivered in the great room his "Lectures on the English Humorists. That "great painted and gilded saloon, with long sofas for benches," as Charlotte Brontë describes it, in spite of the splendid society it had once seen, could hardly have been filled before by so many illustrious people as those who formed Thackeray's audience: Monckton Milnes and Lord Carlisle; Caroline Fox and Charlotte Brontë, Dickens and Leslie, the artist, Hallam and Macaulay and Harriett Martineau, and the rest.

Dickens himself once spoke here, not in one of his readings, but as chairman at the annual dinner of the Dramatic Fund, on February 14, 1866. The rooms have, indeed, been used for a variety of different purposes, and in 1837 we read of the sale by auction here of what was called "The Deccan Booty," including the famous Nassuck Diamond, and the Arcot Diamonds which Warren Hastings had presented to Queen Charlotte, in 1785, a gift that led to much silly scandal at the time, and is supposed to have favourably influenced the royal reception of Mrs. Hastings at Court.

Since those days the rooms have undergone radical changes. Messrs. Robinson and Fisher have long since been established here; and the rest of the premises have been occupied by Prince's Restaurant and a range of shops ending, on the east side, in the old-world house occupied by the Orleans Club. Indeed the once-famous Almack's and the well-remembered Willis's Rooms have undergone as great a metamorphosis as the street itself in which they were situated—the street where Napoleon III. once lodged, and where Fashion still crowds, not to dance or drink "weak tea," but to gaze at the treasures of art which Messrs. Christie have been annually dispersing since they came hither from Pall Mall, in 1823, to No. 8 King Street, formerly Wilson's European Emporium or Museum, and before then the site of one of the notorious gambling hells of this fashionable neighbourhood.

CHAPTER XIII

LONDON FAIRS

THE fairs which were once annually held in London properly take their place among its pleasure haunts, for although in their earliest days they were rather in the nature of commercial *media* than centres of amusement, it was not long before their character changed, and if, as was the case, buying and selling still went on, the shows that gradually became identified with such things in time merged their more business-like characteristics in the fun and revelry which their very name has now come to connote.

At one time a number of such saturnalia took place in various parts of London, just as they did throughout the country. There was, for instance, one held at Brook Green, one at Edmonton,[1] another at Greenwich, and yet another at Westminster, locally termed Magdalen Fair, which had been established in 1257, and was held in Tothill Fields, and, originally limited to three days, was extended by Edward III. to thirty-one.

Among other such-like institutions was Camberwell Fair, which is said to be mentioned in Domesday Book, so ancient was its origin; Peckham Fair, an offshoot of the earlier one at Camberwell; and Stepney Fair, of relatively modern origin, having been inaugurated in 1664, by Charles II., at the instance of the Earl of Cleveland, then Lord of the Manor of Stepney; and others could be mentioned. But the three outstanding ones, outstanding because they were something

[1] Edmonton Statute Fair, 1788, forms the subject of a picture by John Nixon, now in the Victoria and Albert Museum. Greenwich Fair and Brook Green Fair have been perpetuated by Rowlandson in well-known water-colour drawings.

in the nature of civic events, were Bartholomew Fair, Southwark Fair, and Mayfair—the last of which, as we all know, has given its name to the most fashionable quarter of the metropolis.

The annals of *Bartholomew Fair* are extensive and peculiar, so full, indeed, are they that when Henry Morley, in 1859, wrote its history, he found four hundred and ninety odd pages not too much in which to present its innumerable points of interest; and as the fair lasted from the reign of Henry I. to that of Victoria, it can be readily imagined what a wealth and variety of social changes had become attached to it during this long period.

It had its origin in the foundation of the Priory of St. Bartholomew by Rahere, once jester to Henry I., but who, repenting of his light life, made a pilgrimage to Rome, and on his return obtained a charter from his Royal master for the establishment of the religious house. Many privileges were attached to the grant, and among others the right of the Prior to hold an annual Fair at Bartholomewtide for three days; "firm peace," as it was called, being granted to all who should visit the Fair.[1] As Rahere had foreseen, this brought traders and purchasers to Smithfield from all parts of the country, and even those merchants in foreign lands who dealt in cloth[2] and such-like commodities. The stalls and booths for this traffic were erected within the precincts of the Priory, the gates of which were closed each night, and the wares exposed carefully guarded. With the Dissolution a change came over the scene, and the Priory having lost its rights in the Fair, these were transferred to the Lord Mayor and Corporation, in conjunction with Lord Rich, one of Henry's favourites who benefited by the suppression of the religious houses.

[1] Apparently at first the fair was of longer duration; it was limited to three days by an edict of Henry II.
[2] Cloth Fair perpetuates the original intention of the Fair.

As a commercial undertaking the fair continued to hold its own into Elizabeth's reign, but during that period a variety of circumstances combined to militate against its continuance in this respect, and its character gradually changed from being that primarily of a trade centre to that of a centre of pleasure and amusement. The fair, as before, continued to be opened in state by the Lord Mayor and twelve principal alder-men,[1] but few of its former associations were identified with it, and were merely perpetuated by a mock proclamation by certain drapers and clothiers, who marched in procession from their head-quarters—a house with the sign of a Hand and Shears, in Cloth Fair, and announced the opening of the Fair, with appropriate shouting and "snapping of shears."[2]

The situation selected by Rahere for his fair was not merely convenient for its original purpose of trade, but was, as it happened, appropriate when that purpose had become largely identified with amusement. For Smithfield—the Smooth Field of Fitzstephen's chronicle—had from time immemorial been a centre of recreation, where on summer evenings the youth of the city had been wont to run, leap, and wrestle, to contend with sword and bucklers, and to shoot with bows and arrows; while the maidens were accustomed to dance there to the sound of tabors; and no doubt some of those juggling feats represented in old illuminated manuscripts—where we see men walking on stilts, women balancing themselves on swords, and such-like shows—had become incidental attributes of the fair itself, until such time as it entered into the phase when distractions of this kind were almost its only end and aim.

By the close of Elizabeth's reign Bartholomew Fair had become a centre of amusement and practically nothing else; although things were, of course, sold

---

[1] Hentzner's "Travels in England," 1598.
[2] Timbs's "Romance of London."

Y

there as they are in all such places. "Each person," says Strype, "having a booth, paid so much per foot for the first three days. The Earl of Warwick and Holland (a descendant of the Lord Rich to whom partial rights in the fair had been granted) is concerned in the toll gathered the first three days in the fair, being a penny for every burthen of goods brought in or carried out; and to that end there are persons that stand at all the entrances in the fair; and they are of late years grown so nimble, that these blades will extort a penny if one hath but a little bundle under one's arm, and nothing related to the fair."

For a description of what went on, and the "humours" of the place, as they may be termed, Ben Jonson in his play entitled "Bartholomew Fair," first performed in 1614, is one of the best authorities. It is a skit on the mania for sight-seeing which is inherent in human nature, and the gullibility of a certain section of society which is apparently equally perennial. One of the characters, relating the wonders he has seen, remarks: "I have been at the Eagle and the Black Wolf, and the Bull with Five Legs, and the Dogs that dance the Morrice, and the Hare of the Tabor;" while one of the showmen says: "Oh, the motions that I, Lanthorn Leatherhead, have given light to in my time. . . . The Gunpowder Plot— there was a getpenny! I have presented that to an eighteen and twentypence audience nine times in the afternoon. Your home-born projects prove ever the best—they are so easy and familiar; they put too much learning in their things now-o'-days."

All the humour and fun of the fair is represented in this interesting dramatic record of a once-famous event. Adam Overdo, the judge of the Court of Piepowders;[1] Master Daniel Knockem Jordan, the

---

[1] In every fair there used to be a Court of Pie Powder, for the adjustment of disputes arising therefrom. It is suggested that the name comes from *pieds poudreux*—the dusty feet of the frequenters.

horse runner; Master Littlewit, the author of one of the puppet-plays; Busy, and Dame Trash, who keeps a ginger-bread stall, and the rest, all help to produce that atmosphere with which Bartholomew Fair was compact in Elizabethan and early Caroline times. At a later day, in 1641 to be precise, there appeared a now scarce and curious tract entitled "Bartholomew Faire, or Variety of Fancies, where you may find a Faire of wares, and all to please your mind, with the severall enormityes and misdemeanours which are there seene and heard;"[1] and from this we learn incidentally that the place teemed with pickpockets who reaped a great harvest what time the unsophisticated were, open-mouthed, wondering at the strange and weird "enormityes" exhibited. Later, after the execution of Charles I., a booth-play called "A Bartholomew Faring, New, New, New, etc.," here represented from the Royalists' point of view the civil strife that had recently distracted the kingdom.

It was not, however, till the time of Charles II. that the Fair having been extended from three days to three weeks (it had received an earlier extension of a fortnight during the interregnum), really took on it that air of carnival with which it was to be identified for nearly two centuries. Everyone went to it, and the West End was almost as well represented there as were the citizens east of Temple Bar. Needless to say, Mr. Pepys was one of the visitors. Thus on September 2, 1664, we find him there looking at the rope-dancing, and buying combs for Mrs. Pepys to give her maids. He went again, with Creed, six days later and saw the best dancing on the ropes he ever remembered to have witnessed. Three years later he was there again, glad to see it once more, "after missing it two years by the plague." This was

---

[1] In the same year appeared another tract, entitled "Bartholomew Faire, etc.," with a different sub-title, but substantially the same production.

on August 29, 1667, and the next day he paid another visit: "and there among other things found my Lady Castlemaine at a puppet-play, 'Patient Grizill,' and the street full of people expecting her coming out." Indeed, Pepys could not keep away from the place, and again, on September 4, we read of his accompanying his wife and Hewer thither, when they witnessed the performance of some Polichinelli. In the following year he was there three times, fascinated by the rope-dancing of the celebrated Jacob Hall, watching "a ridiculous, obscene little stage-play called 'Merry Andrew';" and, on the last occasion, seeing "several sights; amongst others, the mare that tells money and many things to admiration," and what one thinks he liked best: when the mare "was bid to go to him of the company that most loved a pretty wench in a corner," she came direct to him: "this," he adds, "did cost me 12*d.* to the horse, which I had flung it before, and did give me occasion to kiss a mighty *belle fille* that was exceeding plain, but *fort belle*"—Mrs. Pepys does not appear to have been of the party.

There is evidence even of the sober Mr. Evelyn at least once having visited the "celebrated follies of Bartholomew Fair," in 1648; but such things were hardly as a rule in his way, and this is the only reference to the place in his Diary.

During the reign of Charles II., Bartholomew Fair became a yearly index of the uncurbed hilarity of the people in general, as exhibited after a long period of repression.

The names of some of those who exhibited their powers of amusing have come down to us, and we know that Mat Coppinger, who had been a player and afterwards by degrees descended in the social scale until he was hanged at Tyburn, was for some time a popular favourite here. Joe Haines was another, and so was Tom Dogget, noted for his dancing of the Cheshire Round. Jacob Hall, to whom I have already referred, was notable for his "somersets and flip-flaps," and for "flying over rapiers and men's heads, and through several hoops." He was "the sword servant to His Majesty Charles II.," and was something more to that monarch's favourite, Lady Castlemaine.[1] A more unusual performer was the Dutch lady who, in 1689, astonished the spectators by her vaulting and dancing on the tight-rope, and, as they are described in a contemporary hand-bill, "her side-capers, upright-capers, cross-capers, and back-capers, on the *tight*-rope"; she also walked on the *slack* rope, which no other woman, it was affirmed, could do.

As a matter of fact Bartholomew Fair at this period seems to have resembled not remotely such gatherings at a later day. Impossibly fat women and impossibly intelligent animals fought for mastery in attracting the pence out of the visitors' pockets; freaks of all kinds were exhibited; although to our more sophistic-ated ideas some of the exhibits, then looked upon as special curiosities, seem ordinary enough. But even we in these days might not be unwilling to see "The Wonder of Nature" which was shown here, in 1667, in the person of "a girl about sixteen years of age, born in Cheshire, and not above eighteen inches long, having shed the teeth seven several times, and not a perfect Bone in any part of her, only the Head; yet she hath all her senses to Admiration, and Discourses, Reads very well, Sings, Whistles, and all very pleasant to hear."

There are extant a number of broadside ballads, and other poetical references, appertaining to the shows in Bartholomew Fair at this period. Dr. Wild's "Rome rhymed to Death," 1683, contains some; as does "Roger in Amaze, or the Countryman's Ramble

---

[1] He set up a booth at Charing Cross, and later in Lincoln's Inn, as well as in Cheapside, but had to abandon his performance owing to the complaints of the inhabitants, that they occasioned brawls and general rowdiness.

through Bartholomew Fair," and it is easy to realize by the nature of these that the civic authorities had good reason for taking, as they did in 1678, formal notice of the "Irregularities and Disorders of Bartholomew Fair," and referring the matter to a committee "to consider how the same might be prevented, and what damage would occur to the city by laying down of the same."

As Morley remarks, this is the first hint of suppression that arises in the history of the fair, and he adds that it synchronizes almost simultaneously with the decay of the great annual gathering as a necessary seat of trade. Although it cannot be precisely stated when Cloth Fair actually became non-existent, it had long been waning; and although after some years of the following century (1715) had elapsed we hear of the greatest number of Black Cattle being brought here that was ever known, and so the actual trade part of the fair cannot be said to have become wholly extinct, there is little doubt that it had for long, in the eyes of the general public, become a subsidiary part of the show, and a part that attracted but a few of the citizens.

It is, indeed, during the whole of the eighteenth century that Bartholomew Fair became essentially a pleasure-haunt, almost solely. Ned Ward, writing on the eve of the new century, indicates this; seated at the window of a public-house near by, he remarks: "The first objects, when we were seated, that lay within our observations, were the quality of the fair, strutting round the balconies in their tinsel robes, and golden leather buskins, expressing such pride in their buffoonery stateliness, that I could but reasonably believe they were as much elevated with the thought of their fortnight's pageantry, as ever Alexander was with the thought of a new conquest; looking with great contempt on their split-deal thrones upon the admiring mobility, geering in the dirt at our ostentatious heroes, and their most supercilious doxies, who looked as awkward and ungainly in their gorgeous accoutrements, as an alderman's lady in her stiff-bodied gown, upon a Lord Mayor's festival."

But it would be a mistake to suppose that all the shows exhibited here, were of a negligible character and merely such as were likely to attract and astonish the yokel or more unsophisticated citizen. It began to be the fashion for actors of recognized ability to organize or to take part in some of the entertainments provided, and we find Ben Jonson, afterwards an actor in Cibber's company, performing here in 1694, and Theophilus Cibber playing here in Rome's "Tamerlane." Bullock's great theatrical booth, the largest at that time in the fair, was specially noted for its harlequinades, as well as for its representation of "George Barnewell's fate," that ever-popular tragedy based on citizen life. Theatrical exhibitions grounded on notable current events had long been popular, from a representation of the Gunpowder Plot, to "a little opera called the *Old Creation of the World Newly Revived*, with the addition of the glorious battle obtained over the French and Spaniards by His Grace the Duke of Marlborough;"[1] while Powel's Puppets were also a certain draw, when his dolls performed such things in "Whittington and his Cat," "The Children in the Wood," "Dr. Faustus," and such-like old favourites.

The literature of the period is full of references to the fair and the varied sights to be seen there; and that the theatrical displays alone drew all the Town is evidenced by the fact that during the fortnight the place was open, the regular theatres closed, partly, no doubt, to allow some of their actors to take part in a profitable change of employment, but also obviously because the counter-attraction was too great

[1] A hand-bill of this is among the Bagford collection of such things in the British Museum.

for them to find it worth while remaining open. Mills, Booth, Dogget, and such-like *impresarios* had their regular booths here, and one Timothy Fielding,[1] in conjunction with Hippisley, the actor, set up one for nine successive years. Some afterwards famous histrions began their careers in such booths, and it was at Fielding's that Mrs. Pritchard first achieved success in the author's adaptation of Molière's "Fourberies de Scapin"; while Mrs. Clive and Mrs. Theophilus Cibber were among other ladies who condescended to perform at the fair. In contemporary news-sheets may be found advertisements of the theatrical fare provided here; and the place as a centre for the drama (a drama chiefly selected with a view to the mixed company that congregated at Smithfield) takes a recognized position in the history of eighteenth-century manners and customs.

But, after all, these entertainments were but part and parcel of a vast organism of varied amusements provided annually at Bartholomew Fair: monsters of the most extraordinary and alarming character were shown; acrobatic feats of the most daring description were performed; and all sorts of toys and gimcracks were sold at booths which alternated with those set up for the purpose of pure amusement. Monsieur Sorbière coming to London during the seventeenth century, went there as a matter of course, and found it consisting largely of toyshops, china and picture booths, and ribbon shops, but he could discover no books being sold there. There were many confectioners' shops "where any woman may commodiously be treated"; rope-dancing, too, went on perpetually, and "dexterous cut-purses and pickpockets" were there in abundance. One very saleable article was what was known as a Bartholomew Doll, or a Bartholomew Baby, as it was earlier called; and these often figured in those "fairings" which people

[1] Not Henry Fielding, the novelist, as was once supposed, and by no less an authority than Henry Morley himself.

gave one another. The eighteenth century delighted in dolls, and not merely the childhood of the time, but children of an older growth, and Bartholomew Fair was regarded as an excellent centre for the purchase of such things.

The conjuror and the posture-maker were also regular concomitants of the fair, and one of these named Fawkes is said to have made a large fortune by his art as a prestidigitator. One of his famous feats was to produce an apple tree which, bare at first, within a minute bore ripe apples, a western variation of the mango trick, apparently. In an extant print of Fawkes's booth, a figure in court-dress, looking on, is said to represent Sir Robert Walpole, who is known to have been a frequent visitor here, as were occasionally even members of the Royal Family.

At a later date the most famous of the shows attached to the place was undoubtedly that of Richardson, which may be said to have been a modern successor of a long line of such things, the largest and most important of which hitherto had been that erected for the King's players in 1715. Richardson's booth was a sixpenny show, as were Wombwell's and Atkins's, while all the rest charged but one penny for admission. It was lined with green baize, and lighted by no fewer than 2000 lamps, and the band of men dressed as beefeaters, and the superior character of its theatrical performances, made it the most popular and outstanding of all such entertainments.

How remunerative these were is shown by the receipts in the year 1828, when Wombwell's Menagerie realized £1700, Richardson's Show £1200, and Atkins's £1000; while at a penny admission, such attractions as the Pig-faced Lady produced £150; Ball's Show, £80; Ballard's Show, £89; the Fat Boy and Girl, £140; the Panorama of the Battle of Navarino, £60; and the Chinese Juggler, £50.[1]

[1] These figures are given in Daniell's "Merrie England in the Olden Time."

As in the case of all such places attracting every class of the community, Bartholomew Fair was responsible for much disorderly conduct. It was a happy hunting-ground for all those who lived by their wits and the credulity of the unsophisticated. Organized bands of roughs, such as the once-notorious "Lady Holland's Mob," not infrequently spread terror and confusion throughout the Fair. Horace Walpole uses its name as a synonym for irregularity; and the frequent attempts on the part of the civic authorities to suppress it, or at least to curtail its duration, show how difficult it was found to curb its activities in this direction.

One of the places especially notorious within its precincts was a passage known as "The Cloisters," from King Street to Smithfield. It was lined with small shops occupied by seamstresses and milliners, and during the progress of the fair these were used as raffling shops, a term that concealed but too often rendezvous of a very different character. Defoe's "Moll Flanders" refers to one of these, obviously of this nature; and a writer in "The Observator" for 1703, remarks of them: "The Cloisters, what strange medley of lewdness has that place not long since afforded! Lords and ladies, aldermen and their wives, squires and fiddlers, citizens and rope-dancers, mistresses and maids, masters and apprentices! This is not an ark like Noah's which received the clean and the unclean; only the unclean beasts enter this ark, and such as have the devil's livery on their back"; while Defoe, in his "Reformation of Manners," had, some few years earlier, said much the same thing in verse.

Among the innumerable visitors to Bartholomew Fair was John Thomas Smith, who has left an interesting account of his experiences,[1] and who took good care to leave his watch behind, when he determined

[1] In "A Book for a Rainy Day."

to adventure in its purlieus. There he first saw that remarkable man, Belzoni, who was later to create something like a *furore* with his book on Egyptian Excavations, which he wrote after his showman days were over, and whose Herculean powers were exhibited on more than one unrehearsed occasion.[1]

Bartholomew Fair gradually drew towards its close during the first half of the nineteenth century. Higher rents charged for the ground on which the booths were erected eliminated many of the humbler exhibitors; in 1840, a special committee instituted for letting sites further lessened these, and although it still permitted shows of wild animals, it struck out for some recondite reason the applications of giants and dwarfs. The earlier semi-state opening by the Lord Mayor had, too, gradually become denuded of its once civic importance, and a relatively few insignificant stalls were at last all that remained as the successors of that vast congeries of shows which had drawn all London to Smithfield and had been for long a recognized public institution. At last, in 1850, the Lord Mayor, walking to the appointed gateway, found that there was practically no fair worth opening; and henceforth, for a few years, such a ceremony was dispensed with. In 1855 the Bartholomew Fair of so many memories came to its inevitable end; and, writing in 1859, Mr. Momley is able to state that "the sole existing vestige of it is the old fee of three and sixpence still paid by the City, to the Rector of St. Bartholomew the Great, for a proclamation in his parish."[2]

What Tom Brown wrote many years ago may still be said of the site of Bartholomew Fair's activities:

"Smithfield is another sort of place to what it was in the times of honest Ben Jonson, who, were he to rise out of his grave, would hardly believe it to be the

[1] Notably when he forced his way into the Abbey, at George IV.'s Coronation.

[2] This is no longer paid.

same spot of ground where Justice Overdo made so busy a figure; where the crop-eared Parson demolished a ginger-bread stall; where Nightingale, of harmonious memory, sung ballads; and fat Ursula sold pig and bottled ale."[1]

Southwark Fair

Southwark Fair was for long one of the three great annual fairs held in England, the other two being Bartholomew Fair and Sturbridge Fair, near Cambridge. That at Southwark was long known as Our Lady Fair, but exactly when it was first instituted is a question, and although by a charter[2] of Edward IV. dated November 2 1462, liberty to hold it was granted to the City of London, it has been surmised that probably long before that date it was in existence in an inchoate state. In the reign of Charles I., Southwark Fair is mentioned as being of outstanding importance, to which, says Rymer, "there is usually extraordinary resort out of all parts of the kingdom."

The fair was ostensibly supposed to last for three days, September, 7, 8, and 9, according to Stow, but it would seem that custom had ordained a far longer period for its activities, and it is probable that it continued for about two weeks, as did other similar institutions. As in the case of Bartholomew's Fair, it was declared open by the Lord Mayor and other civic dignitaries with some pomp and ceremonial; the Lord Mayor himself riding to St. Magnus's church, at two o'clock in the afternoon, attended by the sword-bearer, where they were met by the assembled aldermen. After certain prayers had been heard, the cavalcade proceeded over the bridge to St. George's Church, in whose purlieus the fair was held. This

---

[1] There is a large literature connected with the Fair. Morley's book is the standard work on it, but Hone in his "Every Day Book" has left a good account of its later history. Besides this, it enters into innumerable plays and other works dealing with the long period of its existence.

[2] This charter was confirmed by Edward VI., in 1551.

opening, although attended with much ceremony, appears to have been simple enough in itself, if we are to judge from what happened in the year 1741, when, according to the record of Sheriff Hoare, "on September 8 the Sheriffs waited on the Lord Mayor in procession, the City music going before, to proclaim Southwark Fair, as it is commonly called; although the ceremony is no more than our going in our coaches through the Borough, and turning round by St. George's church back again to the Bridge House; and this is to signify the licence to begin the fair."

The fair was held on St. Margaret's Hill, a portion of the thoroughfare now known as Borough High Street, in the immediate neighbourhood of the famous Tabard Inn, and St. George's church. There was no large open space for its accommodation, as in the case of Bartholomew's Fair, but the ſtreets and courts and inn-yards of the vicinity were all requisitioned for the erećtion of booths and shows, which spread themselves throughout the neighbourhood during a hećtic fortnight. When the fair was finally closed, I imagine that this temporary interference with the amenities of the residents, as well as with their businesses, had as much to do with its suppression as the rioting and general immorality it produced which was the oſtensible cause of its being prohibited.

There are not many references to Southwark Fair before the eighteenth century. Pepys, of course, knew it, although he only mentions it twice in his Diary, once when, on September 11, 1660, he speaks of "Landing at the Bear, at the Bridge foot and . . . saw Southwark fair;" and again, on September 21, 1668, when he has something more to say about it: "To Southwarke Fair," he writes, "very dirty, and there saw the puppet-show of Whittington, which was pretty to see; and how that idle thing do work upon people that see it, and even myself too! And thence to Jacob Hall's dancing on the ropes, where I saw such

action as I never saw before, and mightily worth
seeing." Later at a neighbouring tavern he met Hall,
and entered into conversation with him, as, says he,
"I had a mind to hear whether he had ever any mischief by falls in his time. He told me, 'Yes, many;
but never to the breaking of a limb'; he seems,"
adds Pepys, "a mighty strong man."

It is, curiously enough, from Evelyn that we get
a more general idea of the fair at this period. He
visited it on September 13, 1660, and has left the
following record of his experiences there. "I saw in
Southwark, at St. Margaret's Faire," he writes,
"monkies and apes dance and do other feates of
activity on ye high rope; they were gallantly clad *à la
mode*, went upright, saluted the company, bowing and
pulling off their hatts; they saluted one another with
as good a grace as if instructed by a dancing-master;
they turn'd heels over head with a basket having eggs
in it, without breaking any; also with lighted candles
in their hands and on their heads without extinguish-
ing them, and with vessells of water without spilling
a drop. I also saw an Italian wench daunce and
performe all the tricks on ye high rope to admiration;
all the Court went to see her. Likewise was a man who
tooke up a piece of iron cannon of about 400 lbs.
weight with the haire of his head onely."

I have before observed how popular at these fairs
were the representations of current events; one such
exhibition at Southwark Fair was prohibited, however.
In 1692 there occurred an earthquake which was more
or less generally felt on the Continent, and of which
some tremors were even observable in England. But
in Jamaica it proved a veritable disaster, and the
organizers of one of the shows at the following Southwark Fair thought it would make an excellent exhibition there. Apparently, however, it was, to use
Evelyn's words, "so profanely and ludicrously represented in a puppet-play, or some such lewd pastime,"

that Queen Mary, having been informed of it, gave orders "to put downe that idle and vicious mock shew." It has been concluded by some that these laſt words indicate that the fair itself was temporarily at leaſt suspended. It rather seems, however, that it was only the special parody of the Jamaica earthquake that came under the royal ban.

But it was in the eighteenth century that Southwark Fair reached the height of its aćtivity, and it is probably through the work of the great pićtorial satiriſt of that age that it is known to moſt people. For in 1733 Hogarth produced his famous pićture of it, and in that work we not only obtain an excellent general idea of what went on there; but many of those careful and essentially accurate delineations of special features inſtinćt with that allegorical moralizing which was one of the artiſt's moſt notable and outſtanding charaćteriſtics. An examination of the work, or of the engraving which Hogarth made from it, will enable one to realize at a glance how it was frequented by all classes, and also to realize what were some of the principal attraćtions provided for their amusement. We see, for inſtance, Elkanah Settle's "Siege of Troy" being exhibited at Lee and Harper's booth; the wax-work show, portraying "the whole court of France;" Müller, the Leipsic giant, and Violante, the tumbler; the "poſture-maſter," and the "curious Indian birds" of Mr. Fawkes, the conjuror, and Cadman, daringly suspended on his slack-rope; we see, too, the attraćtive young lady, accompanied by a black-boy, beating her drum to gather in patrons to one of the side-shows; a boy playing on the bag-pipes to draw attention to the little puppets he is working by a ſtring with one foot; the man (Figg, the prize-fighter) on the horse with a drawn sword whom I imagine to represent Don Quixote. The people falling headlong from the collapsed scaffold allegorically indicate the "Fall of Bajazet," which was represented at Cibber and Bullock's booth.

The whole picture is instinct with the life and move-
ment, the bustle and the noise, the fun and frolic of
the fair; every countenance displays some dominant
emotion, from surprise and complacency, up to
astonishment and open-mouthed wonder. One might
write pages of description of such a scene, and yet not
come within miles of reproducing the actuality of
Southwark Fair as it is presented to us by Hogarth's
magic brush and graver.[1]

Innumerable advertisements and handbills inform
us of the various shows exhibited at different times here.
Thus we know that at Lee and Harper's great booth,
which was one of the outstanding features of the fair,
a play called "Bateman, or the Unhappy Marriage"
was performed, together with such lighter fare as the
"Comical Humours of Sparrow," "Pumpkin," and
"Sheer going to the Wars." Burlesques were the chief
mainstay of such performances, however, and the
evolutions of Punch and Harlequin and Scaramouch,
and the graceful attitudinizing of Pierrot and Colum-
bine were always attractive.

Just as the company in such places was of the most
mixed character, the peer elbowing the pedlar, and
the duchess cheek by jowl with the "doxy"; so the
entertainments were varied in the extreme, ranging
from theatrical displays given by trained and finished
actors and actresses, to the most elementary kinds of
side-shows, and the most obvious forms of mystification. The fat woman and the five-legged calf fought
for mastery with the polished periods of Mr. Cibber;
Jacob Hall and Cadman exhibited their remarkable
feats next door to some poor wretch who tried to gain
a few honest pennies by tricks in which even the
childhood of the eighteenth century could hardly have

---

[1] The original painting belongs to the Duke of Newcastle. The
print known variously as "Southwark Fair," "A Fair," and "The
Humours of the Fair," although dated 1733, was not issued till 1735.
See Austin Dobson's "Hogarth."

SOUTHWARK FAIR
AFTER HOGARTH
1733

been deceived; what time those who came hither to gain anything but honest pennies, were busily engaged in searching the pockets of the wide-eyed, open-mouthed countryman, who, if he returned to his rural haunts richer in experience, was too often decidedly poorer in pocket.

Nor were other dangers absent, and the fairs were the happy hunting-ground of the prostitutes, who here flaunted their bedizened cheeks, and often passed themselves off on the ignorant or unwary as ladies of *ton*. Drinking, too, was rampant, and the manners of many of the frequenters of such places boisterous and unruly in the extreme. We have seen how this was the case at Bartholomew Fair, and how much cause for anxiety was created in the minds of the civic authorities by such excesses.[1] Many of those who were accustomed to exhibit their shows at Bartholomew Fair were also to be seen at Southwark, and among them Timothy Fielding, who set up his booth, in conjunction with one Reynolds, at the lower end of Blue Maid Alley on Southwark Green, and on one occasion performed "The Beggar's Opera," with a company of comedians from the Haymarket, as we are informed by a contemporary advertisement, which proceeds to state that "there is a commodious passage for the Quality, and coaches through the Half Moon Inn, and care will be taken that there shall be lights, and people to conduct them to their places."

Such shows were in themselves practically as good as those to be seen in the regular playhouses. But, unfortunately for the prosperity of the fair, they were *rari nantes* in the *gurgite vasto* of very different exhibitions, and above all were set up in an environment which, although it attracted large numbers of honest and often notable people, was more amply filled by the

---

[1] It is, however, pleasant to record that many of the booth-keepers were accustomed to collect money for the prisoners in the neighbouring Marshalsea.

z

rag and tag of the town, and by such as depended on mixed companies for the furtherance of nefarious ends.

Southwark Fair had by 1743 become so notorious in this respect that it was ordered to be "cried down" by the bellman. Indeed the justices could no longer disregard its character nor the complaints of those living in the vicinity, and in 1762 it was prohibited by the Common Council, and shortly afterwards formally suppressed (in September 1763) by order of the Corporation,[1] after an existence of just three hundred years.

Mayfair

The word Mayfair connotes something so different from that which it originally indicated that, were we not accustomed to find throughout London equally curious and unlikely derivative transitions, one might well wonder that the heart of fashion should take its title from what was at first a commercial centre and finally became so rowdy a one that it had to be suppressed. But as the chief thoroughfare connected with this area can also boast of no more dignified a designation than that of a lane, one may well be reconciled to the fact that its centre was once identified with a fair.

At first, however, it was not known as Mayfair at all, but as St. James's Fair, and was so called because Edward I. granted to the Hospital of St. James's (where the palace is now) the right to hold a fair in its neighbourhood on the eve of St. James's day, and for six days after. This fair was situated in what were then open fields, and its nucleus is identical with Shepherd's Market, which may be regarded as having been evolved from it. As was usual, St. James's Fair was originally itself a market, and the power to hold it was of considerable annual value to the religious house to whom the privilege had been granted. In course of time, probably at first with a view to attracting people to it, entertainments of a limited and archaic character

---

[1] "London Past and Present."

were given; then, as these prospered, they increased in number and importance, until, in course of time, they came to be the real objective, and having ousted the commercial spirits, remained masters of the field, retaining only such subsidiary buying and selling as helped to add to their emoluments, and were necessary for the refreshment of the visitors.

That St. James's Fair still retained something of its earlier character in the time of Queen Elizabeth is evidenced by what Machyn says of it in his Diary.

"The XXV day of June (1560) St. James's Fayer by Westminster was so great that a man could not have a pygg for money; and the bear (beer) wiffes had nether meate nor drinke before iiij of cloke in the same day. And the chese went very well away for 1ᵈ. q. the pounde. Besides the great and mighti armie of beggares and baudes that ther were."[1] This seems to show that the trade was so brisk that high prices were paid and that there was insufficiency or goods to meet the demands; while the women who sold drinks were so busily engaged as to be unable to get any refreshment themselves till a late hour. There appear to have been no side-shows then, otherwise one imagines they would have been referred to by the chronicler. But be this as it may, there is little doubt that in course of time such things crept in, accompanied by those abuses and irregularities to which they so often gave rise, and thus we find St. James's Fair being suppressed in the year 1664, as "tending rather to the advantage of looseness and irregularity, than to the substantial promotion of any good, common and beneficial to the people."[2]

Once at least before its suppression Pepys visited it, being taken there by his friend, Doling, on July 26, 1660; but he makes no comment on the place, merely remarking that he met there W. Symons and his wife, and Luellin, and D. Scobell's wife and cousin, and

[1] "The Diary of Henry Machyn."
[2] Frost "The Old Showmen and the Old London Fairs," 1874.

with them went off to Woods' "in the Pell Mell (our old house for clubbing)[1] and there we spent till ten at night."

In the following August, Rugge in his "Diurnal," tells us that the fair was kept as usual, but that "many lewd and infamous persons were committed by the King's commands" for infesting it; a good and sufficient reason for its ultimate suppression.

Soon after it had ceased its activities, Lord St. Albans began his building development in the West End, and among other things erected a market-house in the centre of the spot that had been identified with St. James's Fair, "up and down my Lord St. Albans his new building and market-house," writes Pepys, on April 1, 1666, "looking to and again into every place building." This market-house was to become part and parcel of the resuscitated fair, and to be used, in its lower portion, for the sale of toys and gingerbread; and upstairs as a miniature theatre. This, however, was not destined to take place for many years, as it was not till the reign of James II.[2] that a licence was granted for the holding of a fair on May 1 and following fourteen days, in place of the old St. James's Fair. It was in consequence of the month of May being selected that it received the name of Mayfair. When the fair was again revived, its booths and stalls occupied most of the ground as far as Piccadilly and Park Lane and a good way towards Oxford Street. "The open space westward," says Frost, "was covered with the booths of jugglers, fencers, and boxers, the stands of mountebanks, swings, roundabouts, etc., while the sides of the streets were occupied by sausage stalls and gambling tables. The first-floor windows were also, in some instances, made to serve as the *proscenia* of puppet shows."

[1] The first recorded instance of the word.
[2] The *London Gazette* for September 1688 recites the grant "for a market of live cattle to be held in Brook-field, near Hyde Park Corner."

In 1696, according to a newspaper announcement, the first three days of the fair were restricted to the sale of leather and live cattle, and it is stated that "those that bring in leather has (*sic*) their ground this year *gratis*. This Fair," the writer says, "continues yearly at the same time and place, when there is a droll called King William's happy Deliverance and glorious Triumph over his Enemies, or the whole form of the siege of Namur."

Although there were probably many more, only two outstanding shows have been identified with May fair during the year 1702; one of these being Barnes and Finlay's, and the other Miller's, which stood opposite to each other, and carried on an active and noisy rivalry.

It was not long before Mayfair began to equal the fairs of Bartholomew and Southwark in its riotous character. Its central position made it an easy place for young men of family but loose morals to frequent, and the inhabitants of Whetstone Park and the Seven Dials found it equally convenient, and flocked thither. The authorities made some attempt to prevent suspected people from gaining entrance to the place, but the only effect was to provoke something very like a serious riot in the year 1702. Certain women being apprehended as being prostitutes, were promptly rescued by a body of soldiers. The watchmen thus attacked sought the aid of others; many of the frequenters of the fair took sides, and a battle-royal ensued, and was not ended before one of the guardians of the peace (John Cooper) had been killed and three dangerously wounded; while a butcher (Cook), who had shown himself specially active in withstanding the officers of the law, was arrested and eventually hanged on the adjacent Tyburn Tree.[1]

[1] The tumult occurred on May 12. The funeral sermon for Cooper was preached by the Rev. J. Woodward, at St. James's Church, and was afterwards published.

In the following year Mayfair was "presented" by the grand jury of Middlesex, as being a public nuisance; but for some reason nothing was done to suppress it at the time, and for some years it continued to be a source of amusement and profit to many, a cause of apprehension to others, and a veritable nuisance to those unlucky enough to dwell or have their businesses in its vicinity.

That extraordinary *impresario* Penkethman, who, besides being an actor at Drury Lane, owned a theatre at Richmond, and ran shows at Bartholomew and Southwark Fairs, had, I have little doubt, an interest in some of the entertainments given at Mayfair, although his name does not appear in connection with them;[1] and one might give a shrewd guess that it was some such far-reaching influence as his that made the various presentations of the place by the grand Jury of no effect. However, in 1708, notice was at length taken of the complaints which were focussed in their statement "that the yearly riotous and tumultuous assembly in a place called Brookfield, in the parish of St. Martin's-in-the Fields, called May Fair," was "a public nuisance and inconvenience"; and it was accordingly suppressed.

A little vignette of the fair at the beginning of the eighteenth century is contained in a letter of Brian Fairfax dated 1701:[2] "I wish," he writes, "you had been at May Fair, where the rope-dancing would have recompensed your labour. All the nobility in town were there, and I am sure even you, at your years, must have had your youthful wishes, to have beheld the beauty, shape, and activity of Lady Mary when she danced. Pray ask my Lord Fairfax after

---

[1] Since writing this I find an entry in *The Tatler*, for April 1709, which runs thus: "Advices from the upper part of Piccadily say that May Fair is utterly abolished, and we hear Mr. Penkethman has removed his ingenious company of strollers to Greenwich."

[2] In the *Tatler*.

her, who, though not the only lord by twenty, was every night an admirer of her while the fair lasted. There was the city of Amsterdam, well worth your seeing; every street, every individual house was carved in wood, in exact proportion one to another; the Stadthouse was as big as your hand; the whole, though an irregular figure, yet that you may guess, about ten yards diameter. Here was a boy to be seen, that within one of his eyes had Deus Meus in capital letters, as Gulielmus is on half-a-crown; round the other he had a Hebrew inscription, but this you must take as I did, upon trust."

When the suppression of May Fair was an accomplished fact, all sorts of curiosities were sold off as being no longer useful for the purpose of shows there, and probably superfluous in other fairs, where much the same sort of exhibits were to be seen. In *The Tatler* for May 1709, the following humorous paragraph appeared: "May Fair is now broke. . . . but it is allowed still to sell animals there. Therefore if any lady or gentleman have occasion for a tame elephant, let them enquire of Mr. Penkethman, who has one to dispose of at a reasonable rate. The downfall of May Fair has quite sunk the price of this noble creature as well as of many other curiosities of nature. A tiger will sell almost as cheap as an ox; and I am credibly informed a man may purchase a cat with three legs for very near the value of one with four."[1]

One of the reasons for the fair being "broke," as *The Tatler* phrases it, is indicated in a little tract published in this very year (1709) and entitled "Reasons for suppressing the yearly Fair in Brookfield, Westminster, commonly called May Fair." After noticing the re-institution of the fair by Charles II.,

---

[1] I suppose this is the same elephant which Steele refers to in the *Spectator*, when he says he saw it at Bartholomew Fair kneel down and take "the ingenious Mr. Pinkethman" on its back. *Spectator.* No. 455.

it proceeds to say that "In this time sad experience hath demonstrated that this grant, however well intended, hath been of ill consequence, tending to corrupt the *Minds* and *Manners* of very many People; insomuch that it is now one of the most pestilent nurseries of *Impurity* and *Vice*; and one of the most notorious occasions of *Riot* and *Disorder*. Multitudes of the *Booths* erected in this Fair, are not for *Trade* and *Merchandise*, but for *Musick*, *Showes*, *Drinking*, *Gaming*, *Raffling*, *Lotteries*, *Stage-Plays*, and *Drolls*; which are constant and open scenes of *Impiety* and *Profaneness*, and very frequently the stalls of *Vice*, and *Impurities* not to be mentioned."

But although May Fair had earned so unenviable a notoriety and had been presented by the Grand Jury so frequently, it bore a charmed life. It had been suppressed more than once, but somehow it continued its activities after a sufficient period had elapsed for its irregularities to be forgotten or overlooked. It might, however, have seemed that the year 1709 was to witness its final extinction. This, however, was not so, and although in 1721 we read that "the ground upon which the May Fair formerly was held is marked out for a large Square, and several fine streets and houses are to be built upon it,"[1] we know that it had a re-crudescence, and in 1736 a donkey race at the fair is recorded as having drawn crowds of people thither; while two years later we read that "Mr. Shepheard the Builder hath obtained his Majesty's grant for a Market of Live Cattle at May Fair."[2]

Shepherd, whose name is perpetuated in this Market, was about to develop the land he owned here, and no doubt regarded a market as a valuable adjunct to his property. As we can see from Rocque's plan, of 1746,

[1] *London Journal* for May 27, 1721. The square mentioned never materialized.

[2] *Gentleman's Magazine* for March, 1738.

the ground around Shepherd's Market was but
partially built over on its south and west sides, and the
once-famous Ducking Pond is shown almost due west
of Mayfair Chapel (whose site is now occupied by
Sunderland House). The sport of hunting a duck
with dogs used to be a favourite one here, and was
for long perpetuated by name in the little old wooden
public-house known as the Dog and Duck, which
stood close by, partly on the site of Hertford
Street.[1]

The coming of the Market gave a new lease of life
to the fair, which during its annual fortnight became
part and parcel of it; and what a prosperous recrudescence it must have had is proved by the recollections
of a certain Mr. John Carter, who in 1816 communicated them to the pages of the *Gentleman's
Magazine*.

"Fifty years have passed," he writes, "since this
place of amusement was at *its height of attraction*. . . .
The Market house consisted of two stories; first
story, a long and cross aile for butchers' shops, ex-
ternally, other shops connected with culinary purposes;
second story, used as a theatre at fair-time, for dramatic
performances. . . . In the areas encompassing the
market-building were booths for jugglers, prize-
fighters, both at cudgels and backsword, boxing
matches, and wild beasts. The sports under cover
were mountebanks, fire-eaters, ass-racing, sausage-
tables, dice ditto, ups-and-downs, merry-go-rounds,
bull-baiting, grinning for a hat, running for a shift,
hasty-pudding eaters, eel-divers, and an infinite variety
of other similar pastimes;" and he proceeds to particularize such exhibitions as the Mountebank's
Stage, erected opposite the Three Jolly Butchers
tavern, later to become the King's Arms; the Be-
heading of Puppets; the Strong Woman, on whose

[1] For an account of this "sport," once so favourite a one, see Strutt's
"Sports and Pastimes."

bosom an anvil and forge were placed and a horse shoed thereat; and Tiddy Doll, the then renowned seller of ginger-bread, a commodity without which no fair has ever been regarded as quite complete.

But although Mr. Carter, writing in 1816, speaks of half a century earlier as being the heyday of the fair, which would date its high-water mark at 1766, what he saw then must have been in the nature of its swan-song. For two years earlier the Earl of Coventry had purchased Sir Henry Hunloke's residence in Piccadilly (now the St. James's Club); and it was not many years after this that he, being annoyed at the riot and disorder that occurred during fair time at the back of his premises, procured, by what means is not recorded, the abolition of May Fair. Lord Chesterfield, who speaks of living in a neighbourhood of thieves and murderers, among which he no doubt included the butchers of May Fair, must have been pleased at the abolition of the nuisance (as must the then few other residents round about), and may have been instrumental with Lord Coventry in putting an end to it. One person, however, one thinks, would not, had he been alive, have seen its disappearance with so much equanimity, for the Rev. Alexander Keith, to whom I refer, must have done a roaring trade at his chapel close by during the progress of the fair, when he held his "Fleet marriages" at a guinea each [1] in spite of the fulminations of the Bishops, whom he once threatened to *under bury.*

[1] He is known to have conducted 6000 marriages here in a single year.

CHAPTER XIV

THE PLEASURE GARDENS: MARYLEBONE GARDENS, ETC.

THE Pleasure Garden was an essentially eighteenth-century form of recreation in London; true, a few can be traced to a time slightly anterior to that period, such as Lambeth Wells in 1697, Islington Spa in 1684, Sadler's Wells in 1683, Pancras Wells in 1697 and Cuper's Gardens in 1691, but it was with the beginning of the new century that they began an activity as pronounced as it was widespread, and by its close that they were like the sands of the sea in number. As I have shown, and as will be more apparent when we have considered some of those gardens dealt with in this chapter, such places as Ranelagh and Vauxhall were essentially different from the ordinary pleasure gardens of the eighteenth century; and if, as exceptions, the Spring Gardens of earlier days may to some extent be found approximating to the latter, and the later Marylebone Gardens having no little in common with Vauxhall and Ranelagh, these exceptions may be taken to prove the rule.

The annals of these Pleasure Gardens have been detailed, with a wealth of documentary evidence, by the late Mr. Warwick Wroth,[1] and no one dealing with this subject can possibly ignore his invaluable work. Writing in this book on a more extended subject, I can only touch on the many pleasure haunts of which Mr. Wroth has left so complete a record, and I gratefully acknowledge my debt to his indefatigable exertions.

[1] "The London Pleasure Gardens of the Eighteenth Century," 1896.

Of the sixty or seventy odd places of amusement and recreation of this character which formerly existed in the London area, and which are found in groups at Chelsea, and Marylebone, Clerkenwell, and Hampstead, and Highbury, and on the other side of the river from Kennington to Bermondsey and Rotherhithe, the most outstanding, after Vauxhall and Ranelagh, was *Marylebone Gardens;* not only because of its long and prosperous history, but because it was intimately associated, for a time, with the fashionable annals of the day, and because it possessed something in common with those two famous centres that stand like sentinels guarding the manners and customs of all classes during what was socially and decoratively the most interesting period of our history.

Opposite old Marylebone Church, on the east side of the High Street, was once a tavern called the Rose, or the Rose of Normandy, and this formed the entrance to Marylebone Gardens, which reached as far as Harley Street, and whose site is to-day occupied by Beaumont Street, a portion of Devonshire Street and Devonshire Place, and Upper Wimpole Street.

For a number of years there existed a garden with a bowling-green, part of the grounds of the old Manor House, here, to which people in the neighbourhood were wont to resort, and which Pepys is found visiting and finding "a pretty place" in 1668. The tavern attached to this was a notorious gambling centre; and in course of time certain other features were added, such as fireworks on notable occasions, and music, and once, a so-called Flying Man exhibited his prowess here. Such things were a success, and it occurred to the proprietor of the Rose, one Daniel Gough, that he might make something out of the place, in addition to what he gained by the sale of food and drink, by opening it as a regular pleasure resort, with an entrance fee and so forth, and on

T. Donowell del. 1761.   A View of the Orchestra with the Band of Music, the Grand Walk &c. in Marybone Gardens

Engraved by A. Carse.

MARYLEBONE GARDENS

1755

July 12, 1738, we find him doing so and calling it "Marybone Gardens."

Gough had engaged some members of the opera and the theatre orchestras to play good music from six till ten o'clock; and two years after he had opened his gardens, he commissioned Bridge to build him an organ. He had already erected a "Great Room" for balls and supper-parties, and by 1740 Marylebone Gardens may be said to have been well launched and, to use a later phrase, to have caught on. It had its silver tickets (at twelve shillings each, later at a guinea), which admitted two subscribers for the season; and it rather obviously tried to rival the attractions of Vauxhall and Ranelagh. One thing which differentiated it from these haunts was the fact that, as a contemporary advertisement puts it, the proprietor humbly requests that no gentleman will smoke on the walks! Walpole speaks of the statue-lined garden and the fireworks of Marylebone, and Rocque's plan shows how elaborately its grounds were laid out and how extensive they were.[1] This was long after Captain Macheath had frequented it to his undoing, and such deep play went on there, that "money could be picked up on the road," as he says in the "Beggar's Opera."

In 1753 the gardens were considerably enlarged, under the *ægis* of John Trusler, who managed the place for John Sherratt. Trusler had been a cook, and his daughter, inheriting his culinary ability, produced certain almond cheese-cakes, which became a special feature of the place.

That the gardens were well regulated is evidenced by the fact that Sir John Fielding once remarked that Londoners should not require Mrs. Cornelys's entertainments when they had the music and wine and plum-cakes of Marylebone, and the fireworks of

---

[1] By a later plan in the Crace Collection, dated 1756, we see what large alterations and, from the point of public convenience, what improvements, had been made in the place in the intervening ten years.

Ranelagh. He might have added fireworks to the Marylebone Gardens attractions, for they formed a portion of its "shows," and Walpole speaks of seeing them illuminating the sky as he walked at night in his Strawberry Hill grounds.

Here, too, the music was excellent, and many of those who sang at Ranelagh and Vauxhall also gave performances at Marylebone—Lowe, and Baker, and Michael Arne, and Rheinhold; with the famous Defesch as first violin. In 1758, a "burletta" was first performed here: "La Serva Padrona, or the Servant Mistress," and met with such applause that it was frequently repeated; although it only reminded Dr. Johnson of the discords he daily experienced in Bolt Court. Notable people began to visit the place, and Mr. Handel—the "Master of Musick," was to be seen there with his friend Mr. Fountayne. On one such occasion, after listening to the band, the latter suggested that they should go, as the music was "poor stuff," "Yes, Mr. Fountayne," said Handel, "so I thought when I had written it!"

Another notable visitor to the gardens, at least on one occasion, was Dr. Johnson himself, who went there with George Steevens to see the firework display of the famous Torré, with whose exhibition he once compared Gray's poetry, by the bye. It would appear that the evening was wet and the squibs and catherine-wheels were a failure. Johnson, annoyed at what he attributed to the parsimony of the management rather than the vagaries of the weather, proposed to threaten to smash the coloured lamps as a protest, a remark which, being overheard by some young sparks, was immediately acted upon, and something like a riot ensued. Whether it was on this occasion that he made his remark on the "Serva Padrone" is not recorded; but the idea of the learned lexicographer as the protagonist in a destructive onslaught on anything but a piece of bad literature, is amusing.[1]

[1] See Austin Dobson's "Side-walk Studies."

Although Marylebone Gardens was as a rule well
regulated and decent, occasional disturbances were
not unknown there, and we read of a quarrel occurring
between two hot-headed *habitués*, when swords were
drawn, and the result might have had a tragic ending,
but for the interference of the bystanders, which,
however, did not prevent the disputants from settling
their differences with their fists. The Duke of Cumberland, who was a frequent visitor, often behaved here,
we are told, in a scandalous manner[1]; but then he was
not noted for special good behaviour anywhere; and
the fact that there are few instances on record of
people making themselves objectionable at Marylebone is a proof that on the whole the gardens were
far more carefully conducted than were many other
similar haunts at that period. Indeed by the year
1753, when the gardens had been enlarged and
improved, a contemporary writer is able to state that
there was to be seen there, the largest and politest
assembly possible gathered together.

In this year the *Public Advertiser* announced the
extension which had taken place; and also informed
its readers that lights had been erected on the thoroughfare from the Oxford Road, as well as on the foot-path
from Cavendish Square. The fact is the neighbourhood
of the gardens was anything but a safe one after
nightfall. Footpads abounded in those then unfre-
quented parts, and so dangerous was the going and
coming between inhabited London, and what was
then an outlying pleasure haunt, that, in 1741 and
for some years later, a guard of soldiers was provided
to conduct people there, and to see them safely back
between eleven and twelve. The daily news-sheets
provide ample evidence of the danger, to purse and
even person, run, in those times, by people who
adventured a hair's-breadth beyond the inhabited
streets. Nor were the common footpads the only
depredators to be feared, noted highwaymen did not

[1] "Dr. Trusler's Memoirs."

disdain these fields of activity, and if Marylebone Lane was not as much infested by these gentry as Turnham Green and other selected spots, it was simply because the presence of the guardians of the peace, and the numbers going to and from the gardens made it, in comparison, a less safe theatre for their activities. Once, however, Dick Turpin is said to have kissed a young lady, noted for her beauty, in the gardens themselves, and although the anecdote may only rest on tradition, it is quite probable, when one remembers the "gallant" character of that popular scoundrel, and also remembers the assurance with which such as he were wont to exhibit themselves publicly.

It was apparently in 1760 that Marylebone Gardens were first opened to the public on Sundays, when the company were admitted free; and it was then that Miss Trusler's cakes and other dainties were added to by "fruit fresh gathered in the gardens." A contemporary advertisement tells us that that enterprising young lady, who used "none but loaf-sugar and the finest Epping butter" in the concoction of her dainties, was prepared to send her "new and rich seed and plum cakes to any part of the town"; and that she provided these, as well as coffee, tea and chocolate at any time of the day in the gardens.

Three years after this the famous Tommy Lowe, who had sung here earlier and had been a standing favourite at Vauxhall for many years, took over the gardens at a rent of £170; and with him the place entered on a period of five years of harmony. As a singer and musician he naturally paid special attention to the musical attractions, and in addition to the orchestra, he engaged a number of well-known vocalists to perform here. Nollekens remembered being taken by his grandmother "to hear Tommy Lowe sing"; and he tells us that the orchestra stood exactly on the site later to be occupied by No. 17, Devonshire Place.

Among the singers who performed here during Lowe's management were Mrs. Vincent, Mrs. Lampe, and Nan Catley, who, with Miss Smith and Lowe himself, took part in a "Musical Address to the Town," with which the season opened. Besides these, Miss Hyat, Miss Smith, Miss Plenius and Mr. Squibb, Mrs. Collett, Miss Davis, Mrs. Taylor, Mr. Legg, Mr. Raworth, and Mrs. Gibbons appeared here at one time or another under Lowe's direction, at the concerts at which he was an assiduous manager and very frequently a performer. Airs by Handel and Boyce were given, and catches and glees often formed part of the programme. The concerts began at 6.30, and the admission to the gardens (which opened at five o'clock) was one shilling. In 1766 these delights were added to by "an exhibition of bees"; and tea was to be had at eightpence a head. The subscription for the season for two people was fixed at a guinea and a half.

Whether Lowe concentrated too much on his musical programme, or whether want of enterprise, as has been suggested, coupled with a wet season, was the cause, it is a fact that by 1767 he found himself in monetary difficulties, and in the January of the following year he was obliged to assign all his rights in the gardens to his creditors.

Under the new management the place was carried on at a loss, although Miss Davis and Mr. Phillips for a week's singing only received three guineas; while Werner, the harpist, got a guinea less. But the band cost nearly £30 a week, and there must have been many heavy expenses connected with the upkeep of the gardens. Anyhow, notwithstanding receipts for the season of over £2000, there was a deficit of over £250 at its close; and the creditors were probably glad enough when Dr. Samuel Arnold came forward and took the place off their hands. It was under Arnold that Marylebone Gardens reached the apex of

A A

its fame and (although Arnold on his retirement was actually a loser by the venture) what may be termed its prosperity. Arnold himself composed several pieces of music for it, and James Hook, the father of the better-remembered Theodore, wrote some of the songs which were received with so much applause.

Arnold did much to improve the grounds in other ways, and took special trouble to drain them and to construct a covered platform for shelter against the rain. He arranged for firework displays under the direction of such well-known pyrotechnists as Rossi and Clanfield; he engaged Barthelemon to play the violin, and Rheinhold and Charles Bannister and Mrs. Thompson to sing, and it was he who gave Chatterton five guineas for a burletta, called "The Revenge," which, however, was not actually performed till many years later. That good music should have been a feature of Arnold's management goes without saying, and we know that on September 4, 1770, Corelli's fourth Concerto was given here. If many people loved music then, more loved fireworks, and with the famous Torré directing them, such things during the years 1772–4 drew great crowds to the gardens; although people who had begun to live in the neighbourhood were not so delighted by these nocturnal displays and the consequent noise they produced. The "Forge of Vulcan," which was one of the "shows," could hardly have proved welcome to those who night after night heard the expected explosions; but it proved a great "draw" to less-sophisticated visitors; while another pyrotechnic display of which "upwards of 10,000 cases of different fires all lighted at the same time" was a feature, what time martial music was performed in the Temple of Apollo, ravished the Lydia Melfords of the period, and were attractive to even less susceptible minds.

When any special performance was given, the management was accustomed to raise the price of

admission, and as much as five shillings was sometimes charged in place of the usual shilling—this not
without occasional protest on the part of the newspapers, whose writers indicated that the increased fee
was not justified by the few extra lamps and festoons
with which, in July 1774, the gardens were decorated
and the result grandiloquently called a *Fête Champêtre*.

In that curious little work entitled "A Sunday
Ramble," there is anything but an enthusiastic description of Marylebone Gardens on a Sunday, but
it is perhaps hardly fair to judge it from what it
looked like on what was an off day. However, here is
what the writer says of the place under these conditions: "Instead of beholding agreeable walks, beautiful alcoves, and delightful retreats: the garden, as it
is arrogantly stiled, consists of nothing more than
two or three gravel *roads*, and a few shapeless trees.
The places *intended* for company, are the meanest
possible to conceive. . . . Those parts which might
otherwise somewhat resemble a garden, are clogged
with a parcel of rubbish and lumber, for the fireworks of Signor Torré, and other ingenious imitators
of the infernal regions. In short, the whole place is in
the greatest confusion and disorder possible to conceive. I only wonder that the publick have so long
bore with this daring impeachment of their understanding." [1]

As only sixpence was charged for Sunday admission, which included tea, it was perhaps hardly fair
to expect more than our Rambler found. But there is
little doubt that the days of Marylebone Gardens
were drawing to a close. The discovery of a mineral
spring in the gardens gave the management the idea
of making this a further inducement to visitors, and
it was advertised and opened as the Marybone Spa—
one of that numerous band of water-drinking resorts

[1] A Sunday Ramble or Modern Sabbath-Day Journey in and about
London, etc., 12 mo., *circa* 1772.

which were to be found in London at this period. But it does not appear to have been a great success; and with the discontinuance of the concerts (in 1775), although firework displays still held their ground, the place entered on the last phase of its existence. The fact is that as an open-air resort it had outlived its popularity; and the coming of a conjuror and a magic lantern, and above all of lectures, indicates that it was hoped to give it a new lease of life as an indoor pleasure haunt—if any pleasure can possibly be associated with lectures.

The Swan-song of Marylebone Gardens occurred in 1776, when Torré's show was reproduced, and Caillot exhibited his fireworks, and other delights were tried to win back the public to the haunts in which they had once delighted. But, if it did this, it was but for a short time, and at the end of the season, in September, the place was finally closed. Two years later the inevitable building development began, which was to cover the site of the gardens with houses and streets, and finally to obliterate all traces of a place which, if it never attained the vogue of Ranelagh and Vauxhall, has an outstanding place in the social life of the period.

As might have been expected, considering the facilities it then afforded for rural entertainment, the south side of the Thames was in the eighteenth century a great centre for the Tea Gardens and Spa Gardens, as they were called, which were in such request in those days. Sometimes the already known existence of a mineral spring resulted in the formation around it of a pleasure garden where people could find amusement as well as what purported to be health-giving liquid; sometimes a spring of this character was opportunely discovered in such an already formed place of entertainment, generally, as the sceptical will be quick to observe, at a moment when the popularity of the place merely as a pleasure resort was on the wane. If all the springs that were discovered in and about London during this period really possessed the advantages claimed for them, it is a wonder that society ever went to the trouble and expense of journeying to Tunbridge Wells or Bath.

The two moſt important of such places in the South London area were Bermondsey Spa Gardens and Cuper's Gardens; although Finch's Grotto Gardens almoſt rivalled them in popularity and the variety of the attractions it offered the public.

Bermondsey Spa Gardens was situated at a point in the middle of Grange Road, a thoroughfare connecting Long Lane with Southwark Park Road; its site being marked by Spa Road. It was created by one Thomas Keyse, a self-taught artiſt, who, having purchased a tavern called the Waterman's Arms, with some ground surrounding it, opened it as a Tea Garden, where many of his own pictures formed the chief decorations. A few years after the Tea Gardens had been in exiſtence, a mineral spring was discovered in the grounds, and Keyse's place became known as the Bermondsey Spa Gardens, presided over by the cheery hoſt, whose forte (beyond the mere painting of pictures) was the making of cherry brandy.

The place continued to flourish until in 1784, Keyse having obtained a music-licence, and having expended some thousands of pounds on improvements, it was thrown open as a regular pleasure haunt at a shilling admission (raised on special occasions to half-a-crown and even three shillings), with an orchestra, coloured lamps, alcoves and arbours, a sort of miniature Vauxhall.

According to J. T. Smith, Jonas Blewitt, the famous organiſt, composed many of the songs sung here, while the verses were written by Oakman and Harriss; and these and burlettas, duets and interludes, formed the musical fare provided, the chief exponents of which were, however, only local lights.

Sometimes firework displays were given; and a sort of elaborate set-piece representing the Siege of Gibraltar was a favourite spectacle. As the fireworks were sometimes under the direction of Rossi of Ranelagh fame, they may be supposed to have been as good as the pyrotechnic art of the day could make them.

But for many the exhibition of Keyse's own pictures, which were shown in a special gallery, was an inducement to travel so far from London's centre, and the painter once told J. T. Smith that Sir Joshua Reynolds had been to see them more than once.

If not fashionable, the place was at least respectable, and for some years provided entertainment for a not too sophisticated audience, who must not infrequently have left its lamp-lighted groves with a certain fear, although the proprietor had arranged to have the road lighted "and watched by patroles"[1] in order to prevent footpads from preying on the departing guests.

The Bermondsey Spa Gardens waned in popularity towards the close of the eighteenth century, and when J. T. Smith paid it a visit in 1795, he found it practically deserted, except for a few waiters and Keyse himself, who had an interesting conversation with him, a conversation which he records at length in his gossiping book of reminiscences.[2]

Keyse died in 1800; and although the place was carried on for a time by successors, its end came about five years later.

Cuper's Gardens is a far better remembered place, for it was a very favourite resort during the days of the earlier Georges, and its name is known to many who have not the remotest idea where it was situated. As a matter of fact those who go over Waterloo Bridge

---

[1] According to advertisements in the newspapers.
[2] "Book for a Rainy Day."

and down the Waterloo Bridge Road are, after they
have walked a few paces, passing straight through the
centre of what in former times was Cuper's Gardens.
From Rocque's plan we get an excellent idea not
only of the extent of them, but also of the way in
which they were laid out. A landing-stage on the
river called Cuper's Bridge gave access to a lane
which led directly to the entrance, about eighty yards
from the Thames. The gardens extended southwards
nearly to St. John's Church. They were long and
narrow, about 800 feet by 200, and had serpentining
paths among trees and bushes on each side of a long
central alley; on the west side of which was an oblong
piece of water. The buildings attached to the place
were nearer the river on the east side.

As a pleasure haunt Cuper's Gardens dates from
the closing years of the seventeenth century, for it
was first opened for such a purpose by one Boyder[1]
Cuper, in 1691, if not earlier, and walks, decorated
with some of the Arundel marbles, and arbours and a
bowling-green were then sufficient to attract people
thither, many of such patrons coming by boat from
the opposite shore, and landing at a little inn called
the Feathers, which was connected with the place,
and formed a convenient landing-stage for it.

During its earlier days, it seems chiefly to have
been used as a place for walking in and lounging,
by the denizens of the city who much frequented it
during the summer, and by whom it was popularly
known as Cupid's Gardens, a name perpetuated in a
song of the period, and given the place for obvious
reasons.[2]

Music and other attractions were brought to the

[1] So spelt by Wroth, but Nollekens calls him Baydell, and is followed
by Dr. Wheatley. Nollekens says he had been a gardener to the Earl of
Arundel, which would account for his possession of some of the statuary
once at Arundel House.

[2] See "Nollekens and his Times," by J. T. Smith.

gardens in 1738, when Ephraim Evans, once mine hoſt of the Hercules Pillars Tavern, in Fleet Street, took them over in that year, much improved them, and added an orcheſtra which discoursed the airs of Corelli and Handel to the visitors. The entrance was one shilling; but on Sundays, until 1752, when they were closed on that day, the gardens were open free to the public. Evans took ſteps to keep the gardens seleƈt, and for those entering by a gate off St. George's Fields, ſtationed watchmen to guard his visitors againſt footpads.

In 1740 Evans died, but was succeeded by his widow in the management, and it was under her *ægis* that the moſt flourishing period of Cuper's Gardens occurred. People from the Weſt End began to frequent the place; even the Prince and Princess of Wales were to be seen there, and much of the *haut-ton* came hither by water—two of its members, Lord Bath and Lord Sandys, once having their pockets picked here, as Horace Walpole records. Like all such resorts, Cuper's Gardens was a happy hunting-ground for petty depredators, and others who were worse, and, according to one writer, it was hardly a place for the unproteƈted female to visit with impunity.[1]

Although music—and very good music it muſt have been, from the names of the composers and executant that have come down to us—was for a time the chief source of attraƈtion here, Mrs. Evans, who was evidently a woman of resource and energy, realized that the frequenters required something more; and firework displays were organized, and soon became a feature here, advertisements in the newspapers conſtantly making known some novelty in this direƈtion. One time the Gorgon's Head formed a kind of set-piece; at another, Neptune drawn by sea-horses appeared; while in honour of the viƈtory

[1] "The Complete Letter Writer," 1773; quoted in *Notes and Queries*, 7th series.

of Culloden "triumphant arches" glittered with a thousand colours; what time the equally triumphant notes of Handel floated on the summer air, or the gentle melodies of Arne.

The crowds that congregated to see and hear such things were great, and we read of people climbing into the trees the better to see the sights, and of one of them falling headlong among the massed spectators, including, perhaps, the "spirited young thing" who promenaded the gardens dressed as a man, to the wonder of all.

That the moral atmosphere of Cuper's Gardens was not what it should have been, is evident. Mrs. Evans no doubt was anxious to keep it orderly; but such places, when once they take on an air of rakishness, cannot well be regulated by the best-intentioned. So when in 1752 an Act was passed for, among other analogous things, "regulating places of public amusement," Cuper's Gardens fell a victim, and the renewal of its licence was refused. It had, indeed, become, as Pennant says he remembers it, "a scene of low dissipation,"[1] and Mrs. Evans was forced to re-open it in a modified form as a Tea Garden. She, no doubt, hoped gradually to revive its former character as a regular pleasure haunt, and, indeed, in 1755 did so, but only to subscribers, and as a musical centre, by which she sought to evade the actual wording of the Act of three years earlier. Fireworks were also revived under the cloak of the excitement incident to the coronation of George III. But it would seem that these were stopped, as in the following year the place reverted to its Tea Garden state, in which it survived till 1759, when it came to an end with a concert given on August 30, as it was publicly stated, "by a select company of gentlemen for their own private diversion."

Later the ground was taken by Beaufoys, the wine merchants, and it was during their occupancy, which

[1] "Some Account of London," 1813.

began in 1768, that J. T. Smith visited the place, and saw some of the remaining objects which had once decorated the gardens. In 1814, when the ground was required for the south approach to Waterloo Bridge, Beaufoys' works were demolished.

It should not be forgotten that Dr. Johnson's name is associated with the gardens that had such a vogue during part of the eighteenth century. "Beauclerk, and I, and Langton, and Lady Sydney Beauclerk, mother to our friend," he once told Boswell, "were one day driving in a coach by Cuper's Gardens, which were then unoccupied. I, in sport, proposed that Beauclerk, and Langton, and myself should take them; and we amused ourselves with scheming how we should all do our parts. Lady Sydney grew angry, and said, 'an old man should not put such things in young people's heads!' She had no notion of a joke, sir; had come late into life, and had a mighty unpliable understanding."[1]

According to Wilkinson, who was the first to attempt a connected account of *Finch's Grotto Gardens*, which he gleaned from those who actually remembered them, the site they occupied was a triangular piece of ground forming the western side of St. George's Street, Southwark, bounded on the south by the road called Dirty Lane and on the north by a vinegar yard in Lombard Street, at the extremity of St. Saviour's Parish. They were first opened in 1760, from which fact it has been supposed that they were intended to fill the place occupied by Cuper's Gardens down to the preceding year. A medicinal spring had been discovered here, and Thomas Finch, who had inherited the property, which consisted of a house and a well-treed and shrubbed garden, conceived the idea of turning this to account. Over the spring he built a grotto, and by the help of medical advertisement (although later investigations showed that the spring had no more special

---

[1] A long account of Cuper's Gardens will be found in Wilkinson's "Londina Illustrata."

qualities than any of the other innumerable ones in this
district) persuaded people that it was a panacea for all
sorts of ills. Subscribers at a guinea were admitted to
drink the waters and enjoy the entertainments that
were soon organized, entertainments to which casual
visitors had access by payment of one shilling each.

An octagon room, presumably already part and
parcel of the residence, was used as a music room, and
was profusely decorated; an organ was installed, and
an orchestra, and besides concerts, balls and similar
entertainments were given; while special nights were
set aside for Freemasons' gatherings, which were largely
attended. That the place was ever exactly fashionable
is a question. Miss Hardcastle certainly brackets it
with the Pantheon as a place where the nobility resort;[1]
but if this were so, it was but occasionally; and Finch's
Grotto may be regarded as one of those places where the
neighbouring citizens loved to congregate, and where
the absence of the *haut-ton* did not materially detract
from its respectability.

The concerts were certainly good enough, and those
who took part in them popular enough to attract the
West End, for many who sang at Covent Garden and
Drury Lane and Ranelagh and Sadler's Wells were to
be heard here, including the ever-attractive Tommy
Lowe and the charming Sophia Snow, better remembered as Mrs. Baddeley.

On the death of Finch in 1770, he was succeeded
in the conduct of the place by one Williams, who then
changed its name to Williams's Grotto Gardens. He
made a variety of alterations here, but essentially
carried it on on the lines by which Finch had achieved
success. Fireworks duly made their appearance as an
added attraction, and "transparencies" were exhibited
during 1771 and the following year. But notwithstanding the excellence of the fare provided (as attested
by the advertisements which appeared in the public

[1] In "She Stoops to Conquer," Act 2.

prints), the place did not pay its way, and in 1773, or thereabouts, it was closed. The grotto was later demolished, and the shrubs pulled up to make way for a skittle ground as an adjunct to the tavern which still held its own until its destruction by fire in 1795, when another house was erected on its site, in the wall of which was inserted a stone bearing the words

"Here Herbs did grow
And Flowers sweet,
But now 'tis called
Saint George's Street."

Wilkinson gives an engraving of this new tavern, which was first called "The Goldsmith's Arms," but later bore the legend that it was "The Old Grotto new Reviv'd." As in the case of Cuper's Gardens, the coming of a bridge brought about the destruction of this survival of Finch's Grotto Gardens, and when the Southwark Bridge Road was formed, in 1825, the building was pulled down.

Among the other pleasure gardens which once existed in this area, such places as *Belvedere House and Gardens*, Lambeth, which was little more than a tavern with "pleasant gardens," and as such was in existence but for a few years (1781–5); the *Flora Tea Gardens*, sometimes called Mount Gardens, in the Westminster Bridge Road, which the author of the "Sunday Ramble" once visited and found "very orderly," and probably very dull; *The Black Prince*, of which a print by Bowles is extant, showing men playing at trap-ball, for which the place was chiefly frequented; *Marble Hall*, Vauxhall, which was close to the more famous haunt, where in a "long room" facing the river, dancing was indulged in; and *The Cumberland Tea Gardens*, close by, on the banks of the river, a kind of half-way house to Vauxhall, and where in 1779 the proprietor, Smith (they were sometimes known as Smith's Tea Gardens), advertised a "Fête Champêtre," are examples of many of those lesser places of amusement, some of which hardly rose beyond the status of ordinary taverns, although now and again they ambitiously attempted to copy the doings of more outstanding pleasure haunts.

And there were others such as the *Restoration Spring Gardens*, in St. George's Fields, which had existed from the time of Charles II., and was noted for its medicinal waters, which were said to "far exceed" those of the more famous Dog and Duck, close by, but which were shown on analysis to be merely ordinary water. Public credulity, however, enabled these gardens and their spring to exist into the latter part of the eighteenth century, just as many others retained their prosperity for a like reason. Indeed the spring which had helped to make the *Dog and Duck* renowned (I say "helped," because this place had been so early as 1642 noted as the centre for the brutal sport of duck-hunting) was proved to be actually impure, although in the heyday of its prosperity it was known as St. George's Spa, and had a great reputation as a cure for all sorts of ills from sore eyes to cancer. Physicians of repute were found extolling it; the *St. James's Chronicle* once bracketed its excellencies with those of the waters of Buxton and Cheltenham, and Dr. Johnson, on one occasion at least, is known to have recommended its use to Mrs. Thrale.

At a later period, *circa* 1770, the place was altered and improved, the gardens laid out, and music performed in a room in which an organ had been installed. Much custom, too, accrued through the institution of a circus close by; and it was generally much frequented, although, latterly, by such a riff-raff[1] as made its suppression inevitable—a fate which befell it about the year 1799.

Lambeth Wells, situated in what is now Lambeth

[1] In the "Sunday Ramble" and elsewhere, evidence is given of the mixed and rowdy character of its *habitués* towards the close of the eighteenth century.

Walk, was yet another of those haunts which possessed the double attraction of medicinal qualities, and attendant amusement in the form of what one of its advertisements terms "consorts." The shilling concerts, which are thus indicated, were carried on for a few years, from 1697 to 1700, but the Dog and Duck, which had been fatal to other rivals, was the cause of Lambeth Wells losing its patrons, and about 1755 it ceased to exist both as a *pseudo* health-giving centre and a haunt of pleasure.

Two other somewhat similar places once stood on the left-hand side of the Westminster Bridge Road, as one goes south. One of these was called *The Temple of Flora*, the other, *The Apollo Gardens*, or Temple of Apollo. Such classic names were hardly supported by the facts; but there was an attempt, not only to give the Temple of Flora an air of luxury, so far as "elegant" statues and such-like embellishments were concerned, but also to make use of attractions in the form of firework displays, and cascades where the songs of a variety of birds were imitated. As, however, its proprietor, of the name of Grist, was indicted, in 1796, for keeping a disorderly house, the intention of these adjuncts is fairly obvious.

The Apollo Gardens aimed at something better, and concerts, at which reputable and sometimes well-known, performers took part, were given here, and fantoccini exhibited. In the gardens were pavilions and alcoves for those who preferred these to listening to the voices of the singers or the tones of the excellent organ. As the Apollo was, in 1788, managed by Claggett, who had once been lessee of the Pantheon, it may be supposed that under him things were done well. But the place gradually earned a bad name; pickpockets and worse characters seem to have found it a specially profitable resort, and in or about 1793 it was suppressed by order of the magistrates, its proprietor passed through the bankruptcy court, and the Temple itself, after remaining in a ruinous condition for some time, was demolished, and subsequently its site built over.

In Chelsea Ranelagh has obliterated the memory of other pleasure haunts of a smaller though not essentially dissimilar character, and, with one exception, they were not of first-rate importance. *Strombolo House* and gardens was, indeed, quite a minor centre of amusement, although from the fact that it stood just opposite the famous Chelsea Bun House, in Jew's Row (now the Pimlico Road), it has become remembered in connection with the better-known place. It was opened in 1762 as a tea-garden and nothing else, and should thus, perhaps, rather be included in places of refreshment than haunts of pleasure. When it ceased its activities, its site was occupied by the Orange Tea-Gardens, which, in view of the fact that a very small theatre—the Orange Theatre, was connected with them, may be said better to have deserved the name. Davis calls the original tea-garden Stromboli, and says the height of its popularity (which was probably, however, but a local one) was about the year 1788, and it seems probable that it did not continue long after that date.

The *Star and Garter Tavern* and gardens, in the Five Fields, that large tract of land on which Belgrave Square and its surrounding squares and streets are now, did attempt something more, as in 1762 it is found the centre of firework displays in a sort of double honour of the birth of George, Prince of Wales, and the visit of those Cherokee Indians who were taken everywhere to see the most unexpected sights. There were also other attractions provided, and among them Thomas Johnson's equestrian feats were much appreciated by visitors, who afterwards refreshed themselves at the neighbouring Dwarf's Tavern, also owned by the proprietor of the Star and Garter. The heyday of these places was in 1760,[1] and they were symbolical of many

[1] Davis's "Memorials of Knightsbridge."

such minor centres of recreation whither people went, as it was quite the fashion to do, "to drink tea at Pimlico," a phrase that became almost proverbial during the eighteenth century, when, as Gay sings,

". . . Chelsea's meads o'erhear perfidious vows,
And the press'd grass defrauds the grazing cows."

A rather earlier centre of this kind was "*Jenny's Whim*," near Ebury Bridge, which was quite a fashionable resort in the reign of George II., although by 1755 a contemporary writer describes it as being affected by "the lower sort of people." It possessed a bowling-green, a ducking-pond, and a cock-pit, as well as a well-kept garden with the usual alcoves, where, however, unusual accessories were mechanical figures which, on a spring being touched, started suddenly up, to the terror and confusion of many. The entrance fee was but sixpence, and in its prime Jenny's Whim seems to have been the resort of all classes. Lord Granby we know had been there when he joined Lady Caroline Petersham's famous party to Vauxhall, as recorded by Walpole; and according to Angelo, in his "Picnic," "it was much frequented, from its novelty, being an inducement to allure the curious, by its amusing deceptions," by which he alludes to the terrific monsters that lay hidden in its recesses. Towards the close of the eighteenth century it began to decline, and gradually becoming forgotten, it sank to the level of an ordinary tavern till 1804, when it became extinct.[1]

Almost exactly contemporaneous with Strombolo and the Star and Garter at Chelsea, were *Cromwell's Gardens* or *Florida Gardens*, as they were afterwards called, at Brompton. Whether Cromwell ever had any personal association with the place is rather a

[1] It is mentioned in a contemporary novel, entitled "Maids of Honour; a Tale of the Times of George the First"; and in 1755 appeared a satirical tract called "Jenny's Whim; or a Sure Guide to the Nobility, Gentry and other Eminent Persons in this Metropolis."

moot point, and one outside my province here. It is sufficient to say that what had originally been known as Hale House received for some reason its alternative appellation, which ſtuck to it; and when the tea-gardens were formed on part of its site (a site approximately coinciding with the south end of Prince's Gate) they went by this name. The rank and fashion of Kensington and its neighbourhood were wont to come here and wander about the well-kept grounds and take refreshment in the numerous arbours—arbours, as one writer says, that were "well adapted for gallantry and intrigue."[1] It became a haunt for the better class of proſtitutes, and the "Sunday Rambler" had ocular demonſtration of the faċt. But other amusements in the shape of music and equeſtrian performances by Charles Hughes were provided, and later, about 1780, when a Mr. Hiem took over the place and changed its name to the Florida Tea Gardens, a band played twice a week, a bowling-green was formed, and even fireworks and air balloons mounted into the sky.

In those days all this part was nursery gardens and open fields, and the pleasant and, as the age was fond of calling it, "salubrious" air drew as many people here as did the music or the pyrotechnics. In spite of all that he did, however, Hiem was not successful in making the gardens pay their way, and he eventually became bankrupt; the property being afterwards purchased by Maria, Duchess of Glouceſter, who built Maria or Orford Lodge, as it was successively called, on the site, and died there in 1807. Later Canning bought it and changed its name to Glouceſter Lodge.[2] Both the names of Cromwell and Glouceſter are to-day well represented in this quarter, where the orchards and market gardens, and the country lanes, have ceased to be even a memory.

[1] The author of "The Sunday Ramble."
[2] For reasons for identifying Cromwell's Gardens with the later Florida Gardens, see foot-note in Wroth's book, p. 226.

B B

CHAPTER XV

SPAS AND PLEASURE GARDENS

ALTHOUGH, as we have seen, some of the tea-gardens and such-like resorts in south London added to their attractions by the timely discovery of springs whose very ordinary qualities were mistaken by an unsophisticated generation for medicinal properties, and were even, in some cases, recommended by over-optimistic doctors, the majority of such springs were to be found in the northern heights of the metropolis, and did more nearly approximate to the health-giving waters of Buxton and Bath, with which their proprietors were never chary of comparing them.

One of the best known, as well as the oldest, of these was *Hampstead Wells*, whose waters were a source of profit to one, Dorothy Rippin, in the time of Charles II., a period when the exploitation of such things began.[1] With the help of the well-known Dr. Gibbons's assertion that the well possessed excellent chalybeate properties, and advertisements which began to appear at the opening of the eighteenth century, the Hampstead Wells attracted attention, and for the convenience and amusement of those visiting them, various attractions were added, such as a coffee-room, a bowling-green, and, rather unexpectedly, a chapel. In course of time one of those Great Rooms, without which such places were seldom considered complete, was added, and, in

---

[1] There is an undated token issued by this lady, bearing a representation of the well, recorded in Boyne's "Trade Tokens."

Chatelain's view, may be seen facing the Heath. It was on the south side of Well Walk, and was used for concerts and dances from 1701 to 1733; the admission being two shillings and sixpence. The chapel was apparently something in the nature of Keith's in Mayfair, except that a licence was necessary, for on payment of five shillings people could be married there at any hour.

For a time the company at Hampstead Wells appears to have been select, and something of its atmosphere can be gathered from the comedy which Baker wrote in 1706 entitled "Hampstead Heath." But gradually a less desirable kind of people began to affect the place, and by the close of the first quarter of the eighteenth century, they formed the large majority of its frequenters; and the dances were indulged in by demireps and the gambling by card-sharpers. By 1733 the Wells for all practical purposes had ceased to exist, the Great Room having been converted into an Episcopal Chapel, and the gardens deserted. Later an attempt was made to revive the popularity of the waters, and a Long Room was erected,[1] which "Evelina" knew and Samuel Rogers remembered dancing minuets in.[2] The Hampstead Assemblies of this later incarnation of the Wells were, indeed, for a time not unfashionable; but a subsequent attempt (1802) to resuscitate the fame of the once-much-vaunted waters met with no success.

What Hampstead Wells had been, *Kilburn Wells* attempted to be at a later date, and it is about the middle of the eighteenth century that we find them coming into some prominence. They occupied a site in the Abbey Fields near the old Priory, and were situated behind the Bell Inn, whose proprietor was chiefly active in advertising them. A Great Room was, of

[1] Wroth, in 1896, says it was then a private residence called Weatherall House.
[2] "Recollections of the Table Talk of Samuel Rogers," 1856, p. 102.

course, erected, the surrounding grounds were laid out, and everything done, "in the most elegant manner," to attract the public. The efficacy of the waters was conclusively shown by "an eminent physician," in a pamphlet which was presented to the visitors who in one of the rooms were able to amuse themselves by reading a list of the diseases for which the health-giving stream had proved efficacious. As the waters were of a bitter saline taste, people at last apparently came to prefer the diseases, as they ceased frequenting Kilburn and its Wells during the closing years of the eighteenth century.[1]

But purveyors of public amusement did not always rely on medicinal springs as attractions, and *Belsize House*, which Evelyn and Pepys both remembered chiefly for the beauty of its gardens, when it was the residence of Lord Wotton, was one of the places which during the first quarter of the eighteenth century was converted into a pleasure haunt. It was opened in 1720, by one, Howell, for music and dancing, and although it was a considerable way out of London, being situated between what is now Finchley Road and Haverstock Hill, and so isolated that patrols were provided "for timid females and others," it became quite fashionable, and we hear of the Prince and Princess of Wales going to it, in 1721, when they dined in the house and were entertained with hunting and other diversions.

Hunting, indeed, seems to have formed a prominent feature of the entertainments here,[2] and on one such occasion, when wild deer were the quarry, hundreds of coaches brought the "nobility and gentry" to these then remote and rural fastnesses. Races and athletic

---

[1] See Park's "Hampstead," Howitt's "Northern Heights of London," etc., where will be found interesting data concerning the wells and spas in this neighbourhood.

[2] *Mist's Journal*, for April 16, 1720, contains an advertisement of the opening of the place as a pleasure haunt.

sports were also held, and for others who were not interested in such diversions there was plenty of gambling and other attractions, which, pleasant as they no doubt were to many, were looked at askance by the magistrates, who tried to stop unlawful gaming here, and especially by the author of the satire called "Belsize House," who does not hesitate to call it "a nuisance to the land," and is particularly severe on the fops and beaus who daily frequented it, and the women who used it as a place of assignation.

Howitt says the evil reputation of Belsize House increased so rapidly that highwaymen who lay in wait for the gamblers and others increased in an equal ratio, and so perilous had the journey to London become that the patrol, which originally consisted of twelve "stout fellows completely armed," had to be increased to thirty. The house was finally closed in 1745, in which year foot races were advertised, but probably did not take place.

Many of the taverns in the more rural parts of London possessed bowling-greens, and gardens where tea could be had and sometimes other diversions, but to attempt to notice these would be as impossible, if any limit is to be placed on this book, as it would be to speak of the inns and coffee-houses of London. Such places as the famous Spaniards, at Hampstead, comes under this heading, the Spaniards whose landlord, Giles Thomas, saved Caen Wood from the destructive fury of the Gordon Rioters, and whose more peaceful annals include a famous visit there of Mrs. Bardell and her friends. The New Georgia, not far off, was another place of a similar character, although not so well known; and certain others, which sometimes masqueraded under the favourite titles of Spring Gardens and Spas, were really little more : the Shepherd and Shepherdess, in the City Road;[1] the Spring Garden,

[1] As a precursor of the Eagle Tavern, I shall have to refer to this later on.

Stoke Newington; the Black Queen Tea Gardens, Shacklewell; the Devil's House, Holloway, whither anglers resorted in George III's reign, and whose name belied its essentially quiet character.[1] Hornsey Wood House, the Barley Mow Tea Gardens, and the Castle Inn Tea Gardens, Islington; the Adam and Eve Tea Gardens, St. Pancras; the Jew's Harp Tea Gardens, Marylebone (where the Speaker, Arthur Onslow, used to resort); the Yorkshire Stingo, in the same neighbourhood; the Bayswater Tea Gardens (whence Hampton ascended in his balloon, in 1839), and so forth, among them.

Such a place as *Pancras Wells*, however, cannot be so summarily dismissed. Exactly when it was opened is uncertain, but early in the eighteenth century it is known to have secured no little fashionable patronage. The Wells were situated a little south of St. Pancras old church, and, as it was then described, "about a mile to the north of London." From a pen-and-ink drawing in the Crace Collection, we can see how extensive were its formally laid out grounds and how solid and considerable the buildings on them. Attached to the plan is a description of the waters and their efficacy in the cure of all sorts of diseases and ailments, from "the most obstinate scurvy" to "most violent colds." The usual Long Room had been originally designed for the convenience of those drinking the waters, but in course of time it came to be used for dancing, and an advertisement in *The Craftsman*, for July, 5 1722, mentions that "the credit of these wells hath much suffered for some late years, by encouraging of scandalous company, and making the long room a common dancing room . . . due care will be taken for the future that nothing of the kind shall be allowed, or any disorderly person permitted to be in the walks."[2]

1 It was one of the traditional haunts of Claude Duval. Hence perhaps the name Duval changed into Devil.
2 See Clinch's "Marylebone and St. Pancras."

In view of this action on the part of the proprietor, the place appears to have regained the reputation it had for a time lost; and people went there to drink the waters, and no doubt to indulge in a little discreet dancing. It would seem from the fact that nothing much is recorded of it from this period (about 1730) till 1769, when the excellence of the waters began again to be advertised, that its career was of that peaceful and prosperous character connoted by no history; and it was not till after another thirty years that we hear of it being converted into a private residence. It was not an outstanding pleasure haunt, but being situated in what was then quite a rural environment and easily reached by footpaths from Gray's Inn and Islington and Tottenham Court, it was, no doubt, a favourite one, especially as ocular demonstration was shown of the efficacy of its medicinal spring.[1]

A still better remembered resort was *White Conduit House*. When the author of the "Sunday Ramble" made his excursion, "the first garden we visited," he writes, "was that of White Conduit House, which is situated on rising ground, opposite a conduit, from whence it takes its name. The prospect is very extensive, commanding a most agreeable view of the metropolis and the surrounding country. The garden is formed into several pleasing walks, prettily disposed; at the end of the principal one is a painting, which serves to render it much longer in appearance than it really is; and in the middle of the garden is a round fish-pond, encompassed with a great number of very genteel boxes for company, curiously cut into the hedges, and adorned with a variety of Flemish and other paintings. There are likewise two handsome tea-rooms, one over the other, as well as several inferior ones in the dwelling-home."

---

[1] It was a cure for stone, and evidences of its purgative properties in this respect were to be seen in the shop of one Bristowe, a goldsmith, near Bride Lane, Fleet Street.

It was converted into a pleasure resort about the year 1745, and nine years later the proprietor, Robert Bartholomew, enlarged and improved the gardens and, as cricket was played in an adjoining field, kept a supply of bats and balls for that purpose.

Bartholomew carried on the place till his death in 1766, and catered for a public which, if not fashionable, was respectable, and, on Sundays, crowded its walks and drank its tea, coming from their city shops and houses to do this, as is indicated in a poem on the subject which appeared in *The London Chronicle* for 1760. Special modes and manners were associated with it, and Wroth tells us that "curtseys, bows and compliments were the order of the day," and that "a White Conduit method of effecting an introduction was for the gallant 'prentice to tread on the lady's train, to apologize profusely, and finally to suggest an adjournment for tea in one of the arbours," where they not only consumed the beverage, but partook of the loaves ("White Conduit Loaves" was a London cry for many years) for which the gardens were famous.

Among notable visitors there were Oliver Goldsmith, who once found himself without the wherewithal to pay his bill,[1] and at a much later date, George Cruikshank, who was to be seen, sketchbook in hand, jotting down its "humours" and the faces that attracted him.

After Robert, Christopher Bartholomew carried on the gardens, and once having won money in a lottery, he gave a great public breakfast to commemorate the event. This concession to Fortune did not, however, beguile her smiles subsequently, and Christopher, continuing to gamble in lotteries, lost the whole of his once large savings.

Although the White Conduit House was a favourite resort during the eighteenth century, it was not till

---

[1] The incident is recorded by Forster in his "Life of Goldsmith."

the following one that any serious attempt was made to provide regular entertainments here. In 1824, however, a band-stand was set up, and bowls and archery were instituted. Balloons also began to rise from the grounds, the Grahams and Hampton making various successful ascents during the years 1824–1844. Fireworks also became a feature and gala fêtes were occasionally organized.

So ambitious, indeed, had the management, under Messrs. Sharpe and Warren, who carried it on from 1811 to 1828, become, that it is found being advertised as "the New Vauxhall: White Conduit Gardens," and evening concerts, variety entertainments, and firework displays made it increasingly popular; while the appearance of such people as Chabert, the Fire-eater, in 1826, and Mrs. Bland, the singer, were hailed with delight by the company, which, in spite of its diminishing rurality owing to building, still patronized it.

In 1826 the licence was only granted on condition that the gardens should close at 11.45, and that no masquerades or fireworks should be permitted, a proviso probably made on account of the residential quarter then arising around. The prosperity of the place, however, continued, and in 1829, its accommodation being found insufficient, a new hotel, with a large dancing-room, was erected on part of its grounds. The "New Minor Vauxhall," as its proprietors now termed it, seems gradually to have deteriorated, and both Hone and Dickens speak of it in anything but flattering terms.[1] Its licence was refused in 1832, and two years later its proprietor was fined for the rowdy conduct of some of the audience.

White Conduit House was on its last legs; but by the aid of jugglers and ballets, farces and dioramas, and such-like variety entertainments, it lasted till 1849, when a ball given for the benefit of the check-takers marked its close. It was soon afterwards pulled down;

[1] "Every Day Book," and "Sketches by Boz."

its site being approximately covered by the White Conduit public-house, now No. 14 Barnsbury Road, and its name further perpetuated in that of a thoroughfare linking up Barnsbury Road with Cloudesley Road, Islington.

The *Belvidere Tea Gardens*, Pentonville, the successor to the seventeenth-century place of entertainment called Busby's Folly, where the Society of Bull Feathers Hall met in 1664, later to be known as Penny's Folly, is chiefly noted for the performances of Zucker and his "Learned Little Horse," just as *Dobney's Bowling-Green* was famous for the equestrian audacities of Price in 1767 and Wildman in 1772,[1] and for the fact that it possessed a racquet-court which was its principal attraction and remained so into the second half of the last century. The *Castle Inn Tea Gardens* in the same district was notable for nothing except tea and light refreshment; although as it was in Colebrooke Row, Lamb may have visited it; while the *Canonbury House Tea Gardens* would perhaps not be remembered but for the fact that the house itself, Canonbury Tower, dating from the sixteenth century and still standing, was let as cheap lodgings to literary men and others during the eighteenth century, and is, in this connection, indissolubly associated with Goldsmith.

Of *Copenhagen House*, between the Caledonian Road and York Road, something more must be said, because as a house of entertainment it had a seventeenth-century genesis, although its fame in this respect dates from a later period.

[1] Equestrianism was at one time in the public eye, and at the Three Hats, Islington, Johnson and, later, Sampson gave exhibitions of their skill in this direction, from 1758 to 1772. This caused the Three Hats to have a reputation, which for some people was enhanced by the presence of an excellent skittles alley. Cricket was also played here, and there is a drawing by Rowlandson showing some nude women indulging in the same!

What was the authentic origin of the name it is difficult to determine, but Howitt may be right when he
indicates that a Dane, living in London in the reign
of James I., opened the place as a pleasure resort for
those of his countrymen who were also domiciled in
this country. In the map attached to Camden's Britannia
(1695) the name is spelt Coopen-Hagen, and in the
Gardner collection was a picture showing what the
house appeared like in the eighteenth century. During
that period it was much resorted to by those who
played skittles and Dutch-pins, and by others who
made it the objective of tea-drinking. Its views over
the surrounding country were unrivalled; but the house
was rather isolated, a fact, no doubt, which accounted
for a daring burglary being perpetrated there, when a
Mrs. Harrington was the landlady, in 1780, of which
Hone has left a long and interesting account. This
incident, terrifying as it must have been at the time,
was not without its advantages to Mrs. Harrington;
for a subscription was opened for her benefit, and the
curious were attracted to the place in such numbers
that a Mr. Leader, who owned the house, erected a
special room for the better accommodation of the
visitors, where they could drink tea, and a room below
where those who wished could smoke. Another addition
was a Fives Court, and Hone relates how the first
game ever came to be played here, by a young Shropshire woman named Tomes, who helped Mrs. Harrington in the house, and a fellow native named Hick-
man, who was a butcher at Highgate. The game
caught on, and among other exponents of it who came
to play at Copenhagen House was John Cavanagh.
As readers of Hazlitt's "Memoir of Cavanagh" remember, the writer affirms that the player was unsurpassed
and unapproachable in his skill: "His eye was certain,
his hand fatal, his presence of mind complete." After
a time Robert Orchard became landlord (1795), and
as he was a member of the London Corresponding

Society, a fraternity of advanced reformers, meetings of the associates, sometimes numbering, it is said, no fewer than 40,000, met in the fields around Copenhagen House, John Thelwell being one of the chief speakers. After Robert Orchard came one Tooth, who filled the neighbourhood with a rough and brutal class of people by inaugurating rough sports, bull-dog fighting being one of them, and bull-baiting another, until he was stopped by the magistrates in 1816. Tooth's successor was a very different sort of man, and under his *ægis* Copenhagen House, from 1816 to 1830, was a favourite resort of the people who flocked thither, in the summer-time especially, to drink tea and gambol in the hay-fields.[1] As such a centre of mild amusement and recreation it existed down to 1852, when, together with a large area around, it was purchased by the Corporation for the purpose of erecting the Metropolitan Cattle Market, which duly arose some years later.

One other somewhat similar haunt in this district was *Highbury Barn*, originally a place of great antiquity, but which as a pleasure resort was represented by a small cake and ale-house dating no further back than 1740. It has, however, a literary association as having been not infrequently the objective of Goldsmith and his friends on their "Shoemakers'" holidays; whence, after dinner, they would often adjourn to White Conduit House. Many people came here, and to other somewhat similar places—Cream Hall and the rest— to drink milk warm from the cow, and eat syllabubs, as they used to do in the Five Fields.[2]

Custom thus pouring in, Highbury Barn developed from a small ale-house to a regular tavern with tea-

[1] See Tomlin's "Perambulation of Islington," Nelson's "Islington," Howitt's "Northern Heights of London," etc.

[2] The late Sir Algernon West's mother remembered, as a child, doing this; see Sir Algernon's "Recollections."

gardens and so forth; no little of its increased prosperity being due to Mr. Willoughby, the proprietor,
who died in 1785, and was succeeded by his son, who
still further improved the place by the addition of a
bowling-green, a trap and ball ground, and such-like
popular diversions. In course of time an adjacent barn
was transformed into the inevitable Great Room, and
here monthly assemblies, chiefly patronized by the
local population, and great dinners held by clubs and
such-like associations, were given.[1]

In 1818 Highbury Barn was sold, and became a
popular tea-garden resort; while some years later, under
fresh management, it almost rivalled Cremorne in its
varied entertainments; for although the immense feasts
which had once made it *sui generis* no longer took place,
the securing of a dancing licence in 1856 gave it the
means of developing in a fresh direction, and with the
erection of a monster dancing platform a Terpsichorean
air was given to it, and people disported themselves
under the lamps which surrounded the vast floor,
which was almost entirely open to the sky. In 1860
Archibald Hinton, who had been carrying it on for
many years, gave it up, and one Edward Giovanelli
having erected a covered-in hall for dancing and added
other improvements, including a theatre in the grounds,
made a success of it for a time with his varied attractions, among which Blondin and the Siamese Twins
figured.

As in the case of most of these haunts, riotry and
general disorderliness became rampant at night, and
the neighbouring residents having opposed the renewal
of the dancing licence, this was refused in 1870. The
place went on without it for a year, but when the
proprietor (now a Mr. E. T. Smith, who had succeeded
Giovanelli) was unable to secure one again, Highbury

[1] In 1800, eight hundred people partook of a dinner here, and in
1841, no fewer than 3000 were thus entertained at the Licensed
Victuallers' Dinner. Sayer published a view of the place in 1792.

Barn was closed; and after a decade buildings covered the site of what had been for long a prosperous and outstanding pleasure haunt.

I have said that the presence of springs gave rise to many of the places of entertainment which gradually grew out of the collocation of people who frequented them originally from hygienic motives, and Clerkenwell was another centre of these; indeed there were few districts in which such springs (seldom as medicinal as their owners were anxious to have believed) did not exist.[1] In Clerkenwell, however, there congregated in remarkable profusion "wells" and "spas," as well as other places of public resort. Many of these latter were of such a subsidiary character that they can be dismissed with a few words. Of such was the *English Grotto*, or the Grotto Garden, Rosoman Street, with which it was probably identical. Extant views of this place show it to have been but a wooden erection, sheltered by some lofty trees, and having a flagstaff indicating the presence of the Grotto which, about 1769, had been constructed by a man named Jackson, who was a well-known adept at this kind of garden decoration. In the grotto was a fountain, but if this was served by a spring, it does not appear that Jackson ever claimed chalybeate properties for it. The place was, doubtless, one of those houses of refreshment for people resorting to its then rural neighbourhood, and a charge of sixpence was made to such as wished to see the proprietor's handiwork. Another place of a not dissimilar character was the *Mulberry Garden*, although it was on a more extensive scale, and a band played there, and even fireworks were occasionally let off. It had its long room, and sometimes men of fashion made an excursion to it to play ninepins or skittles. As from 1745 to 1752 (after which the place is no longer

[1] See, *inter alia*, "Springs, Streams, and Spas of London," by S. A. Foord, 1910.

heard of) it was kept by a Mrs. Bray, reported to have been one of the fattest women in London, she may have provided a "sight" in herself, in an age which delighted in abnormality of any kind.

Merlin's Cave, near the New River Head (Merlin's Place perpetuated its name), was a Sunday resort for many years from 1735, when it is first said to have been constructed. It was obviously an imitation of the cave made for Queen Caroline in the gardens at Richmond with which the thresher-poet, Stephen Duck, is associated, but possessed a skittle-ground which was probably its chief source of attraction.

The "*Lord Cobham's Head*," in Cold Bath Fields, where the Farringdon Road is to-day, opened in 1728, possessed a canal in which carp and tench were stocked, and anglers used to go there for this sport, and sometimes lodge in the house connected with the place. In this house, at a later date, 1744, an organ was erected, and concerts and balls held. Later these were discontinued, and the "Lord Cobham's Head" carried on its existence as an ordinary tavern till 1811, when it was sold. It took its name from the neighbouring mansion of Sir John Oldcastle, Lord Cobham, which, having become ruinous, had been demolished just half a century earlier.[1]

The name of the *Bowling-green House*, which stood at the back of the Foundling Hospital, indicates its later, rather than its earlier, significance; for in the seventeenth century it was a noted haunt of gamesters, and is so mentioned in 1676: "Just twenty years later, it had become so notorious, that it was raided by soldiers and constables, and those found on the premises were carried before the magistrates and fined."[2]

---

[1] It also gave the name to the "Sir John Oldcastle" Tavern and Gardens, another place of entertainment similar to the "Lord Cobham's Head," close by, where concerts were given, and fireworks displayed during the middle of the eighteenth century.

[2] Malcolm's "Manners and Customs of London."

It was not, indeed, till 1756 that one Barras, having acquired the place, opened it as a centre for bowls, a very fine green having been laid out. As such it continued till 1811, when its site was built over. Refreshments could, of course, be had there, but the bowling-green appears to have been its one and only source of amusement.[1]

The *Adam and Eve Tea Gardens,* in the Tottenham Court Road, situated in a district long known for its attractions as a holiday resort, and mentioned so early as 1628 by George Wither in this connection, was in existence in 1718, and probably earlier, and during the holding of Tottenham Fair and "The Gooseberry Fair," as it was called, did a great business in catering for the wants of the visitors. Indeed it probably attracted many from the noisier amusements of these gatherings, as it had its long room furnished with an organ; its pleasant and ample grounds, in which bowls and skittles could be played; and its alcoves for tea-parties. No doubt it flourished during the eighteenth century, but it was in the latter part of that period that an event occurred which gave it a fresh advertisement; this was the unexpected descent of Lunardi in his balloon there, on May 13, 1785. The circumstance is recorded in the contemporary newspapers, and we read of the æronaut being surrounded by a great crowd which had rushed to the spot, and being carried in triumph on the shoulders of some of his admirers.

Notwithstanding the gradual building development in this quarter at the beginning of the nineteenth century, the Adam and Eve remained unmolested; but its *clientèle* had sadly changed for the worse by that time, and magisterial interference resulted in its being closed for a period. Although, in 1813, it was re-opened, it was only as an ordinary tavern, a descendant

[1] The Spring Garden at Stepney, which was in existence in 1702 till 1764, had not even this recreation, but was a favourite Sunday resort during that period.

of that shown, on the left, in Hogarth's "March to Finchley," and the precursor of a more ambitious house erected in 1869.[1]

Of the actual wells or spas which remain to be dealt with, three take an outstanding position: *Islington Spa*, Sadler's Wells, and Bagnigge Wells. The first is, perhaps, the least known and its history is the least extensive, but it was once a famous resort, and so early as 1684 its "sweet gardens and arbours of pleasure" are found commemorated in a poem bearing its name. The discovery of a chalybeate spring in or about 1685, by a Mr. John Langley, who purchased the place (he also bought a rhinoceros at about the same time, as the *London Gazette* informs us), first brought it into notice, and it was opened as Islington Wells, a name that was coupled with that of the New Tunbridge Wells, and was later (1754) converted into Islington Spa, although the New Tunbridge Wells was still often applied to it. One of the many poems written on the place shows its uses in those days

> "Of either sex whole droves together,
> To see and to be seen flocked thither,
> To drink—and not to drink the water,
> And here promiscuously to chatter."

For many years it held its own as a Spa without the varied attractions of the neighbouring Sadler's Wells; but although many came here solely to drink the waters, far more did so to promenade in the grounds, where the rustle of lute-strings and the tapping of snuff-boxes, the *airs vainqueurs* of the fine gentlemen

---

[1] I may mention that close by was the Cold Bath, which in 1785 was advertised as possessing medicinal qualities. The Peerless Pool, in the region of Old Street and the City Road, the Perillous Pond of the sixteenth and seventeenth centuries, was in 1743 opened by one Kemp as a bathing place, and was greatly resorted to by aquatic 'prentices and others. It was frequented till 1850, and is to be found mentioned in all sorts of histories of London. A handbill of it, dated 1846, shows what a well-arranged and delightful place it must then have been.

and the side-long glances of the be-rouged ladies, formed a marked contrast with the worsted-stockinged paterfamilias from the city with his ample spouse, and the open-mouthed wonder of the young girl in her teens. The man of fashion and the 'prentice elbowed each other in the walks, and bullies and decoys and ladies of dubious antecedents and more than dubious callings, lurked in the alleys; what time the valetudinarians were drinking the waters, and a resident physician was listening to the tale of their ailments. Sir Fopling Flutter and Sir Courtly Nice ogled the pretty girls, and mamma drew them away beneath the protection of her frown. Some went at once to the raffling shops and lost and won (generally the former) their money with a modish air or with unconcealed chagrin as their characters or upbringing prompted. At eleven o'clock dancing began in the Great Room, and the strains of music drowned the clatter of tongues.

After a period of depression, during which the place lost for a time its fashionable vogue, its fortunes revived largely owing to the fact that in 1733 the Princesses Amelia and Caroline suddenly took to coming here regularly to drink the waters. A salute of guns heralded the arrival of the royal ladies, and so great an impetus to the place resulted that no fewer than sixteen hundred people were sometimes to be seen here on a single morning. Pictures of the Wells began to appear on the fans which Pinchbeck produced, and as the charming vignettes to the printed songs which were popular there.

The vagaries of fashion are no better exemplified than in the annals of Islington Spa. After this burst of popularity, it suddenly became *démodé*, till 1750, when a new lease of life was given it, and for another twenty years ran a prosperous course. Later it degenerated into a "genteel" tea-garden, but fashion seems to have deserted it, and a Mr. Holland, who

was responsible for this recrudescence, became bankrupt seven years later. Subsequently it was run by one
Howard, who added a bowling-green, and tried to
exploit the water-drinking to its fullest extent. After
a time, however, both this and its other attractions
ceased to exert their whilom power over a fickle public;
the times were changing and, after some of the buildings had been pulled down in 1810, a period ensued
when the water remained the only attraction, and that
to diminishing numbers of patrons. In 1840 Spa
Cottages were built on the site of what had once been
a haunt of all classes and which had passed through
many vicissitudes.[1]

Before speaking of Bagnigge Wells one or two
lesser haunts should be noticed. Of these *The Pantheon,
Spa Fields*, is given in a contemporary magazine as
being patronized by the mobility in contradistinction
to that in Oxford Street affected by the nobility.[2]
It was a large circular building with galleries running
round the interior, and was first opened in 1770.
The company that assembled here was the reverse
of fashionable, although, especially on Sundays,
numerous enough, and it found refreshments in an
adjoining tea-room; while the gardens were full of
seats and convenient alcoves; and statues and a fish-
pond added to its *agrémens*. For some reason, however,
the Pantheon had but a short life, and half a dozen
years after it had been opened it was closed, and the
Countess of Huntingdon's Spa Field Chapel eventually
occupied its place.

Near by was *The London Spa*, which had had a
seventeenth-century origin, and under its energetic
proprietor, John Halhed's direction, a more or less

---

[1] The elder Colman wrote a play called "The Spleen or Islington
Spa," printed in 1776, after being performed at Drury Lane; and two
medical treatises on the efficacy of the waters were published. See
Cromwell's "History of Clerkenwell."

[2] *The Macaroni and Theatrical Magazine* for January 1773.

prosperous career, partly through the advocacy of the medicinal qualities of its spring by Robert Boyle. After going out of favour for some years during the earlier part of the eighteenth century, it revived in or about the year 1720, and May Day (according to a contemporary print) used to be kept here with much fun and jollity; while the Welsh Fair held in the neighbouring Spa Fields is said to have brought custom to the place, people coming to eat roast pork and drink the ale, both of which were specialities of it. By the year 1754, however, the efficacy of the natural waters appears to have been forgotten in the satisfaction produced by less innocuous beverages, and the house passed into a fresh existence as a tavern and little more.

The *New Wells*, close by, demand little notice. Here, indeed, the chief attraction was not a spring at all, but a theatre where a variety show was given for a number of years, dating from about 1737. Entrance to the entertainment, which began at five o'clock, was purchased merely by the consumption of a certain quantity of wine or punch. As time went on, other attractions were added, and we hear of a miniature Zoological Gardens being formed here, and a Merlin's Cave, and such-like features; what time feats of skill and agility, giants and dwarfs, and so forth were exhibited in a sort of rivalry with the Sadler's Wells entertainment near by. By 1750 the activities of the place, which were not without vigour and variety, ceased, and John Wesley, two years later, took it and turned it into one of his chapels.

In the curious little book from which I have already once or twice quoted—"The Sunday Ramble"—there is a pretty frontispiece depicting *Bagnigge Wells*, "drawn on ye spot." Beneath it are printed the following lines, which summarize concisely the character of this once-famous place:

"Salubrious Waters, Tea, and Wine,
Here you may have, and also dine;
But, as ye through the Garden rove,
Beware, fond Youths, the Darts of Love."

Bagnigge Wells stood slightly to the east of the Gray's Inn Road, on a spot now partly occupied by the premises of Messrs. Holland, Hannen, and Cubitts. The original structure is said traditionally to have been one of the many residences of Nell Gwynn; others think it was a place of entertainment as early as 1680; but for all practical purposes its history begins in the second half of the eighteenth century, when its proprietor, Hughes, discovering the medicinal properties of a well in its gardens, opened the place as a "Spa" in 1759, and forthwith did all he could (even to publishing a pamphlet on the subject) to popularize his discovery and to entice people to drink the waters there. He charged threepence for one drink, and half-a-guinea a season to those who made a habit of the practice.

Of the Long Room, a spirited representation exists, published by Bowles in 1772,[1] indicating something of the character of the apartment and also the fact that fashionable people had by that time begun to resort to Bagnigge Wells. In this room was an organ, some mirrors of that distorting kind which are so provocative of mirth, and other ornaments dear to a decorative period. Every day there was a performance on the organ, and the instrument and its regular executant, Charles Griffiths, are shown in a humorous print called "The Bagnigge Organist." Previously to 1772 these performances were also given on Sundays, but in that year they were prohibited by the magistrates not as nocuous in themselves, but as tending to make the place too attractive!

For the first forty years of George III.'s reign

[1] It is entitled "The Bread and Butter Manufactory, or the Humours of Bagnigge Wells" (see Frontispiece).

Bagnigge Wells remained not only popular but fashionable. People came here in their hundreds to partake of breakfast or to drink the waters; while in the afternoons a still gayer crowd was to be seen here, and it seems to have been a special objective of the citizens' ladies, who regarded the place as the last word of modish resort, and

" . . . drinking tea on summer afternoons
At Bagnigge Wells with china and gilt spoons."

was by many thought to be the *ne plus ultra* of *bon-ton*.

The author of "The Sunday Ramble" has something to say about the place on his own account, and he quotes more which the friend who accompanied him had to tell from his recollections.

"When," he says, "my friend had informed me of these particulars, I proceeded to take a view of the place, which I found to consist of several beautiful walks, ornamented with a great variety of curious shrubs and flowers, all in utmost perfection. About the centre of the garden is a small round fish-pond, in the midst of which is a curious fountain, representing a Cupid bestriding a swan, which spouts the water through its beak to a great height. Round this place, and indeed almost over the whole garden, are genteel seats for company; which my friend said we should undoubtedly find quite full in the afternoon, notwithstanding their prodigious number. At a little distance from the pond is a neat cottage, built in the rural style; and not far from that, over a bridge leading across a piece of water that pours through part of the garden, is a pretty piece of grotto-work, large enough to contain near twenty people. Besides which, there is a small house, and several seats placed by the water-side, for such of the company as chuse to smoke or drink cyder, ale, etc. which are not permitted in the other parts of the garden. Having sufficiently admired this agreeable place, I did not wonder at my friend's encomiums, though they at first seemed to be rather exaggerated."[1]

It need hardly be said that in a resort such as this, where all classes mixed together, and the dame from Cheapside brushed shoulders with the high-born lady from St. James's, the member of White's with the "cit" from the Minories, the young girl fresh from the paternal acres in Shropshire with the sempstress and mantua-maker from Whitechapel and the Seven Dials, there mingled others who came for purposes of their own, and the pickpocket of both sexes, and the lady of easy ethics from Whetstone Park were to be found plying their varied trades. The notorious "Sixteen String" Jack Rann appeared here in a dress as audacious as his manner, and as he flaunted his scarlet coat, tambour-waistcoat and laced hat, he no doubt little thought that in the space of four months he would be hanging from Tyburn Tree. But even on this occasion he ran a risk of his life, for he is said to have behaved so badly that some outraged gentleman threw him out of one of the windows of the Great Room.

After the close of the eighteenth century Bagnigge Wells lost its fashionable air, and was resorted to almost entirely by the lower classes; and in 1813, on the advent of a new proprietor, the gardens were considerably curtailed; a sale subsequently taking place of many of the adjuncts which were then found superfluous. But in the following year the place was again opened, at threepence entrance, and although concerts were given, they failed to attract sufficiently to make it successful. Various people tried to galvanize the place into a pleasure haunt, although admittedly of a very different character from what it had been during the forty years of its prosperity. They were, however, a succession of failures; although in 1838 the lessees, a Mr. and Mrs. Foster, provided for a benefit night quite a galaxy of musical talent. Three

[1] "The Sunday Ramble."

years later the end came with an evening performance (on March 26, 1841) of comic songs, glees and so forth. A few years afterwards a modern tavern was erected on the site of Bagnigge Wells, and in 1850 this was run by the suggestively named Mr. Negus as mine host.

Bagnigge Wells was responsible for quite a little literature (besides being the subject of many pictures) and "Bagnigge Wells—a poem," by an anonymous writer, although Hawkins is supposed to have written it, published in 1779, largely unfit for quotation as it is, is valuable as possessing many foot-notes full of humour, sarcasm, and general information. Many songs, too, were written eulogizing the place, where, as some ironically-minded person once put it:

> "Cits . . . repair
> To swallow dust and call it air."

Sadler's Wells.

Mazzinghi, in his "Histoire de Londres," 1793, giving a list of the then existing pleasure haunts of the metropolis, places Sadler's Wells, not among "the most frequented tea gardens," where Bagnigge Wells finds a place, but among the "theatres"; and Goede, fourteen years later, speaks of it as such, being "pleasantly situated and neatly embellished."[1] And such it was. But as its earlier history is associated with the discovery of a medicinal spring here by a Mr. Sadler, so early indeed as 1683, and the exploitation of the place originally as a "Spa," I make no apology for including it in this section of my book, instead of in that allotted to the London playhouses.

As in the case of Bagnigge Wells, the discovery of the health-giving properties of the water (concerning which Dr. Thomas Guidot published a pamphlet in 1684) was purely fortuitous; but Sadler, having found it out, set about making the most of it.

[1] "The Stranger in England," Vol. 2.

As he took every means to advertise the place, calling it first "Sadler's New Tunbridge Wells,"[1] a name that, however, soon became shortened, the place began to be patronized, especially as the proprietor, from the first, made entertainments of music, acrobatic displays, and such-like amusements a feature of his Spa. He laid out the gardens, too, in an attractive way, and in their centre constructed a marble basin from which people could drink the waters. It was not long before the fame of these spread and crowds came daily to partake of them, to see posture-makers go through their intricate performances, and to hear, sometimes a lady (like the maid in Coleridge's dream —in this case a Miss Pearson) playing on the dulcimer. So popular did the place become, indeed, that the proprietors of Epsom Wells and Tunbridge Wells took fright at the rivalry, and, went so far as to get a pamphlet written against the new-comer. Not, apparently, without some effect; for we are told that by 1687 Sadler's Wells had become deserted by the water-drinkers, and its amusements were not seemingly sufficient to attract others. An attempt at a revival was made in 1697; but, although anglers[2] went there, as they continued to do down to the nineteenth century, and others were attracted by the rural attributes of the place, this sort of patronage was not a paying one, and from about this time the proprietor began to seek public support on other grounds than those of medicine.

We read of vocal and instrumental concerts being given here in 1698, and following years; and that the place already possessed some of the characteristics of a playhouse, is evidenced by the fact that "a brightly-

[1] It has in consequence been often confounded with Islington Spa, which, as we have seen, was also known as New Tunbridge Wells.

[2] There is a print showing some people fishing here in 1796; it appeared in Woodward's "Eccentric Excursions," published in that year.

painted gallery in the saloon used for the entertainments appears to have been occupied by the quieter
portion of the audience, who were able from thence
to survey the pit below . . . filled, according to Ned
Ward, with butchers, bailiffs, prize-fighters, and
house-breakers."

At this time Sadler's Wells had become known as
Miles's Music Room, from one James Miles, who,
with a certain Francis Forcer, was then the joint-
proprietor; and was the resort, we are told, of "stroll-
ing damsels, half-pay officers, peripatetic tradesmen,
tars, butchers, and other musically inclined." But it
was not without its occasional excitements, and in
1712 a brawl here resulted in a tragedy—a Frenchman
killing an English naval lieutenant as the sequel to a
quarrel.

When Miles died, young Forcer, a son of Francis,
became the head of the concern, and did much to
improve it in every way. What the old theatre (if it can
be so called) looked like, is shown by a vignette
attached to the well-known view of the later Sadler's
Wells, given in "Londina Illustrata." It was merely
one of those Long or Great Rooms with which nearly
all the "Spas" and "Wells" were provided; and it was
in it that Winifred Jenkins was so frightened at the
tumbling and rope dancing that she thought herself
bewitched.[1]

Forcer did something, but Rosoman, who became
proprietor in 1746, did far more, and apart from
various changes in the internal economy of the place,
the introduction of novelties, and the regulation of the
going and coming of the visitors and their convenience
when there, it was he who in 1765 demolished the old
room and built a new theatre, part of which still exists,
on its site.

The accompanying illustration shows the picturesque appearance of that theatre, a theatre which, with

[1] See "Humphrey Clinker."

SADLER'S WELLS THEATRE
1825

one exception, was the only one in London that had never been burnt down.

Here Mrs. Lampe and Tommy Lowe sang: here Spinacuti[1] introduced his remarkable monkey to wondering audiences; here Jenny Warner and the better-known Joseph Grimaldi, the clowns, made their audiences rock with laughter, and Richer, the wire dancer, made them hold their breath. Songs and plays written by the Dibdins, father and son, were given here to packed houses, which frequently held members of the Royal Family. Later, Braham, not yet having discarded his original Abraham, sang as a boy, and here, in 1801, Edmund Kean appeared under the disguising title of "Master Carey." Even pony-races, on a track formed from the stage and encircling the pit, were given, a regular race-course being constructed in the grounds at a later date. In those grounds, too, balloon ascents were made, notably by the Grahams in 1838; and the ubiquitous Belzoni here exhibited his amazing physical strength.[2]

As a playhouse the most notable period of Sadler's Wells was from 1844 to 1862, when it was under the able management of Samuel Phelps. Then Shakespeare's plays were given with the same success as has attended them at the Old Vic—"Hamlet" alone, Wroth tells us, being performed four hundred times.

To come almost to our own days, in 1879, Mrs. Bateman came to Sadler's Wells from the Lyceum, and thoroughly reconstructed the place, which later, as everyone knows, became a music-hall, and is now apparently awaiting a further palingenesis as a home of the "legitimate."

[1] A curious contemporary print shows Spinacuti surrounded by his monkey in all its quaint attitudes, *circa* 1768.

[2] For an interesting notice of this remarkable man, see Smith's "Book for a Rainy Day."

CHAPTER XVI

SPAS AND PLEASURE GARDENS (*continued*)

THE general impression seems to be that such pleasure gardens as have existed in London are practically confined to the eighteenth century, with a few dating from still earlier times. As a matter of fact, however, the nineteenth century provides a very large number of such places, but with one or two exceptions they were not exactly fashionable, although people of fashion may occasionally, as we know they did, have patronized them from motives of curiosity. These later pleasure haunts were to be found in all parts of London, but the immense building development that began during the first quarter of the century, and has never entirely ceased, resulted in their often being relegated to distant outskirts of the city.

One of these pleasure gardens stands out from the rest, and is known, at least by name, to numbers who would be hard put to it to say where it existed; others were of such a minor character that even their names, much less their sites, are no longer remembered; and it is with Cremorne that the nineteenth century can chiefly rival the Ranelagh and Vauxhall, the Marylebone and the Bagnigge Wells, the Cuper's Gardens, and the White Conduit House, of an earlier day.

Cremorne.

Whistler has made Cremorne both famous and picturesque. Famous, because without his wonderful reconstruction of its distant atmospheric charm, it might have been forgotten by an age whose sight has been blurred by many successive manifestations of the pleasure-lust; and picturesque, because he has shed a halo of romance and faery (almost) over what must have been in itself essentially commonplace. The more detailed etchings which his pupil, W. Greaves, has left of its Entrance Gates, its Fireworks Gallery, and its Dancing-platform, reveal that florid and rococo style of decoration and design which the period (the 'seventies of the last century), when these valuable reminders were made, delighted in. Other contemporary illustrations confirm the essentially vulgar character of Cremorne's setting, a vulgarity which, from all accounts, was not absent from its performances nor from many who frequented it.

Cremorne was situated at Chelsea on the banks of the Thames, slightly to the west of Battersea Bridge. There had originally been a house on this site erected by Theophilus, Earl of Huntingdon, which passed successively through the hands of Lord Powerscourt, the Dowager Countess of Exeter, Sir Richard Littleton, the Duke of Bridgwater and Lord Cremorne, the last of whom spent large sums on improving it, as well as its surrounding grounds. In course of time the property came into the possession of Granville Penn, a relation of Lady Cremorne, who sold it to that extraordinary adventurer, Charles Randon de Berenger, who called himself the Baron de Beaufain, but who was called by many others the swindler he really was.[1] But he was also a man of resource, an inventor and a skilled shot among other things, and he it was who, getting together a number of supporters, opened Cremorne House grounds as the Cremorne Stadium, in 1832. From a charming lithograph published in that year, we obtain a good idea of the well-treed grounds, with a shooting butt in the distance, and a number of

[1] He was the head and front of the great Stock Exchange hoax of 1814, in which Lord Cochrane and others became involved.

sportsmen congregated round a tent in the foreground, preparatory to trying their skill as shots.
Here, for a subscription of two or three guineas,
members could be coached by the Baron in shooting
and other "manly exercises"; and a portion of the
grounds was allocated to ladies, who had their own
clubroom attached. It is interesting to remember that
golf was one of the sports indulged in here, and the
fact is emblematically perpetuated by George Cruikshank in the design he made for the "Chelsea Stadium
Shield," in 1834.

The place, notwithstanding the energy and resource
of its only begetter, the Baron, was never really a
success; but for nine years it managed to exist, its
sporting characteristics being re-inforced by occasional
firework displays, *fêtes champêtres*, balloon ascents,
and such-like attempts to interest a wider public than
that represented by the subscribers. In 1843 it was
closed, but almost immediately re-opened under the
flamboyant *ægis* of that extraordinary character, Renton
Nicholson, notorious for many things, but chiefly as
the presiding genius or judge of that mock court
called the Judge and Jury, which was sometimes held
at the Garrick's Head in Bow Street, of which Nicholson
had become the proprietor in 1841, and sometimes
at the Coal Hole and the Cider Cellars.[1]

By the aid of flaming advertisements he tried to
galvanize Cremorne into popularity, and one great
show, which he grandiloquently called a "Thousand
Guineas Fête," and which lasted three days, with a
mock tournament, no doubt inspired by the famous
Eglinton Tournament of 1839, and a variety of other
amusements, was insufficient to make the place a
paying concern, at least in Nicholson's hands.

Followed a period when it was managed by Little-
john and Tom Matthews, and Green, the aeronaut,

---

[1] See the "Dict. of Nat. Biog." for an account of Nicholson's very
variegated career.

made innumerable balloon ascents there, sometimes with sensational adjuncts, as when he was on one occasion accompanied by a lady and a leopard, and another when the very lively Lord George Beresford was one of the passengers.

But Cremorne did not come into its own till 1846, when T. B. Simpson became the manager for James Ellis, who had purchased the concern. Simpson, once a waiter at the Albion in Russell Street, was, like his famous Vauxhall namesake, a man of shrewd business capacity and, as George Augustus Sala once termed him, "a kindly and generous gentleman," and he ran the place as a pleasure garden with much success for a number of years. He spent money lavishly but wisely, and although his opening fête cost some £5000, it proved to be wisely laid out.

An interesting plan of the gardens as they were in 1846, when Simpson came to their management, and as they substantially remained till their close in 1877, gives a good idea of their extent and formation. They covered some twelve acres of ground and abutted on the river and on the King's Road, their north and south boundaries. From the former they could be entered by a landing-stage and river gate, later to be made a very elaborate iron-work structure, as Greaves's etching shows; and hundreds of people used this way, coming by steam-boat from the east and west, when steam-boats were still a paying proposition, and the river, as a highway, had not come to be neglected.

In the grounds was an immense orchestra, something on the lines of that at Vauxhall, and around it a vast circular dancing platform, on which gentlemen in frock-coats and top-hats, and ladies in crinolines and coal-scuttle bonnets, may be seen gyrating in the print published in 1847.[1]

On the left of the main entrance was a Pagoda of

---

[1] In *The Pictorial Times*, for June.

immense proportions, and elsewhere, dotted about among the trees, were buildings of a kind familiar to *habitués* of exhibitions of a later date, refreshment rooms, kiosks, bandstands, temples, Swiss châlets and such-like adjuncts. But notwithstanding the presence of these, the charm of Cremorne was that it remained essentially rural, and its avenues and ancient trees gave it a picturesqueness which was sadly to seek in such places as the Earl's Court Exhibitions of our own day.

Among other attractions was a piece of water; and the more sophisticated found a circus and a theatre, and a miniature play-house where marionettes, introduced in 1852, disported themselves and were a favourite show.[1]

Suppers could be had at two shillings and sixpence a head, and if the vaunted sherry, "free from acidity and highly recommended to invalids," was not all that it claimed to be, the general company which frequented Cremorne were probably not aware of the fact. For the chief end and aim of the majority was dancing, and I have been told by those who knew the place that it was "the thing" not to indulge in this till after the fireworks had been let off; the earlier part of the evening, so far as this was concerned, being left to the clerks and their young ladies, who had to retire earlier than was necessary in the case of the *jeunesse dorée* and their female friends.

The usual time for opening was from three or four in the afternoon, and a certain number of people were to be found there during daylight hours; but it was in the evening that Cremorne became crowded and, as time went on, mixed, as all such places do become. It also became gradually rather too much encumbered by side-shows, and, as Wroth remarks, had a tendency to resemble, in this respect, a fair; but it was essentially a place of light-hearted amuse-

[1] See Wroth's "Cremorne and Later London Gardens."

Interior of the Banqueting Hall

CREMORNE
THE BANQUETING HALL
CREMORNE GARDENS.
ABOUT 1845

ment, and the garrulousness of age has come to
represent it as a devil of a place, not dissimilar from
the Jardin Mabille and the Bal Bullier of Paris.
This is probably doing it an injustice. That it was
easy to make acquaintance with charming young
ladies who had mislaid their mothers or their aunts
there, is, no doubt, the fact; and although there was
a dignified master of the ceremonies, his aid was
probably seldom invoked or required for intro-
ductions; but much the same might be said of any
place where the youth (and not only the youth) of
both sexes mingle; and I don't suppose that Cremorne
was any worse than haunts not dissimilar of our own
day.

Whistler, as I have said, has perpetuated those
fireworks for which it was famous and which the
producers—Mortram and Duffell—regularly sent
shooting and banging into the summer air, as they do
—if they do still—at the Crystal Palace, to the prolonged ohs—and ahs—of the assembled crowd.

But the fireworks were only one feature of Cremorne. Special entertainments were constantly being
arranged by the indefatigable Simpson and his
coadjutors. Now it was an Aquatic Tournament, or
a Naval Fête; anon "the Italian Salamander," as he
was called, emulated Shadrech and his companions
in passing through a fiery furnace unharmed; sometimes special balloon ascents were organized, and it
was from here that the veteran Green made his three
hundred and sixty-fifth ascent, on August 2, 1847;
once, too, in 1852, a Madame Poitevin went up
seated on a heifer, as Green had done, at Vauxhall,
on a pony two years earlier; but in the latter instance
the magistrates interfered and stopped future performances of a like character.

The delight in balloons and parachutes (the latter
sometimes attended by loss of life) was at this time
at its height, and Cremorne was a favourite place

D D

for the exhibition of such things; numbers of ascents being made from its grounds.

For those who preferred theatrical entertainment the playhouse offered farces and vaudevilles and ballets; while in the concert-room popular singers, such as Samuel Cowell, Robert Glindon and Jack Sharp performed between 1846 and 1850; and the eccentric Herr von Joel ranged the gardens and turned up in unexpected places, giving his curious vocal imitations or yodelling, which at first produced a sensation, but from over-repetition finally only a sensation of boredom, as those who remember him have attested.

Notwithstanding that in 1857 the Chelsea Vestry tried to stop its licence on account of the character of many of its frequenters and the general disturbance of the late hours by its noise, Cremorne was not quite so bad as its critics would have had the authorities suppose. A passage in Wroth's account of the place may appositely be quoted here, because it probably shows exactly the mixed atmosphere of the gardens and the varied class of their frequenters:

"Cremorne," he says, "was never able to parade in the newspapers that array of fashionable and distinguished personages who 'last night visited Vauxhall.' It was not, for one thing, a place that ladies (in the strict sense of the word) were in the habit of visiting, unless perhaps (as Mr. Sala puts it) 'in disguise and on the sly,' or, at any rate, under the safe conduct of a husband, or a brother. Ladies of some sort were, no doubt, considerably in evidence there, though we are not to think of Cremorne as so entirely given over to 'drink, dancing, and devilry,' as its sterner critics declared. If it was a place for the man about town, it also attracted a number of worthy citizens and country cousins who went there for an evening's pleasure with their wives and daughters, and were 'not particular.' A livelier element was imported by the medical student—a high-spirited race made responsible in those days for the sins of many non-medical youngsters—by Oxonians and Cantabs, by temporarily irresponsible clerks and shopmen, and 'flash' personages of various kinds."

This gives a very fair picture of what Cremorne must have been during its palmy days, although a drawing by M'Connell, dated 1858, and entitled "Cremorne Gardens in the Height of the Season," shows the most respectable and *haut-ton* crowd parading its walks or seated taking refreshments at its little circular tables; while at a later date Lady Dorothy Nevill is able to tell that she occasionally went to some of the special fêtes given here, "when the gardens presented much the same appearance as Vauxhall in its palmy days"; but she says that at the last of such fêtes "considerable disorder prevailed on account of a number of the usual frequenters obtaining admission and squirting ink at the ladies' dresses as a sign of their displeasure at the intrusion of another society than their own. In consequence of this," she adds, "no more of these fêtes were held, the gardens being entirely abandoned to the class which eventually caused their end."[1]

In 1861,[2] on the retirement of Simpson, his place was taken by the once well-known E. T. Smith, a man whose name is identified with many of the theatres and other entertainments of his day, and who was a born *impresario*. He inaugurated his management by presenting to an astonished public the lady (Selina Young) known as "the female Blondin," who

[1] "Leaves from the Notebooks of Lady Dorothy Nevill."
[2] "In the 'sixties," says Wroth, "some charming little folding programmes were issued, printed in colour, and presenting on every page a view of Cremorne. Portions of the programme were ingeniously cut out, so that on the front page there was a view up the long walk, flanked by its trees and lamp-bearing goddesses, right to the great fountain." These programmes have, as such things are wont to do, become very scarce, and owners of them would do well to treasure them."

was billed to cross the Thames on a tight rope. She had partially done so, in the presence of a vast crowd, when it was found that some ruffian had cut the guy-ropes, and she was only saved from falling into the river by the presence of mind with which she caught hold of the rope and gradually lowered herself into a boat. On a subsequent occasion she fell at Highbury Barn, and was crippled for life.

Another of Smith's "shows" was a recrudescence of the tournament idea, in 1863, which was held on July 8;[1] and following days, and owing to the fine weather was as great a success as the famous Eglinton one had been a failure.

Still other attractions, organized by the resourceful manager, were the Man Frog, and the Beckwith family in their natatory exhibitions; and the captive balloon in which anyone who was ready to pay ten shillings could ascend, and which, on one occasion, soared aloft bearing a female centenarian from the Fulham Workhouse, free of charge.

With the opening of the 'seventies John Baum became lessee, and although he was not of the calibre of Smith, he did more for the dramatic features of Cremorne, largely developing these and erecting a new theatre where Offenbach's and Auber's musical dramas were performed with much success, with a large ballet, and an excellently conducted orchestra under the direction of Jules Rivière.

Baum's management was, however, marked by one disastrous episode, when De Groof, "the flying man," making an ascent on July 9, 1874, attached to a balloon, fell with his machine in Sydney Street, Chelsea, and died shortly after; an event which caused a widespread sensation at the time. In other respects, too, Baum had much anxiety with regard to Cremorne. It had become, if not habitually riotous, at least

[1] There is an account of this in the *Illustrated London News,* for July 18, 1863.

a sort of recognized centre for riotry on special occasions, and the storming and wrecking of the bars characterized one of these disturbances on the night of Oaks day.

From now onwards, indeed, it was seldom without some unpleasant feature of this kind. Race days, and Bank Holidays, the Boat Race and any special occasion were caught at as an excuse for unlimited drunkenness and shameful rowdyism, until the Chelsea Vestry and Canon Cromwell, the Principal of St. Marks Training College, jointly took steps to put it down, not, of course, without the ridicule that is generally cast at those who try to improve manners and to combat public abuses.

They had a rather curious coadjutor in a Mr. Alfred Brandon, a tailor, who produced a pamphlet of doggerel verse, entitled, "The Trial of John Fox, or Fox John, or the Horrors of Cremorne," in 1876. Baum's attention was drawn to what he considered a libel, and he brought an action against the sartorial poet, but only obtained a farthing damages. This and the fact that he was already much in debt, and ill, caused him to withdraw his application for a further licence, on October 5, 1877, much to the delight of those who were prepared to oppose it, and the astonishment and annoyance of many to whom the gardens were a happy hunting-ground.

Cremorne was thereupon closed, and in the following year its fixtures, and stores of wine, and so forth, were sold by auction, as well as the timber, the plants, the statuary, and, indeed, everything that was saleable; and the site was eventually built over. As a pleasure haunt it had existed more or less feverishly for some thirty odd years; and in spite of the raffish character it in time came to earn, it formed one of those open-air places of amusement and recreation which we seem now entirely to have dispensed with. If its name does not recall the picturesqueness of a period when Vauxhall and Ranelagh were the *mode*, it is at least probable that it will remain as long as these as a later landmark in London's various manifestations of pleasure-seeking, and as one hardly less interesting in the annals of such haunts.

It is a curious thing that almost as well remembered by name as Cremorne, is *Rosherville*; for Rosherville, although near London, was not strictly a London pleasure haunt at all; at least no more than the Star and Garter at Richmond or the Ship at Greenwich were; and therefore the Gravesend Rosherville, "the place for a day's pleasure," the objective of so many excursion steamers, the elysium of a class not too fastidious in its amusements, needs but to be named, and passed by as being outside our present purview.[1]

A pleasure haunt that does, however, require some notice, for it existed from 1824 to 1882, was the *Eagle Tavern*, with its Grecian Saloon or Theatre, in the City Road.

About the middle of the eighteenth century there existed at this spot a humble ale-house called the Shepherd and Shepherdess, whose gardens were among the resorts of the middle classes, until the coming of the City Road, in 1761, took from it that rurality which had been one of its chief assets. For years, however, the actual tavern with its diminished attractions was carried on, until about the year 1825, when it was demolished, and on or near its site the Eagle Tavern arose, having been built by Thomas Rouse, who had become the owner of the property a few

---

[1] I may, however, note that the place was so called from the name of its projector, Mr. Jeremiah Rosher, and that Gaspey, in the book on London he wrote for Tallis* calls it "a kind of Cheltenham in miniature." Dancing and fireworks were features of the place, which, from two little views given in the above work, would appear to have been diversified and picturesque.

---

* "Tallis's Illustrated London," by William Gaspey, 2 vols., *circa* 851.

years previously. Rouse, who is said to have been originally a bricklayer, had quite a genius for building, and the Eagle was his first attempt in this direction.

Attention was quickly drawn to the place through Rouse arranging for Green and Harris,[1] the æronauts, to make some of their balloon ascents from its gardens —gardens that were likewise the scene of the annual meetings of the Devon and Cornish wrestlers and single-stick exponents.

That Rouse was a man who knew when to take occasion by the hand, is proved in a curious way. When, in 1831, the authorities wished to dispose of certain fittings and temporary ornamentation used in parts of Westminster Abbey, on the occasion of William IV.'s Coronation, he came forward and purchased them, and converted them into an ornamental entrance to his pleasure-garden, taking care to advertise the fact as a means of exciting curiosity, and thus attracting further patronage. But he did more than this, for in the same year he built the Grecian Saloon, as it was called, and installed in it an organ and an automatic piano; while he commissioned an artist, Phillips, a pupil of Clarkson Stanfield, to decorate the walls with allegorical paintings.

Having thus enlarged and beautified his premises, Rouse re-opened them in the spring of 1832, and visitors crowded to the place to dance in what was called "The Grecian Tent," to wander about the be-lanterned gardens, to listen to the band, or to wonder at the cosmorama and the fountains, what time a conjuror or a tight-rope dancer performed in one part of the grounds, and Miss James or Miss Smith, perennial favourites, delighted audiences in another.

[1] Harris's ascent from here, in 1824, resulted in his death. See that very scarce book : Major Chambre's "Recollections of West End Life," 2 vols., 1858.

The audiences were of vast proportions, and in the daily papers as many as 5000 or 6000 are mentioned as being present on a single night. That they were not of a fashionable character is true, but they were a happy and amused, and, on the whole, well-conducted crowd, and when Mr. Samuel Wilkins went there, he found a large number of them "eating and drinking as comfortably as possible."[1]

In 1838, another Coronation year, by the way, Rouse projected fresh improvements; and from that time, when the place was also called the Coronation Pleasure Grounds, onwards it may be said to have entered on the second phase of its successful career. Round the gardens was now formed a covered promenade; a new tavern was built, and an additional ballroom added; while the saloon, in which a larger organ had been installed, was wholly remodelled and re-decorated.

This saloon was opened on New Year's Day, 1838, with a concert, in which Moncrieff, the dramatist, took part, the catholic nature of which may be estimated by the fact that airs from Rossini and other classic composers were interspersed with popular comic songs. But Rouse had greater ambitions than this, and it was not long before he began to present complete operas here, among them the "Barber of Seville," "La Gazza Ladra," "La Sonnambula," "Don Giovanni," and so on.

They were successful in one way, but the cost of their production made them unremunerative; however, what Rouse lost on them, he gained by his tavern and other attractions. He was certainly the means of introducing and making popular in the East End good music, and should, therefore, be remembered as a pioneer and a public benefactor.

But he did not rely solely on this æsthetic entertainment, and if the Eagle Tavern, with its Grecian

[1] See "The Sketches by Boz."

Saloon, had one marked characteristic, it was variety. All sorts of attractions were to be found there. There Flexmore, the clown, delighted old and young; there Robson created a *furore* with his singing of "Villikins and his Dinah," in 1853 and following years.

But by this time Rouse, the ever-popular proprietor, had retired (1851), and was succeeded in the management by Benjamin Oliver, who called himself Conquest. True to his predecessor's musical proclivities, Conquest opened with a production of "A Midsummer Night's Dream"; and made his career as manager notable by the presentation of ballets so excellent and complete that they were said to have only been surpassed by those at Her Majesty's Theatre. In this he was helped by his wife, who happened to be a beautiful dancer herself and a good teacher of others—the others including that exquisite exponent of the art—Kate Vaughan, and the three Miss Conquests.

Dancing among amateurs was then at the height of its popularity, although the measures then trodden were very different from those now in vogue, and while the visitors delighted in watching ballets on the stage, they were also more than ready to enjoy themselves in less skilful manifestations; and for their convenience a new monster platform, capable of holding 500 people, was erected, and was nightly patronized; sometimes by people in fancy dress, for masquarades were occasionally permitted. I say permitted, because the utmost care was taken to prevent them degenerating into the rowdyism often rampant at Vauxhall on similar occasions. The fact that they were not encouraged by the management, however, proves that it found no little difficulty in preserving the decency and order at which it aimed.

At a later date, George Conquest, the son of Benjamin Oliver, was largely responsible for the introduction of the romantic drama lightened by pantomime, and after having exhibited his remarkable powers as a quick-change artist and a capable actor during his father's management, he succeeded him in 1872, and five years later built and opened (October, 1877) the new Grecian Theatre, with a company in which he himself, Harry Nicholls and Miss M. A. Victor, that excellent actress, figured.

When Conquest went to the Surrey Theatre, he sold the Eagle to a Mr. T. G. Clark, in 1879. From this time onwards, the place declined in public favour. Clark was not a success as a manager, and he was, besides, faced by the fact that a certain class of puritanical firebrands suddenly discovered that the Eagle was a rowdy, ill-conducted place, the haunt of vice and the resort of the wicked. It was, no doubt, like all such centres, not immaculate; but the charges brought against it were as undoubtedly exaggerated. However, it was attacked, and in 1882 the Salvation Army purchased it, and religious services were held where erst had danced the light-hearted of an earlier generation. The amusing part of the whole thing was that it was discovered that by law the Salvation Army was obliged to keep up the old drinking licence, and it had to do so—no doubt with much profit. Finally the Salvation Army gave up its rather anomalous possession, and in 1899 the large Eagle Tavern was demolished, and a smaller house was erected, in the following year, on its site. A view, published about 1838, shows how imposing, if rather rococo, were the appearance of the pleasure gardens attached to the Eagle Tavern, with their oriental pinnacled structures and their gas-lamps of mammoth design. The whole place is but a memory even in its somewhat remote regions, where the inhabitants would be hard put to it to solve the problem as to what was exactly meant by that enigmatic "Pop goes the Weasel" with which the Eagle and the City Road are identified in the once-popular song.

Among other pleasure haunts of a not dissimilar character which flourished about the same time was *The Albert Saloon and Royal Standard Pleasure Gardens*, as they were rather clumsily styled, which stood not far away, to the north, from the Eagle itself; and which one Henry Bradley started in 1838, somewhat on the lines of its more redoubtable rival. The place was advertised to accommodate 10,000 people; and all sorts of entertainments were to be found there, from concerts and theatrical performances, to occasional balloon ascents. Although as a theatre it could not rival the Eagle, it had some success with pantomimes, especially when the then-popular clown, Paul Herring, appeared in them. It continued to be run for a few years, but even in the 'forties we are told that its popularity had begun to wane, and in 1857 it was closed.

Another pleasure resort was that formed by the ample grounds attached to the New Globe Tavern in the Mile End Road. It was called *The New Globe Pleasure Grounds*, and a charming little picture of it was made by H. M. Wichelo, about 1846. The gardens were very much be-shrubbed, and walks surrounded a large lawn. Fountains and statues and arbours give it that essential air which all such places had at a time when nature itself was never thought to be complete without the adventitious aid of such adornments. Concerts and sometimes ballets were performed for the benefit of those who frequented the place; and at least once Coxwell, the aeronaut, was advertised to make an ascent here, in 1854. Wroth gives an amusing story of what happened. It appears that Coxwell's balloon had just been oiled when he received his unexpected order, and he realized that it would be dangerous to go up in it. However, the crowd was expectant, and it would have been equally dangerous to disappoint those who began to clamour for the show to begin. Finally, after some delay, when it was quite dark, the balloon ascended in a glory of attendant fireworks, and a figure was seen leaning over the side with a flag in its hand; what time a man might have been observed, muffled up, hastily making his way out of the grounds. It need hardly be said that the mysterious hurrying figure was Coxwell himself, and that the occupant of the balloon was a dummy!

All over London, during the earlier half of the last century, were scattered a number of these pleasure gardens, all of which had more or less a resemblance to each other, in that they were places where people could lounge about, partake of refreshment, and often "assist," in the French sense of the word, at such entertainments as were provided by the proprietor; sometimes in the form of ballets, music, pantomimes on a restricted scale, balloon ascents, tight-rope dancing, conjuring, and so forth. They formed, indeed, open-air equivalents to the variety shows of to-day; but many of them were of so subsidiary a character as really to be little more than adjuncts to the taverns with which they were generally connected: the *Sir Hugh Myddelton's Head*, near Sadler's Wells; the *Mermaid*, at Hackney, which had a regular assembly-room, and where balloon ascents were a feature; the so-called *Weston's Retreat*, in Kentish Town, which posed as a miniature Cremorne, became a nuisance to the neighbourhood, and was finally absorbed, in the 'sixties, by the Midland Railway; *Chalk Farm*, where pony-racing and rifle-shooting took place, and whose original tavern was demolished in 1853; the *Eel-Pie House*, Highbury, noted for its wrestling-matches, dog-fights, and rat-killing matches, which differentiated it from many of its congeners, although people resorted there to eat the eel-pies for which the place was, at least locally, famous; and the *Panarmonion Gardens*, at Battle Bridge, King's Cross, formed by a company on the dusty wilderness then existing in that region, and containing a "Suspension

Railway," a view of which, *circa* 1830, is extant, which had, however, but a temporary popularity; although the little theatre attached to it was opened and re-opened under new names—the Cabinet, the King's Cross Theatre, among them, with an optimism worthy of a better cause.

Elsewhere in London, especially in the regions about Chelsea and the river, various centres of amusement existed; and there were few taverns in those parts that had not their adjacent gardens which went not infrequently by high-sounding names, although as a rule the sign of the inn itself was found sufficient to indicate their existence to the local *clientèle* which chiefly patronized them.

One of these is rather outstanding because its name at least is known to those who are unacquainted with many others existing at this period. This was the *Red House*, at Battersea, facing the river at the spot where the Victoria Suspension Bridge crosses it. Being by the water-side, it had naturally an aquatic air, and boat-races in connection with it were frequent, one of the most curious being that in 1852, when a Mr. John Garratt and a Mr. Hollyoak emulated Barry the clown's earlier performance in 1844 by competing in a race in washing-tubs, from the Old Swan to the Red House.

But the Red House was a resort for other than boating amusements; and it is chiefly famous for its pigeon-shooting matches, in which the best shots in London were wont to take part. A kind of fair was also held in the adjoining fields at Easter time, which, although prohibited in 1823, was revived some twelve years later, and continued till 1852, when it was suppressed, much to the satisfaction of those who had long reprehended its viciousness. It seems to have been not very dissimilar from other fairs; how-ever, as one reverend gentleman did not hesitate to say that "if ever there was a place out of hell which

surpassed Sodom and Gomorrah in ungodliness and
abomination, this was it," one supposes that he muſt
have had some rather extraordinary experiences there.

If ever one regrets the demolition of the old landmarks of London[1] and the subſtitution of hideous
objeɕts in their place, it muſt be in remembering the
piɕturesque old Red House, as it appears in Rorke's
beautiful colour-print published in 1845, and then
looking at the bridge which is what we have in its place.

There are one or two other forms in which our
forbears were wont to take their pleasures, in London,
and which may be conveniently alluded to at the close
of this chapter. I have said that the Thames[2] in earlier
days was used not only as a commercial highway,
but as a pleasure resort. In the sixteenth, seventeenth,
and eighteenth centuries it was in the heyday of its
popularity, not only as a means for reaching the
various centres of entertainment on its banks, but as
a pleasant change from the narrow, noisy ſtreets of old
London. Even in the earlier years of the nineteenth
century it preserved something of its charaɕter in this
respeɕt, and that old gaudily-decorated barge the
"Maria Wood," which made excursions from the city
to such places as Kew and Richmond (in my youth
I remember to have seen it doing so), was a kind of
peripatetic successor to the ſtationary "Folly," as it
was called, which was sometimes moored near
Cuper's Stairs, opposite Somerset House, sometimes
near the Savoy, and occasionally at Bankside,
Southwark.

This "Folly" was really a kind of glorified house-
boat, having cabins below and a large space for
walking or sitting, above. At each corner of this

[1] It was purchased, in 1850, by the Government for £11,000, and
demolished in order that its site might be included in Battersea Park.

[2] In the "Diary of Amusements" (Picture of London, 1826), we read,
under July 3, that a silver cup given by the proprietors of Vauxhall
Gardens, was *sailed* for by gentlemen's pleasure-boats; and that the
famous Doggett's coat and badge was rowed for on August 1, as it ſtill is.

promenade was a turret supported by columns,
beneath which were seats. When exactly it was first
put on the Thames is uncertain, but the statement,
in "London Past and Present," to the effect that it
originally made its appearance in William III.'s reign,
is obviously incorrect, as Pepys, in 1668, speaks of
spending a shilling there in the April of that year.
According to Tom Brown,[1] this "whimsical piece of
architecture" was constructed "as a musical summer-
house for the entertainment of quality, where they
might meet and ogle one another . . . but the
ladies of the town, finding it as convenient a rendezvous
for their purpose . . . dash'd the female quality out
of countenance and made them seek a more retired
conveniency." Brown describes how he once went to
see it, and from the company he found assembled
there, it is pretty clearly proved that the "Folly" was
decidedly not a place *virginibus puerisque*. Indeed he
speaks of the scene as a confused one of "folly, madness
and debauchery." Occasionally, however, it was more
respectable, and once at least had a royal visitor, when
Queen Mary honoured it by her presence, an event
which induced its owner to call it "The Royal Diversion," and to try to substitute that name, but without
success, for its more generally received and far more
appropriate one.

Its moral decadence began with the coming of
the eighteenth century, and then for two or three
decades it went on with its intrigues and its drinking
and its gambling (it possessed what was called a
Golden Gaming-Table, which auriferous adjunct led
largely to its undoing), until on account of the scandal
attached to it owing to the obvious reasons for its
popularity, it was suppressed and chopped up for
firewood.[2] Hatton[3] says it took its name "perhaps from

[1] "Amusements Serious and Comical."
[2] Sir John Hawkins in a MS. note in his "History of Music."
[3] "New View of London," 2 vols., 1708.

the foolish things there sometimes acted"; but it seems more probable that it was so called with a view to the encouragement of such things. It need hardly be said that the very respectable "Maria Wood" had nothing in common with the "Folly," except that it was a floating pleasure haunt, just as was the Chinese junk which, in 1848, was moored nearly on the same spot, and which attracted thousands of curious sight-seers, Charles Dickens among them. At first the junk was stationed at Blackwall; but when the London season began, it was towed up the river to its station near Waterloo Bridge.[1]

Another form of amusement, common enough all over the country, and having its chief manifestation so close to London as Epsom, was and is racing; but it will be news to some people that there have been several subsidiary race-courses actually in London itself, and one which was for a time quite outstanding. Yet this is the fact; and had John Williams and Thomas Dixon, in the latter years of the seventeenth century, succeeded in their plan to form an amphitheatre in Lincoln Inn's Fields, ostensibly for the exercise of the trained bands of the city, I might have had to record a miniature course in that legal stronghold; for such places have a way of degenerating from their solemn beginnings, and although Williams and Dixon sought powers to close all the theatres on Bankside and stop all plays during one day in the week for the most excellent motives, one feels that had this application been successful and continuous, some daring spirit would have come forward and projected another kind of entertainment here, especially as it would thus have been freed from dramatic rivalry.

But this is, of course, conjectural; while the racing of ponies at the Spa Gardens, Bermondsey "for a

---

[1] Walford's "Old and New London," where there is a woodcut of the vessel.

silver cup,"[1] in 1802, and similar races at Sadler's Wells, where a regular course was laid out both in 1806 and 1826 with grandstand, judge's box, and everything complete, the ponies being ridden by jockeys of "great celebrity"; as well as at Belsize House and on Hampstead Heath, during the eighteenth century, are facts. But these were confessedly limited courses, the length of a race at Belsize House, for instance, being six times round, and were restricted apparently to ponies. There was, however, a race-course in London of far more ambitious proportions, no less indeed than two and a half miles in circuit, and it was situated at Notting Hill, just west of Ladbrooke Grove, on which it abutted. A plan of the *Hippodrome*, as it was called, dated 1841, gives its outlines and shows its exact extent, while a woodcut of a few years earlier indicates the high mound that rose on its grounds, around which part of the course ran. The place was projected and carried out by a Mr. John Whyte, in 1837, and was first opened on June 3 of that year. The entrance was fixed at one shilling, and the pedestrian spectators could obtain a splendid view of the whole course from the dominating mound to which I have referred, and which, in the woodcut, is shown crowded with people.

That the Hippodrome was placed on a fashionable footing from the beginning, is evidenced by the fact that two such outstanding members of the "ton" as the Earl of Chesterfield and Count D'Orsay consented to act as the first stewards, and that many notable people, including some of the Royal family, were to be seen there. Everything appears to have been done to make "the London Epsom," as it was called, really a sporting centre without those adjuncts which

---

[1] See Picture of London, 1802, under "Almanack of Pleasures." Of course racing in "The Ring" in Hyde Park, under the Stuarts, was a regular amusement, and attracted crowds of sightseers. It may be said to have been the precursor of modern racing.

E E

vitiate so many race meetings. For instance, no gambling or drinking booths were permitted, although various kinds of beverages were obtainable at the entrance. Valuable cups were offered as prizes, and in the pages of Bell's Life will be found, for 1837 and following years, the regulation details of the horses, jockeys, weights, etc.

According to various authorities, there was only one circumstance that affected the select character at which the proprietor aimed, and that was the presence across the ground of a public right of way, and this was taken advantage of by the usual crowd of hawkers, gipsies and such-like gentry, together with others less acceptable, who are to be found at most race-meetings.

In the year following the opening of the course, efforts were made to seek Parliamentary powers to close this right of way; and at first with promise of success, but opposition was rampant, and many cogent, and some extremely ridiculous, reasons were forthcoming in opposition—several of the latter probably concealing the puritanical outlook of those who regard horse-racing as only a step to perdition. The matter was allowed to drop; but by cutting off a considerable portion of the ground the proprietor was able to exclude the right of way from his area. This, however, naturally much affected the *agrémens* of the course; and together with the fact that the soil was so full of clay as to make it impossible to train horses here during any but the dry seasons, was no doubt the main reason for the closing of the race-course in 1841.

The site is now covered by streets and houses, and the large open space has become a thickly populated district; but it seems regrettable that this earnest attempt to give London a race-course, and a select one at that, should have resulted in financial loss to its projectors (a Mr. Connop appears to have become the proprietor, or "lessee," as he was called, when,

in 1845, he appeared in the Bankruptcy Court[1]),
and that its open space should have been obliterated
in favour of bricks and mortar.[2]

One other form of amusement, somewhat analogous
to that of racing, in that its chief attraction was
equestrianism, was the circus. London has always
been rich in such things, and circuses and hippo-
dromes have often been adjuncts to more far-reaching
exemplifications of the entertainment cult. But notwithstanding the frequency with which these are to
be met with in the pleasure annals of London, one
only of them has remained as an outstanding name,
and that one is Astley's.

The origin of Astley's was humble enough, for in
1774, Philip Astley having rented a piece of ground
in the Westminster Bridge Road, erected a temporary
wooden building made of deal boards, and there, to
the music of a drum and two fifes, began his exhibition
of feats of daring equestrianism.[3] It was at first an open
arena, surrounded by covered rows of seats to which
the price of entrance was two shillings; one shilling,
originally sixpence, admitting to stands outside the rails.

Owing to success not only in connection with his
show, but in other ways,[4] Astley was able to convert
his rather archaic amphitheatre into a roofed edifice
in 1778, and in the following year to open it as the
Amphitheatre Riding House. In the mornings it was
utilized as a riding school, and Astley, who is said to
have been one of the handsomest men of the day, and

[1] See Wroth's "Cremorne and Later London Gardens."
[2] St. John's Church now stands on the summit of the mound.
[3] A good account of Astley's Circus is to be found in Wilkinson's
"Londina Illustrata"; of it and of the man himself, in that very scarce
book "Historical and Descriptive Accounts of the Theatres of London,"
by E. W. Brayley, with beautiful coloured prints by Havell, published
in 1826; where a view of the later entrance is given.
[4] He picked up a diamond ring at the foot of Westminster Bridge,
which, being unclaimed, he sold for a large sum.

was undoubtedly one of the most skilful of equestrians, soon had as much business in this way as he could wish. In the afternoons and evenings the regular equestrian performances took place.

And so things went on till 1786, when Astley entirely refitted his amphitheatre, and gave it a new name: "The Royal Grove," a name that six years later was destined to be superseded by yet another: "The Royal Saloon, or Astley's Amphitheatre." At this time the show was so good that even Horace Walpole, generally fastidious and suspicious of novelty, says that it was better than he expected.

When the place was opened in the evening other items beyond equestrianism were to be found on the bills, and rope-dancing, transparencies, fireworks, and acrobatic feats alternated with the horses and their daring and accomplished rider.

In 1794, the disaster which has overtaken so many places of amusement befell Astley's, and on August 17, it together with a number of adjoining houses, was burned to the ground. Indeed the place proved singularly susceptible to fire, for having been rebuilt, it was again burnt down in 1803; and yet a third time in 1841. In the second conflagration the mother of Mrs. Astley perished in the flames; while as a consequence of the third, the famous horseman, Ducrow, went mad from grief at the losses he had sustained.

At the time of the second fire Astley was in France, whither he had gone to superintend a theatre he was running in Paris. He was there kept a prisoner by Napoleon, and he only heard of his loss later, on managing to escape into Germany. The new theatre he built was called "Astley's Royal Amphitheatre of Arts," the patronage of the Prince of Wales and the Duke of York having been secured.

Astley died in 1814, and was succeeded by his son, John, who was as fine a horseman as his father, but hardly so impressive a personality as the man who is said to have been responsible for the erection of no fewer than nineteen different playhouses in various parts, and who had initiated and brought to perfection a then novel form of entertainment.

For many years Astley's continued to draw all and sundry with its variety shows, in which quasi-theatrical performances on the stage, including wonderful performing animals, weird freaks of both sexes, and suchlike things, were varied by exhibitions of horsemanship in the arena, which was situated in the space usually allotted to the stalls.

In 1821 John Astley died in Paris, curiously enough in the same house and in the same bed in which his father had expired just seven years earlier, when a Mr. W. Davis, who had been associated with him in the management, carried it on alone till 1824, in which year it was leased to Ducrow. Here the spectacular entertainment of "The Battle of Waterloo" was given for many weeks with great success, the part of Napoleon being sustained by Gomersall, as all readers of the Bon Gaultier Ballads will remember.

Books on London of the period grow lyric over the excellence and beauty of Astley's second theatre, but we should not probably be greatly astonished at it. However, it seems to have been well arranged and commodious, and that and the rather florid decoration then in favour, were as much as the *habitués* required.

After the third fire, a Mr. Batty erected yet another theatre, capable of holding 4000 people; and this, in 1862, was converted by Mr. Dion Boucicault into what he called "The Theatre Royal, Westminster," although, of course, it was not in Westminster at all.

Dickens, in his "Sketches by Boz," and Thackeray, in "The Newcomes," have both perpetuated the once-famous Astley's; and the importance that was attached to it as an outstanding place of entertainment is indicated by the fact that it not only crops up in all sorts of ways in the literature of the period, but in the "Pictures of London," and such-like productions, it is always referred to with an enthusiasm that in these days, when circuses are a thing of the past, seems quite astonishing.

In one's own younger days Hengler's, to be followed by Sanger's, had taken the place of the once-famous Astley's, and the latter has been prominent, in a peripatetic way, down to more recent times. But neither could quite claim that unique place which their prototype occupied for so long.

One other circus must be mentioned, for although it existed but for a short time, it was projected by that William Batty whom we have met just now as once the lessee and builder of the fourth Astley's. This enterprising man, taking advantage of the Great Exhibition of 1851, opened in that year a Hippodrome which went by his name, nearly opposite the Broad Walk in Kensington Gardens, and between part of Victoria Road and Victoria Walk, then a recently developed residential district.[1] Batty opened his Hippodrome, in May 1851, with a troupe brought over expressly from Paris, and the performances, which took place in the evening, and for which the lowest admission was sixpence, were Roman Chariot Races, executed by three brothers named Debach, each of whom drove six horses, and races of unmounted Barbery horses. But other attractions were added, among them the inevitable balloon ascents, for which the services of such well-known exponents as Hampton and Graham were requisitioned.

With the closing of the Great Exhibition the end came to Batty's Hippodrome, which thereupon and for a number of years later was used as a riding school.

[1] Victoria Road was formed about 1847. Loftie's "Kensington."

CHAPTER XVII

THE OPERA, AND OTHER MUSICAL HAUNTS, ETC.

THERE was, perhaps, never a time when music was so popular in this country as during the second half of the eighteenth century. Then, the great Handel was domiciled among us; then, Italian opera first seriously came to these shores; [1] then, the tender airs of Domenico Scarlatti, and Geminiani, Porpora, and Veracini, and the rest of that rich school, tinkled on innumerable harpsichords and spinets; then, Dr. Arne was producing his operas and inimitable songs to show that we had a successor to Purcell, and a rival to imported melody.

Society then went mad over La Faustina, Cuzzoni, Senesino, and Farinelli, and the rest, and was divided into hostile camps in its varied patronage of these foreign singers; while the supporters of native talent formed yet another body which saw with alarm an alien inrush and found support in "The Beggar's Opera" as a kind of manifesto against imported talent. As time went on, the people from high to low burst into an orgy of glee-singing and such-like forms of the melodious spirit; and probably at no period in our social annals have we so nearly approximated to the really musical standpoint of Germany or Italy as we did when George, Prince of Wales, who, as Mrs. Robinson assures us, had so good a voice, and who, besides, could play creditably on the 'cello, was leading the nation in melodious, if sometimes boisterous, song.

---

[1] Of course Italian music had been heard before in England. Pepys records listening to some at Lord Brounker's house in 1667, and Purcell acknowledges his debt to the Italian masters.

Indeed, the Royal Family showed themselves generally ardent and discriminating patrons of music. George III. had inherited the love of it from his father, Frederick, Prince of Wales, who was also a 'cello-player of no mean ability, and it was he who, by his patronage of the concerts of Ancient Music and his indefatigable attendance at oratorios, set an example which was one of the few which he did set that society followed. If there is one thing marked about the character of George III., it is his love of music, and the Farmer King would sit for hours playing the tender airs of Handel on that spinet which during his last, sad, remote years was one of the few delights left to his vagrant senses.

In the pages of Dr. Burney's "History of Music" and in those of Hogarth's "Memoirs of the Opera," and elsewhere we can read of that period when melody, vocal and instrumental, was predominant, when the Ancient Music rivalled Covent Garden, and the Haymarket rivalled both; when the Hanover Square Rooms were to our forbears what the Albert Hall and the Queen's Hall are to us; when the comparative claims of Bononcini and Handel were discussed by the Fashion, and violent disputes arose over the merits of Farinelli and Cuzzoni and Senesino, of Gabrielli and Mingotti and Guadagni; while the great organ in the Abbey and a voiceful choir rose triumphant, and drowned the quarrels in the tremendous choruses of "The Messiah."

The opera, was, of course, one of the recognized headquarters of the musical spirit, and thus properly comes within our purview as a pleasure haunt. Opera has had three recognized homes in London, one in the Haymarket, another at Drury Lane, and yet another in Covent Garden. The first takes precedence, on a question of dates, although it is the last which has preserved till our own day the musical character which marked it from its inception.

The Haymarket Opera House

This house has been known variously as the Queen's Theatre, the King's Theatre, Her Majesty's Theatre and His Majesty's Theatre, and is to-day wholly identified with dramatic art. It had its origin in the building which Vanbrugh erected on this site and which was opened on April 9, 1705,[1] with a performance of Dryden's play "The Indian Emperor." At first the house was used as a theatre, but a few years later, an effort being made by many influential people in London to establish a recognized home for Italian Opera (certain performances in "the Italian manner" had already taken place at Drury Lane), the Queen's Theatre in the Haymarket was hired, and Handel was appointed director, with full powers to engage well-known performers. With this object he went to Dresden and secured the services of the then famous Senesino. Returning to this country, he set himself to composing a number of operas, all of which were performed at the Haymarket during the years 1721-8.

But although this went on for some seven years, the opera-house appears to have been the scene of continual disputes and intrigues. Handel was emphatic and domineering, the Italians were *difficile*, and Senesino was one of the ring-leaders in the dissensions that arose. Then Cuzzoni and La Faustina were ladies who were continually at loggerheads, and Colley Cibber did not overstate the case when he wrote: "These costly canary birds contaminate the whole body of our music-loving public with their virulent bickerings. Ladies refuse to receive visits from friends who belong to the opposite musical party. Cæsar and Pompey did not excite the Romans to more violent partisanship than these contentious women."[2]

[1] Mrs. Tofts had sung Italian songs at the Lincoln's Inn Theatre two years previously, and her rivalry with Margherita de l'Epine, anticipated the dissensions between the Italians who came to England at a later date.
[2] "Apology for his own Life."

At last things came to a head with a disgraceful public squabble on the stage of the Haymarket opera-house, between Cuzzoni and La Faustina, a quarrel which had been preceded by such incidents as that recorded in the *London Journal*, for June 10, 1757: "A great disturbance happened at the opera, occasioned by the partisans of the two celebrated rival ladies, Cuzzoni and Faustina. The contention at first was only carried on by hissing on one side and clapping on the other; but proceeded at length to the melodious use of catcalls and other accompaniments, which manifested the zeal and politeness of that illustrious assembly. The Princess Caroline was there, but neither her royal highness' presence, nor the laws of decorum, could restrain the glorious ardour of the combatants." Among the supporters of Cuzzoni was Lady Pembroke, and the following epigram was accordingly written on the event:

> "Old poet's sing that hearts did dance
> Whenever Orpheus play'd;
> So, to Faustina's charming voice
> Wise Pembroke's asses bray'd."

lines that were doubtless inspired by Lady Burlington or Lady Delawar, or some other of the band that supported La Faustina.[1]

In view of such things, Handel had nothing else to do but close the Haymarket Opera House, and Cuzzoni returned to her native land, whence she was destined once again to visit our shores in 1750, when she was given a benefit at the same house. La Faustina also went back to Italy in 1732, and was heard no more in England. Handel, nothing daunted, determined to reopen the opera house on his own

---

[1] Horace Walpole tells us of the difficulty his mother had on the question of precedence, when, on one occasion, she received "the rivals" at her house. See, too, Hogarth's "Memoirs of the Opera."

ITALIAN OPERA HOUSE
HAYMARKET
1825

responsibility,[1] and with this purpose went abroad again in search of vocal talent; but his new venture, in which he was associated with Heidegger, was not a success, and after running for four years was obliged to close.[2]

It was in 1729 that Handel had opened here with his new, and not very distinguished, company, and although he had the constant patronage of the King and Queen, his attempt was a failure. The opposition operas at Lincoln's Inn Fields and Covent Garden were hitting his venture severely, and by the year 1739–40 operas ceased to be performed here. In 1741, however, owing to the interest taken in it by Lord Middlesex and others, performances were resumed, not only of opera but also of oratorios; while on the off days balls and such-like entertainments were organized.

The success of the place was as intermittent as the character of the fare provided was varied. Opera held its own, not without much opposition from other places which, like the Pantheon, opened their doors to this form of amusement; and successive proprietors and managers, Sheridan among the former, Le Texier and Gallini among the latter, were continually faced with active rivalry or half-hearted support.

Thus matters went on during the better part of the century, when, in 1789, the house was burnt to the ground, not without suspicion of arson, Gallini, then the manager, offering a reward of £300 for the apprehension of some suspected person. The damage was computed at £70,000. On April 3, 1790, the foundation stone of a new house, designed by Novosielski, was

---

[1] It had before been subsidized, and Handel had been the general director of the concern, which was then called the Royal Academy of Music. It must be, of course, remembered, that theatrical performances also took place at the Haymarket Opera House intermittently during the time it was also used for musical matters; while occasional ridottos and so forth were given here.

[2] Naumann's "History of Music."

laid, what time opera was given at the Little Theatre, in the Haymarket, opposite. The new building was opened in March 1791, but owing to a licence for opera being refused, its performances were restricted to ordinary music and dancing.

In 1816–18,[1] the house was enlarged by Nash and Repton; the once well-known colonnade being added in 1820. Opera returned to it and was carried on successfully for some years, such famous singers as Mario and Grisi, Tamburini and Persiani appearing here. When, however, in 1847 a schism took place, and these great ones went off to Covent Garden, the glory of the Haymarket as a home for opera departed. Twenty years later it was again burned to the ground, but rebuilt in the space of a year from the designs of Lee. Trouble, however, again arose in connection with the proprietor's rights, and the place remained unused for no fewer than nine years. In 1878 it re-opened, and for a number of years plays, and occasional operas, were given there.

Subsequently, as most of us remember, Her Majesty's, as the house had come to be called, was demolished, and the present theatre, His Majesty's, arose on its site in conjunction with the vast Carlton Hotel; the only thing linking it with past days being the arcade that runs up its west side from Pall Mall to Charles Street.

Covent Garden

Another home of opera in London was, and is, as I have already indicated, *Covent Garden*. I have already had something to say about this famous house in an earlier chapter, just as I have about Drury Lane. In both these operas were performed during the eighteenth century, and both formed at various periods strongholds for the opposition to the companies per-

[1] There is an interesting view by Rowlandson and Pugin of the interior of the opera before its reconstruction, in Ackermann's "Microcosm of London."

forming at the Haymarket. For instance, "Camilla," "after the Italian manner," was given here in 1706, and the music by Bononcini was being played here, while that of his rival, Handel, was performed at the other house. Later, in 1735, Handel himself went to Covent Garden; while "the nobility" who headed his competitors took possession of the Haymarket. George III. strenuously supported him, subscribing £1000 to the Covent Garden venture, and frequently being present at the performances. Indeed, opera resolved itself into a determined feud between the two houses, both of which for a time ruined themselves in the struggle; and meanwhile Italian opera fell into discredit, being succeeded by the English ballad form, which was always more congenial to the taste of the general public.

In spite of the temporary extinction of foreign opera at Covent Garden, that house has continued down to our own day as the headquarters of this form of musical expression. It has outlived all its rivals: the Haymarket; the occasional bursts of activity in this direction of the Drury Lane and Lincoln's Inn Fields playhouses; even the attempt made in our own day by Mr. Oscar Hammerstein to establish an opera-house in Kingsway.

Certain later outstanding features in the career of Covent Garden as the home of opera may be summarized. Thus it was here in 1861 that Adelina Patti made her *début*; here that, under the management of Sir Augustus Harris (1888–96) the De Reszke brothers and Madame Melba first appeared; and in 1907, under the *ægis* of the Royal Opera Syndicate, which had taken over the management just ten years earlier, that Madame Tetrazzini made her first triumphant appearance.

Nor is this the only way in which Covent Garden has catered to the public love of music, for after the opera season, the Promenade Concerts used to be given here, as well as in the so-called Floral Hall adjoining; and it was only in recent years that they were transferred to the Queen's Hall, in Langham Place, where the Sunday Concerts, under the direction of Sir Henry Wood, used to be rivalled in attraction by those at the Albert Hall, under Sir Landon Ronald, until these were superseded by other Sunday Concerts conducted by various people, but essentially on the same lines as their predecessors.

The Hanover Square Rooms

The name of Gallini has been mentioned in connection with that gentleman's conduct for a time of the Haymarket Opera House, and it was he who built that concert room at the north-west corner of Hanover Square (No. 4), long famous in musical annals as *The Hanover Square Rooms*, or alternatively the Queen's Antient Concert Rooms. Gallini acquired the property, including the house that stood on it, from Lord Dunmore, in 1773. It had till then been occupied by Lord Dillon, and when Gallini entered into possession, he pulled down the mansion and erected on its site his music-room which remained till the end of the nineteenth century, when it was in its turn demolished. The principal apartment was ninety feet long by thirty-five wide, and was beautifully decorated by the graceful art of Cipriani. It held seating accommodation for eight hundred people.

Gallini, who was associated with Bach and Abel, those two excellent musicians who were for so much in the advancement of music in this country during their day, and of whom many interesting reminiscences will be found by the curious in the memoirs of Mrs. Papendiek, began his concerts in 1775,[1] and for many years carried them on with much success, being warmly

---

[1] The gentlemen's tickets were black; the ladies' red. Chairs only set down at the Hanover Square entrance; later another door was made in Hanover Street for the convenience of those attending the concerts.

patronized by George III. and Queen Charlotte, who were never tired of attending the concerts, as readers of Fanny Burney's Diary will remember.

In 1791 Joseph Haydn arrived in London, and it was at the Hanover Square Rooms that six of his Grand Symphonies, "The Surprise" being among them, were given at concerts organized by Salomon; the papers announcing that "Mr. Haydn will be at the Harpsichord and compose for every night a new piece of music." From 1804 onwards for more than forty years the "Antient Music," as it was called, was given here with unfailing regularity and unfailing success; while in 1846 the Amateur Musical Society was established here, among its performers being the Duke of Leinster, Sir Archibald Keppel, the Earl of Arundel and Sir Percy Shelley, the latter two playing the trumpet. Here, too, at an earlier date (1828) the Royal Academy of Music began its activities. Indeed down to 1874 the Hanover Square Rooms were intimately associated with the furtherance of the art in London; and there is no spot in the metropolis so closely identified with chamber-music as that on which a modern building has replaced the once-famous and popular music rooms.

An interesting vignette of what the Great Room looked like when it was inaugurated on February 1, 1775, is provided in a letter from Mrs. Harris to her son, afterwards 1st Earl of Malmesbury. Writing on February 3 she says: "Your father and Gertrude attended Bach's[1] Concert, Wednesday. It was the opening of his new room, which by all accounts is by much the most elegant room in town; it is larger than at Almack's. The statue of Apollo is placed just behind the orchestra, but it is thought too large and clumsy. There are ten other figures or pictures bigger than life. They are painted by some of our most eminent artists;

[1] This was not, of course, the great John Sebastian, but Johann Christian, one of his many children.

such as Weſt, Gainsborough, Cipriani, etc. These
pictures are all transparent, and are lighted behind,
and that light is sufficient to illuminate the room without any luſtres or candles appearing. The ceiling is
domed and beautifully painted with alto-relievos in
all the piers. The pictures are chiefly fanciful; a Comic
Muse painted by Gainsborough is moſt highly spoken
of. 'Tis a great ſtroke of Bach's to entertain the town
so very elegantly."

As so often happens in such cases, some of the
neighbours in Hanover Square were not so pleased
at the musical incursion into their faſtnesses, and we
hear of Lord Hillsborough, Sir James Porter, and other
residents in Hanover Square, banding together to
take action againſt what they considered a nuisance.
Although the jury was said to have found a true bill
againſt Bach, the matter muſt have been settled out
of court, for the Hanover Square Rooms continued
their successful career for many a long year after
this.

We have seen that Haydn was here in 1791; in
the following year Hummel, "Maſter Hummel from
Vienna," as he was advertised, gave his firſt benefit
concert in London here; the tickets for which, half-a-
guinea each, were to be had of him at his lodging at
12 Green Street, Leiceſter Fields.

At this time, it may be intereſting to record, the
fashion of wearing swords with full dress obtained:
and even performers at concerts were provided with a
special type of weapon which was in charge of "a
sword-bearer," as he was called. When the player
went on to the platform he was handed this sword,
which he fixed to his side; in retiring from his performance, he took it off and returned it to the sword-
bearer, who hung it up in the green-room till it
should again be required.

In 1804, as I have ſtated, the Concerts of Antient
Music, which had hitherto been given in the Totten-

ham Street Rooms,[1] were removed to Hanover Square. They received their name from the fact that one of the rules laid down was "that no music composed within the previous twenty years should be performed." The Directors, who were amateurs of social standing, chose the programmes, which largely consisted of works by Handel, and George III. took a deep interest in these concerts, sometimes writing out the programmes with his own hand. He was a constant attendant, and on one occasion when Cramer was conducting, he sent a messenger to him with these words, "Tell young Cramer to keep his eye on me, and watch my hand, with which I will give him the true time of the various compositions." At another time, after his recovery from his mental illness, he selected every piece of Handel's having reference to madness or blindness, and added "God Save the King" to the list.[2]

It was in 1823 that the Royal Academy of Music gave its first concert in the Hanover Square Rooms, on July 5, with one of Haydn's symphonies as the *pièce de résistance*. In 1828 Sterndale Bennett, then aged twelve, made his precocious appearance here, and, dressed in the special uniform adopted by the Academy, played one of Dussek's pianoforte concertos.

Another musical body that first used the rooms at a later date (1833) was the Philharmonic Society, which continued to give performances here till 1869; and in connection with it as well as the Antient Music, and Royal Academy, many notable people performed in these now demolished rooms: Thalberg, in 1836; Liszt, in 1840; and Rubenstein, then "Master Antoine Rubenstein, aged eleven," in 1842. It was, also, in this year that Mendelssohn here conducted his Scotch Symphony for the first time in England.

[1] This had previously been known as Pasquale's concert room; after which it was taken and enlarged by the Directors of the Antient Music. It subsequently became a theatre (see *ante*).

[2] See "Musical Haunts in London," by F. G. Edwards, 1895.

F F

Two years later he led five of the Philharmonic Concerts, at one of which, on May 27, 1844, his "Wedding
March" was first heard in this country. It was on this
occasion that Joachim, then only thirteen, played
Beethoven's Violin Concerto entirely from memory,
to the obvious delight of Mendelssohn, who was
conducting. A critic, writing of the performance, has
told us how the youthful violinist, "played with the
utmost self-possession, and obtained on his instrument
the firmness, certainty, and command, and, above all,
the *style*, of an artist of thirty-five."

During this same season, another great instrumental-
ist, who was later to be so identified with Joachim in
concerted music, Piatti, achieved great success—a
success which he continued down to our own days at
the Monday and Saturday " Pops," at the old St.
James's Hall.

For some years the famous conductor, Michael
Costa, led the orchestra at the Hanover Square Rooms,
but on his resignation, in 1854, Richard Wagner was
engaged for the following year; and here, on March 12,
1855, he made his first appearance before a London
audience.[1] In 1856, Sterndale Bennett was conducting
in the place he had first appeared in sixteen years
earlier, and it was during this season (on April 14)
that Madame Schumann gave her initial performance
in England, playing Beethoven's "Emperor" Sonata,
and some of Mendelssohn's "Variations."

With a concert given by the students of the Royal
Academy of Music, Sterndale Bennett conducting,
in December 1874, the Hanover Square Rooms, as a
home for music, came to an end; the building not long
after being taken and opened as the St. George's
Club, which later migrated to 2 Savile Row.

[1] This, however, was his second visit to London, he having been
here in 1839, when he lodged at an inn in old Compton Street, Soho—
"The King's Arms"—but was so annoyed at the organ-grinders that he
left after a week.

A picture of the Hanover Square Rooms as they appeared in 1843 shows that the concert hall had a domed ceiling, was flanked on one side by tall windows, and lighted by six large chandeliers as well as by other lights fixed to the walls. The whole of one end was occupied by the orchestra, behind which stood an organ. There were two wide gangways, and the seats in the centre faced the performers, those at the sides being at right angles to them. Two columns supported the roof at the end furthest from the orchestra; and the little woodblock from which I gather this information indicates the place crowded with a well-dressed gathering of music-lovers.[1]

The Argyll Rooms

Another harmonious pleasure haunt in the London of those days was *The Argyll Rooms*, which occupied the building with its classic circular adjunct, at the north-east corner of Little Argyll Street, in fact, at No. 246 Regent Street.

The Argyll Rooms were built in 1818 by Nash as part of his great Regent Street scheme (now with yesterday's seven thousand years, alas!). At first they appear to have been intended for balls and masquerades and such-like amusements, for which purpose, indeed, they were originally used; but intermittently with such frivolities the Philharmonic Society was accustomed to hold its concerts here, as it had done in a former building on the same site. Previously to this, however, in 1812, Domenico Corri, the son-in-law of Dussek, gave a concert here, performing, with the aid of his pupils, Pergolesi's "Stabat Mater"; this solemn entertainment being followed, rather surprisingly, by a ball.

In the following year the Philharmonic Society came

[1] The Prince Consort took great interest in these concerts, and often selected the programmes; so, in 1848, did the Duke of Wellington—not with such success.

into existence and its first concert was given here, with Cherubini's "Anacreon" as the chief item in the programme; an item which was so vociferously received that, we are told, the performance was repeatedly interrupted by the loudness and continuance of the applause. Another musical event at the Regent Street rooms, in the same year, was the appearance of Samuel Wesley, who played on an organ specially constructed for his use on this occasion.

During Nash's rebuilding of Regent Street the Philharmonic Society had to hold its concerts else-where; but in 1820 it was back in the newly con-structed rooms, and in that year Spohr made his initial appearance in England here. It is an interesting fact that it was on this occasion that a *baton* was first used by a conductor, hitherto the first violin under-taking that office, as one sees him often doing in small orchestras to-day. When Spohr suddenly drew forth his wand at the rehearsal, it produced something like a sensation, a sensation which was repeated at the concert itself.

In 1824 Liszt, then a boy of fourteen, made his first appearance in London at the Argyll Rooms, astonishing everyone by his extraordinary technique, even at that tender age, and still more by proclaiming his readiness to play variations on a theme which anyone in the audience might give him. The following year was notable here for a performance of Beethoven's "Choral Symphony"; and 1826 for the conducting by Weber of one of the concerts.[1]

We have seen that Mendelssohn was conducting at the Hanover Square Rooms in 1842; just thirteen years earlier he had made his first appearance before a London audience at the Argyll Rooms, when he led his C. Minor Symphony, on May 25, 1829, and after that he was seen and heard on various occasions here

[1] He died ten days later at 103 Great Portland Street, where he was staying in March 1826, as the guest of Sir George Smart.

during the season, of which he has left us some records in his "Letters"; occasions on which he and his compositions were received with tumultuous applause.

On February 6, 1830, the Argyll Rooms[1] were destroyed by fire, although a steam engine, more or less on modern lines, was used for the first time to combat the flames. The musical library belonging to the Philharmonic Society was, however, happily saved; but when the place was rebuilt, as from Tallis's views, 1838, we see it was much on the old lines, the Society had migrated to the Hanover Square Rooms, and harmony left an ever-increasingly commercial thoroughfare.

There have in the past been various other pleasure centres in London associated with music. One of a humble character, but no less an earnest attempt to popularize and extend the art was the residence of the famous "musical small-coal man," Thomas Britton, which was situated at the corner of Aylesbury Street and Jerusalem Passage (later it became the Bull's Head tavern), behind the Sessions House, in Clerkenwell. There is no necessity to give a biographical account of Britton, who was a remarkable man, as such data are easily available. It is sufficient to say that in the upper part of a kind of stable, the lower portion of which was used for his coal-dépôt, Britton, in 1678, established a musical club, where, on every Thursday, for a period of no fewer than forty years, he gave his concerts, free at first, but afterwards at a yearly subscription of ten shillings. What sort of man Britton was may be best estimated by the knowledge of those whom he persuaded to perform in his loft. Well, in the first place, no less a one than Handel played on the organ for him; Dr. Pepusch fingered a

[1] The other Argyll Rooms, where the Trocadero is now, was a very different place, notorious in all sorts of ways, noisy but not musical ones, among them.

virginal, built by Ruckers and supposed to be the finest instrument of the kind in Europe; Banister played the violin, and Wollaston, the painter, and others assisted; while fashion, headed by the Duchess of Queensberry, left for awhile its wonted haunts, and found in the glorious harmonies of Handel and the gentle airs that Pepusch won from the virginal, a change from the more florid pleasures of Vauxhall and Ranelagh, and for a time forgot the glories of St. James's and Mayfair, in the musical palace which the stable in Aylesbury Street, Clerkenwell, had for the time become.

In those days anything abnormal was apt to be regarded as suspect, and Britton was by many looked upon as a charlatan, which he was not, and even a magician, which in many respects he was. All one can say is that he was a pioneer, and in the humble, dirty, sordid surroundings of Clerkenwell, he inaugurated a work which came to its full flower in the Philharmonic Society, the Concerts of Antient Music, and the Monday Pops of our own day.

Yet another centre of musical activity was, of all places, Crosby Hall. Few people associate with that venerable piece of antiquity anything but an historic scene and a literary event; for Richard III., is here said to have been hailed as king, and here, if tradition is correct, More wrote his "Utopia." The less historically-minded remember the place chiefly as a restaurant, to which base uses it had come before it was carted away. Such, however, as have seen the picture of it as it was in 1845 will recall that at one end an organ was embedded in the wall, with an ample loft in front of it; and this gives to Crosby Hall a musical *aura* which for a time did pervade it.

In 1842, to be precise, a Mr. Dando initiated here some quartette concerts which became, at the period, a feature in London's musical world. It was he who erected the organ, and, in addition to the quartettes, recitals were given on the instrument—once (on June 3, 1844) its keys being touched by the great Mendelssohn himself.

During the 'forties Miss Mounsey gave a series of sacred concerts at Crosby Hall, and at one of these, which took place on January 8, 1845, she presided at the organ, and Mendelssohn's "Hear my Prayer," for the copyright of which he had received the munificent sum of four pounds (!) was first performed in this country.

Exeter Hall

There remains one other musical centre of the past to be mentioned, and in many respects it is the best remembered of all, for it was destined to be the home of oratorio in London for nearly half a century. *Exeter Hall* has had many uses, and to-day has entered upon the strangest use of all. Its religious meetings; its social-welfare gatherings, as they may be called, and so forth have, perhaps, somewhat obliterated the outstanding position it once occupied in the musical world, and thus as one of the pleasure haunts of the metropolis.

It was erected in 1831, through the exertions of Mr. Henry Pownall, and from the designs of Mr. J. P. Gandy-Deering, at a cost of £30,000. From the first it was intended for the benefit of religious and scientific bodies, and was used as such; but in 1834 a three days' Amateur Musical Festival was held here. The fact that an orchestra had to be specially constructed and an organ installed indicates that among the purposes for which the hall was intended, music did not occupy a place. On the occasion of this first concert no fewer than 733 performers took part, and selections were given from "The Dettingen Te Deum," the "Creation," the "Messiah" and "Israel in Egypt." Two years later another musical festival was held here, under the direction of Sir George Smart, what time the Sacred Harmonic Society, having proved to the satisfaction of the proprietors that music was a science as well as an art, was allowed to hold its concerts within the walls. The first of these took place on June 28, 1836, with a rendering of the "Messiah," which was so successful that henceforth oratorio held its own in Exeter Hall for many years.

I may shortly summarize some of the principal musical events that occurred here. Thus in the March of 1837 Mendelssohn's "St. Paul" was given, the composer being among the audience; and so popular did it prove that a second performance was held in the following September. In 1842 the Sacred Harmonic Society gave a concert at which Mendelssohn played on the new organ that had been installed; while, in 1847, the "Elijah," which its composer had carefully revised since it was first performed at Birmingham in the previous year, was given four times, the Queen and Prince Albert being present at one of the performances.

Until 1848 the conductor at these concerts had been Joseph Surman, but in that year he was succeeded by Michael Costa, who continued to lead the orchestra till 1879; and inaugurated that system of conducting which has since obtained.

Another musical association with Exeter Hall was that of John Hullah's singing classes, which were started in 1841, and were so successful that he wanted the whole place to himself, and would have liked the Sacred Harmonic Society to seek quarters elsewhere. In addition to his "lessons," Hullah gave performances in the Large Hall, notable among these being the series of historical concerts (1847), showing the evolution of English vocal music.

On the founding of the New Philharmonic Society, in 1852, that body also gave concerts in Exeter Hall, at some of which Berlioz conducted, Sivori played the violin, and Piatti the 'cello. But of all the concerts held here, probably none created such a *furore* as those at which Jenny Lind sang to packed audiences; when the passages and the staircases were crowded to suffocation, when people struggled and fought, as we see them doing in Doyle's picture[1] when the popular favourite was singing at the Haymarket Opera House, to catch a note from the magic throat of the Swedish nightingale.

With the season of 1879–80, the Exeter Hall Concerts came to an end; and the lease of the place was purchased by the Y.M.C.A.

Other later musical pleasure haunts include the *St. James's Hall*, to which I have already referred, which was built by Owen Jones, in that Hispano-Mauro style of which he was an outstanding exponent, in 1858; and which for many music-lovers was indissolubly associated with the Monday and Saturday Popular Concerts (Pops, as they were called), which were carried on under the *ægis* of the house of Chappell down to the 'nineties, and at which all the great musical exponents of the time were at one time or another heard; the concerted music led by Joachim, with Piatti, Ries and others supporting him, being a feature. In another part of the building the popular Christy Minstrels gave their ebonized performances, and not infrequently the strains of Beethoven or Schumann were discordantly interrupted by the distant applause of those who preferred a different sort of entertainment. In summer-time, too, when windows were opened for necessary ventilation, the roar of Piccadilly made itself dominant in the concert-hall, and one has seen M. de Pachmann stop in the middle of a piece in a sort of mute agony and despair at the alien sounds that were wafted into inharmonious concords with the notes of a Chopin prelude.

To-day music is chiefly represented by the Prome-

[1] "Manners and Customs of ye Englishe," where other musical events are amusingly portrayed.

nade Concerts which have lived through much ſtress since those early days when Jullien, with his flowing locks and ample shirt-front, his turned-up wriſt-bands and his *air vainqueur*, conducted them as he conducts them in Doyle's little picture; and by the Saturday and Sunday concerts at the Albert Hall and the Queen's Hall, besides those smaller centres such as the Æolian Hall, the Wigmore Hall, the Central Hall, Weſtminſter (where the Bach Choir performs), and so forth.

Vocal music has always appealed to a larger public than inſtrumental, and the theatre appeals to a ſtill larger. It thus happens that although we have but a handful of concert-rooms in London, and the performances in them are limited to a few days a week, there are playhouses and music-halls (which, by the way, have little to do with music)[1] in every ſtreet almoſt, (some ſtreets seem all theatres), where performances are given every day (sometimes twice) and are always crowded; while the cinema has become another power in the world of amusement, and for one class of the community has become the moſt popular of all.

[1] The Alhambra and Empire music-halls, as well as many others, are known to most people, and the popular favourites from Cinquevalli (that wonder) and Chirgwin, the white-eyed Kaffir, downwards, are in many instances household words. In the past, places like the Holborn Casino, the Piccadilly Saloon, etc. were subsidiary pleasure haunts, and as such are mentioned in Schröder Devrient's Autobiography (1868–75) *inter alia*.

CHAPTER XVIII

EXHIBITIONS, ZOOLOGICAL GARDENS, ETC.

In these few laſt pages I want to say something about the various pleasure haunts which did not fall conveniently into a place in the preceding chapters. Some of these are of the paſt which is becoming rapidly hiſtoric (the Victorian era to many seems apparently almost archaic), some are of to-day, and their hiſtory muſt await a later period for proper exposition.

No account of the London pleasure haunts could be considered quite complete without something being said regarding those exhibitions which have from time to time been organized and which have met with such varying success. The greateſt of all, because it was a forerunner, was *The Great Exhibition of 1851*. That vaſt undertaking has overshadowed all succeeding attempts in a similar direction. It ſtands as the culminating point of the Victorian era; in a way it *is* the Victorian era exemplified in terms of glass; and when one gazes at its framework on the Sydenham heights, the vaſt bulk of the Cryſtal Palace, which, as Leigh Hunt remarked, is not a palace and is not cryſtal, seems to dominate the landscape somewhat as the Victorian era (in spite of detractors) dominates the landscape of our later island ſtory.

The Great Exhibition of 1851, although it had had forerunners on less ambitious lines in France, and had even been preceded in our own country by shows chiefly technical and commercial, was the firſt attempt to bring together under one roof the products of various lands, and to give zest to commercial activity by exciting the interest and curiosity of the people. It owed its inception, materialization and success to the initiative and determined courage of Prince Albert. What he desired was that this exhibition should be "a whole world of nature and art collected at the call of the queen of cities—a competition in which every country might have a place, and every variety of intellect its claim and chance of distinction. Nothing great, or beautiful, or useful, be its native home where it might; not a discovery or invention, however humble or obscure; not a candidate, however lowly his rank, but would obtain admission, and be estimated to the full amount of genuine worth."

On January 3, 1850, the Royal assent was formally accorded to the scheme, and a week later the Commissioners held their first meeting. One thing was dominant in the conception of the scheme, and that was its international character, by which the barriers, as Cobden once said, which had separated diverse nations should be broken down. Apart from the immense labour of setting the machinery of such a vast undertaking in motion, there were two primary things to be settled: one, what building to adapt or construct; the other, the site to be chosen. A competition for plans was inaugurated, with the result that some two hundred and fifty were presented for consideration. From the chaos of these emerged that of Joseph Paxton, the famous gardener at Chatsworth, which, although at first coldly received by the Committee, with the exception of Prince Albert and Sir Robert Peel, was at last adopted. This immense erection of iron and glass was based on Paxton's great conservatory at Chatsworth. It was, in fact, a gigantic conservatory, so large that full-grown trees could be included in it, and so spacious that the exhibits from all the ends of the earth and the thousands that daily visited them were able to find space within it.

The spot chosen for its erection was that large open space in Hyde Park between the Albert Hall (which was not then, of course, in existence) and Kensington Palace; and soon those great iron girders and supports began to arise, while the mystic fabric, if not raised in "majestic silence," was at least set up without the aid of bricks and mortar, and with a minimum of scaffolding being required in its erection. The interior was decorated where necessary by Owen Jones and some 500 painters; and the whole structure was set up with such rapidity that from September 26, 1850, to the middle of the following January, sufficed for its completion, and by the appointed day of opening, May 1, everything was ready. The Exhibition was inaugurated by Queen Victoria in state. The doors had been opened at nine o'clock and the 20,000 ticket-holders flocked into the place. So admirably had the arrangements been made, however, that we are told there was no undue crushing in any part of the building, and the great ceremony passed off with a clockwork-like regularity that indicated, perhaps, more than anything, the foresight and labour of those responsible for the arrangements.

In a letter which Queen Victoria wrote to the King of the Belgians on May 3, Her Majesty's delight and satisfaction at the success of the Exhibition, which was really a personal triumph for Prince Albert, are expressed in no measured terms. She speaks of May 1 as being "the *greatest* day in our history," and the ceremony "the *most beautiful* and *imposing* and *touching* spectacle ever seen," and she adds, "the triumph of my beloved Albert."[1]

The Exhibition, which remained open till the autumn, was visited by no fewer than six million people. The actual closing day was October 11; and the financial success of the undertaking may be estimated by the fact that after all expenses had been

[1] "Letters of Queen Victoria," 3 vols., 1908.

paid there remained a sum of over £200,000 to be applied to the promotion of industrial art.

During the five months the Exhibition remained open it was the most popular pleasure resort in London; and the variety of the crowds and their cosmopolitan character (which, by the way, *Punch* made the subject of humorous cartoons and jokes) gave an opportunity for all sorts of people to make money by catering to their material wants. One of those who did so was the famous *chef*, Soyer, who took Gore House just opposite (where the Albert Hall is now), then but recently vacated by the gorgeous Countess and the still more gorgeous dandy, and turned it into a restaurant under the name of the "Symposium of all Nations." Here were provided international feasts, banquets and private dinners of every description; and various entertainments were given in the highly decorated and splendid rooms. The gardens were beautifully laid out and adorned with statues, etc.; while the interior of the house testified to the clever art of Madame Soyer as a painter. With these attractions, coupled with the great name of Soyer himself, and advertised by that past master in the art, George Augustus Sala, the place for a time did well; but the Great Exhibition was but for a season, and that season was, too, Soyer's only one. At the close of it his temporary success ended; and in due course the "Baronial Hall" and "The Encampment of all Nations," and such-like reconstructions of Lady Blessington's erstwhile famous dwelling, were sold and the house itself in due course demolished.[1]

The Commissioners of the Great Exhibition purchased the site together with much surrounding ground partly covered by the gardens of other houses, nursery

[1] It is said that the average attendance of visitors was 1000 a day, and that the takings amounted to £21,000; nevertheless so great had been the expenses that Soyer was out of pocket by £7000 at the closing of his venture.

grounds, market gardens, etc., and eventually the Albert Hall and other public buildings arose there, and were in time to become the nucleus of other exhibitions which were popular as pleasure resorts in their day.

At a later time such manifestations of the amusement cult combined with the more serious objects of trade and commerce succeeded each other at Earl's Court, where successive exhibitions, each dealing with a special phase of social life, were held and were popularly known by such names as The Fisheries, The Healtheries, the Colinderies, and such-like absurd names, which disguised, as in the case of the last-named, which was really connected with our Colonies, their identity past all seeming. Later still the White City, under the *ægis* of Mr. Imré Kiralfy, had for a time a vogue; and in these days Wembley has taken the place of these earlier shows.

It has not been my intention in this book to say anything at length regarding existing pleasure haunts, and thus such places as Hurlingham and Ranelagh and Queen's Club, Lords[1] and the Oval and Lillie Bridge, with a large etcetera, must be passed over with this bare allusion. But a few words must be said, in conclusion, concerning the two Zoological Gardens of London, one of which is world-famous; the other almost wholly forgotten.

The Zoo, as it is termed, in Regent's Park, belonging to the Zoological Society, which was instituted in 1826, and incorporated by Royal Charter three years later, was opened to the public in 1828. Since those days such vast improvements and additions have

---

[1] Those who are interested in the history of Lord's will find it fully and admirably set out in "Lords and the M.C.C.," by Lord Harris and F. C. Ashley-Cooper; while an excellent account of "The Oval" is contained in "The History of Kennington," by H. H. Montgomery, Bishop of Tasmania, 1889.

been made to the place that its projectors would hardly know it. The great Lion House, the Mappin Terraces, the recently formed aquarium, are but a few of the features added to the Gardens which have always been one of London's chief pleasure resorts.

The other Zoological Gardens was, in a way, still more so, because in it was incorporated a Music Hall and other extra-zoological attractions. The Surrey Zoological Gardens, as it was called, was formed by a Mr. Cross, who acquired a site in Panton Place, Kennington, which was transformed into a "zoo" in 1831–2 for the reception of his menagerie, formerly housed in Exeter 'Change, in the Strand,[1] and on the demolition of that building in 1829, in the King's Mews at Charing Cross. The Surrey Zoological Gardens were first opened to the public in the August of 1831, "under the immediate patronage of her most gracious majesty Queen Adelaide." But that they were anything but complete then, is proved by the almost contemporary statement that since that time "rapid progress has been made in the erection of suitable and imposing structures for the various inmates."[2] Among the features of the place was a circular conservatory, three hundred feet in circumference; a grotto for the eagles, a smaller conservatory for the monkeys, a rustic "Refectory," a hermitage, and such-like adjuncts. A collection of the "large carnivorous animals" was exhibited; and near by was "a building of considerable dimensions, *with suitable padlocks*, for the more domesticated animals"; while constant additions are spoken of as being made by purchase and by donation.

---

[1] Cross occupied "the entire range of the floor above Exeter 'Change." Here the elephant, Chunee was shot in 1826. Hone, in his "Every Day Book," gives an interesting account of the animal, and Hood wrote a poem on its death. Byron records going to Exeter 'Change "to see the tigers sup."

[2] Kidd's "New Guide to 'the Lions' of London."

The grounds covered fifteen acres, and in them was a lake of three acres. In addition to the attraction of wild beasts, birds, etc., a collection which was a very good one, fêtes and special exhibitions were held here during the summer, and in 1837 displays of fireworks were introduced. A beautiful lithograph by Havell, published in 1832, shows how picturesque the place must have been, at least in its initial stages, with its large lake and as yet unsophisticated character. Here giraffes were first seen in England (1836); here the South London Horticultural Society held its flower-shows from 1837 onwards; here the first panorama was displayed; here the inevitable balloon ascents took place; here orchestral concerts were given; all of which things must have surprised the denizens of the forest safely caged behind Mr. Cross's iron bars.

In 1844 Cross was succeeded by William Tyler as proprietor, and under the new management a large orchestra was erected, in which Jullien and his band of three hundred performers discoursed eloquent music. Later, when the Surrey Music Hall Company acquired the property, a music-hall was erected, and opened in 1856 with a performance of the "Messiah"; and in this hall, where Clara Novello, Sims Reeves, and others had charmed large audiences, the Rev. C. H. Spurgeon rather surprisingly appeared in the following year to electrify them in another direction. Indeed that hall has witnessed many strange tenants, among them the patients of St. Thomas's Hospital, in 1862, when that Institution had to leave its old headquarters in Southwark and before it entered into possession of those on the Embankment.

By the 'seventies the Surrey Zoological Gardens had become a centre for concerts, ballets, etc., in fact a kind of Cremorne. But they did not last long after this, and the end came in 1877; the final entertainment in the theatre, which had risen on the site of the old music-hall, burnt down in 1861, took place on

G G

August 14 of that year. The site was soon after built over, and Delverton, Suffield, Tarver, and Berryfield Roads run through it; its name being alone perpetuated by the Surrey Gardens Hotel.

As I close these pages one other pleasure haunt swims into my ken: The Westminster Aquarium, which was opened in 1876. That large red-brick, stone-faced building was designed by Mr. A. Bedborough, and was 600 feet long by 160 wide. It had a theatre at its west end called "The Imperial." But it was the Aquarium itself, lined with tanks to which few people paid any attention, with its concerts and its dancing Zulus, its swimming ladies, and, above all, its Zazel being shot out of a mammoth cannon, that comes back to memory, with Peall *v.* Mitchell playing billiards upstairs, in those non-spot-barred games which seemed interminable! Many things have happened in this quarter since those days: an immense Central Hall, with its vast dome, has arisen on the site of The Aquarium; Tothill Street is changed out of all recognition; yet when one passes along it, one seems to hear the ghostly click of balls, and a voice asking Zazel if she is ready; a tiny reply issuing from the interior of the great gun; a terrific report; and there is the beautiful little athlete being projected into the air above a thousand up-turned faces, and descending safely into the net which catches her in mid-air. . . . What an aquarium it was!

INDEX

451

Index

H H